Management
Decision Making

A Network
Simulation Approach

Management
Decision Making
A Network
Simulation Approach

A. ALAN B. PRITSKER

President
Pritsker & Associates, Inc.

C. ELLIOTT SIGAL

University of California
San Francisco

Prentice-Hall, Inc., Englewood Cliffs, New Jersey 07632

Library of Congress Cataloging in Publication Data

Pritsker, A. Alan B.,   (date)
    Management decision making.

    Bibliography: p.
    Includes index.
    1. Decision making—Data processing. 2. GERT
(Network analysis) I. Sigal, C. Elliott (Charles
Elliott) II. Title.
HD30.23.P75   658.4'034   82-5377
ISBN 0-13-548164-3   AACR2

Editorial production/supervision
  by *Gretchen Chenenko*
Cover design by *Mario Piazza*
Manufacturing buyers: *Joyce Levatino*
  and Anthony Caruso

Printed in the United States of America

10 9 8 7 6 5 4 3 2 1

ISBN   0-13-548164-3

Prentice-Hall International, Inc., *London*
Prentice-Hall of Australia Pty. Limited, *Sydney*
Prentice-Hall Canada Inc., *Toronto*
Prentice-Hall of India Private Limited, *New Delhi*
Prentice-Hall of Japan, Inc., *Tokyo*
Prentice-Hall of Southeast Asia Pte. Ltd., *Singapore*
Whitehall Books Limited, *Wellington, New Zealand*

DEDICATED TO:

Charles D. Hoyt, Jr., and Richard L. Smith,
friends and colleagues
who have helped to educate me (AABP)

My loving wife Ruth (CES)

Contents

II Q-GERT SYMBOLS, ROUTINES, AND PROGRAMS *17*

IV LOGISTICS AND INVENTORY CONTROL *261*

V NETWORK DECISION MODELING AND PROJECT PLANNING *339*

VI NETWORK GRAPHICS *471*

Preface

Computer simulation has long been practiced by management scientists as a relatively inexpensive way to experiment with systems. Now, corporate and operations managers have found repeated successes for modeling and simulation in resolving manufacturing problems [199]. This book presents these findings and concentrates on the presentation of network models and their use.

Network simulation has truly come of age. Since the development of PERT and CPM in the mid-1950s, managers have benefited from using network diagrams as aids in decision making. Throughout the 1960s and 1970s, advanced simulation techniques permitted the refinement of computer approaches to decision analysis. Several network simulation packages were developed and applied to a wide variety of problems in management and engineering. Solutions too complex for analysis were obtained in unprecedented time frames. With this rapid development of technique, however, there coexisted a need for a single reference documenting the use of network modeling and simulation in the decision-making process. This book provides such documentation.

In order to focus clearly on the use of network simulation, we have used one particular network language throughout the text. The choice of the Q-GERT network language is based on its advanced capabilities, its ready availability, and its proven success in application.

A fundamental premise of this book is that networks can effectively be used in management decision making. Viewed in this perspective, the book presents a novel approach to management decision making. This approach involves obtaining an understanding of the problems and concerns related to the decision to be made. This includes a definition of the environment of the decision, a specification of the measures by which a good decision will be judged, and the building of a model that forecasts the measures of performance for each decision alternative.

A supplementary purpose of the book is to demonstrate that a single modeling vehicle can be used to portray a large class of problem situations that are of concern to management. Problem situations from the following areas are addressed: project planning, production scheduling, risk analysis, logistics analysis, and inventory planning. It is shown that Q-GERT networks are useful for describing, understanding, and communicating these problems at different levels of management. By providing a common modeling framework, decision makers can obtain a greater understanding of the modeling process and of models. Throughout the book, examples emphasize how the network simulation approach focuses on performance measures, key decision elements, and the use of computer simulation results to solve problems.

The modeling philosophy of Q-GERT leads to a systems approach to problem resolution that consists of four steps. First, a system is decomposed into its significant elements. Second, the elements are analyzed and described. Third, the elements are integrated in a network model of the system. Fourth, system performance is assessed through the simulation of the network model. The evaluation of the network model is accomplished through the use of a computer program called the Q-GERT Analysis Program or Q-GERT processor. The Q-GERT Analysis Program employs simulation procedures to obtain statistical estimates of the performance measures required for decision making. The Q-GERT Analysis Program is written in ANSI FORTRAN IV. It has been compiled and run on a wide class of computers and its portability has been demonstrated. The program is available from Pritsker & Associates, Inc., P.O. Box 2413, West Lafayette, Indiana 47906.

This book has been written to be self-contained, and only minimal prerequisites are required of the reader. The material in the book is primarily at the junior–senior college level. It can be used to introduce the concepts of decision making, modeling, and simulation. Alternatively, the material in the book can be used at the graduate level to integrate and explain problem solving, industrial engineering, management science, and operations research techniques.

The book is organized into six parts. Part I introduces management decision making and the role that can be played by network modeling in the decision-making process. Part II contains a summary of the Q-GERT network language. The four chapters included in Part II contain information on network symbols, support routines, input procedures, and output reports. Procedures for storing the outputs in a data base for future use are detailed in Chapter 5.

Part III deals with decision making and model building related to production planning. The first chapter in Part III, Chapter 6, presents the basic concepts of production planning, including performance measures and their use, and basic procedures for modeling production systems to obtain the planning performance measures. Chapter 7 describes how network models can be developed to evaluate scheduling and sequencing procedures. Models for evaluating material handling systems are described in Chapter 8. Material handling systems considered are conveyors, pipelines, and overhead cranes. Special topics related to production planning are detailed in Chapter 9. These include labor-limited queueing situations, maintenance and inspection processes, and order routing. Five applications of Q-GERT network models that have been used for decision making within a production planning context are presented in Chapter 10.

Part IV is concerned with logistics and inventory control. The terminology and modeling requirements associated with logistics systems analysis are presented in Chapter 11. This chapter presents modeling concepts for integrating reliability, maintainability, supply, transportation, personnel and training, and support equipment and facilities into a single system study. An example of decision making for a logistics system at an Air Force depot is presented. Chapter 12 defines reliability and quality control concepts in terms of Q-GERT network models. The chapter makes explicit the concepts involved in these areas and can be used for explaining such concepts to management. Chapters 13 and 14 address the central questions of inventory control: when to place orders and how much to order. Q-GERT models for periodic review and transaction reporting (continuous review) inventory control procedures are developed. The modeling of back orders and lost sales is also included. Diverse methods for characterizing the demand for units in inventory are presented, and a consideration of how to model multi-commodity inventory systems is considered.

Part V provides a detailed presentation of risk analysis and project planning. In Chapter 15, the concepts and procedures associated with decision trees, decision networks, risk assessment, and shortest-route problems are presented. Q-GERT network models for these areas are described, and the procedures for using such network models in management decision making are explored.

Chapters 16 through 19 are devoted to project planning with the basic concepts, terminology, and performance measures contained in Chapter 16. Procedures are provided for estimating project completion-time distributions, activity start times, activity criticality indices, and project cost for network models of the PERT/CPM variety. Chapter 17 combines the concepts of risk and decision making into project planning, and it illustrates how Q-GERT network models can be employed for decision making in a project planning context when increased uncertainty due risk and failure are included. Chapter 18 presents information on the scheduling of activities in a project planning context. Procedures for making the scheduling computations, including estimates of activity slack, are given. In addition, analyses of project plans under the condition of limited resources are made. Applications of Q-GERT network modeling for decision making in project planning are presented in Chapter 19.

Part VI is concerned with network graphics. Procedures for using advanced graphic capabilities for building models, portraying the operation of systems, and for displaying performance measures are described. The potential impact of computer graphics on management decision making is portrayed. The combined use of computer graphics and network modeling will provide the foundation for new organizational and behavioral procedures for management decision making.

The material in this book covers a wide spectrum of applications, network models, and statistical developments. We have drawn on the research and contributions of many people. Several of the applications and analysis projects of Larry Moore, Ed Clayton, and Chuck Taylor have been used directly. Gary Whitehouse reviewed the manuscript, and we have used material from his book on decision and risk analysis. The material on nuclear fusion forecasts is taken from the work of John Vanston. Charlie Standridge, Ken Musselman, and Steve Duket provided detailed comments on the manuscript that significantly improved its readability. The material that describes the use of simulation data languages in conjunction with network languages is based on research by Charlie Standridge.

Chapter 11 is based on the work of Lt. Col. Robert Mortenson and Capt. Victor Auterio. The material included in Chapter 20 on statistical analysis of probability distributions and the study of McClellan Air Force Base is derived from the work of Ken Musselman, Bob Hannan, Bill Penick, and Bob Mortenson. Obtaining graphical outputs from network simulation languages was developed based on the work of Steve Duket and Jerry Sabuda. The material on Q-GRAF for interactively building Q-GERT models and for displaying output traces is based on the developments of Jerry Sabuda.

Insights into production and scheduling applications have been obtained through discussions with Jim Wilson, Randy Sadowski, Richard L. Smith, and Bill Stewart. Throughout the years, we have received support from many individuals interested in the development of a network language for describing management decisions. Our discussions with Ed Clayton, Steve Duket, Salah Elmaghraby, Hank Grant, Larry Moore,

Charlie Standridge, Gary Whitehouse, Jim Wilson, Phil Wolfe, and Dave Wortman have been significant. We gratefully acknowledge the contributions of all the individuals named above and thank them for their contributions, assistance, and encouragement.

A. Alan B. Pritsker
West Lafayette, Indiana

C. Elliott Sigal
San Francisco, CA

1

Introduction

1

Management Decision Making

1.1 THE DECISION PROCESS

A decision is a selection of a course of action. A decision process specifies the steps leading to the making of such a selection, the final step in the decision process. In this book we are interested in the process leading to management decision making. We assume that managers and systems analysts working together can develop implicit or explicit objectives associated with decision problems, can formulate alternative choices, and can define performance measures to evaluate decision outcomes. Furthermore, assigning qualitative or quantitative values to performance measures is a part of the decision process. Our view of the decision process follows the paradigm shown in Figure 1-1, which is similar to the one given by Thrall et al. [200].

The starting point in the decision process is the existence of a problem situation. For some problem situations, decision making can proceed immediately without any intervening steps. Other problem situations need to be converted into a problem definition consisting of a system specification, performance measures, and objectives. After defining the problem, decision making could be initiated. A line with a double arrow is shown between problem situation and problem definition. This is meant to indicate that based on the problem definition, the understanding of the problem situation could change. That is, iterations between problem situation and problem definition could take

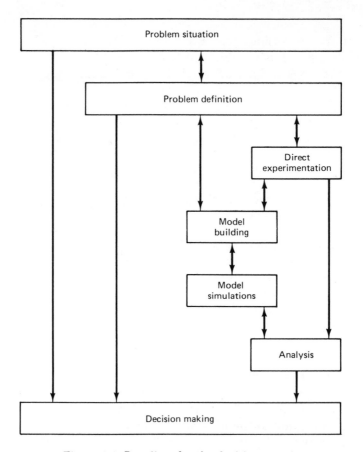

Figure 1-1 Paradigm for the decision process.

place. Throughout the description of Figure 1-1, lines with double arrows are used to indicate such an iterative process.

There are two other paths from problem definition to decision making: direct experimentation and model building. Direct experimentation includes observations and measurement on the defined system, which, after analysis, could lead to decision making. The last route to making a decision involves model building, model computations, analysis, and then decision making. It is this route which the material in this book best supports.

With the advent of computers and advanced simulation software, the steps in the decision process described can be facilitated through the use of these new tools and techniques. The foundation of the approach presented herein emphasizes the building of a model on which simulations can be performed. The building of the model includes a definition of the environment of the decision, a specification of the measures by which a good decision will be judged, and the forecasting of values of the measures of performance for each decision alternative by simulating (exercising) the model on a computer. Decision making in this context is illustrated throughout this book with emphasis on problem definitions and model building.

1.2 CATEGORIZING MANAGEMENT DECISION MAKING

Decisions can be categorized into three levels: strategic planning, management control, and operational control [26]. *Strategic planning* is the process of deciding on the objectives of an organization, on changes in these objectives, on the resources used to obtain these objectives, and on the policies that are to govern the acquisition, use, and disposition of resources. *Management control* is the process by which managers assure that the required resources are obtained and used effectively and efficiently in the accomplishment of the organization's objectives. *Operational control* is the process of assuring that specific tasks are carried out effectively and efficiently. A list of problem situations categorized by these three levels is presented in Table 1-1.

For each of the levels we can identify three types of decision: structured, semistructured, and unstructured [16,26]. *Structured deci-*

TABLE 1-1 Areas of Decision Making for Procedural Systems

Strategic planning
1. Design of new processes
2. Design of new policies
3. Determination of effect of different priorities
4. Design of new systems
5. Forecast of production levels
6. Determination of required resources
7. Estimation of cost of alternatives

Management control
8. Determination of how to improve throughput
9. Determination of effect of changes in resource capacities
10. Determination of effect of delays in raw materials
11. Determination of how to relieve bottlenecks
12. Determination of effect of change in demand
13. Determination of effect of equipment failures
14. Determination of system efficiency

Operational control
15. Determination of capacity
16. Determination of bottlenecks
17. Determination of operational requirements
18. Assessment of in-process inventories
19. Determination of utilizations
20. Determination of critical operation rates
21. Determine best staffing configurations

sions are those which are understood well enough to be automated. *Semistructured decisions* are those which involve some judgment and subjective analysis and are sufficiently well defined to enable the use of models. *Unstructured decisions* are those for which the alternatives, objectives, and consequences are ambiguous. Our main thrust is on decisions that are semistructured at each of the three levels presented above. The types of models presented are intended to assist managers in making decisions about problems which are sufficiently large and complex to require the aid of a computer, but which involve judgment and subjective analysis by the manager. Because of this, the decision maker should be drawn into the problem definition and model building stages of the decision process.

To support the decision process, a data base will be required. The integration of the decision maker, decision models, and decision support data base constitutes a decision support system (DSS). A pictorial view of the organization of these subsystems is shown in Figure 1-2.

In this book, heavy reliance on examples is made to show how model building blocks are used on the semistructured decisions in strategic planning, management control, and operational control. The interfaces between the decision model subsystem and the decision support data base and decision maker subsystems are described. However, the emphasis is on the decision model subsystem.

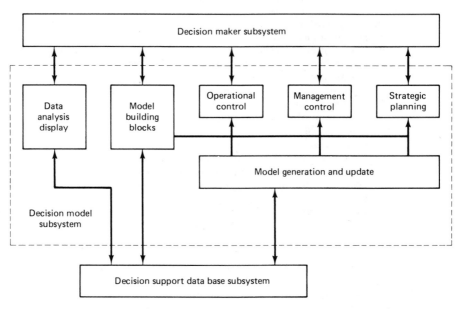

Figure 1-2 Conceptual framework of a decision support system. (From Ref. 187.)

1.3 MODELING FOR DECISION MAKING

Models are *descriptions* of systems. In the physical sciences, models are usually developed based on theoretical laws and principles. The models may be scaled physical objects (iconic models), mathematical equations and relations (abstract models), or graphical representations (visual models). The usefulness of models has been demonstrated in describing, designing and analyzing systems. Many students are educated in their discipline by learning how to build and use models. Model building is a complex process and in most fields is an art. The modeling of a system is made easier if (1) physical laws are available that pertain to the system, (2) a pictorial or graphical representation can be made of the system, and (3) the variability of system inputs, elements, and outputs is manageable.

Industrial engineers, managers and administrators, management scientists, and operations researchers deal primarily with *procedural systems*. These individuals and their respective fields are attempting to bring order out of chaos with respect to the modeling and analysis of procedural systems. For our purposes, procedural systems can be thought of in terms of information flow and decision making with respect to the implementation of stated or implied policy. Emphasis is placed on improving performance through procedural changes or through new designs regarding scheduling, sequencing, distribution, allocation, layout, and similar functions (see Table 1-1). The modeling of procedural systems is often more difficult than the modeling of physical systems, for the following reasons: (1) few fundamental laws are available; (2) procedural elements are difficult to describe and represent; (3) policy statements are hard to quantify; (4) random components are significant elements; and (5) human decision making is an integral part of such systems.

In modeling procedural systems, the specification of the proper elements to include in the model is difficult. It is recommended that a dialogue between the model builder and the decision maker be established at the earliest possible time. The model building process should be considered as an iterative one. "First-cut" models should be built, analyzed, and discussed. The time that elapses between the establishment of the purpose for building a model and the production of outputs of the first-cut model should be kept as small as possible. In many cases this will require heroic assumptions and a willingness on the part of the modeler to expose his or her potential ignorance of the problem situation. In the long run, it should pay off, as modeling inaccuracies will be discovered more quickly and corrected more efficiently than would be possible otherwise. Further, discussions that include tentative projections tend to clarify issues and to promote suggestions.

A good modeler draws the decision maker into problem-solving activities for three reasons: to ensure that a proper problem formulation has been developed, to assist in determining the system details that can be omitted from the model, and to set the stage for implementing the results of the analysis. In this light, an analyst should consider reformulating the purpose for which the model was built and, if necessary, rebuild the model. The modeling vehicle advocated in this book, Q-GERT, has been designed to be used in this mode [154].

1.4 DECISIONS AND DECISION MAKERS

All decision makers are not alike nor should they be. Let us characterize decision makers with respect to how they might use a decision support system (DSS) if one were available. The *hands-off* user reads reports that are automatically generated by the DSS but is not in direct contact with it either through requests or knowledge of the underpinnings of the DSS. This user's approach is to assume that with the facts, a good decision can be made.

A second type of decision maker is the *requester*. This type of user employs an intermediary to use the DSS. He or she frames the questions, interprets the results, and uses the answers to make decisions. The requester is not knowledgeable as to how the answers are obtained but knows that they provide additional information that is helpful in making decisions.

The third type of decision maker is of the *hands-on* variety. This type of user views the DSS input device as an extension of himself or herself and employs direct on-line access to the system using predetermined interfaces and models. Through direct interaction, he or she asks such questions as: "Why can't I get a particular type of information?" "Shouldn't a model be built that provides me with an estimate of the rate of return?" The hands-on user learns about the DSS by using it and provides inputs that can cause the DSS to adapt to his or her needs.

The fourth type of decision maker is the *renaissance* decision maker. This type of user functions as part of a team and does not feel uncomfortable talking in terms of data base systems and modeling, but is at home when making decisions. The renaissance decision maker knows how to set requirements for information, can prescribe the types of reports he or she wants, and can ask questions concerning the details of a model. In addition, this approach can avoid the expenditure of large amounts of time and possible degradation of objectivity that is sometimes associated with a decision maker who builds and uses his or her own models.

1.7 DECISION MAKING USING Q-GERT

A Q-GERT network model is a graphical picture that characterizes the decision points and algorithms that affect the time-varying behavior of the system-defining variables. These variables relate to transaction flow and the time at which milestones (nodes) are reached.

Information can be obtained directly from the network diagram relating to the structural aspects of a system's operation. This type of information provides a basis for a qualitative assessment and understanding of the mechanisms that are under the control of decision makers.

When data are available, a quantitative view of the actual flow of the transactions through the Q-GERT network model can be made and a further understanding of system operation obtained. Such a view indicates the quantity of flow, queue buildups, bottlenecks, and to some extent, server and resource utilization. The standard outputs from the analysis program provide quantitative measures of these variables.

Decision making using Q-GERT involves an assessment as to whether the system meets design requirements with respect to the types of questions posed in Table 1-1. To evaluate alternatives, structural changes or parameter changes are made to the network and their impact determined. The sensitivity of the outputs to such changes is easily assessed and a comparison between alternatives can be made on a statistical basis. Typically, changes are made to the model which can be implemented in the real system and assessments are made until a satisfactory system operation is found. This evaluation of alternatives until a satisfactory alternative is found follows the "satisficing" approach to problem solving [116]. Throughout the decision-making process, objectives and requirements are continually reevaluated to determine if different goals are more appropriate for the problem situation under study.

1.8 INFORMATION PROCESSING AND DATA BASES

Data base capabilities have grown extensively in the past five years. Information-processing computers exist in most corporate settings. The availability of timely and accurate data and their conversion into knowledge is no longer a futuristic dream. The time has come for decision makers, analysts, and designers to employ such knowledge to resolve the problems facing them. Network modeling is one method for converting the data stored in data bases into the knowledge required for management decision making. It is because of the current state of information processing and data bases that the need for the material in this book becomes so important. Network models can now be used for business and manufacturing systems in the same manner that models have always been employed for physical systems.

1.9 PROBABILITY CONCEPTS IN DECISION MAKING

There are many unknowns in decision making. The future cannot be forecast with certainty and all variables associated with a decision cannot be characterized explicitly. Because of this lack of complete information, decision making inherently requires judgments and probabilistic assessments.

Consider the question of whether the selection of an alternative will result in a correct decision. There may be a chance that the selected alternative is not as good a choice as some other alternative or that a negative value results from the selection. The recognition that there is a chance of a negative return is a first step in accepting probability concepts within the decision-making process. The chance can be characterized on a subjective or a relative frequency basis. A subjective probability is based on a decision maker's feeling about a situation. Thus, if a decision maker believes that there is 1 chance in 10 that an adverse result will occur, the subjective probability estimate is 0.1. A probability based on a relative frequency counts the number of times the adverse result occurred divided by the number of times it could have occurred. In this case, the decision maker considers all similar decisions and estimates the fraction of the decisions that were made correctly.

The recognition of the potential for a negative value should not interfere with the implementation process once the decision is made; that is, once an alternative is selected, the decision maker must stand behind it. Psychologically, the chances of a positive return are improved by the forcefulness of the decision maker in presenting the alternative selected. However, the implementation strategy needs to be sensitive to critical contingencies [133] and to be adaptive to meet the needs of the company and personnel affected.

Potential reasons for the occurrence of a negative return could be an unanticipated environmental state or an incorrectly forecasted future state. A catastrophic event, low demand, or poor weather could also be the cause. Currently, weather prediction, catastrophic events, and economic forecasts are considered from a probabilistic viewpoint.

When models are used to assist in the decision-making process, variables in the models can be defined in probabilistic terms. For example, the demand for a product could be characterized as a random variable and the probability distribution associated with that random variable could be a part of the model. The underlying assumptions associated with different random variables have been described [154] and depicted graphically. A program has been developed to aid in selecting a distribution to use in a model [137]. Alternatively, a histogram of data collected for a situation can be employed.

By combining a probabilistic characterization of the variables included in a model with a probabilistic forecast of possible future states, estimates of the probability of making a correct selection or incorrect selection can be computed. This probability, coupled with the magnitude of the outcome associated with the alternative, provides the decision maker with a risk assessment for an alternative.

Network models provide the structure for including in the decision-making process each of the probabilistic concepts listed above. The use of probabilistic concepts in the model is determined by the model builder. It is not always necessary to include advanced concepts in models nor is it necessary for the decision maker to be cognizant of all the details associated with each probabilistic concept. In fact, a network structure is ideal for representing probabilistic concepts in a form that is understandable to managers.

1.10 STATISTICAL CONCEPTS IN DECISION MAKING

There are three areas in which statistical concepts are important in decision making: (1) comparing the returns associated with alternatives, (2) determining the probability that an outcome may be beyond a prescribed limit, and (3) projecting the value of an outcome due to a change in one or more input values.

To compare alternatives on a statistical basis, hypotheses are established and statistical tests of hypotheses are performed. These statistical tests provide a means for specifying whether a return from one alternative is superior to a return from another alternative. If the hypothesis is that the returns are the same, a statistical test of hypothesis provides an estimate of the probability that the values of the outcomes are different when the alternatives are indeed the same. This is referred to as a *Type I error*. In some instances, it is possible to estimate the probability that the alternatives are different when the outcomes are similar. This is a *Type II error*. These types of errors relate to the probability of making a correct decision that was discussed in Section 1.9. When many alternatives are involved, the statistical procedures associated with the design of experiments, including analysis-of-variance (ANOVA) techniques, are used.

To determine the range of the value of an outcome for an alternative, a confidence interval should be derived. A confidence interval is specified by a lower limit and an upper limit defined to contain a theoretical value with a prescribed probability. The establishment of a confidence interval is a standard procedure in statistical analysis.

The third area for the use of statistical concepts involves building a model that relates output values to input values. The statistical technique of regression analysis is often used to estimate such a relationship [102, 157]. Regression analysis procedures are described in detail in most statistics books and courses [121].

In building models for management decision making, it is not necessary to have an extensive background in statistical concepts. However, it is important to know that such concepts exist and that additional information can be gleaned from the outputs of models. In this book we do not dwell on statistical procedures, although we do advocate their use wherever possible.

1.11 WILL MANAGEMENT ACCEPT MODELS?

It is often stated that an essential ingredient of successful management decision making is management "know-how." Management know-how apparently relates to the ability of the manager to understand what is going on in his or her environment [29]. For management to accept the outputs of models as inputs to the decision-making process, the models must augment and complement the manager's understanding of the problem situation. Another way of stating this is that a manager will accept models if the models provide new knowledge. The knowledge that the manager requires is a "know-how" concerning the selection of the correct alternative even though conditions may change.

In the preceding sections of this chapter, we have described a decision process that includes a network modeling phase that leads to new knowledge. Our experience with Q-GERT has demonstrated that management will accept models and that they will make decisions based on the information, analysis, and presentations from such models.

Semistructured problem situations are complex and require in-depth study. Managers recognize the need for a decision support system that includes a modeling capability that can be used in a broad spectrum of such problem situations. Network modeling, and Q-GERT modeling in particular, provides such an analysis vehicle. This book documents our experiences in using Q-GERT in this mode and lays a foundation for management's acceptance of models.

1.12 EXERCISES

1-1. Define the following terms used in Figure 1-1: problem definition; direct experimentation; model building; model simulations; analysis; and decision making. Specify a problem situation and relate the definitions to your approach in reaching a decision.

1-2. Specify potential performance measures for each of the areas of decision making listed in Table 1-1. Categorize the performance measures with respect to their use in strategic planning, management control, and operational control.

1-3. Compare accounting models with models used for decision making.

1-4. List the functions that are required for the model generation and updating blocks shown in Figure 1-2. Define the procedures for performing these functions and interrelationships between the functions.

1-5. Describe and characterize a procedural system. Give an example of a procedural system and discuss policies associated with the system. Define a sequence of steps that would facilitate the implementing of the policies.

1-6. Find five existing policy statements. Analyze the statements and identify elements that make them difficult to translate into operational guidelines.

1-7. In Section 1.4, decision makers are categorized by the following terms: hands-off; requester; hands-on; and renaissance. Relate the positions within a firm to these types of decision makers. Relate courses you have taken to these types of decision makers. Identify tools and techniques that could be used by each type of decision maker.

1-8. Describe network modeling procedures with which you are familiar and discuss how they separate modeling tasks from analysis tasks.

1-9. Discuss the information requirements for building a network model in comparison to the data requirements to analyze a network model.

1-10. Design output formats for presenting performance measures associated with one of the areas of decision making listed in Table 1-1.

1-11. Discuss how advances in data base systems might have an impact on decision making and modeling for decision making.

1-12. Describe how you would react to a manager who indicated that he or she was not interested in the probability that an adverse outcome would be obtained but was only interested in whether it would occur.

1-13. Discuss the ramifications of the analyst who makes the following recommendation to the plant general manager. "My model specifies that we should purchase two cranes, which will result in an increase in throughput of 30%. This increased throughput after deducting the cost of the cranes provides a 10% increase in net profit."

1-14. Discuss the use of regression analysis, analysis of variance, and tests of hypothesis with respect to a decision problem with which you are familiar.

1-15. Write a treatise on the subject "Will management accept models?"

Q-GERT Symbols, Routines, and Programs

2

The Q-GERT
Network Language

2.1 INTRODUCTION

A Q-GERT network consists of nodes and branches. A branch represents an activity that involves a processing time or a delay. Nodes are
placed before and after activities and are used to model milestones, decision points, and queues. Flowing through the network are items referred to as transactions. Transactions can represent physical objects,
information, or a combination of the two. A set of attributes is used to
describe and distinguish transactions.

Different types of nodes are included in Q-GERT to allow for the
modeling of complex systems which include queueing and project
management characteristics. Transactions are directed through the network from one node to another according to the routing characteristics
associated with each node type. The modeling of the flow of a transaction through all possible paths in a network is referred to as a *process-
oriented* or *process-interaction* modeling approach [64,157]. The nodes
and branches of a Q-GERT model are used to describe the operations
and procedures of the system.

Let us be more specific about a network model. Transactions origi-
nate at source nodes and travel along the branches of the network. Each
branch has a start node and an end node.

Transactions moving across a branch are delayed in reaching the end node associated with the branch by the time to perform the activity that the branch represents. When reaching the end node, the disposition of the transaction is determined by the node type, the status of the system, and the attributes associated with the transaction. The transaction continues through the network until no further routing can be performed. Typically, this occurs at sink nodes of the network but may occur at any node.

The Q-GERT processor employs a simulation procedure to analyze the network. The simulation procedure involves the generation of transactions, and the processing of the transactions through the network. As transactions flow through the network model, observations are made of travel times, the status of servers and queues, and the times at which nodes are released. Furthermore, statistical analysis of these data is embedded directly in a Q-GERT network model. The statistics computed are summarized in a report that is prepared and printed automatically.

This chapter summarizes the characterization of (1) objects and information by transactions and resources; (2) activities by branches; and (3) milestones, queues, and decision processes by nodes. Q-GERT input procedures and output reports are described in Chapters 4 and 5, respectively. For detailed information on Q-GERT procedures, the reader is referred to Pritsker [154].

2.2 ACTIVITIES

Let us now describe the activities of a network in more detail. Each activity in a Q-GERT network is assigned a time description. The time is specified by a *function type* and a *parameter identifier*. For constants, the function type is CO and the parameter identifier is simply the value of the constant. Thus, a delay of 100 would be shown as (CO,100). For function types that relate to random variables, the identifier is a parameter set number that specifies which set of parameters are to be used in the function. For example, a function type could be the normal distribution and the parameter set number could be given as 2, that is, (NO,2). This would specify that the activity time should be a sample from a normal distribution with the parameters of the normal distribution maintained as the second set of parameters for the network. A list of the available distribution and function types and their codes is given in Table 2-1.

TABLE 2-1. Distribution and Function Type Codes and Parameter Identifiers for the Q-GERT Network Language

Code	Description	Identifier
AT	The value of an ATtribute of a transaction is to be assigned as activity duration time	Attribute number
BE	BEta distribution	Parameter set number
BP	Beta distribution fitted to three parameters, as in PERT	Parameter set number
CO	COnstant	Value of constant
ER	ERlang distribution	Parameter set number
EX	EXponential distribution	Parameter set number
GA	GAmma distribution	Parameter set number
IN	INcremental assignment	Initial value
LO	LOgnormal distribution	Parameter set number
NO	NOrmal distribution	Parameter set number
PO	POisson distribution	Parameter set number
TR	TRiangular distribution	Parameter set number
UF	User Function	User function number
UN	UNiform distribution	Parameter set number
US	User Subroutine	User subroutine number

An activity is represented by a branch as follows:

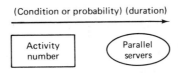

The duration of an activity is prescribed above the branch in the manner discussed previously. A routing condition or a probability is also assigned to the activity if necessary. This is explained in Section 2.4. Below the activity, an activity number is placed in a square if there is a need to refer to the activity elsewhere in the network.

The number of transactions that can concurrently be processed by the activity is unlimited unless the activity is a server. In the latter case, the number of parallel servers represented by the activity is prescribed in a circle below the activity which limits the number of concurrent transactions engaged in the activity to the number of parallel servers. Furthermore, a queue must precede the activity as a place where transactions can wait when all servers are busy processing transactions.

2.3 TRANSACTIONS

In a process approach to systems modeling, transactions play a fundamental role. The view of the system requires focusing on a single transaction and modeling all possible happenings to that transaction during its flow through the system.

As they flow, transactions pass through nodes in a network, where they may be assigned or reassigned new attributes values. The attributes can be used to distinguish between types of transactions and to differentiate between transactions of the same type. Attributes are used to affect three fundamental aspects of network logic:

1. The specification of the time required for an activity to process the transaction
2. The ranking of transactions in queues
3. The routing of transactions

By using attributes, a modeler can incorporate complex logic in a Q-GERT network. This capability results from having a network process transactions differently based on their attribute values.

Value assignments to attributes can be made at any node in the network. For each assignment to be made, three items of information are required: the attribute number, the function type, and the parameter identifier (see Table 2-1). A plus sign appended to the attribute number specifies that a value is to be added to the current value of the attribute. A negative sign appended to the attribute number indicates that a value is to be subtracted from the current value of the attribute.

2.4 TRANSACTION ROUTING

Transactions are delayed in their flow through the network by activities. At the end of each activity is a node. Different types of nodes are used to specify the logical disposition of the transaction. The transaction may be required to wait at the node or it can be immediately routed from the node. No explicit time delay is associated with a node. If the transaction is not required to wait at the node, the transaction may be routed over activities that emanate from the node in accordance with routing specifications prescribed for the node. Although the type of routing is associated with the node, the values and conditions related to routing are identified with the activities emanating from the node. Four types of routing can be specified at a node: deterministic; probabilistic; conditional, take-first; and conditional, take-all. Each of these will now be described.

2.4.1 Deterministic Routing

When a transaction is to be routed along each activity emanating from a node, deterministic routing is prescribed. Deterministic routing specifies that a duplicate transaction be created for each activity emanating from the node. Each duplicated transaction contains the same information, that is, the same attribute values. Each duplicate of the transaction is treated individually and can represent whatever the modeler specifies. For example, a transaction could represent a part and its duplicate could be an invoice.

Node types are available in Q-GERT to accumulate, assemble, or match transactions into a single unit when required. In this way, duplicate transactions that have been created by deterministic routing can be merged again into a single transaction.

2.4.2 Probabilistic Routing

Probabilistic routing of a transaction entails the selection of one activity from a set of activities based on the relative frequency with which an activity should be performed. Probabilistic routing is used to categorize transaction flow in accordance with the percentage of transactions that flow over a given portion of a network. Alternatively, probabilistic routing can be used to represent the fraction of time a specific type of activity duration is to be employed for transactions departing from a node. A probability value is assigned to each activity emanating from a node that has been specified to have probabilistic routing. In addition, the probability values can be determined dynamically by taking them from the attributes of the transaction to be routed.

2.4.3 Conditional Routing

Conditional routing specifies that transactions are to be routed over activities emanating from the node based on a condition prescribed for the activity. Two types of conditional routing are included in Q-GERT:

1. Route the transaction over the first activity whose condition is satisfied.
2. Route the transaction over each activity whose condition is satisfied.

TABLE 2-2. Condition Codes for Routing Transactions over Activities

Condition codes[a]

   T.$\mathcal{R}$.V
   T.$\mathcal{R}$.Ak
   Aj.$\mathcal{R}$.V
   Aj.$\mathcal{R}$.Ak
   Ni.R
   Ni.N
   NAj.R
   NAj.N

where T = current simulation time (TNOW), that is, the time at which conditional routing is taking place

   V = a constant value

   Aj and Ak = values of attributes j and k of the transaction for which routing is being determined

   $\mathcal{R}$ = a relational operator; the possible operators are LT, LE, EQ, NE, GT, and GE

   Ni = node number i

   NAj = node number specified by the value of attribute j of the transaction for which routing is being determined

   R stands for released

   N stands for not released

Examples

Specification	Route Transaction through Activity If:
T.LT.10.0	Current time less than 10
T.GT.A3	Current time greater than attribute 3
A2.EQ.4.0	The value of attribute 2 is equal to 4
A2.NE.A3	The value of attribute 2 is not equal to the value of attribute 3
N5.R	Node 5 has been released
NA3.N	Node number specified by attribute 3 has not been released

[a]There are 28 possible condition codes that can be specified for an activity.

These two conditional routing types are referred to as conditional, take-first and conditional, take-all, respectively. Again, the routing type is associated with the node but the conditions that specify which activities are to be taken are on the activities directly. Table 2-2 provides a summary of the conditions that may be specified for activities emanating from nodes for which the conditional routing characteristic is specified.

2.4.4 Routing Symbolism

The output side of a node is depicted by one of the four symbols shown here to indicate graphically the type of routing to be performed when a transaction is to leave the node:

Routing types

         □

| Deterministic | Probabilistic | Conditional, take-first | Conditional, take-all |

For deterministic routing, no condition or probability is associated with the activities emanating from the node. For probabilistic routing, either the probability value or the attribute number containing the probability value is associated with each activity emanating from the node. For conditional branching, one of the conditions listed in Table 2-2 is specified. If no condition is prescribed, the routing condition is assumed to be satisfied in all cases.

2.5 NODE TYPES

In Q-GERT, there are seven fundamental node types. It is interesting that only a small number of nodes is required even when modeling varied and complex situations [120,182]. Flexibility in modeling is obtained in Q-GERT by building onto the fundamental node types the concepts of attribute assignment and transaction routing.

Four node types in Q-GERT are employed to model the decision processes, milestones, and events associated directly with the flow of transactions through a system. These node types are referred to as the basic node, the queue node (Q-node), the selector node (S-node), and the MATCH node. Three node types are defined in Q-GERT for relating resources to transactions during their flow through the network. A resource is an entity that is required by a transaction in order to continue its movement through a network. First, we describe the node types associated with the flow of transactions independent of resource considerations.

2.5.1 Basic Node Type

The basic node type in Q-GERT is as follows:

Regular
Statistics
Source
Sink

R_f = first release requirement
R_s = subsequent release requirement
S = statistics or marking
C = choice criterion

The release requirement specifies the number of transaction arrivals that must occur before the functions prescribed by the node and routing from the node can be performed. The release requirement is broken into two parts: requirement for a first release and the requirement for any subsequent release. Thus, if $R_f = 2$ and $R_s = 1$, it is required that two transactions arrive before the node is released for the first time but only one transaction arrival is required for the second, third, or further release of the node.

In the middle portion of the node, a specification is made with regard to a choice criterion (C) which indicates how attributes are to be kept when more than one transaction is required to release the node. The possibilities are: keep the attribute set of the first-arriving transaction; keep the attribute set of the last-arriving transaction; keep the attribute set of the transaction with the biggest or smallest value of a specified attribute. For example, S/1 says to keep the attribute set of the transaction that had the smallest value of attribute 1.

For the basic node type, a specification is made that marking or statistics collection is to be performed. Marking involves the assignment of the time at which the transaction passes through the node to a specially designated attribute called the mark (M) attribute. Statistics collection, when specified, automatically collects and summarizes data for one of the following quantities:

Time of first release of the node, F

Time of all releases of the node, A

Time between releases of the node, B

The interval of time from when the transaction releasing the node was marked until the node was released, I

The delay involved in releasing a node due to a multiple transaction arrival requirement, D

Also, associated with each node is a node number which is used as a labeling mechanism.

There are four special cases or uses of the basic node type and each is given its own name. One use of the basic node type is as a SOURCE node which creates transactions and routes them into the network. For SOURCE nodes, no first release requirement is needed, that is, $R_f = 0$, as a first transaction always starts at a SOURCE node. Also, for SOURCE nodes, marking is always performed, that is, S = M. A self-loop or branch around a SOURCE node is the typical manner to model time between transaction arrivals. This concept is shown here for node 5, where a transaction is to arrive every 10 time units.

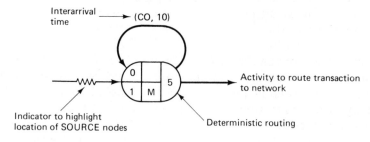

A SINK node has the basic node description for which the S parameter is specified as one of the statistical collection types. For SINK nodes, arriving transactions that release the node decrement a counter which prescribes the number of arrivals to SINK nodes necessary to complete a single run or experiment of the network. A STATIS-TICS node is identical to a SINK node with the exception that there is no run termination counter associated with a STATISTICS node.

When statistics are not collected and a node is not a SOURCE node, we refer to the basic node type as a REGULAR node. Transactions passing through a REGULAR node may be marked but beyond that, no special processing is done. The breakdown of the basic node type into four functional categories is a convenience for the modeler, as it assists in documenting the specific purpose associated with a particular use of this node type.

2.5.2 Queue Node (Q-node)

A Q-node represents a waiting line or buffer storage area where a transaction may be halted in its flow through the network until a server or resource is available to process the transaction. In its most basic form, a Q-node precedes an activity that represents a prescribed number of parallel, identical servers:

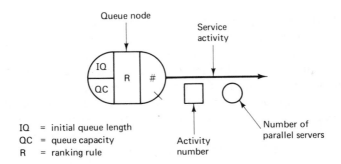

When a transaction arrives at a Q-node and one of the servers is available, the transaction passes through the Q-node and goes immediately into service. If all servers modeled by the activity are busy, the transaction waits at the Q-node if space is available in the waiting area. The size of the waiting area is specified by the queue capacity (QC) parameter of the Q-node.

Transactions waiting in the queue area are ranked in importance according to the ranking (R) specification of the Q-node. The possible ranking rules are: first-in, first-out, FIFO or F; last-in, first-out, LIFO or L; big value of attribute i, B/i; and small value of attribute i, S/i. The ranking rule specifies the order in which transactions will be removed from the queue when a server or resource is available to process the next transaction residing in the queue. Each Q-node is given a node number and an initial number of transactions residing in the queue, IQ. When $IQ > 0$, it is presumed that all servers following the Q-node are busy initially and that there are IQ transactions waiting in the queue at the beginning of the run. Each of the initially waiting transactions have all their attribute values set to zero.

When a transaction arrives to a Q-node that is at its capacity, the arriving transaction will balk from the Q-node or be blocked. Balking is indicated by a dash–dot line and points to the node to which the balking transaction is routed. Blocking requires that the activity preceding the Q-node be a service activity. When blocking occurs, the transaction on which service was completed cannot move and the server completing the service is blocked and not made available to process another transaction. The symbolism for blocking is a double line preceding the Q-node. The balking and blocking symbols are as follows:

— · —· —· —· →   Balking indicator

|| Blocking indicator

If a Q-node has a finite capacity but neither balking or blocking is indicated, the transaction arriving when the queue is full is lost to the system.

Attribute assignments can be made at a Q-node and, if prescribed, will be assigned to a transaction when it is taken out of the queue. Probabilistic routing from the Q-node is a special case and is permitted only when the service activities following the Q-node have the same activity number and the same number of parallel servers. In this way, a single service operation can be modeled by multiple branches to allow different types of service to be performed by the same server(s). Conditional routing from a Q-node is not permitted, as it could result in transactions waiting in a queue and a server being idle.

2.5.3 Selector Node (S-Node)

The decision regarding the routing of a transaction to one of a set of parallel queues or to one of a set of nonidentical servers is modeled in Q-GERT by a selection procedure prescribed at an S-node. Specifically, the conditions when an S-node is needed are the following:

1. When a transaction is to be routed to one of a set of parallel queues, what rule should be used to select the queue to which the transaction should be routed?

2. When a transaction arrives at a queue that has two nonidentical servers drawing transactions from it, what rule should be used for selecting the server to process the transaction?

3. When a service activity completes the processing of a transaction, what rule should be used for selecting the next transaction to be assigned to the server if the parallel queues that precede the server have transactions waiting in them?

Following is the graphic symbol for the S-node.

S-nodes have node numbers that are placed on the right-hand side of the node. On the left-hand side of the node, a Queue Selection Rule and a Server Selection Rule are specified. The Queue Selection Rule specifies the procedure by which a transaction is routed to or from queues based on the status of the network. The procedure is invoked when a transaction arrives at an S-node or when a service activity emanating from an S-node completes the service on a transaction. The Server Selection Rule is invoked when a transaction arrives at a Q-node and a choice from among free servers is necessary.

The list of rules for selecting from among Q-nodes at an S-node is given in Table 2-3. The Queue Selection Rules are used in two modes: to route transactions to one of a set of parallel queues; and to obtain a transaction from a set of parallel queues preceding a server or servers. The queue selection rule of the S-node is used to compare characteristics of Q-nodes. This should not be confused with the ranking of transactions within a Q-node, which is prescribed by the ranking rule associated with a Q-node. By separating the selection procedure from the ranking procedure, Q-GERT provides for a dual-level ranking and ordering system relating to transactions and sets of queues.

In network modeling, Q-nodes and S-nodes are connected by dashed lines. This indicates that decisions and procedures, not activities, are employed in the transfer of transactions from a Q-node to an S-node, or vice versa.

The list of priority rules associated with an S-node for selecting from a set of parallel service activities is shown in Table 2-4. The priority rule prescribed for an S-node will be invoked whenever a transaction arrives to a Q-node preceding the S-node and more than one server is available following the S-node. The S-node is used to distinguish and to select from among activities representing nonidentical

TABLE 2-3. Priority Rules Associated with S-nodes for Selecting
from a Set of Parallel Queues

Code	Definition	Numeric Code
POR	Priority given in a preferred order	1
CYC	Cyclic priority—transfer to first available Q-node starting from the last Q-node that was selected	2
RAN	Random priority—assign an equal probability to each Q-node that can be selected	3
LAV	Priority given to the Q-node which has had the largest average number of transactions in it to date	4
SAV	Priority is given to the Q-node which has had the smallest average number of transactions in it to date	5
LWF	Priority is given to the Q-node for which the waiting time of its first transaction from its last marking is the longest	6
SWF	Priority is given to the Q-node for which the waiting time of its first transaction from its last marking is the shortest	7
LNQ	Priority is given to the Q-node which has the current largest number of transactions in it	8
SNQ	Priority is given to the Q-node which has the current smallest number of transactions in it	9
LNB	Priority is given to the Q-node which has had the largest number of balkers from it to date	10
SNB	Priority is given to the Q-node which has had the smallest number of balkers from it to date	11
LRC	Priority is given to the Q-node which has the largest remaining unused capacity	12
SRC	Priority is given to the Q-node which has the smallest remaining unused capacity	13
ASM	Assembly mode option—all incoming queues must contribute one transaction before a processor may begin service (this can be used to provide an "AND" logic operation)	-14
NQS	User-written function for queue selection	15

parallel servers. If more than one branch emanates from an S-node, only single servers can be specified for the activities following the S-node.

When an S-node precedes a set of parallel queues, balking can occur from the S-node if all the following Q-nodes are at their capacity. Similarly, an S-node can block an incoming server if routing to Q-nodes is not possible due to limited queue capacity. Multiple S-nodes may be associated with a single Q-node. This permits the modeling of a transaction that is to wait at a Q-node for the first server that is available

Code	Definition	Numeric Code
POR	Select from free servers in a preferred order	1
CYC	Select servers in a cyclic manner	2
RAN	Select servers by a random selection of free servers	3
LBT	Select the server that has the largest amount of usage (busy time) to date	4
SBT	Select the server which has the smallest amount of usage (busy time) to date	5
LIT	Select the server who has been idle for the longest period of time	6
SIT	Select the server who has been idle for the shortest period of time	7
RFS	Select randomly from free servers according to preassigned probabilities	8
NSS	User-written function to select service activity	9

where the set of possible servers is not associated with a particular S-node. In this case, a preferred order for interrogating the S-nodes is employed based on the order in which the S-nodes are specified when describing the Q-node (see Chapter 4). When multiple S-nodes are associated with a Q-node, any of the servers following any of the S-nodes will refer back to the Q-node in which the transaction resides, and the transaction becomes a candidate for selection when any of the servers becomes available.

The ASM queue selection procedure is different from other Queue Selection Rules, as it involves the assembling of waiting transactions for a server. In this case the selection process requires that at least one transaction be in each Q-node prior to the start of the service activity. A special form of the dashed-line connector between Q-nodes and S-nodes is used for this, as shown on the next page. In this example, node 23 will extract transactions from Q-nodes 20, 21, and 22 only if there is at least one transaction in each of the Q-nodes. A single transaction will be assembled and the attributes of the assembled transaction will be set to the attributes of the transaction that has the biggest value of attribute 1. The assembled transaction is processed by activity 4, where the combined transaction incurs a normally distributed delay in accordance with the parameters specified by parameter identifier 3. The choice criterion associated with the S-node is required only when it is used to assemble transactions.

This section has illustrated the concepts and use of the S-node. The S-node provides the important function of routing transactions to

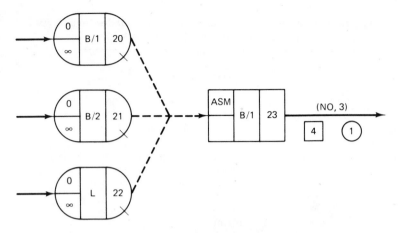

Q-nodes and to servers when a choice exists. Since routing is performed in accordance with rules, no routing type is ever specified with the output side of the S-node. The S-node performs a decision function and no time delay is associated with the processing of a transaction through S-nodes. As with all node types, attribute value assignments can be made at S-nodes.

2.5.4 MATCH Nodes

A MATCH node in Q-GERT forces transactions to wait in specified Q-nodes until each Q-node has a transaction that has a specified attribute value. The MATCH node removes these "matched" transactions from the Q-nodes and routes each transaction individually. A MATCH node differs from an S-node with the ASM Queue Selection Rule in that the MATCH node requires that the transaction in the different queues have a common attribute value.

The Q-GERT symbolism for a MATCH node is as follows:

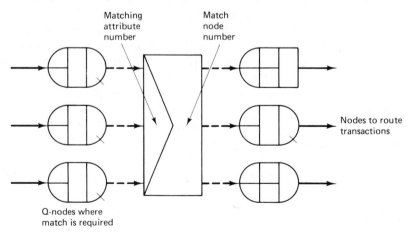

The attribute number to be "matched" is placed in the left-hand portion of the symbol. No choice criterion is necessary, as each transaction is routed separately when a match occurs. The Q-nodes associated with the MATCH node are connected to the input side of the MATCH node with a dashed line. The nodes to which the transactions are to be sent are connected to the output side of the MATCH node with a dashed line. Recall that dashed lines represent direct transfers and are not to be considered as activities.

A Q-node can be associated with more than one MATCH node but may *not* be associated with both a MATCH node and an S-node. Also, *the initial number in the queue for a Q-node associated with a MATCH node must be zero.*

2.6 RESOURCES

A resource in Q-GERT is an entity that is required by a transaction before it can proceed through a network segment. The Q-GERT modeler can define different resource types. For each resource type, there is an available number of units, that is, a capacity. For example, technicians can be defined as resource type 2 and we can declare that 10 technicians are available for allocation to job transactions.

Resource types are defined through the use of a resource block which appears on the network as a legend. The resource block provides general information regarding the resource, such as resource number and label, resource capacity, and an ordered list of ALLOCATE node numbers where the resource units can be allocated to transactions.

A transaction requesting resource units waits in a Q-node until sufficient units of the resource are available for allocation to it. The allocation of resource units to transactions occurs at ALLOCATE nodes. When a resource unit is allocated to a transaction, the transaction is removed from the Q-node and routed to a node following the ALLOCATE node. An allocated resource unit is in use until a transaction makes it available by passing through a FREE node. At the FREE node, resource units are made available and are reallocated at ALLOCATE nodes. A preferred order is used to determine which ALLOCATE node is to attempt to allocate the freed resources.

The third node type associated with resources is the ALTER node, which permits the changing of the resource capacity, that is, the total number of units of a resource that can be allocated concurrently.

2.6.1 ALLOCATE Node

An ALLOCATE node is used to allocate resources to transactions that arrive to or are waiting in Q-nodes that precede the ALLOCATE node. When a transaction arrives at a Q-node preceding an ALLOCATE node and the required resources are available, the resources are allocated. If the resources are not available, the arriving transaction waits in the Q-node until other transactions make resources available by passing through a FREE or ALTER node.

The symbol for the ALLOCATE node is as follows:

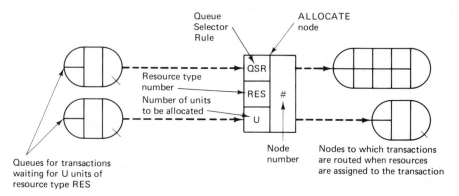

On the input side of the ALLOCATE node, the following information is prescribed:

1. A Queue Selection Rule (QSR), which can be any of those prescribed for an S-node (see Table 2-3) except the ASM rule
2. The resource number, RES, of the resource to be allocated
3. A constant number of units, U, of RES to be allocated to each transaction at the ALLOCATE node

When sufficient units of a resource can be allocated and a transaction has been selected from one of the preceding Q-nodes, the transaction is removed from the Q-node and routed to a specific node associated with that Q-node that is on the output side of the ALLOCATE node and connected to it by a dashed line. When resources are allocated at the ALLOCATE node, they are made unavailable. Value assignments can be made at ALLOCATE nodes. Frequently, the resource type and number of units allocated are assigned as attributes of a transaction passing through the ALLOCATE node to allow decision making based on these values. Since each transaction is routed individually, no routing type is associated with the ALLOCATE node.

2.6.2 FREE Nodes

The FREE node allows a transaction to make resources available. At the FREE node, the resource type and the units of the resource to be freed are prescribed. These quantities can be specified by numeric values or by attribute numbers. Thus, the resource number and the number of units to be freed can be carried as attributes of the transaction arriving to the FREE node. Note that the transaction arriving to the FREE node need not have had resources allocated to it and that the transaction will be routed from the FREE node. Routing of the transaction that arrived to the FREE node can be DETERMINISTIC, PROBABILISTIC, or CONDITIONAL. A list of ALLOCATE nodes can be associated with a free node where the resources freed are to be reallocated. The symbol for the FREE node is as follows:

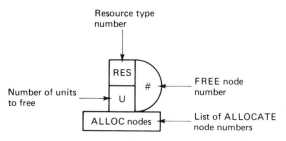

The ALLOCATE node list specified below the FREE node prescribes the order in which ALLOCATE nodes are to be polled in order to reallocate the freed resource units. Added to this list will be any ALLOCATE nodes given in the general resource block for the specified RES type. If it is desired not to concatenate the general list of ALLOCATE nodes, a delimiter (–1) should be prescribed at the end of the ALLOCATE node list given below the FREE node.

2.6.3 ALTER Nodes

The ALTER node is placed in the network at locations where it is desired to cause a change (positive or negative) in the capacity of a resource type. Each transaction that arrives to the ALTER node causes an alteration in the resource capacity. At the ALTER node, the resource number and the change requested can be prescribed as constants or attribute numbers. Branching from an ALTER node can be DETERMINISTIC, PROBABILISTIC, or CONDITIONAL. A list of ALLOCATE nodes can be associated with the ALTER node to indicate where an increase in resource capacity is to be allocated.

When the capacity of a resource type is increased, a polling of ALLOCATE nodes is started to determine if transactions waiting at Q-nodes preceding each ALLOCATE node can use the newly available units of resource. When a capacity decrease is requested, it is satisfied immediately if a sufficient number of resource units are not in use. If this is not the case, the portion of the requested decrease not satisfied is queued. As resource units are freed at FREE nodes, any queued capacity decrease is satisfied prior to the reallocation of the freed resource units.

The symbol for the ALTER node is as follows:

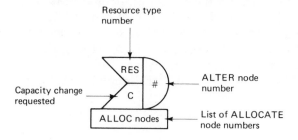

2.7 NODE MODIFICATION

Nodal modification involves the replacement in the network of one node by another node when an activity is completed. The replacement of a node specifies that the functions performed at the node *after it is released* are replaced by a new node. Only nodes that are released can be modified, that is, the basic node type. The functions that are replaced involve the collection of statistics, the assignment of values to attributes, and the method for routing transactions. For example, if node 7 is replaced by node 10, any transaction that causes node 7 to be released is transferred to node 10 and the functions and routing specified for node 10 are applied to the transaction. A dotted line from the node being replaced is used to indicate nodal modification with an arrow pointing toward the node being inserted. The activity number causing the modification is placed in a square next to the dotted line.

The graphical symbolism indicating that node 7 is to be replaced by node 10 when activity 3 has been completed is shown here.

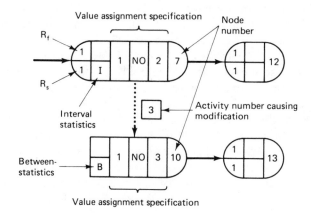

For this network segment, activity 3 is not shown but is presumed to be part of the total network. A transaction arriving to node 7 releases node 7. If activity 3 has not been completed, interval statistics are collected, and a value is assigned to attribute 1 of the transaction that is a sample from a normal distribution having parameters as specified by parameter set 2. The transaction is then sent to node 12. However, if activity 3 was completed prior to the time that the transaction arrived at node 7, node 7 is released, but the functions associated with node 7 are now replaced by the functions specified by node 10. Thus, between statistics are collected, and a value is assigned to attribute 1 of the arriving transaction that is normally distributed with parameters as specified by parameter set 3. The transaction is then routed to node 13 from node 10.

In the illustration above, the input side of node 10 was not drawn to indicate that the input functions performed at a node are not replaced when a nodal modification occurs. This example illustrates how a new value can be assigned to an attribute of a transaction and how the routing of a transaction can be changed, based on the completion of an activity. From an applications standpoint, activity 3, the instigator of the modification, could be modeling the passage of time or a learning process after which transactions are processed in a more efficient manner.

In Q-GERT, reinserting a node by a network modification is allowed. For example, in the illustration above, node 10 could be modified to node 7 when activity 4 is completed. It may be desired to construct a network involving a series of nodal modifications which specifies that node 7 is replaced by node 8 when activity 1 is completed and node 8 is replaced by node 9 when activity 2 is completed. These serial modifications are as follows:

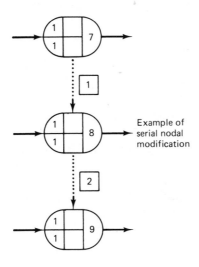

Example of serial nodal modification

For this specification, the order in which activities 1 and 2 are completed affects the nodes kept in the network. If, in the example above, it is desired to have node 9 in the network when activities 1 and 2 are completed regardless of the order in which the activities are completed, it is necessary to construct the following Q-GERT network segment:

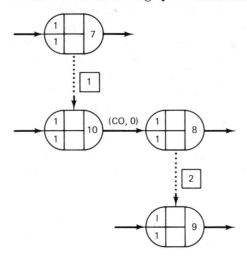

2.8 Q-GERT SYMBOL SUMMARY

This chapter has described the symbols that constitute the Q-GERT network language. A summary of all Q-GERT symbols is presented in Figure 2-1. Basically there are seven node types, as pictured in the left-hand portion of Figure 2-1. Activities are depicted by a directed branch. Service activities must be preceded by a Q-node or an S-node, which, in turn, has preceding Q-nodes. Service activities limit the number of concurrent transactions flowing through them. Activities that are not preceded by a Q-node allow an unlimited number of concurrent transactions to flow through them.

The assignment of values to attributes can be made at any node. The node symbol is extended to show the value assignment information. Transaction routing from a node is indicated by the shape of the right-hand side of the node. Four routing types are available in Q-GERT, as indicated in Figure 2-1. All four types may be used with any of the basic nodes and the FREE and ALTER nodes. Conditional routing is not permitted from Q-nodes. Connectors are used to route transactions through SELECTOR, MATCH, and ALLOCATE nodes; that is, node-to-node transfers are performed for each transaction.

The three remaining Q-GERT symbols indicate balking (a dash-dot line), blocking (a pair of parallel lines), and nodal modification

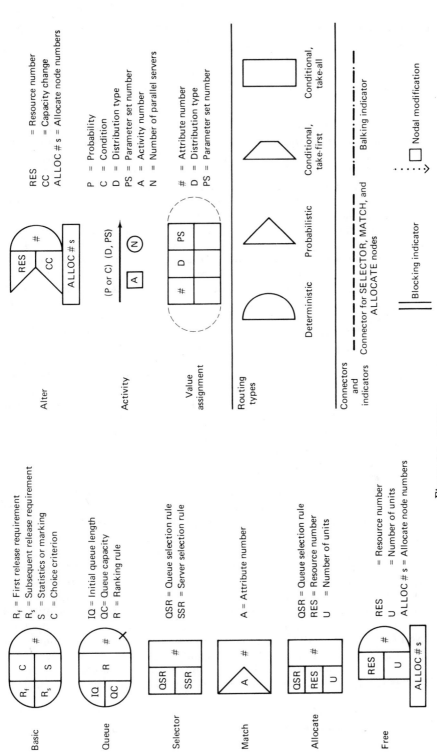

Figure 2-1 Q-GERT symbols summary.

39

(a dotted line). Figure 2-1 illustrates the compactness of the Q-GERT symbol set.

2.9 EXERCISES

2-1. Develop a Q-GERT model for the following situation. Assembled television sets move through a series of testing stations in the final stage of their production. At the last of these stations, a control setting on the TV sets is tested. If the setting is found to be functioning improperly, the offending set is routed to an adjustment station, where the setting is adjusted. After adjustment, the television set is sent back to the last inspection station, where the setting is again inspected. Television sets passing the final inspection phase, whether for the first time or after one or more routings through the adjustment station, pass on to a packing area. The time between arrivals of television sets to the final inspection station is uniformly distributed between 3.5 and 7.5 minutes. Two inspectors work side by side at the final inspection station. The time required to inspect a set is uniformly distributed between 6 and 12 minutes. On the average, 85% of the sets pass inspection and continue on to the packing department. The other 15% are routed to the adjustment station, which is manned by a single worker. Adjustment of the control setting requires between 20 and 40 minutes, uniformly distributed. Based on the model, list five decisions that are incorporated into the model that can be analyzed using the model. Estimate performance tendencies that you feel would be associated with changes caused by decisions affecting the model.

Embellishments: Modify the Q-GERT model of the inspection and adjustment stations to accommodate the following changes:

(a) An arrival of television sets to the inspection station involves two television sets to be inspected.

(b) The adjuster routes 40% of the adjusted sets directly to packing and 60% to the inspectors.

(c) By adding a step to the inspection process, it is felt that the probability of sending a set to the adjuster can be decreased to 0.10; the added step takes 5 minutes. Redraw the network to indicate these changes.

2-2. A paint shop employs six workers who prepare jobs to be spray painted. The preparation operation is lengthy compared to the spraying operation; hence, only two spraying machines are available. After a worker completes the preparation of a job, he or she proceeds to the spraying machine, where the worker must wait, if necessary, for a free spraying machine. The preparation time is normally distributed with a mean of 20 minutes and a standard deviation of 3 minutes. Spraying time is uniformly distributed between 5 and 10 minutes. A Q-GERT model of this situation is to be developed to obtain estimates of the utilization of the workers and the spraying machines for five 8-hour days. Also to be determined is the length of time required to prepare and paint a job. It is assumed that jobs to be prepared and painted are always available to the workers.

Embellishment: Include in the model a drying operation that is to be performed after painting. Drying requires 15 minutes and does not require a worker. Include this operation in your Q-GERT network. With this addition, what changes would you expect in the statistical quantities of interest?

2-3. A machine shop operates 8 hours a day, 5 days a week. There are 54 machines in the machine shop and management maintains a work force of 50 operators. The machines are subject to failure and when a machine fails, another machine, if available, is put into service. A failed machine is serviced by a repairman, if one is available. Travel times by the operator to a different machine, and the repairman to a failed machine are considered negligible. An aggregate model of this situation is to be built. Data have been collected on all machines as a group. The time between failures for any machine has been determined to be exponentially distributed with a mean of 157 hours. Repair times are also based on aggregated data and the time required to repair any failed machine for any repairman has been determined to be uniformly distributed between 4 and 10 hours. Develop a Q-GERT model to estimate the average number of operators busy, the average number of repairmen busy, the number of machines in a backup status, and the number of machines waiting for repair.

Embellishments:

   (a) Develop the Q-GERT network for the situation decribed above, assuming that four machines are initially in a failed state.
   (b) Develop a cost structure that will allow management to decide the number of repairmen required to service failed machines. Redevelop the Q-GERT network to obtain the data to support the management decision process associated with the determination of the number of repairmen to keep on the payroll.

2-4. Explain the differences among the terms accumulation, assembly, and matching. Specify why different Q-GERT concepts are required to model these operations. Develop one example of each operation in a practical situation.

2-5. Build a series of hierarchical models using Q-GERT concepts and symbols for a manufacturing facility. At the most aggregate level, consider the facility as a single server that processes orders. As a first level of disaggregation, consider that three operations are involved in processing orders: order receipt, producing a product, and packing and shipping. At the next level of disaggregation build Q-GERT models for portraying order receipt, production, and packing and shipping. Discuss how each of the models may be used to solve different managerial problems.

2-6. Compare the similarities and differences associated with each of the following set of Q-GERT constructs: Service Activity and Resource; Conditional Branching and Node Modification; Entity representing a server and Service Activity; an Entity and a Resource; a Q-GERT network model and a simulation program.

2-7. Describe each of the rules employed at a selector node (S-node) in your own terms. Identify situations in which you think these rules would be appropriate. Develop two rules that are not available to be specified at an S-node.

2-8. ALLOCATE nodes 10, 11, and 12 are referenced at FREE node 7. Describe the decision processes implied by the following situations:

   (a) At ALLOCATE node 10, Q-nodes 13 and 14 are referenced and a POR rule is used at ALLOCATE node 10. A first-in, first-out ranking procedure is specified for Q-node 13, and a high-value-first based on attribute 2 is specified for Q-node 14.

(b) At ALLOCATE node 11, Q-nodes 14, 15, and 16 are referenced, each of which has a last-in, first-out ranking procedure specified. The queue selection rule used at ALLOCATE node 11 is cyclic.

(c) At ALLOCATE node 12, only Q-node 20 is referenced. A low-value-first based on attribute 4 is specified for Q-node 20.

2-9. In Q-GERT, there are seven node types. Explain the significance associated with such a small number of node types. Discuss the symbolism used within Q-GERT from a human factors standpoint. Discuss how you would explain the Q-GERT symbols to the following individuals: your supervisor; the dean of the business school; your spouse or potential date; a 13-year-old sibling.

3

Q-GERT Support Routines

3.1 INTRODUCTION

The network modeling of systems using Q-GERT involves the use of Q-GERT symbols and procedures. The Q-GERT symbol set was designed to allow the modeling of a wide class of problems without requiring any programming by the modeler. Many problems can be resolved using only the network features of Q-GERT. However, as a Q-GERT modeler encounters more complex systems with special characteristics, a need may develop for user-written program inserts that model such specialized situations.

This chapter describes the procedures for a user of Q-GERT to include FORTRAN subprograms in a Q-GERT network model. Included in Q-GERT are standard subprograms for accessing Q-GERT data and for performing Q-GERT functions. These subprograms are designed to assist the user in writing programming inserts. In this chapter, these subprograms are defined. In addition, the internal Q-GERT variables that define the status of nodes, activities, transactions, and resources are provided. Throughout the chapter, we assume that the reader has a familiarity with FORTRAN, computers, and simulation techniques and terminology.

3.2 MODELING STRATEGY

As a modeling procedure, we recommend that a model be built without programming inserts. This "first-cut" model may require aggregation of details to a high level. By approaching a problem in this manner, a segregation of network modeling constructs and detailed programming aspects involved in model building can be made. This simple procedure can significantly decrease the design and development problems inherent in any computer programming effort. By making the programming effort subservient to the modeling task, a clear definition of the requirements and functions that need to be programmed usually results. In fact, the structure imposed by Q-GERT which specifies where programming inserts may be made can be a tremendous help in building models of complex situations. As in the case with most methodologies that impose structure, it is at the cost of flexibility. Q-GERT, however, has the structure to allow for the orderly development of a model, yet provides sufficient flexibility to enable the building of models that have the fidelity necessary to produce a solution to the problem being studied.

3.3 LOCATION OF PROGRAMMING INSERTS
IN Q-GERT MODELS

Q-GERT defines network constructs (nodes, branches, and information transfers) and the rules for combining these constructs into a network model. Q-GERT also prescribes three locations where a modeler may call a user-written function,† *function UF*. These are:

1. As an activity duration
2. As a value assignment specification at a node
3. As a queue selection rule at an S-node or ALLOCATE node or a server selection rule at an S-node

In the first case, function UF replaces the function type specification that is normally associated with the duration of the activity. In the second case, function UF replaces the function type specification that normally specifies the mechanism by which a value is assigned to a specific attribute of a transaction passing through the node. In the third case, function NQS replaces the Queue Selection Rule and function NSS replaces the Server Selection Rule.

†In this section we reference only function UF(IFN). However, subroutine US(ISN, DTIM) could be invoked as an alternative.

When using function UF, the parameter identifier in these situations is a user function number. The code letters UF are used to indicate that a user function is to be employed at a branch or node. The notation (UF,IFN) indicates that user function number IFN is to be employed. For example, the following network segment indicates that user function 2 is to be referenced every time service activity 3 is started.

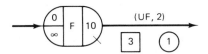

In user function 2, the time required to perform service activity 3 must be specified. Also, the user may code in function 2 other decision elements such as the halting of ongoing activities, the reassignment of attribute values, and the replacement (modification) of nodes in the network.

The symbolism for prescribing the use of a user function at a node is as follows:

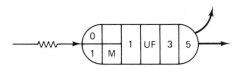

At node 5, user function 3 is used to compute a value that will be assigned to attribute 1 of the transaction flowing through node 5. Through user function 3, the modeler can adapt the network model to meet specific conditions that exist when a transaction passes through node 3.

The purpose of the user function number is to differentiate calls to the user-written function UF. The specification for the user-written subroutine US is identical to UF. Subroutine US is typically used to code complex decision situations, whereas function UF is used to compute activity times or attribute values.

3.4 GENERAL FORM FOR CODING USER-WRITTEN SUBPROGRAMS: UF, US, NQS, NSS

All user-written subprograms called by Q-GERT have a similar structure. We describe this structure for function UF since it is the most commonly used of the subprograms. The syntax for subroutine US and functions NQS and NSS are given at the end of this section.

The layout of function UF is shown in **Figure 3-1**.

```
            FUNCTION UF(IFN)
            Common and Dimension Statements
            GO TO (1,2,3),IFN
          1 Calculate a value for user function 1
            GO TO 100
          2 Calculate a value for user function 2
            GO TO 100
          3 Calculate a value for user function 3
        100 CONTINUE
            RETURN
            END
```

Figure 3-1 General format for function UF.

This is not a FORTRAN listing but a representation of the typical form for writing function UF. Normally, the first executable statement in UF is a computed GO TO statement based on the value of the function number passed to UF as an argument. In this way, separate sections of UF are used to model different aspects of the system.

In the remainder of this chapter, information is provided on (1) definitions of Q-GERT variable names, (2) procedures for accessing the Q-GERT subprograms for sampling from different density functions, and (3) subprograms capable of performing complex Q-GERT functions, such as nodal modifications, activity halting, event scheduling, and attribute assignment. Throughout the chapter any reference to function UF also applies to subroutine US. The syntax for US is

SUBROUTINE US(ISN,DTIM)

where ISN is the user subroutine number and DTIM is the value the user sets in the subroutine to be used as a duration or value assignment.

The functional form for NQS and NSS is

FUNCTION NQS(NODE)

FUNCTION NSS(NODE)

where NODE is the node number for which the NQS or NSS selection rule is specified. The user must specify NQS as the selected Q-node number in function NQS and NSS as the selected service activity number in function NSS. NQS and NSS must be set to zero if no selection can be made.

TABLE 3-1   Selected List of Q-GERT Variable Definitions

Variable Name[a]	Definition
NDE	Number of attributes associated with a transaction; NDE counts the mark time as an attribute
NFTBU(NODE)	Node number at which statistics collection, value assignments and branching occurs when NODE is released
NREL(NODE)	For Q-node, current number in queue; for S-node, queue selection code (numeric); otherwise, number of remaining requirements for nodal release
NRELP(NODE)	For Q-node, initial number in Q-node; for S-node, numeric queue selection code (see Table 3-2); otherwise, number of requirements for first release of NODE
NREL2(NODE)	For Q-node, maximum capacity of queue; for S-node, numeric server selection code (see Table 3-2); otherwise, number of subsequent requirements to release NODE
NRUN	Current run number, that is, NRUN = 3 signifies that the third simulation of the network is being performed
NRUNS	Total number of runs requested
NTC(NODE)	The number of transactions that have passed through node NODE since time TBEG; if NODE has been replaced by another node, NTC(NODE) is not increased
PARAM(I,J)	Jth value of parameter set I (see Table 4-4)
TBEG	Time at which data collection is to begin (TBEG is input on GEN card)
TNOW	Current simulation time

[a] In the list of variables, the argument NODE denotes the current node number, which is normally known to the user through his or her knowledge of the location of the call to UF or US.

3.5 DEFINITIONS OF Q-GERT VARIABLES

Table 3-1 lists the Q-GERT variables† that can be used directly in function UF if the labeled COMMON block QVAR, shown below, is included in function UF.

```
COMMON/QVAR/NDE,NFTBU(100),NREL(100),NRELP(100),NREL2(100),NRUN,
1NRUNS,NTC(100),PARAM(100,4),TBEG,TNOW
```

The current simulation time is TNOW, and it is one of the most important Q-GERT variables. The current run number, NRUN, is useful for changing decision rules between runs. NRUNS is defined as the total

†QVAR is shown for the 100-node version of the Q-GERT processor.

TABLE 3-2 Codes for Distribution Types, Queue Selection, and Server Selection

Distribution Types	Queue Selection	Server Selection
1 COnstant	1 POR	1 POR
2 NOrmal	2 CYC	2 CYC
3 UNiform	3 RAN	3 RAN
4 ERlang	4 LAV	4 LBT
5 LOgnormal	5 SAV	5 SBT
6 POisson	6 LWF	6 LIT
7 BEta	7 SWF	7 SIT
8 GAmma	8 LNQ	8 RFS
9 Beta-PERT	9 SNQ	9 NSS
10 User subroutine	10 LNB	
11 TRiangular	11 SNB	
12 ATtribute value	12 LRC	
13 INcremental	13 SRC	
14 User function	-14 ASM	
	15 NQS	

number of runs to be made and is used to check when all runs have been completed. The other variables listed in Table 3-1 are not used as frequently.

3.6 NUMERIC CODES ASSOCIATED WITH FUNCTION TYPES, QUEUE SELECTION RULES, AND SERVER SELECTION RULES

Table 3-2 presents the numeric codes used in the Q-GERT processor that correspond to the alphabetic descriptors for function types, queue selection rules, and server selection rules. The Q-GERT processor translates the alphabetic information that is specified on input to the numeric codes shown in Table 3-2. When accessing these values in function UF, it is a numeric value that will be returned. (The use of numeric codes internally within the Q-GERT processor is based on the efficiency of the computer to process numeric values.)

3.7 FUNCTIONS AVAILABLE FOR OBTAINING SAMPLES FROM PROBABILITY DISTRIBUTIONS

Table 3-3 presents the functions that are included in Q-GERT for obtaining samples from probability distributions. The modeler may use these functions in UF to obtain samples directly. For example, to ob-

TABLE 3-3 Probability Distribution Functions for Use in UF

Function Name and Arguments[a]	Description
BE(J)	Beta distribution using parameter set J
DPROB(CP,VAL, NVAL,ISTRM)	Discrete probability distribution where CP is a vector of cumulative probabilities for values stored in the vector VAL; NVAL is the number of values in the distribution and ISTRM is the random number stream to be used
DRAND(ISTRM)	Pseudo-random number generator using stream ISTRM
ER(J)	Erlang distribution using parameter set J
EX(J)	Exponential distribution using parameter set J
GA(J)	Gamma distribution using parameter set J
LO(J)	Lognormal distribution using parameter set J
NO(J)	Normal distribution using parameter set J
PO(J)	Poisson distribution using parameter set J
TR(J)	Triangular distribution using parameter set J
UN(J)	Uniform distribution using parameter set J

[a] All functions return real values. REAL FUNCTIONs are used for LO and NO. A real representation of an integer is returned from FUNCTION PO.

tain a sample from a normal distribution with parameters as specified by parameter set 2, the following statements would be used in function UF:

REAL NO

SAMP=NO(2)

With these statements, SAMP is a sample from a normal distribution with a mean and standard deviation as specified by parameter set 2 (the first and fourth parameters of the parameter set).

The samples obtained from any of the functions listed in Table 3-3 will always be between the minimum and maximum values specified by the modeler. The minimum and maximum are contained in the parameter set as the second and third values, respectively. Any value that is below the minimum value causes the sample to be set at a minimum value. Similarly, any value greater than the maximum value causes the sample to be set at the maximum value.

The names selected for the functions that obtain samples from probability distributions correspond to the input codes for distribution types. FORTRAN requires that user-defined variable names be different from these function names.

3.8 PARAMETER CHANGES REQUIRED WHEN USING LOGNORMAL, BETA, GAMMÁ, BETA-PERT, OR TRIANGULAR DISTRIBUTIONS DIRECTLY IN FUNCTION UF

The values of parameters stored in the parameter sets for sampling from the lognormal, beta, gamma, beta-PERT, and triangular distributions are different from the parameter specifications listed in the standard Q-GERT input fields. The standard input values are automatically modified by Q-GERT. When the functions are called in UF, it is the modeler's responsibility to ensure that the correct parameter values are used when obtaining samples from the distributions noted above. To accomplish a change of parameters (which should only be done once), the following subroutines are provided.

Subroutine CPLO(JP)	Changes values of parameter set number JP to values required for sampling from a lognormal distribution
Subroutine CPBE(JP)	Changes values of parameter set number JP to values required for sampling from a beta distribution
Subroutine CPGA(JP)	Changes values of parameter set number JP to values required for sampling from a gamma distribution
Subroutine CPTR(JP)	Changes values of parameter set number JP to values required for sampling from a triangular distribution

3.9 SUBROUTINE UI

Before each analysis run for a network, the Q-GERT processor calls subroutine UI to allow the modeler to initialize user-defined variables and to create special initial conditions. Subroutine UI is called after all the Q-GERT data records for a run have been processed. Note that if 10 runs are requested, subroutine UI will be called 10 times.

3.10 SUBROUTINE UO

After each analysis run for a network, the Q-GERT processor calls subroutine UO to provide the modeler an opportunity to perform any end-of-run computations or to output user specified information. By testing for NRUN being equal to NRUNS in subroutine UO the last run can be detected, and special outputs for all runs can be prepared and written in subroutine UO.

3.11 SPECIAL SUBPROGRAMS FOR USE WHEN CODING FUNCTION UF

Since Q-GERT is a FORTRAN program, the number of special functions that can be provided for assisting the user in the coding of function UF is open-ended. The following sections present subprograms associated with transactions, Q-nodes, activities, servers, statistics, auxiliary attributes, resource information, and resource operations. Some of the subprograms perform the function of retrieving a value for a Q-GERT variable. These are included for user convenience.

3.11.1 Subprograms Associated with Transactions

The subprograms relating to transactions are listed in Table 3-4. These subprograms deal mainly with the acquisition of or the setting of attribute values for a specific transaction. The transaction at a node or

TABLE 3-4 Subprograms Associated with Transactions

Subprogram	Use and Definition of Arguments
Function GATRB(J)	Returns GATRB as the value of the Jth attribute of the transaction currently being processed
Subroutine GETAT(ATT)	Returns the vector ATT($\cdot$); ATT(J) contains the value of the Jth attribute associated with the transaction currently being processed; the user must dimension ATT in UF
Subroutine PATRB(ATTR,J)	Assigns the value ATTR to attribute J of the current transaction
Subroutine PTIN(NODE,TIME, TIMEM,ATT)	Puts transaction in the network at node NODE at time TNOW+TIME; the mark time of the transaction is TIMEM and the attributes of the transaction are given by ATT(I), I=1,...,(NDE-1); ATT must be dimensioned in UF
Subroutine PUTAT(ATT)	Assigns the values contained in ATT to the attributes of the current transaction; the user must dimension ATT in UF
Function TMARK(IDUM)	Returns TMARK as the time the current transaction was last marked; IDUM is not used

the transaction being routed from a node is referred to as the *current transaction*. The subprograms are designed to acquire or to set the attribute values of the current transaction. Also listed in Table 3-4 is subroutine PTIN, which is used for inserting (putting) a transaction into the network.

Subroutine PTIN(NODE,TIME,TIMEM,ATT) creates a transaction and puts it in the network where TIMEM is the mark time for the new transaction and ATT is a vector containing the attributes of the new transaction. The transaction is scheduled to arrive at node NODE at TNOW+TIME.

3.11.2 Subprograms Associated with Q-nodes

The first six functions listed in Table 3-5 are related to Q-GERT variables associated with Q-nodes: CAPQ(NODE), RCAPQ(NODE), XNINQ(NODE), NOFQ(IDUM), AVEWT(NODE), and TINIQ(NODE). CAPQ, RCAPQ, and XNINQ are included to assist the modeler by providing real values of the capacity, remaining (unused) capacity, and number in the queue. (When these functions are used, the labeled COMMON block QVAR need not be included in function UF.) The function NOFQ permits the determination of a Q-node associated with a service activity. The functions AVEWT and TINIQ provide a means to obtain intermediate values of average waiting time and integrated number in the Q-node. These values can be used for routing and decision making during a simulation run.

There are subprograms in Q-GERT for locating transactions, copying attributes, and removing and inserting transactions with respect to Q-nodes. To find the location of a transaction in Q-node NODE with a specified attribute value, function NFIND is used. The arguments to NFIND are described in Table 3-5. The value of NFIND is an internal location of the transaction that the Q-GERT processor recognizes. The location information is used to copy or get (remove) the transaction from its current Q-node. Thus, function NFIND and subroutine COPYQ or GETQ are normally used together. The use of NFIND in conjunction with GETQ is as follows:

NTRAN= NFIND(10.0,0,0,3,1)

IF (NTRAN.EQ.0) GO TO 100

CALL GETQ(NTRAN,3,ATT,TM)

These statements identify NTRAN as the location of a transaction in Q-node 3 whose first attribute is equal to 10.0. If no transaction in the queue has its third attribute equal to 10, NTRAN is set to zero. The transaction is removed from Q-node 3 by the call to subroutine GETQ

TABLE 3-5 Functions Associated with Q-Nodes

Subprogram	Use and Definition of Arguments
Function AVEWT(NODE)	Computes the average waiting time of all transactions passing through Q-node NODE from time TBEG; assumes that the waiting time for each transaction currently in the Q-node is the entire waiting time of the transaction
Function CAPQ(NODE)	Returns CAPQ as the capacity (maximum number of transactions allowed) of Q-node NODE
Function NOFQ(IDUM)	Returns NOFQ as the number of the Q-node associated with the service activity just completed; IDUM is a dummy argument and is not used
Function RCAPQ(NODE)	Returns RCAPQ as the remaining capacity of Q-node NODE
Function TINIQ(NODE)	Computes the time integrated number in Q-node NODE from time TBEG to time TNOW; to compute the average number in Q-node NODE divide by (TNOW-TBEG)
Function XNINQ(NODE)	Returns XNINQ as number of transactions currently in Q-node NODE
Function NFIND(VALUE, MCODE,IS,NODE,NATR)	Returns NFIND as transaction identifier (or zero if none) of a transaction in Q-node NODE whose NATR attribute satisfies the relation specified by MCODE; the relations for MCODE are: MCODE = 0: NATRth attribute equal to VALUE ±0.0001 *VALUE MCODE = 1: maximum value but greater than VALUE MCODE = 2: minimum value but greater than VALUE MCODE = 3: maximum value but less than VALUE MCODE = 4: minimum value but less than VALUE MCODE = 5: highest priority in queue with NATRth attribute greater than VALUE MCODE = 6: highest priority in queue with NATRth attribute less than VALUE IS identifies the starting point for the search, with IS = 0 indicating the first transaction in the queue
Subroutine COPYQ(IDTR, NODE,ATT,TM)	Copies attributes of transaction IDTR into the ATT vector and defines TM as its mark time

TABLE 3-5 *(cont.)*

Subprogram	Use and Definition of Arguments
Subroutine GETQ(IDTR, NODE,ATT,TM)	Removes transaction IDTR from Q-node NODE and sets ATT vector to attributes of the removed transaction and TM to its mark time
Subroutine PUTQ(NODE, ATT,TM)	Puts transaction in Q-node NODE whose attributes are in the vector ATT and whose mark time is TM

with a first argument of NTRAN. When removed, the attributes of the transaction are placed in the user array ATT and the mark time of the transaction is set into the user variable TM. To put this transaction into Q-node 4, subroutine PUTQ would be used as indicated by the statement

CALL PUTQ(4, ATT, TM)

3.11.3 User-Defined Nodal Modifications: Subroutine NODMOD(NOUT,NIN)

To allow the modeler to make nodal modifications based on the status of the system, subroutine NODMOD(NOUT,NIN) is included in the Q-GERT processor. Thus, if it is desired to replace node 5 by node 7 when user function 3 is activated, the following statement would be included in function UF:

3 CALL NODMOD(5,7)

3.11.4 Subprograms Associated with Activities

Three subroutines, STARTA(NODE,NACT), HALTA(NODE, NACT,REMTI,ATT), and XTEND(NACT,TIME), are provided for starting an activity, halting an activity, and for extending the duration of an ongoing activity. The subroutine SNACT is used to obtain the time until the next activity completion occurs, and, if desired, the stopping of that activity. The function NACTY(IDUM) provides the user with a means to obtain the number of the activity that released a node, and subroutine PACTY enables the user to obtain a list of ongoing activities at any time during a run. The definitions of these subprograms are given in Table 3-6.

Subroutine STARTA(NODE,NACT) causes activity NACT to be started. The variable NODE defines the start node number of activity NACT. When subroutine STARTA is called from function UF, an end-

TABLE 3-6 Subprograms Associated with Activities

Subprogram	Use and Definition of Arguments
Subroutine HALTA(NODE, NACT,REMTI,ATT)	Halts activity NACT scheduled from node NODE if it is ongoing when HALTA is invoked; sets REMTI to the remaining time until completion and ATT(·) to the attributes of the transaction associated with the activity
Function NACTY(IDUM)	Returns NACTY as the activity number associated with the activity just completed or started; IDUM is not used
Subroutine PACTY	Prints a list of ongoing activities when called
Subroutine SNACT(ICA, NACT,REMTI)	For the next activity to be completed, SNACT returns the next activity number as NACT and the remaining time until completion as REMTI; if ICA is set to 1 by the user, SNACT also cancels the completion of the activity; if ICA is set to 0, only the values of NACT and REMTI are set
Subroutine STARTA(NODE, NACT)	Causes activity NACT emanating from node NODE to be started, that is; the subroutine schedules an end-of-activity event for activity NACT
Subroutine XTEND(NACT, TIME)	Causes the time of completion for activity NACT to be extended by the value of TIME; if NACT is not ongoing, the requested extension is ignored (*Note:* NACT can be a service activity)

of-activity event for activity NACT is scheduled. It is presumed that the attributes of the transaction currently being processed are to be duplicated and associated with the transaction passing through activity NACT.

Subroutine HALTA(NODE,NACT,REMTI,ATT) causes activity number NACT whose start node is NODE to be stopped. The time remaining to process the transaction currently associated with activity NACT is returned as the value of REMTI. If NACT is not ongoing, REMTI is set to a negative value. The attributes of the transaction associated with NACT are returned in the vector ATT(·).

Subroutine XTEND(NACT,TIME) is used to extend the completion time for activity NACT by TIME time units.

Subroutine SNACT(ICA,NACT,REMTI) is used to obtain information or to cancel the next activity to be completed. With ICA equal to zero, only the activity number NACT, and the remaining time, REMTI, are set. When ICA is set to 1, the activity completion event is taken off the event calendar, and NACT and REMTI are set. When no activities are scheduled for completion, SNACT sets NACT to zero. Thus, to clear the event calendar, the following statements would be used:

$$7 \text{ CALL SNACT(1,NUMAC,REMTI)}$$

$$\text{IF (NUMAC .NE. 0) GO TO 7}$$

With these statements, SNACT is called to cancel the next activity completion until all events are removed from the event calendar; that is, a zero is assigned to NUMAC.

Function NACTY(IDUM), when called from the user function employed at a node, returns the number of the activity that caused the node to be released. When called from an activity, it returns the activity number. The argument of function NACTY,IDUM, is not used.

3.11.5 Subprograms Associated with Service Activities

The five subprograms listed in Table 3-7 are available for ascertaining and changing the status of service activities. The status of a service activity can be obtained by using function ISTUS(NODE, NSERV), where NODE is the Q-node or S-node that precedes the service activity and NSERV is the service activity number. The function TISS(NODE,NSERV) makes available to the user the time-integrated status of service activity NSERV, from the time the run began, TBEG, to the current time, TNOW. To obtain the amount of remaining service time for a service activity, function REMST(NSERV) is used. This function returns the amount of time before server number NSERV completes his or her next service. If service activity NSERV is not ongoing, a value of zero is returned as the remaining service time.

To stop a service activity being performed by server NSERV, subroutine STSER(NSERV) is called. Each call to this subroutine stops one service activity. If a number of service activities are in progress for server NSERV, the transaction whose service is nearest completion is stopped. In addition, the transaction being served is deleted from the system. The status of the server number NSERV is updated so that if items are waiting in the queue of NSERV, the server would be made busy. If no items are waiting, the server is made idle.

If it is desired to stop service and route the transaction on which service was stopped to another node, subroutine STAGO(NSERV, NEWN,TIME,ICATT,ATT) is called. This subroutine performs a function similar to subroutine STSER, with the addition that the transaction on which service is stopped can be routed to node NEWN with a time delay of TIME. By setting the argument ICATT to 1, the attributes of the rerouted transaction are changed to ATT. The mark time of the transaction is not changed. If ICATT is zero, no change is made to the attributes of the transaction. When subroutine STAGO is called, the status of server NSERV is updated according to the condition of the

TABLE 3-7 Subprograms Associated with Servers

Subprogram	Use and Definition of Arguments
Function ISTUS(NODE, NSERV)	Returns ISTUS as the status of the service activity NSERV whose Q-node or S-node is NODE; the value of ISTUS is assigned as follows: +N number of busy servers 0 server is idle <0 server is blocked
Function REMST(NSERV)	Returns REMST as the service time remaining on service activity NSERV; if NSERV is idle, a value of zero is returned; if there are parallel service activities, REMST is set to the smallest remaining service time
Subroutine STAGO(NSERV, NEWN,TIME,ICATT, ATT)	Causes server NSERV to stop processing a transaction and sends transaction stopped to node NEWN with a time delay of TIME; if ICATT is set to 1, the attributes of the transaction are changed to the vector ATT; the status of server NSERV is then updated according to the condition of the Q-nodes preceding it; if NEWN = 0, the transaction is lost to the system; if server NSERV is idle, no action is taken
Subroutine STSER(NSERV)	Stops service by server NSERV, deletes transaction from system and updates status of NSERV
Function TISS(NODE, NSERV)	Computes the time integrated status of server(s) NSERV from time TBEG to time TNOW; NODE is the start node of the activity representing NSERV; NODE can be either a Q-node or an S-node; to compute the average utilization divide by (TNOW– TBEG)

Q-nodes preceding it. If a number of service activities are in progress for server NSERV, the transaction whose service is nearest completion is stopped.

3.11.6. Functions for Accessing Resource Information

Five functions are included in the Q-GERT processor for accessing resource-related information. These functions are described in Table 3-8. Functions ICSRA, ICSRU, and ICCR can be used to make decisions based on the current status of resource availability, use, and capacity, respectively. For example, attribute values can be assigned and transactions routed based on current resource status. Also, transactions can be put into the network using subroutine PTIN when prescribed resource conditions are detected.

TABLE 3-8 Functions for Accessing Resource Information

Function Name	Definition
ICSRA(NRES)	Integer value of Current Status of Resource type NRES Availability, that is, the number of units of NRES not in use (allocated)
ICSRU(NRES)	Integer value of Current Status of Resource type NRES being Used
ICCR(NRES)	Integer value of Current Capacity of Resource type NRES
TIRA(NRES)	Time-Integrated Number of Resources Available of resource type NRES
TIRU(NRES)	Time-Integrated Number of Resources Used of resource type NRES

The functions for obtaining the time-integrated values associated with resource availability (TIRA) and utilization (TIRU) allow average values to be computed by dividing the time-integrated values by the time period over which statistics have been collected (TNOW–TBEG). In this way, decisions based on average use and average availability can be included in a model.

3.11.7 Subprograms for Performing Resource Operations

Three subprograms are included in the Q-GERT processor for allocating, freeing, and altering resources directly from a user function. These subprograms are described in Table 3-9.

Function IALOC is used to allocate resource units to the transaction passing through the node for which the user function was called. The value returned from function IALOC should be checked to deter-

TABLE 3-9 Subprograms for Performing Resource Operations

Subprogram Name	Definition
Function IALOC(NRES, NUNIT)	Attempts to allocate NUNIT units of resource type NRES to the current transaction; if the units are allocated, IALOC is set to 1; if the units are not allocated, IALOC is set to 0
Subroutine FREE(NRES, NUNIT,NODES)	Frees NUNIT units of resource type NRES to be allocated at the ALLOCATE nodes specified in the vector NODES(·)
Subroutine ALTER(NRES, NUNIT,NODES)	Alters the capacity of resource type NRES by NUNIT units; if NUNIT is greater than 0, capacity is increased and the newly available units are attempted to be allocated at ALLOCATE nodes specified in the vector NODES(·)

mine if the units requested were available for allocation. When IALOC is returned with a value of 1, the NUNIT units were allocated to the current transaction. Otherwise, the units were not allocated.

Subroutines FREE and ALTER perform functions identical to the FREE and ALTER nodes. These subroutines are included to enable the freeing and altering of resource units within a user-written program insert. The vector NODES, which is the third argument to both subroutines, corresponds to the ALLOCATE node list as placed below the FREE and ALTER nodes. When a zero value is encountered for an ALLOCATE node number, the general list of ALLOCATE nodes given in the RESOURCE block is polled. Thus, if NODES(1) equals zero, the ALLOCATE nodes prescribed in the RESOURCE block are polled. To avoid polling the ALLOCATE nodes in the RESOURCE block, a –1 should be placed after the last ALLOCATE node given in the vector NODES. When using subroutines FREE and ALTER in function UF, the user must provide a DIMENSION statement containing an array corresponding to the vector NODES($\cdot$).

3.12 USER-COLLECTED STATISTICS

Routines are available in the Q-GERT processor that allow the user to collect data on any system variable. The data collected may be based either on the observed value of a variable or on the time-persistent behavior of a variable. In addition, data can be organized into cells in order to obtain histograms that portray the relative frequency with which a variable is within a range of values. Table 3-10 gives a list of subroutines available in Q-GERT for user-collected statistics. The following sections provide a discussion of the routines and their use.

3.12.1 Collection of Statistics Based on Observations

Statistics based on the observation of variables are collected, reported, and initialized through three subroutines: COL, COLP, and COLC.

Subroutine COL(XX,ICLCT) is used to collect the sample value of a variable. The variables are given numeric codes that are communicated to subroutine COL by its second argument (ICLCT). The value of the sample is passed to COL by its first argument, XX, and must be of type REAL. Five quantities are stored in an internal array of the Q-GERT program for each ICLCT variable. The name of this array is UOBV(ICLCT,J), J=1,5. In general, row ICLCT is used for values of variables with code ICLCT. The statement CALL COL(YY,3) causes YY to be added to the sum of other values and is stored in UOBV(3,1). The square of YY is added to the sum of squares of other values and is stored in UOBV(3,2). In addition, when COL is called, the number of observations stored in UOBV(3,3) is increased by one, and the mini-

TABLE 3-10 Subroutines for User-Collected Statistics

Subroutine Name	Description[a]
COL(XX,ICLCT)	Collects sums and sums of squares of values XX for variable number ICLCT
COLP(ICLCT)	If ICLCT=0, print statistics for all variables; if ICLCT>0, print statistics for variable number ICLCT
COLC(ICLCT)	If ICLCT=0, clear the entire statistical storage array UOBV($\cdot$,$\cdot$); if ICLCT>0, clear row ICLCT of UOBV
TIM(XX,ISTAT)	Integrates the values XX over time for variable number ISTAT
TIMP(ISTAT)	If ISTAT=0, print statistics for all variables; if ISTAT>0, print statistics for variable number ISTAT
TIMC(ISTAT)	If ISTAT=0, clear statistical storage array UTPV ($\cdot$,$\cdot$); if ISTAT>0, clear row ISTAT of UTPV
HIS(XX,IHIST)	Increments the number of times the value XX has fallen in a specified range for variable number IHIST
HISP(IHIST)	If IHIST=0, print a histogram for all variables; if IHIST>0, print a histogram for variable number IHIST
HISC(IHIST)	If IHIST=0, reset all values regarding histograms to zero; if IHIST>0, reset the values for variable IHIST with regard to histograms to zero
CLEAR	Initialize statistical storage arrays UOBV and UTPV and reset the histogram storage area to zero

[a]When using these subroutines, the variables ICLCT, ISTAT, and IHIST are assigned numeric codes by the user to distinguish among different variables on which statistics collection is to be performed.

mum and maximum values of YY are retained in UOBV(3,4) and UOBV(3,5) respectively.

The user can obtain output statistics based on the values collected by COL by calling subroutine COLP(ICLCT). If subroutine COLP is called with ICLCT=0, a report of all COL variables is generated. If ICLCT is greater than zero, a statistical report is printed for the ICLCT[th] variable. The report consists of estimates of the mean, standard deviation, standard deviation of the mean, the minimum and maximum values observed, and the number of observations on which the statistics are based. The values stored in UOBV($\cdot$,$\cdot$) are not altered when these statistics are reported. COLP is called with a zero argument automatically at the end of all runs to obtain a report on all COL statistics.

Subroutine COLC(ICLCT) is used to reset or clear the statistical storage array UOBV. If subroutine COLC is called with ICLCT equal to zero, all rows of UOBV are cleared. If ICLCT is greater than zero, only row ICLCT of UOBV is cleared. Q-GERT contains a call to COLC with ICLCT=0 prior to the start of run 1. If separate statistics are desired on each run, COLC should be called by the user in subroutine UI.

3.12.2 Collection of Statistics for Time-Persistent Variables

Statistics based on time-persistent variables are collected, reported, and initialized through three subroutines: TIM, TIMP, and TIMC.

Subroutine TIM(XX,ISTAT) is used to collect statistics based on time-persistent variables. The argument XX is a value for the variable of interest and is of type REAL. ISTAT is the index for the ISTAT[th] time-persistent variable.

When TIM is used, the variable in question is assumed to have maintained a constant value over a time interval. This type of variable is referred to as a time-persistent variable. An example of a time-persistent variable would be the number of transactions being processed. The number of transactions has a constant value from the time of arrival of a transaction until the next arrival or next departure of a transaction. The length of the time interval from arrival to departure dictates the weight assigned to the value of the variable in computing its average over the entire run. Subroutine TIM integrates the value of the variable over the time interval. The statement CALL TIM(XISYS,2) collects the integrated value of the number in the system identified by code 2 by updating the following six quantities in the array UTPV(2,J), J=1, 6: the sum of the time-integrated values; the sum of the time-integrated values squared; the time of the last change; the minimum value observed; the maximum value observed; and the value for the next time interval, which is XISYS. Through input data or in subroutine UI, an initial value is assigned to XISYS. Changes to XISYS must be made prior to the call to subroutine TIM; hence, XISYS will be the number in the system for the next time period.

Subroutine TIMP(ISTAT) is used to print a statistical report on time-persistent variable statistics. If subroutine TIMP is called with ISTAT equal to zero, a report for all time-persistent statistical variables is generated. If ISTAT is greater than zero, a report is printed for the ISTAT[th] variable only. A statistical report is automatically prepared at the end of all runs if subroutine TIM is used.

Subroutine TIMC(ISTAT) is used to reset or clear the statistical storage array UTPV. If subroutine TIMC is called with ISTAT equal to zero, all the rows of UTPV are cleared. If ISTAT is greater than zero, only row ISTAT of UTPV is cleared. Q-GERT calls TIMC at the beginning of each run with an argument of zero. The variable UTCLR(ISTAT) is set equal to the time at which TIMC was last called with argument ISTAT or with an argument of zero.

3.12.3 Histograms

Histograms are computed, reported, and initialized through three subroutines: HIS, HISP, and HISC.

Subroutine HIS is used to determine the relative frequency with which a variable falls within a set of prescribed limits. It is normally used for observed valued variables. The number of cells, the upper limit of the first cell, and the width of each cell of the histogram are user data inputs for each histogram (see Chapter 4). If histogram 1 is for the variable TISYS, the statement CALL HIS(TISYS,1) would add one observation to the cell that represents the interval in which the TISYS value occurred.

Subroutine HISP(IHIST) is used to print the histograms for the variable desired. If subroutine HISP is called with IHIST equal to zero, histograms for all variables for which histogram information is collected are printed. If IHIST is greater than zero, a histogram for the IHIST[th] variable for which histograms are to be produced is generated. Histograms are automatically printed at the end of all runs.

Subroutine HISC(IHIST) is used to zero or clear the statistical storage array associated with histogram data. If subroutine HISC is called with IHIST equal to zero, the statistical storage area for only the IHIST[th] variable is cleared.

3.12.4 Clearing of All User-Collected Statistical Storage Arrays

Subroutine CLEAR is used for clearing the entire user statistical storage area. A call to this subroutine will perform the same function as separate calls to HISC, TIMC and COLC, each with an argument of zero. The most recent time at which subroutine CLEAR was called for the Ith time-persistent variable is maintained as the variable UTCLR(I).

The user statistical storage area is automatically cleared by the Q-GERT processor at the beginning of each network analysis. Also, the storage array for statistics based on time-persistent variables is automatically cleared at the start of each run of each network simulation, as these statistics are meaningful only for a single simulation run. If averages over a set of runs are desired for time-persistent variables, the analyst can call subroutines COL and HIS in subroutine UO.

3.13 AUXILIARY ATTRIBUTE PROCESSING SUBROUTINES

To augment the attribute storage and retrieval system included in the Q-GERT processor, three subroutines are provided to allow the Q-GERT

TABLE 3-11 Subroutines for Auxiliary Attribute Processing

Subroutine Name	Description
INITA(ARRAY,NEXTR, NATT,NROWS)	Initializes the two-dimensional array, ARRAY, which has NATT columns and NROWS rows; sets next row to store auxiliary attributes, NEXTR, to one
STORA(ATT,ARRAY, NEXTR,NATT)	Stores NATT values of auxiliary attributes as defined in the vector, ATT, in row NEXTR of ARRAY; resets NEXTR to the next row in ARRAY that can be used to store auxiliary attributes
FREEA(NRFRE,ARRAY, NEXTR,NATT)	Makes row NRFRE of ARRAY available for storing auxiliary attributes; resets NEXTR to NRFRE

user to initialize and maintain user-defined arrays for storing attributes of transactions. The subroutines allow the user to employ different arrays for storing attributes for different types of transactions. The three subroutines included in Q-GERT are described in Table 3-11.

Subroutine INITA is used to initialize an array that has NROWS rows and has up to NATT auxiliary attributes per transaction. Subroutine INITA establishes NEXTR as the first row in which a set of auxiliary attributes will be stored.

Subroutine STORA is used to store the values of the auxiliary attributes as defined in the vector ATT into row NEXTR of the auxiliary attribute array ARRAY. The number of attributes placed in row NEXTR is NATT. The user, before employing subroutine STORA, must define the vector ATT to have NATT values. In addition, the row number should be saved in which the auxiliary attributes will be stored. This row number can be employed as a regular attribute of a transaction and thus a transaction's auxiliary attributes can be identified through this pointer to the row number of ARRAY. Subroutine STORA internally changes the value of NEXTR after being called, so that it is important for the user to access the value of NEXTR before the call to STORA.

Subroutine FREEA is used to free up row NRFRE of the auxiliary attribute array ARRAY. Row NRFRE becomes the next row of ARRAY in which auxiliary attributes will be placed; that is, the value of NEXTR is updated to be equal to NRFRE. In this way, the rows of ARRAY are used dynamically to store auxiliary attributes of transactions.

3.14 DUMMY SUBPROGRAMS

A dummy subprogram is one that includes only RETURN and END statements. Dummy subprograms included in Q-GERT are:

1. Function UF
2. Subroutine US
3. Subroutine UI
4. Subroutine UO
5. Function NQS
6. Function NSS

By including dummy subprograms, a user need not write these subprograms if they are not used in a model. Should they be included, it is the user's responsibility to ensure that the written subprograms are loaded and not the dummy routines. The method of processing employed by most computer systems performs the loading correctly.

3.15 RESTRICTION ON USE OF USER SUBPROGRAMS THAT CAN START ACTIVITIES

FORTRAN IV does not permit recursive calls to subprograms. Care must be taken so that the code written in function UF does not result in a call to UF. This can occur when subroutine PTIN, STARTA, STSER, or STAGO is used. These subroutines would be called in UF within a specific function number. If an activity is started based on such a call, and if the activity started had the distribution type UF, function UF would be called again with a new function number. This second call to UF would be a recursive call and is not allowed in standard FORTRAN IV. Recursive calls can be avoided if function UF is used only to compute attribute values or activity times and subroutine US to code decision logic. The Q-GERT error code 87 normally results when such a recursive call is made.

3.16 SUMMARY

This chapter has presented procedures for including FORTRAN inserts into Q-GERT models. With such procedures, Q-GERT becomes a highly flexible modeling and simulation tool. Following is a list of tables included in this chapter to facilitate locating information about Q-GERT subprograms.

3.17 EXERCISES

3-1. Discuss the orientation and viewpoint required of a modeler when defining a system in terms of the Q-GERT symbols. Discuss the differences between structural information requirements of modeling and the detailed data required to characterize activities. Indicate the constructs necessary to portray procedures and functions within a systems model.

3-2. Explain why it is not necessary to have a precise problem formulation including all data elements when building a Q-GERT model. Compare this approach to the one used when developing an analytic model, in which the problem formulation and all data descriptions must be precisely stated before the modeling effort can begin.

3-3. Describe three locations where management decision making can be included within a Q-GERT model. Discuss the limitations with regard to the types of management decision making that can be included within Q-GERT models.

3-4. Discuss the differences in the use of FUNCTION UF(IFN) and SUBROUTINE US(ISN,DTIM).

3-5. Write SUBROUTINE UI to change parameter set 3 so that it provides the correct parameters to obtain samples from a triangular distribution. The model to be run is for 20 runs. At the beginning of each run the user variable RATE is to be set equal to a sample obtained from a normal distribution whose parameters are described in parameter set 1. The value of the sample will be used in FUNCTION UF, which is not to be written as part of this exercise.

3-6. Write statements to perform the following functions. (Only the statements, not their location in any subprogram, are required.)
   (a) Access the third attribute of the transaction currently being processed when the statement is invoked. Store the third attribute in a local variable AT3.
   (b) Access all attribute values of the transaction currently being processed and store them in the vector ATT.
   (c) Set the third attribute of the current transaction to a value of 10.

(d) Store the mark time of the current transaction in the variable ARRTIME.

(e) If the number of transactions in Q-node 7 is greater than 5, cause a transaction to arrive at node 10 in 5 time units, whose mark time is the current time and whose first two attribute values are 17 and 4, respectively.

(f) If the remaining capacity in Q-node 7 is less than 2, replace node 6 by node 7.

(g) If the average number in Q-node 7 is currently greater than 5, increase the capacity of resource 3 by 2 units.

(h) If the average utilization of service activity 1, whose corresponding Q-node is node 3, has been greater than 10, cause any transaction being processed by server 1 to be routed to node 15 with a time delay of 10 units.

3-7. For the one-server, single-queue situation, it has been determined that the service time remaining on a transaction changes based on the number of transactions waiting. If a new arrival causes more than five transactions to be in the queue, the service time remaining is decreased by 0.10 minute for each waiting customer greater than five, including the new arrival. In no case, however, can the remaining service time be decreased by more than 50%, and the remaining service time can be decreased only once; that is, if two transactions arrive during the servicing of a transaction, only the first arrival causes a decrease in the remaining service time. Assume that interarrival times are exponentially distributed with a mean of 2 time units and service time is exponentially distributed with a mean of 1.7 time units.

3-8. Jobs arrive at a machine tool on the average of one per hour. The distribution of these interarrival times is exponential. During normal operation, the jobs are processed on a first-in, first-out basis. The time to process a job is normally distributed with a mean of 0.5 and a standard deviation of 0.10 hour. Processing times are never less than 0.25 hour or greater than 2 hours.

In addition to the processing time, there is a setup time that is uniformly distributed between 0.2 and 0.5 hour. Jobs that have been processed by the machine tool are routed to a different section of the shop and are considered to have left the machine tool area.

The machine tool experiences breakdowns during which time it can no longer process jobs. The time between breakdowns is gamma distributed with a mean of 20 hours and a standard deviation of 2 hours. When a breakdown occurs, the job being processed is removed from the machine tool and, after a 0.1-hour delay, is placed at the head of the queue of jobs waiting to be processed. The service time for the job preempted by the machine breakdown is the remaining service time plus an additional setup time which is again uniformly distributed.

When the machine tool breaks down, a repair process is initiated which is accomplished in three phases. Each phase is exponentially distributed with a mean of 0.75 hour. Since the repair time is the sum of independent and identically distributed exponential random variables, the repair time is Erlang distributed.

Build a Q-GERT model to analyze the machine tool, to obtain information on the utilization of the machine tool and the time required to process a job. Make five runs using the Q-GERT processor, with each run being for a 6000-time-unit duration. Obtain outputs from each run.

Q-GERT Input Procedures

4.1 INTRODUCTION

The analysis of a Q-GERT network is performed by the Q-GERT processor through simulation techniques. A Q-GERT network model is transmitted to the Q-GERT processor through data input records. Input records are also used to define control information related to the experimental design and analysis to be performed on the network. In this chapter, the simulation procedures employed to analyze a Q-GERT model are discussed. The input requirements for the Q-GERT processor are then detailed. Tables are provided that define each input record, default value, and option.

4.2 THE Q-GERT PROCESSOR

The Q-GERT processor employs discrete event procedures to simulate the flow of transactions through a network. Basically, only one event type is included in the program: the arrival of a transaction at a node. All the decision logic that can occur when a transaction arrives at a node is included in the program and appropriate actions are taken based on the network model provided by the analyst, including the collection of statistical quantities.

The Q-GERT processor begins an analysis by identifying the

source nodes in the network. At each source node, a transaction is generated and marked and then routed according to the routing characteristics prescribed for the source node. The performance of activities over which a transaction is routed is simulated by selecting a time for the activity in accordance with the distribution type and parameter values prescribed for the activity. An event corresponding to the arrival of the transaction at the end node of the activity is scheduled and placed on an event calendar.

When all source nodes have been considered in this fashion, time is advanced to the time of the next (first) event which is removed from the event calendar. The type of node to which the transaction is arriving is examined. If it is a basic node type, the number of incoming transactions to release the node is decreased by 1. If the node is not released, that is, it requires more incoming transactions, no further action is taken and time can be advanced to the next event time. If the node is released, statistics are collected, marking is performed, and attribute values are assigned as necessary. Then the transaction is routed along the activities emanating from the node just released. If the node has deterministic routing, identical transactions are routed along each activity emanating from the node. If the node has probabilistic routing, a selection of one activity is made using a pseudo-random number generator. For conditional routing, the conditions are tested and activities are taken accordingly. For each activity selected, an activity duration is completed and the transaction is scheduled to arrive at the end node at the current time plus the activity duration. This arrival-of-transaction event is placed on the event calendar. After all activities have been selected and their associated events scheduled, the next event is removed from the event calendar and the process is repeated.

Each time an event is taken from the event calendar, the time of the event is compared to a total time allocated for the simulation. If all time has expired, the simulation run of the network is considered to be completed. Similarly, when a transaction arrives at a sink node, a check is made to see if the simulation run is completed because the prescribed number of sink nodes has been released. If the run is not completed, the process described above continues. When a run is completed, summary statistics for one run of the simulation are obtained.

When a transaction arrives at a Q-node, a slightly more complex decision process is involved. First, a check is made to see if the queue is full. If it is, the transaction either balks from the Q-node or blocks its current service activity. If it balks and there is no balk node prescribed, the transaction is deleted from the system. If a balk node is prescribed, the transaction is scheduled to arrive at the balk node in zero time. If blocking occurs, the service activity that just completed processing the transaction is not made available for processing another transaction.

If the queue is not full but the servers (or resources) following the queue are all in use, the transaction is placed in the queue according to the queue ranking rule specified for the Q-node. If a server (or resource) is available, the transaction is scheduled to arrive at the node following the service activity at the current time plus the service time. Statistics are maintained on the number of transactions in the queue and the utilization of servers (or resources).

When a transaction completes a service activity, additional processing must be performed. Not only must the transaction be routed to the end node of the service activity, but the disposition of the service activity must be considered. The logic involved in determining the disposition of the service activity involves examining the Q-node associated with the service activity. If no transactions are in the Q-node, the service activity is made idle. If transactions are waiting at the Q-node, the first one is removed from the Q-node and it is routed along the service activity, that is, the transaction is scheduled to arrive at the end node of the service activity. If, before removing the transaction from the Q-node, the Q-node was at its maximum capacity, a check is also made to unblock any service activities preceding the Q-node. If an S-node precedes the service activity, a process similar to the above is used. In this case, the S-node examines each Q-node in turn in accordance with its Queue Selection Rule.

When a transaction arrives to a FREE or ALTER node, the node is always released. The disposition of the resource units associated with the node is determined. These resource units are allocated to transactions waiting at Q-nodes that precede the ALLOCATE nodes in the list associated with the FREE or ALTER node released.

A MATCH node is released only when each Q-node preceding it has a transaction with a given attribute value. When this occurs, each transaction is routed to a specfied node on the output side of the MATCH node.

This brief description of the Q-GERT processor illustrates the initiation and routing of transactions through the network. In the next section, the procedures for describing a network to the Q-GERT processor are discussed in detail.

4.3 FREE-FORM INPUT FEATURES

The input to the Q-GERT processor is format free. Such a free-form input permits fields of data to be punched on a card or typed at a terminal without column restrictions. A set of fields that pertain to a specific Q-GERT element or symbol is called a record. For example, a record would be a description of node 7. The record identifier is always placed in field 1 and requires at least three characters. The specific characteristics of free-form input are as follows:

1. *Blanks.* Blanks are ignored except in the analyst and project name fields. Hence, information may be placed in any column of the input record.

2. *Field termination.* All fields except the last are terminated by commas.

3. *Multiple values in a field.* Selected fields may have a second value which sometimes is optional. These values are separated by a slash (/). For example, nodes and activities are assigned numeric identifiers but can also be given alphanumeric labels. Also, for some queue ranking procedures, it is necessary to specify an attribute number.

4. *Continuation of records.* Continuation of records on additional lines is permitted. If the last nonblank character of a line is a comma, it is assumed that additional fields of the input record are contained on the next line. Fields may *not* be split between lines. A continuation line contains no identifier and the additional fields may be included anywhere on the line. Continuation lines may themselves be continued. However, an input record may not exceed 49 fields.

5. *Record termination.* An asterisk is used as the record terminator. If no asterisk is present and the last nonblank character on a line is *not* a comma, an end of input record is assumed. The use of an asterisk is preferred for clarity. Also, comments can be placed on a line following the asterisk even if placed in column 1.

6. *Insignificant characters.* Characters not significant in an alphanumeric field will be ignored. Accordingly, for added clarity and for documentation purposes, the user may specify additional characters if desired (parentheses, asterisks, slashes, periods, and commas are not permitted). Alphanumeric fields may be of any length that will fit on a single line but must not start with a digit.

7. *Numeric data.* Any numeric data may be input as an integer or as a real number.

   a. If an integer is input for a field specified as real, the real equivalent of the integer value is used.

   b. If a real is input for a field specified as integer, the decimal portion of the real field is truncated and the integer equivalent of the truncated result is used.

8. *Default values.* Default values are defined for all nonessential input fields. To indicate that the default value is to be used for a certain field (or that a field is not applicable in a given context), the user should do one of the following:

a. *Omit the field.* Omission of a field is indicated by a comma or by blanks followed by a comma.

b. *Skip to the next user-specified input field.* If the user lists the number (enclosed in parentheses) of the next field for which he or she wishes to specify information, all intermediate fields will be bypassed and will assume default values.

For example, if the line

$$QUE,3/CUSTQ,(8)1.*$$

is input, the following interpretation will be made:

Field 1 = QUE

Field 2 = 3 with label CUSTQ

Fields 3 through 7 will assume default values

Field 8 = 1

Fields 9 and above will assume default values

c. *Terminate the record* before giving a value for the field. For instance, in the preceding example, Fields 9 and 10 assume default values since no values were specified after Field 8 (there are 10 fields associated with record type QUE).

[*Note:* A field left blank is not automatically assumed to contain the value zero (unless zero is the established default value for the field); therefore, when a zero value is intended, it should actually be specified.]

9. *Error checking.* Each input record will be read, listed, and scanned for errors. Default values will be assumed for fields containing errors. Nonfatal errors will be flagged as warnings and *will not* prevent execution. Errors flagged as fatal will cancel execution.

4.4 INPUT RECORDS FOR Q-GERT SYMBOLS AND CONCEPTS

The input for each Q-GERT node type and activity requires one record. Whenever values are assigned to attributes at a node, a separate input record is employed that references the node by number. Also, the parameter values associated with a parameter set are placed on a separate record with a reference to the parameter set number. For each resource type and each activity causing a nodal modification to occur, a separate input record is required. Table 4-1 lists the three-character identifiers associated with records describing Q-GERT symbols and concepts.

Except for the value assignment (VAS) identifier, the first three letters of the concept name are used as the input record identifier.

TABLE 4-1 Record Identifiers for Q-GERT Concepts

Record Identifier	Q-GERT Concept
ACT	ACTivity
ALL	ALLocate node
ALT	ALTer node
FRE	FREe node
MAT	MATch node
MOD	MODification of nodes
PAR	PARameter set
QUE	QUEue node
REG	REGular node
RES	RESource
SEL	SELector node
SIN	SINk node
SOU	SOUrce node
STA	STAtistics node
VAS	Value ASsignments

Since only the first three characters are significant, additional characters can be used if increased readability is desired. For example, the Q-GERT processor interprets QUEUE as QUE.

Table 4-2 presents the detailed information regarding each of the records listed above. Note that a default value for a field is given in brackets and options, where possible, are listed within parentheses. In situations where the number of options is too large to include in the table, they are provided separately in Table 4-3. The definitions of parameter fields for the PAR record for the different distributions allowed in Q-GERT are provided in Table 4-4.

When two entries are possible in a single field, both a slash and a dashed line are shown in the field box of Table 4-2, with the data requirement for the second entry in the field specified below the dashed line.

It should be noted that connectors (dashed lines), balking (dash-dot lines), and blocking (parallel lines) are specified implicitly by providing fields on the appropriate record to indicate that the concept pertains. Thus, connectors between Q-nodes and S-nodes are input as a list of S-nodes on the QUE record and a list of Q-nodes on the SEL record. Similarly, balking and blocking are shown directly by the data provided in Field 7 of the QUE record and Field 6 of the SEL record.

4.5 INPUTS FOR SIMULATION CONTROL

Five input record types are provided for specifying information detailing conditions under which the Q-GERT processor is to analyze the Q-GERT network. Most of the control information is contained on the

TABLE 4-2 Q-GERT Input Records for Graphic Concepts[a]

Field

1	2	3	4	5	6	7	8	9	10
ACT	Start node	End node	Distribution or function type (see Table 4-3) [CO]	Parameter set or constant [0.0]	Activity number/ -------- Label	Number of parallel servers [1]	Probability or attribute number or order [.5]	Condition code (see Table 4-3) [Ni.R] i=start node	
ALL	Node number	Queue selector rule [POR]	Resource number [1]	Resource units required by waiting transactions [1]	Q-node/ Routing node [transaction destroyed]	(Repeats of Field 6)			
ALT	Node number	Branching (D,P,F,A) [D]	Resource number (i,Ai) [1]	Resource capacity change (i,Ai) [1]	Associated ALLOC nodes*	(Repeats of Field 6)			
FRE	Node number	Branching (D,P,F,A) [D]	Resource number (i,Ai) [1]	Resource units to be freed (i,Ai) [1]	Associated ALLOC nodes	(Repeats of Field 6)			
MAT	Node number	Matching attribute	Q-node/ -------- Routing node	(R e p e a t s	o f F i e l d 4)				
PAR	Parameter identifier [0]	Parameter 1 [0]	Parameter 2 [-10^{20}]	Parameter 3 [10^{20}]	Parameter 4 [0]	Stream number [10]			
QUE	Node number/ -------- Label	Initial number in queue [0]	Capacity of Q-node [∞]	Branching (D,P) [D]	Ranking (F,L,S,B) [F]/ -------- Attribute [M]	Block or node number for balkers (B,j) [balkers destroyed]	Upper limit of first cell [N]	Width of histogram cell [N]	Following S-nodes or match nodes or allocate nodes

TABLE 4-2 (cont.)

					Field				
1	2	3	4	5	6	7	8	9	10
REG or SOU	Node number	Initial number to release [1]	Subsequent number to release [∞]	Branching (D,P,F,A) [D]	Marking (M) [M if SOU, no M if REG]	Choice criterion (F,L,S,B) [L] / ------- Attribute [M]			
RES	Resource number/ -------- Label	Resource units available [1]	Associated ALLOC nodes	(Repeats of Field 4)					
SEL	Node number/ -------- Label	Queue selection rule (See Table 4-3) [POR]	Server selection rule (See Table 4-3) [POR]	Choice criterion (S, B) [B] / -------- Attribute [M]	Block or node number for balkers (B,i) [balkers destroyed]	Associated Q-nodes	(Repeats of Field 7)		
SIN or STA	Node number/ -------- Label	Initial number to release [1]	Subsequent number to release [∞]	Branching (D,P,F,A) [D]	Statistics desired (F,A,B,I,D) [F]	Upper limit of first cell [N]	Width of histogram cell [N]	Choice criterion (F,L,S,B) [L] / -------- Attribute [M]	
VAS	Node number	Attribute number [1]	Distribution type (see Table 4-3) [CO]	Parameter identifier [O]	(Repeats of Fields 3, 4, and 5)				

[a]Default values are given in brackets [ ]. If no default is indicated, data for the field are required. Options for a field are given in parentheses (·). A slash (/) and dashed line indicate that the field may contain two entries where the slash and second entry are optional. An N indicates no histogram will be collected.

TABLE 4-3 Code Options for Q-GERT Specifications

Distribution and Function Types (See Table 2-1)		Parameter Values[a] (See Table 4-4)			
Code	Key	1	2	3	4
AT	Attribute	—	—	—	—
BE	Beta	μ	a	b	σ
BP	Beta-PERT	m	a	b	—
CO	Constant	μ	—	—	—
ER	Erlang	μ/k	a	b	k
EX	Exponential	μ	a	b	—
GA	Gamma	μ	a	b	σ
IN	Incremental	—	—	—	σ
LO	Lognormal	μ	a	b	σ
NO	Normal	μ	a	b	σ
PO	Poisson	$\mu-a$	a	b	—
TR	Triangular	m	a	b	—
UF,US	User subprogram	—	—	—	—
UN	Uniform	—	a	b	—

Routing Condition Codes (See Table 2-2)		Queue Selection Rules (See Table 2-3)		Server Selection Rules (See Table 2-4)	
Code	Key	Code	Key	Code	Key
T.$\mathcal{R}$.V	Time .$\mathcal{R}$. Value	POR	Preferred order	POR	Preferred order
T.$\mathcal{R}$.Ak	Time .$\mathcal{R}$. Att k	CYC	Cyclic	CYC	Cyclic
Aj.$\mathcal{R}$.V	Att j.$\mathcal{R}$. Value	RAN	Random	RAN	Random
Aj.$\mathcal{R}$.Ak where $\mathcal{R}$=(LT;LE;EQ; NE;GT; or GE)	Att j.$\mathcal{R}$. Att k	LAV	Largest average number	LBT	Largest busy time
		SAV	Smallest average number	SBT	Smallest busy time
		LWF	Longest waiting of first	LIT	Longest idle time
Ni.R	Node i Released	SWF	Shortest waiting of first	SIT	Shortest idle time
Ni.N	Node i Not Released	LNQ	Largest number in queue	PFS	Probabilistic from free servers
NAj.R	Node Aj Released	SNQ	Smallest number in queue	NSS	User written
NAj.N	Node Aj Not Released	LNB	Largest number of balkers		
		SNB	Smallest number of balkers		
		LRC	Largest remaining capacity		
		SRC	Smallest remaining capacity		
		ASM	Assembly mode		
		NQS	User written		

[a]—, not used; μ, mean; σ, standard deviation; m, mode; a, minimum or optimistic time; b, maximum or pessimistic time.

The parameters required to sample from the distributions[a] are described below. The parameter values for the lognormal (LO), triangular (TR), beta (BE), gamma (GA), and beta-PERT (BP) are modified to simplify random sampling. Thus, parameter sets for these distributions must not be used for any other distributions; i.e., a parameter set for a lognormal distribution must only be used for sampling from a lognormal distribution.

For COnstants, no PAR card is used; the value of the constant is taken as the value given to the parameter identifier

For NOrmal, LOgnormal, BEta, and GAmma distributions

Parameter 1   The mean value
Parameter 2   The minimum value
Parameter 3   The maximum value
Parameter 4   The standard deviation

For UNiform distribution

Parameter 1   Not used
Parameter 2   The minimum value
Parameter 3   The maximum value
Parameter 4   Not used

For EXponential distribution

Parameter 1   The mean value
Parameter 2   The minimun value
Parameter 3   The maximum value
Parameter 4   Not used

For ERlang distribution

Parameter 1   The mean time for the Erlang variable divided by the value given to parameter 4
Parameter 2   The minimum value
Parameter 3   The maximum value
Parameter 4   The number of exponential deviates to be included in the sample obtained from the Erlang distribution

For POisson distribution

Parameter 1   The mean minus the minimum value
Parameter 2   The minimum value
Parameter 3   The maximum value
Parameter 4   Not used

Care is required when using the POisson since it is not usually used to represent an interval of time; the interpretation of the mean should be the mean number of time units per time period

For BP and TRiangular distributions

Parameter 1   The most likely value, m
Parameter 2   The optimistic value, a
Parameter 3   The pessimistic value, b
Parameter 4   Not used

[a] A sample is obtained from a distribution such that if a sample is less than the minimum value, the sample value is given the minimum value. Similarly, if the sample is greater than the maximum value, the sample value is assigned the maximum value. This is not sampling from a truncated distribution but sampling from a distribution with a given probability of obtaining the minimum and maximum values.

GEN (General) record, which contains fields for defining the analyst's name, project label, and current date. The condition to be used to terminate a run as well as the number of runs to be made are prescribed on the GEN record. The time from which statistics will be kept and the types of output reports to be prepared are also specified. Fields are provided on the GEN record that allow statistics to be recorded after a warm-up period, the tracing (printing) of all end-of-activity events and/or only those associated with specified nodes, and four computer execution options. Table 4-5 provides a description of each field of the GEN record along with default values.

Fields 1 through 8 are self-explanatory. Field 9 is used to specify a run termination condition based on sink node releases. Field 10 specifies a run termination condition based on simulation time. If values are given for both Fields 9 and 10, the first condition that is met will terminate the run. In Field 11, the number of runs to be performed is specified. Each run is an experimental replication and will be terminated in accordance with the conditions specified in Field 9 or Field 10.

The types of output reports desired from the Q-GERT processor are indicated in Field 12. Output reports are described in Chapter 5. The output report option allows the user to obtain statistics on a run and statistical estimates over all runs. On each run, averages for the run are computed and each average is considered as one observation for a multiple-run analysis. A summary report contains a statistical analysis of the run averages. In addition, statistics on the individual release time of nodes are maintained for the first run. A special report on these first-run values is printed whenever the user requests an output report for individual runs. The reporting options are:

F   a report for the first run and a summary of all runs (default value)

E   a report for each run and a summary of all runs

C   a report for each run and a cumulative report up to the end of each run

S   only a summary report for all runs

If the time from which statistics are to be kept is specified as a value other than zero, the Q-GERT processor will reinitialize all statistical storage arrays at the time specified in Field 13 of the GEN record. In essence, all data values collected up to this specified time are discarded and will not be included in the computation of run or summary statistics. Field 14 is used to specify the maximum number of attributes associated with a transaction flowing through the network. This value is used as a control to ensure proper allocation of space to transactions flowing through the network. The Q-GERT processor automatically adds one attribute for the mark time and the value specified in Field 14 should not include space for the mark time attribute.

Two types of tracing are included in Q-GERT: event and nodal. An event trace is a printout of all start and completion times of activities for the specified set of runs requested by the inputs in Fields 15 and 16 of the GEN record. When a trace is obtained, information on

TABLE 4-5 Description of Data Fields for the General Project Information Record (GEN)

Field Number	Description	Default Value
1	Record type, GEN	Required
2	Analyst name consisting of up to 12 alphanumeric characters	12 blanks
3	Project name or number up to 12 significant characters	12 blanks
4	Month number	1
5	Day number	1
6	Year number	2001
7	Number of STAtistics nodes	0
8	Number of SINk nodes	0
9	Number of sink node releases to end a run of the network	Value in Field 8
10	Time to end one run of the network	1.E20
11	Number of runs of the network	1
12	Indicator for output reports in addition to the final summary report (F, first run; E, each run; C, cumulative summary reports at end of each run; S, summary only)	F
13	Time from which statistics will be kept on each run	0.0
14	Maximum number of attributes associated with each transaction flowing through the network (not including the mark time attribute)	0
15	Run number for beginning of event tracing	0 (no tracing)
16	Run number for ending of event tracing	Value in Field 15
17	Run number for beginning of nodal tracing (If other than zero, a TRA record is required)	0 (no tracing)
18	Run number for ending of nodal tracing	Value in Field 17
19	Indicator that only input records with errors are to be listed (E, records with errors to be listed)	All input records listed
20	Execution option (El, no execution and only input is to be examined; E2, no execution if any input discrepancies; E3, no execution if fatal input discrepancies; E4, same as E3 with the echo check suppressed)	E3

the transaction associated with the event is also printed. A nodal trace is a printout of start and completion times of activities for selected nodes as specified on a TRA record, and for selected runs as specified in Fields 17 and 18 on the GEN record. An event trace portrays the sequence in which activities are performed. A nodal trace portrays the decisions, value assignments, and branching that occurs at a given node. Both event and nodal traces can be obtained for any run of the network.† A TRAce record is used for specifying a set of node numbers for which every event associated with the nodes is to be printed. Field 1 contains the characters TRA and the following fields contain the node numbers separated by commas for which nodal traces are desired. An asterisk should follow the last node number.

Fields 19 and 20 of the GEN record are used to specify run-time options. An E is placed in Field 19 if only the records that contain input errors are to be listed. Otherwise, all input records will be printed. Field 20 is used to control the execution of the simulation analysis by the Q-GERT processor. If only a check of the input records is desired, the El option is employed. E2 and E3 do not initiate the simulation analysis if there are any input discrepancies or if there are fatal input discrepancies, respectively. Option E4 is used to suppress the printout of the input data and is employed only when production runs are being made. The input data printout organizes the Q-GERT network model in accordance with Q-GERT symbols and concepts. This completes the discussion of the general control information and the run-time tracing capabilities of Q-GERT.

Three additional input records are used for simulation experimental control. The BEG* record is used to indicate that a complete Q-GERT network has been described and that a set of runs is to be made. A FIN* record is used to indicate that all Q-GERT data records have been scanned. The BEG* record is used only when more than one network model is to be analyzed by the Q-GERT processor during one job submission. Thus, after a complete network description is given, a BEG* record indicates the end of data for the network and that the beginning of the data for the next network will follow.

One of the main experimental controls associated with simulation analysis involves the specification of the random number streams to be used in obtaining samples from statistical distributions. The random number stream is set for each sampling process in Field 7 of the PAR record. In Q-GERT, the random number seed initialization record, SEE, is used to specify a first or starting value for each random number stream. In Field 2, the stream number is given for which a seed value is to be prescribed. The next field, Field 3, consists of a seed value and, if desired, a specification that the same seed value should be used on each simulation run.†† This latter specification is made by having a slash (/) and 'I' follow the seed value. If no slash is used in a field or an 'N' fol-

---

†A trace for a specific time period during a run can be obtained by setting the Q-GERT variable ITRAC=1 to start the trace and setting ITRAC=0 to stop the trace. The setting of ITRAC is done in a user function and the labeled COMMON block that contains ITRAC must be included in function UF.

††Using the same seed on different runs is commonly used in experimental designs [157]. The number of digits prescribed for the seed value depends on the number of bits in each computer word.

lows the slash, no resetting of the seed value is performed. The fields for the SEE record are as follows:

Field

1	2	3	4	5	6	7	8
SEE	Stream number	Seed [0] / ------- Initialization (I, N) [N]			(Repeats of Fields 2 and 3)		

As an example, the record

SEE,1,8751329/I,2,4138977,10,/I*

prescribes that stream 1 have an initial seed value of 8751329 and be reset at the beginning of each run, stream 2 have a seed value for the first run of 4138977 and should not be reset, and stream 10 should take the default seed value and should be reset for each run. Streams 3 through 9 will take default seed values and will not be reset. Q-GERT allows for 10 streams with the tenth stream used internally for probabilistic routing and as the default stream number.

4.6 INPUTS FOR USER STATISTICS COLLECTION

When the data collection subprograms COL, TIM, and HIS are employed by the user, statistical quantities are collected and printed as part of the summary report. To provide labels for identifying the statistical estimates obtained and for providing related numerical information, input record types are provided for each of the user statistics collection methods. The fields for the statistics collection records are shown in Table 4-6.

For the COL record, the numeric code employed when calling subroutine COL is given in Field 2 together with a label identifying the

TABLE 4-6 Input Records for User Statistics Collection

		Field		
1	2	3	4	5
COL	Numeric code/label	(Repeats of Field 2)		
TIM	Numeric code/label	Initial value	(Repeats of Fields 2 and 3)	
HIS	Numeric code/label	Number of cells [10]	Upper limit of 1st cell [0.0]	Width of histogram cell [1.0]

variable on which statistics are collected. Each additional field of the COL record is used in the same manner as Field 2.

Information concerning time-persistent variables is provided on the TIM record. This record is similar to the COL record with the addition that an initial value for the variable at the beginning of a run must also be specified. Thus, the numeric code and label for the variable is prescribed in Field 2 and the initial value in Field 3. Repeats of these two fields can then be used on the TIM record or, if desired, additional TIM records can be employed.

When subroutine HIS is employed, an HIS input record is necessary. Field 2 is used to define a numeric code and a label for the histogram. The number of interior cells for the histogram is specified in Field 3, and the upper limit of the first cell is specified in Field 4. The width of each cell is specified in Field 5. Each cell of the histogram is open at the lower end and closed at the upper end, that is, if a value is observed that is equal to a cell breakpoint, it will be included in the lower-numbered cell.

The number of cells specified on the HIS record is the number of interior cells for the histogram. The Q-GERT processor automatically includes a cell for those values from negative infinity ($-\infty$) up to and including the upper limit of the first cell, and a cell that goes from the upper limit of the next-to-last cell to infinity ($+\infty$). The last breakpoint for the histogram cells is defined in accordance with the following equation:

last cell breakpoint

$$= \text{upper limit of first cell} + \text{number of cells} \times \text{width of a cell}$$

4.7 INPUT PROGRAM FOR Q-GERT PROCESSOR

The sequencing rules for input records to the Q-GERT processor were designed for maximum flexibility. There are only four rules to be followed:

1. A GEN record must be first.
2. The START node of an activity must be defined before it is referenced on an ACT record.
3. A resource must be defined before it is referenced on an ALL, ALT, or FRE record.
4. Nodes and activities must be defined before they appear on MOD records.

These four sequencing rules are easy to follow and permit alternative ways for preparing the input records. Two common approaches for input record preparation are to portray the network in the order that the nodes and activities appear on the network or to include all records of the same type together. For the latter approach, the sequencing rules require that resource blocks be defined first, then node records, followed by ACT records, and MOD records last.

The program setup for submitting a job to the Q-GERT processor is as follows:

Job control cards for program submission and compilation

User-written subprograms

Job control cards to access and link Q-GERT processor

Q-GERT network and control records

Data values read in subroutine UI

Data values read in user functions or user subroutines

Data values read in subroutine UO

Job terminator

The specification above is for a single network which is to be analyzed for a single run. If data values are to be read in on each run, the three lines above the job terminator need to be repeated for each run on which they apply. If several networks are to be analyzed through one job submission, the last five lines above the job terminator need to be repeated for each network to be analyzed. If user subprograms are included in the model, the job control records associated with the program submission must include the information necessary to compile the subprograms and to link them with the previously compiled version of the Q-GERT processor.

4.8 SUMMARY

A complete description of the Q-GERT input requirements and specifications has been provided in this chapter. The inputs for Q-GERT can be prepared with little or no programming background. After gaining experience with the input procedures they can be routinely applied. In fact, the input procedures can be automated as will be described in Chapter 20.

4.9 EXERCISES

4-1. Draw a flowchart that depicts the logic and processing involved when the Q-GERT processor is invoked.

4-2. Describe the roles of the following input delimiters within the Q-GERT processor: blank, comma, asterisk, slash, and parenthesis. Discuss the use of an asterisk (*) as the first character of a record.

4-3. Prepare input statements that will be required to obtain the output statistics presented in Figure 5-4 for the model presented in Figure 5-3.

Embellishment: Redo the input statements so that they are organized by statement type or by transaction movement through the network.

4-4. Prepare a record to define the initial random number seeds to accomplish the following: for stream 1, the default seed is to be reinitialized at the beginning of each run; for stream 2, the seed value for the first run is to be 7816923 and the number is not to be reset at the beginning of each run; the seed value for stream 7 is to be defaulted and the default value is to be used at the beginning of each run; for stream 10, the seed value is to be 2943712 on the first run and 9672133 on the second run and no initialization is to be performed after the second run.

4-5. Prepare the input required to perform the planning study for the multiproduct, multiline production system described in Section 6.4. The inputs should be developed to obtain outputs that could be used in deriving the statistics shown in Table 6-2.

Q-GERT Outputs

5.1 INTRODUCTION

The Q-GERT processor is essentially a transformation mechanism that takes the inputs described in Chapter 4 and combines them in accordance with the Q-GERT network model of the system to produce outputs that can be used for decision making. Since both the inputs and the network model contain probabilistic features, the output from the Q-GERT processor will be estimates of statistical quantities. The purpose of this chapter is to provide the statistical background necessary to interpret the Q-GERT outputs, to describe the various types of outputs obtainable, and to discuss the potential for storing the Q-GERT outputs in a data base for future processing.

5.2 OUTPUT VARIABLES

A Q-GERT network model can represent complex mathematical operations to be performed on the input variables. This is the case even for small networks, as illustrated in Figure 5-1 for networks consisting of two branches in parallel. For situation (a), the release time of node 2 is the maximum of the activity times, that is, max $\{t_1, t_2\}$, whereas in case (b), the release time of node 4 is the minimum of the activity times, that is, min $\{t_3, t_4\}$. When this form of nonlinearity is combined with other Q-GERT model nonlinearities due to queueing, selecting, re-

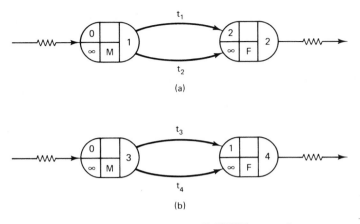

Figure 5-1 Nonlinearities in Q-GERT networks.

source allocating, and routing, the resulting models are analytically untractable.†

As described in Chapter 4, the Q-GERT processor employs simulation methods to obtain sample values in accordance with the logical and computational specifications implied by the Q-GERT network structure. The sample values pertain to the node release times, transactions transit times, service activity utilization, resource utilization, and Q-node statistics. To understand the statistical estimates obtained for these quantities, a brief background regarding these variables is presented in the following sections.

5.3 OUTPUT-VARIABLE TYPES

The output variables of Q-GERT fall into three categories: those variables whose value is maintained for a period of time, those for which an observation is taken, and those on which a count is made. Examples of the first type of variable are the number of transactions at a Q-node and the number of servers or resources being used. Such variables are referred to as time-persistent variables. Examples of the second type of variable are the time a node is released and the transit

†An analytical approach has been developed only for Q-GERT network models consisting of all nodes of the following type:

Networks, consisting of only this node type, model systems that are classified as semi-Markov processes. The GERTE program has been developed to analyze such networks and employs advanced signal flowgraph theory to obtain output values [153].

time of a transaction as it journeys from one node to another in the network. Observations or samples are taken of these variables in order to compute statistical estimates. The third type of variable represents a count of the number of times a specific event occurs. An example of this type of variable is the number of transactions balking from a Q-node.

In a single run of the Q-GERT processor, it is desirable to obtain statistical estimates of the quantities noted above. At the most fundamental level, a trace that details the start time and the end time for each activity performed during a run can be obtained as an output from the Q-GERT processor. The trace contains the information required to obtain estimates on all the variables described above. In fact, the trace can be used to portray every status change that occurs in a run. As will be described in Section 5.4, one procedure for obtaining Q-GERT outputs is to store the trace in a data base which is accessed at a later time to compute any desired statistical estimates. This approach would be equivalent to the current industrial practice of maintaining records on the time of every event occurrence during the operation of a system. Another use of trace information is to drive a graphics terminal in order to represent pictorially the flow and storage of transactions through the network. A prototype vehicle for doing this is described in Chapter 20.

Because trace data can be voluminous, the common practice is to summarize the data during a run. Statistical estimates relating to the operation of the system are then computed based on these summary values. In the following sections, we describe the statistical estimates that are the outputs of the Q-GERT processor which characterize the performance variables previously described.

5.3.1 Statistical Estimates for Q-nodes

Consider first those variables which maintain a value over a time interval such as number of transactions in a Q-node. For a given run, this variable will appear as shown in Figure 5-2. To obtain an estimate

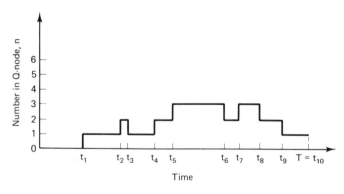

Figure 5-2 Example time history of number in a Q-node.

of the average number in the queue, each value is weighted by the fraction of time it had that value during the run. The equation for making this computation is

$$\bar{n}_T = \sum_{n=0}^{\infty} n f_n$$

where $\bar{n}_T$ is the average over T time units and f_n is the fraction of time that the variable had the value n. f_n is equal to the sum of the time intervals for which the variable had the value n divided by the total length of the simulation run. In the example shown in Figure 5-2, we have: $f_0 = t_1/T$; $f_1 = [(t_2 - t_1) + (t_4 - t_3) + (t_{10} - t_9)]/T$; $f_2 = [(t_3 - t_2) + (t_5 - t_4) + (t_7 - t_6) + (t_9 - t_8)]/T$; and $f_3 = [(t_6 - t_5) + (t_8 - t_7)]/T$.

Other values printed in addition to the average for a run are the minimum and maximum value observed during the run, and the value of the variable at the end of the run (referred to as the current number of the summary report). For Q-nodes, an estimate of the average time spent in the queue by a transaction $\bar{w}$ is also printed and is computed by the equation

$$\bar{w} = \bar{n}_T \frac{T}{A}$$

where T is the length of the simulation run and A is the number of arrivals to the Q-node. This equation is a direct consequence of Little's formula [192, 195].

5.3.2 Statistical Estimates for Servers

Server utilization, the average number of servers busy, is computed in the same manner as average number in a Q-node. If the server is blocked, he or she is not considered as being utilized. For single-server activities, the maximum (longest) consecutive period of idleness and busyness are printed. If the service activity involves multiple servers, the maximum number of servers concurrently idle and concurrently busy are reported. These values are taken directly from the run and are not normalized in any manner. Because of this, longer runs can be expected to have larger maximum values. When a server can be blocked, the average time blocked is computed as the total time blocked divided by the total time for the run. Also maintained is the longest period during the run that the server was in a blocked status.

5.3.3 Statistical Estimates for Resources

Resource utilization is another variable that is time persistent as the number of resources in use remains at a constant value until another resource unit is allocated, freed, or the capacity of the resource is changed. Statistical estimates of the average number of resources in use and the average number of resources available are computed and printed. Both averages are necessary as the capacity of a resource can change through the use of ALTER nodes. Also printed out for a given run are the number of resources in use at the end of the run, the maximum number of resources simultaneously in use during the run, the number of resources available at the end of the run, and the maximum number of resources simultaneously available. As discussed above, the maximum values observed during a run should be compared with values obtained from runs of the same length.

5.3.4 Statistical Estimates for Nodes

Statistics based on observations always reference the node at which the statistics are collected. Thus, if statistics are for the transit time of a transaction, the node at which the transit time statistics are collected is the reference point on the Q-GERT output. For these variables, an average which is the sum of the observations divided by the number of observations is computed using the formula

$$\bar{r} = \frac{\displaystyle\sum_{i=1}^{I} r_i}{I}$$

where r_i = observation of the variable
I = number of observations
$\bar{r}$ = average of the observations

Also computed and printed for these variables are the standard deviation of the observations and the number of observations. It should be noted that the observed values can be highly correlated since sequential node release times (or sequential transaction transit times) can be highly correlated. For example, the value of the twentieth transaction's transit time is probably related to the value of the nineteenth transaction's transit time since there is a high likelihood that they resided in queues concurrently. Thus, although the standard deviation provides information concerning the spread of the observations, the value observed and computed for a single run should not be used for setting confidence intervals on the theoretical mean. Because of the high correlation anticipated between observed values, Q-GERT has been designed to obtain statistical estimates of the variation of the average by making multiple runs since each run is an independent replication of the experiment.

5.3.5 Statistical Estimates for Count Variables

The third type of variable for which statistical estimates are made are count variables. One such variable is the number of transactions balking from a Q-node. A normalized value for this variable is calculated by dividing the total number of transactions balking by the time period for the simulation run. In this way, an estimate of the average balking rate is made. The average balking rate is important as it specifies the arrival process to the node to which the transactions are routed when they balk. In many instances, transactions leave the system and the average balking rate can be used to model the arrival process to other network models that portray the system to which the transaction is balking.

Another count variable is the number of times a node has been released. The value of this variable for a run is printed at the end of a run. These counts are useful in determining traffic flow patterns of the transactions and indicate whether a node was released during a run. This latter information is used when making multiple runs to estimate the probability that a node is released. The probability is estimated as the number of times the node is released at least once in a run divided by the number of runs made.

5.3.6 Statistical Estimates over Multiple Runs

As alluded to above, the Q-GERT processor has been designed to obtain statistical estimates based on replications. For each replication or run, the average for the run is used as a single observed value. The average over all runs is then computed. For example, in M runs there are M values of the average number in the queue. These M values are summed and divided by M to compute a grand average. The minimum average and the maximum average over the M runs are also reported. An estimate is also made of the standard deviation of the averages which provides information on the spread in the average values that could be obtained. The central limit theorem applies in this situation and we can expect the distribution of the averages to approach the normal distribution. Each of the replications are made independently and, therefore, we estimate the standard deviation of the grand average as the standard deviation of the averages divided by the square root of the number of replications. This quantity is printed out for each of the statistical estimates made over the multiple runs.

On the summary report for all runs, the extreme values observed are also printed. Thus, the maximum number in a Q-node in any of the runs is reported. Similarly, the maximum consecutive idle time, maximum consecutive busy time, and longest period blocked are printed for service activities. The design of the Q-GERT processor to obtain estimates over multiple independent runs facilitates the use of standard statistical hypothesis-testing procedures [101, 121].

5.4 HISTOGRAMS

To transform observed values into a more manageable form, it is common to group them into classes or cells. The data are then summarized by tabulating the number of observations that fall within each cell. This kind of table is called a frequency distribution table or, if graphically presented, a histogram. A histogram normally gives a good overall picture of the data. Typically when preparing histograms, the cumulative frequency is also obtained by successively adding the frequencies in each cell.

In Q-GERT, histograms are produced on request for each Q-node and each statistics or sink node. Four columns of data and a graph are contained on each histogram. The four columns of information are:

OBSV FREQ   The observed frequency with which the variable of interest was within a specified range, that is, the number of times that the variable of interest was in a specified range.

RELA FREQ   The relative frequency that a variable had a value in a specified range. The relative frequency is equal to the observed frequency divided by the total number of observations.

CUML FREQ   The cumulative frequency, that is, the number of values for the variable that were less than or equal to the value of the upper bound of the cell divided by the number of observations.

UPPER BOUND OF CELL   The value that defines the topmost point of the cell. All cells are closed at the high end, that is, if a value of the variable equals the upper bound of cell I, the observed frequency for cell I is increased by 1. The first cell of each histogram has a range from negative infinity to the upper bound of the first cell. The last cell of a histogram has a range from the upper bound of the next-to-last cell to infinity.

Histogram outputs can be requested for the following two situations: (1) at statistics and sink nodes on the first run if multiple values are observed; and (2) at statistics nodes, sink nodes, and Q-nodes for average values over all runs. The user has the option of specifying the width of each histogram cell. If no cell width is specified, a histogram is not printed. If a zero cell width is specified, Q-GERT sets the upper limit for the first cell to zero and the width of a cell to one for a first-run histogram and computes appropriate values for the histogram of averages based on values obtained from the first run. If a positive width is prescribed, Q-GERT uses the input values for the first run unless no first-run report is requested. To prescribe the upper limit and width for a histogram over all runs, a negative value is specified for the cell width which Q-GERT interprets as the negative of the cell width for the average values obtained over all runs.

5.5 REPORT TYPES

The statistical estimates and histograms described in the previous sections can be obtained on a variety of Q-GERT reports. As discussed in Chapter 4, the reporting options are:

1. Prepare and print a report of the first run and a summary report over multiple runs.
2. Prepare a report for each run and a summary report over all runs.
3. Prepare a report of each run and a cumulative summary report for every run.
4. Prepare only a summary report over all runs.

The most general of the reporting options is the cumulative one which prescribes that individual reports for each run and summary reports up to and including that run are to be prepared. The individual run reports provide a picture of the transaction flows, nodal releases, and queue, server, and resource utilizations for a single experiment. On the cumulative reports the results from these individual experiments are averaged to illustrate the variability among experiments. It is the information on the cumulative report that can be used in statistical hypothesis testing. The information on the individual run reports more closely corresponds to data values from the real system. The reason for this is that in the business environment, a replication of a time period is normally not feasible. In those actual situations where time can be divided into subintervals, statistical estimates similar to those on the cumulative report would be obtained by considering each subinterval as a replication.

An illustration of the statistical estimates obtained from the

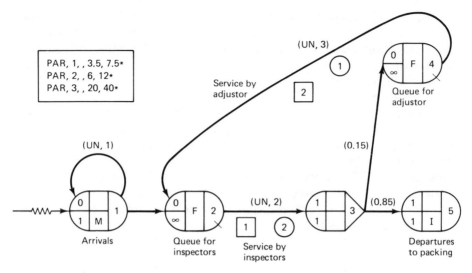

Figure 5-3 Q-GERT model of inspection and adjustment stations.

Q-GERT processor for the network displayed in Figure 5-3 is shown in Figures 5-4 through 5-6. Two runs were specified and the cumulative report option selected. From Figure 5-4, the time for a transaction to be processed through the network is 11.67 minutes on the average. This is based on 81 observations that occurred during a 480-minute run. The average number of transactions waiting at the INSP-QUE node was 0.12 and the average number waiting at the ADJ-QUE node was 0.04. The average waiting time associated with transactions at these nodes was 0.66 and 2.76 minutes, respectively. Server type 1 involves two parallel servers and, on the average, 1.61 of them were busy. During run 1, both servers were idle concurrently and both were busy concurrently as shown under the headings "MAX.IDLE" and "MAX. BUSY." Server 2 involved a single individual and he was busy, on the average, 33% of the time. During the 480-minute run, there was a period where he was idle 156 consecutive minutes. For a period of 29 minutes, he was continuously busy.

Following the server utilization section of the report, information is provided on the number of transaction passages through each node. For node 1, the source node, there were 84 transaction passages during the 480-minute run. Parameter set 1 specifies that the activity from node 1 back to node 1 is uniformly distributed between 3.5 and 7.5. This gives an average time between arrivals of 5.5 minutes, and we would expect 87.27 transactions to arrive in 480 minutes. Of the 84 arrivals, 81 departed the network as can be seen by the number of transaction passages through node 5 (this value is also seen as the number of observations for node 5 in the node statistics section of the report). The three transactions that arrived that did not complete the network are in the following locations: one is in Q-node 4, one is

```
GERT SIMULATION PROJECT TV-INS-ADJ-1 BY PRITSKER
              DATE  2/  1/ 1982

     ***RESULTS FOR RUN     1***

  ELAPSED TIME FOR RUN =     480.0000


              **NODE STATISTICS**
     NODE     LABEL      AVE.      NO OF    TYPE OF
                                   OBS.     STATISTICS

      5     SYS-TIME    11.6744     81.        I


          **NUMBER IN Q-NODE**               ** WAITING TIME **
                                                 IN QUEUE

     NODE    LABEL      AVE.    MIN.  MAX.   CURRENT      AVERAGE
                                             NUMBER

      2     INSP-QUE   0.1236   0.    2.       0        0.6666
      4     ADJ-QUE    0.0402   0.    1.       1        2.7596


            **SERVER UTILIZATION**

   SERVER    LABEL    NO. PARALLEL   AVE.      MAX. IDLE          MAX. BUSY
                        SERVERS             (TIME OR SERVERS) (TIME OR SERVERS)
      1     INSPECT        2        1.6145      2.0000            2.0000
      2     ADJUST         1        0.3251    156.3385           29.2310


   NODE    TRANSACTION
            PASSAGES

     1         84
     2         89
     3         88
     4          6
     5         81

         PRINTOUT OF ONGOING ACTIVITIES
              AT      480.00

   ACTIVITY END      END        ACTIVITY
       TIME         NODE         NUMBER

       481.98         1            0
       483.39         3            1
       488.42         2            2
```

Figure 5-4 Output report presenting results from run 1.

being served by server 1, and one is being served by server 2. The information concerning the transactions being served at the end of a run is contained in the ongoing activities report that follows the transaction passages report. For this run, it is seen that there is a transaction being processed by server 1 that is scheduled to arrive at node 3 at time 483.39. The other ongoing activities are interpreted in a similar manner. Activities without activity numbers are printed with a zero value for the activity number. By examining the transaction passages and ongoing activities section of the report, transaction flow paths through the network can be investigated. This is a good procedure for verifying that the Q-GERT network portrays the operation of the system under study.

In Figure 5-5, the output report presenting results for the Q-GERT network presented in Figure 5-3 for a second run are shown. Comparing the outputs for runs 1 and 2 indicates that the statistical variation between runs is high. This should not be entirely unexpected, as there are many sources of variability in the network model. The probabilistic

RESULTS FOR RUN   2

ELAPSED TIME FOR RUN =   480.0000

NODE STATISTICS

NODE	LABEL	AVE.	NO OF OBS.	TYPE OF STATISTICS
5	SYS-TIME	19.1470	80.	I

NUMBER IN Q-NODE   ** WAITING TIME **
                            IN QUEUE

NODE	LABEL	AVE.	MIN.	MAX.	CURRENT NUMBER	AVERAGE
2	INSP-QUE	0.3549	0.	2.	1	1.7036
4	ADJ-QUE	0.9692	0.	3.	1	27.3652

SERVER UTILIZATION

SERVER	LABEL	NO. PARALLEL SERVERS	AVE.	MAX. IDLE (TIME OR SERVERS)	MAX. BUSY (TIME OR SERVERS)
1	INSPECT	2	1.8341	2.0000	2.0000
2	ADJUST	1	0.8871	39.4601	264.4678

NODE	TRANSACTION PASSAGES
1	85
2	99
3	97
4	16
5	80

PRINTOUT OF ONGOING ACTIVITIES
        AT   480.00

ACTIVITY END TIME	END NODE	ACTIVITY NUMBER
480.98	3	1
484.61	3	1
485.35	1	0
499.04	2	2

Figure 5-5 Output report presenting results from run 2.

branching at node 3 and the feedback of units to Q-node 2 constitute a large source of statistical uncertainty concerning a transaction's movement through the system. Since only 15% of the transactions that arrive are routed back to Q-node 2 through Q-node 4 only a small number of transactions flow through the feedback path (7 in run 1 and 17 in run 2 counting the number being served and in Q-node 4). This source of variability must be considered when making decisions for the system that the network represents.

The elapsed time for each of the runs described above was 480 minutes. This represents an 8-hour day. If the system operates in a fashion where each 480-minute day is independent of the previous day, the outputs given in Figures 5-4 and 5-5 provide appropriate estimates for the period of interest. However, if there is a carryover from one day to the next, a longer simulation period can be used to decrease the variability in the estimates. The appropriate procedure to apply is

GERT SIMULATION PROJECT TV-INS-ADJ-1 BY PRITSKER
DATE 2/ 1/ 1982

FINAL RESULTS FOR   2 SIMULATIONS

AVERAGE NODE STATISTICS

NODE	LABEL	PROBABILITY	AVE.	STD.DEV.	SD OF AVE	NO OF OBS.	MIN.	MAX.	STAT TYPE
5	SYS-TIME	1.0000	15.4107	5.2839	3.7363	2.	11.6744	19.1470	I

AVERAGE NUMBER IN Q-NODE

AVERAGE WAITING TIME

NUMBER IN Q-NODE

NODE	LABEL	AVE.	STD.DEV.	SD OF AVE	MIN.	MAX.	AVE.	STD.DEV.	SD OF AVE	MIN.	MAX.	MAX.
2	INSP-QUE	0.2393	0.1636	0.1157	0.1236	0.3549	1.1851	0.7333	0.5185	1.6145	1.8341	2.0000
4	ADJ-QUE	0.5047	0.6569	0.4645	0.0402	0.9692	15.0624	17.3988	12.3028	0.3251	0.8871	3.0000

AVERAGE SERVER UTILIZATION

EXTREME VALUES

SERVER	LABEL	NO. PARALLEL SERVERS	AVE.	STD.DEV.	SD OF AVE	NO. OF OBS.	MAX. IDLE (TIME OR SERVERS)	MAX. BUSY
1	INSPECT	2	1.7243	0.1553	0.1098	2.	2.0000	2.0000
2	ADJUST	1	0.6061	0.3974	0.2810	2.	156.3385	264.4678

Figure 5-6 Output report presenting cumulative results for runs 1 and 2.

dependent on the system operation and the type of analysis to be performed.

To combine the results from the first two runs, a cumulative summary report for the two simulations is obtained by specifying the "C" report option. The cumulative report, which is, in essence, a summary report over the first two simulations, is shown in Figure 5-6.

Most of the values presented on a cumulative report are similar to those presented on the run report. The average values are the average of the run averages and the standard deviation provides an estimate of the variability of the averages. The column headed "SD OF AVE" is computed as the standard deviation divided by the square root of the number of observations. The "MIN." and "MAX." columns provide estimates of the smallest and largest values of the averages over all runs. As can be seen from Figure 5-6, the cumulative report presents extensive information concerning the operation of the system based on independent simulations representing separate runs or days. The cumulative report in this instance would be used for decision making concerning daily activities.

5.6 STORING Q-GERT OUTPUTS IN A DATA BASE

During the last two decades, significant progress has been made in the management and control of data. Typically, data base systems are used for storing actual observations obtained from a system. Since a Q-GERT model can be considered a system, the use of data base techniques for storing data obtained from the Q-GERT processor could be extremely advantageous. The use of a data base language in conjunction with Q-GERT augments the standardized outputs readily obtainable from the Q-GERT processor. It allows a Q-GERT user to save values from past runs, to make comparisons among the outputs from different scenarios, to perform analysis of experiments that have been designed in accordance with statistical design procedures, and to employ the outputs of various Q-GERT models as inputs to other simulation statistics and optimization programs.

In this section, we describe how the simulation data language, SDL, can be used in conjunction with Q-GERT to build a data base that supports the performance of the functions listed above [191]. The use of other data base languages in conjunction with Q-GERT is feasible. However, since SDL has been designed with simulation studies in mind, its use is more direct. SDL and the routines to access the Q-GERT run statistics are not part of the standard Q-GERT processor; hence, the description presented herein should be considered for the advanced Q-GERT user. SDL is not employed in the analyses performed in this book as it requires a separate software package [190].

5.6.1 Routines to Access Run Statistics

Within any user function or subroutine, values of Q-GERT variables can be accessed, and stored in a data base using SDL functions. Thus, all observations of variables of interest can be stored in the data base. Once in the data base, SDL provides functions for performing the statistical calculations necessary to obtain the standard Q-GERT outputs. Furthermore, statistical summaries computed by Q-GERT can be stored in the data base. For user-defined statistics, there are arrays where the values are stored and their transfer to the SDL data base is direct.

In order to obtain run statistics that are generated for nodes, queues, resources, and servers, the following four subroutines have been written (these are not part of the standard Q-GERT processor).

Subroutine	*Definition*
GNSTA(NODE,STVAL)	This subroutine gets the node statistics for node number NODE and stores the values in vector STVAL
GQSTA(NODE,STVAL)	This subroutine gets the node statistics for Q-node number NODE and stores the values in vector STVAL
GRSTA(NRES,STVAL)	This subroutine gets the statistics for resource number NRES and stores the values in vector STVAL
GSSTA(NACT,STVAL)	This subroutine gets the statistics for activity number NACT and stores the values in vector STVAL

The subroutines defined above return the vector STVAL with the following run statistics:

STVAL(1) = sum of all values

STVAL(2) = sums of squares of all values

STVAL(3) = number of observations or time period for computing the average

STVAL(4) = minimum value observed

STVAL(5) = maximum value observed

Given that the data desired to be stored in the data base can be accessed during the operation of the Q-GERT processor, it is only necessary to understand how to use SDL to store such values, operate on the values, and prepare reports based on the values. The following sections provide an overview for accomplishing these tasks.

5.6.2 A Data Base Language for Simulation

The Simulation Data Language, SDL [190], has been developed to aid simulation modelers in performing data management and control activities on a set of data obtained from a simulation study. The SDL commands are designed to organize, manage, and manipulate data. The organization of the data is accomplished by defining relations, that is, a matrix of rows and columns. The columns specify what values are to be stored and the rows specify how these values relate to one another.

During a computer run of a Q-GERT model, the variables describing system performance are stored, using SDL functions, into the defined relations. All stored data values are preserved by SDL in a data set on the computer being used. Thus, these data values are available both during a model run and after many such runs have been completed.

SDL allows the results of the statistical analysis to be retrieved from within Q-GERT user functions. This capability allows dynamic, complex decisions to be incorporated within models. For example, in the model of a production facility, the performance in week 1 may influence the production strategy employed in week 2. SDL commands can be used in the model to collect observations of the desired performance variables, perform statistical computations on these observations at the end of week 1, and retrieve the results of these computations. Thus, the needed decision could be made based on the observed values. Since the results of these computations can be automatically stored in the data base by SDL, a report could be generated at the end of a model run to quantify how the decision had been made and the quantities on which it was based.

SDL consists of more than 120 commands. However, these commands may be classified into 12 categories:

1. Housekeeping
2. Defining the data organization
3. Storing data
4. Retrieving data
5. Computing statistics
6. Building histograms
7. Plotting

8. Reporting
9. Deleting data
10. Loading data
11. Editing and updating data
12. Creating non-SDL data sets

Figure 5-7 shows the relationship between the categories of SDL commands (arrows), data stored in an SDL data base (circle), and the data management needs of simulators (boxes). Arrows pointing into the data base indicate that the command places data into the data base. Conversely, arrows pointing away from the data base indicate that the command uses data previously placed in the data base without removing the data from the data base.

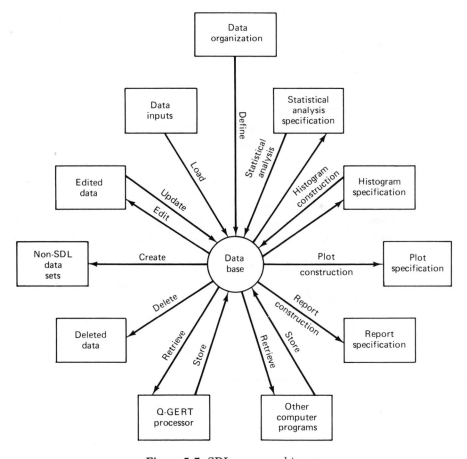

Figure 5-7 SDL command types.

When used with Q-GERT, SDL commands may be used in two modes of operation:

1. Within Q-GERT user-written routines by invoking SDL subprograms to store data in and retrieve data from an SDL data base.

2. By writing programs in the SDL operation invocation language (OIL) to define the data organization, compute statistics, build histograms, plot data, report data, delete data, load data, edit and update data, and create non-SDL data sets. The OIL is used to query the data base; that is, it is a query language for its users.

5.6.3 Storing Statistics and Observations in an SDL Data Base

SDL has two commands for storing statistics in the data base from the Q-GERT user-written subprograms. One of the commands stores statistics for observed quantities that are not weighted by time. This command places statistics, for each run, one variable at a time, in a special SDL relation for storing statistics. The statistics stored are the mean, the variance, the minimum, the maximum, and a count of the number of observations. Examples of Q-GERT variables for which this command would be used are transaction passage times and nodal quantities, such as interval, first, all, delay, and between observations.

A second command is for statistics computed with time-persistent conditions in the model. Examples of variables for this command are the number in queue and the utilization of servers and resources. To use the statistics storing commands, a Q-GERT user would make use of the Q-GERT subprograms described in Section 5.6.1 to retrieve the desired values and then would invoke the appropriate SDL subprogram to store the values in the data base.

SDL provides commands for recording a time history of model performance. One command stores selected attributes of a transaction and the performance measures for the transaction such as its passage time. A second command provides for recording histories of time-persistent conditions in the system such as the number of transactions in queues and the number of resources utilized.

5.6.4 Analyzing Stored Observations of System Performance

SDL provides commands for performing statistical analysis of observations of system performance that were previously stored in the data base. The commands allow many analyses to be made over time without rerunning the models as long as the Q-GERT outputs were stored in the SDL data base.

SDL has four commands which compute statistics from data stored in a collect relation. These commands would be written in SDL's query language which is called OIL, operational invocation language. Each of the commands computes the average, variance, minimum, maximum, number of observations/total observation time, sum of observations, and the sum of the squared observations as well as allowing the data to be partitioned into one or more subsets called batches. The commands allow missing observations to be ignored and data from transient, initial warm-up periods to be deleted.

The first statistics analysis command considers a batch to correspond to a Q-GERT run. This command produces statistics for each of the model runs. Statistics over model runs can be computed using other commands. Thus, a replication analysis with censored data can be performed.

The second statistical analysis command partitions the data from a model run into one or more subinterval sets. This command is used to perform subinterval analysis on collected data.

The third statistics analysis command allows statistics to be tabulated by a specified value or set of values of attributes. In this way, for example, statistical estimates on transactions for which attribute 2 is equal to each of several specified values can be computed.

The fourth statistics analysis command allows the user to have direct control of how batches are constructed by coding the last observation in a batch.

SDL also provides commands for creating, updating, and displaying of system performance data stored in a data base. Four histogram-producing commands are available which correspond to the four statistical analysis commands discussed above.

5.6.5 Reporting Stored Data

SDL provides commands for building reports from the data stored in a data base, that is, a report generator capability. Two types of commands are available. The first prepares a report of the data in a format predetermined by SDL. The second allows the user to design the report format to be used. Each report consists of four sections: page header, column header, data, and footnotes. Page headers, column headers, and footnotes may have as many lines as the user desires. The content of each line is given by the user as part of the general description of the report. In addition, the user may specify the spacing to be used on the report.

5.7 SUMMARY

In this chapter, an overview of the types of variables that Q-GERT uses as a basis to evaluate system performance has been presented. The analysis of the observations of these variables and their integration into reports have been described. A discussion of the potential use of a simulation data language to create a data base for output analysis in conjunction with the Q-GERT processor has been given. In the remainder of this book, illustrations of the use of the output variables and the report types are provided to demonstrate their significance in achieving improved decision making.

5.8 EXERCISES

5-1. Define the three types of variable on which Q-GERT maintains statistics. What statistical quantities are computed for each type of variable?

5-2. Draw a graph that illustrates the number in a system over a 20-time-unit period in which five customers arrive. The following pairs of numbers represent the arrival and departure times for each of the five customers:

$$(1, 5); \qquad (3, 6); \qquad (5, 10); \qquad (9, 19); \qquad (10, 20)$$

Demonstrate for this situation that Little's formula relating the average number in the system to the average time in the system holds. Repeat the demonstration for the average number in the queue and the average time in the queue.

5-3. Explain why the central limit theorem applies when statistical estimates are obtained over multiple runs.

5-4. Verify the correctness (or incorrectness) and provide a rationale for the following statements:

(a) As the elapsed time for a run increases, larger expected values should be obtained for the estimates of the maximum idle time and the maximum busy time for a server.

(b) Estimates from the Q-GERT processor over multiple runs facilitates the use of standard statistical hypothesis-testing procedures.

(c) Histograms for sink nodes will always be part of the Q-GERT summary report.

(d) A negative value is never specified for the cell width of a Q-GERT histogram.

(e) The method of computing server utilization depends on the number of parallel servers represented by an activity.

5-5. Write subroutine UO to produce the output report presented in Figure 5-4.

5-6. For Figure 5-4, perform a transaction balance that demonstrates that all arriving transactions have been processed or are in process at the end of the simulation. Make the computations to show that Little's formula has been used in computing waiting times in the queue under the assumption that transactions currently in the system have a departure time equal to the end time for the simulation run. Show the computations that were made in order to compute the standard deviation of the average of the two runs for nodes 2 and 4 (SD OF AVE).

5-7. Develop a set of commands that you would like to see in a query language to obtain data from a data base in which the Q-GERT outputs are stored. Design a set of formats for presenting the data to managers, engineers, and statistical analysts. Indicate which commands should be available to all users.

III

Production Planning

6

Production Planning – Basic Concepts

6.1 INTRODUCTION

A production system is an organized collection of personnel, materials, and machines that operates within a well-defined work space. Inputs to the system include raw materials and orders for manufactured goods. Manufactured items are the outputs of the system. The diagram in Figure 6-1 depicts a production system. Work space, labor, and machines are referred to as system resources. Because of its importance, material handling equipment is often considered separately from other machines.

In this chapter, a thorough discussion of system performance measures for a production system is given. Procedures for estimating these performance measures using Q-GERT networks are described. The Q-GERT concepts for modeling the machines of a production system are presented and illustrations of the use of these concepts are provided.

6.1.1 System Performance

Resources are considered as the structural elements of the system. Through the structured elements flows a stream of material which is converted by the resources into finished product. The performance of a production system is measured by its effectiveness and efficiency in

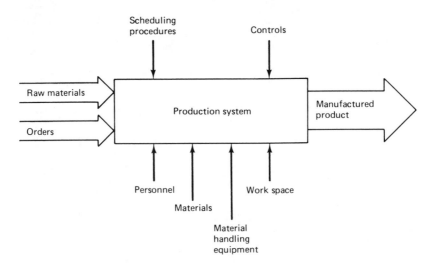

Figure 6-1 Diagram of a production system.

making this conversion. Performance measures can be grouped into four categories:

1. Measures of throughput
2. Measures of ability to meet deadlines
3. Measures of resource utilization
4. Measures of in-process inventory

Throughput is the output produced in a given period of time. Another name for this measure is the production rate. However, the term "rate" is often avoided, as it implies continuous output, which is not always the case. *System capacity* is often defined as the maximum throughput that can be obtained.

The ability to meet deadlines is measured by product lateness, tardiness, or flowtime. *Lateness* is the time between when a job is completed and when it was due to be completed. *Tardiness* is the lateness of a job only if it fails to meet its due date; otherwise, it is zero. *Flowtime* is the amount of time a job spends in the system. In some cases, the total time it takes to complete all jobs is of importance. This time is referred to as the *makespan*. All of these measures are indications of the effectiveness and efficiency of the system, including its scheduling procedures, in satisfying customer orders.

As mentioned previously, system resources include personnel, materials, machines, and work space. The *utilization* of these resources, as measured by the fraction of time they are productive, is another measure of system effectiveness. Measures of resource utilization relate the degree to which a system is operating at capacity.

The final category of performance measures is concerned with the buildup of raw materials and unfinished parts during production. This buildup, called *in-process inventory* or work in process (WIP), is usually due to parts waiting for available resources. Since inventory requires storage space, often a critical resource in itself, and also ties up capital, in-process inventory requirements are of great importance in production planning.

This discussion has dealt solely with system performance measures without a reference to system objectives. Our interest here is in evaluating the performance of systems in light of specified objectives, where objectives are determined by management for a particular situation. Objectives are satisfied when system performance measures reach prescribed levels. The measures outlined above provide the basis for evaluating diverse objectives. By concentrating on performance measures, we bypass the question of identifying the objectives of production planning, which by necessity are situation dependent. For example, it has frequently been noted that the objectives of a production system are highly dependent on the production volume (high or low).

In many situations, objectives are set in terms of cost effectiveness or system profitability. The measures of performance described above provide the inputs for measuring cost effectiveness and system profitability without requiring system-specific data regarding costs and revenues. Consequently, we present methods for obtaining estimates to insert into profit equations rather than specific profit or cost performance measures.

6.1.2 Factors Affecting Performance

In the system diagram of Figure 6-1, we viewed scheduling procedures as a system input. It is a special input in that the procedures are under the designer's or analyst's control. By varying operating procedures, such as scheduling of work, the sequencing of machines, and routing of work within the system, we can improve the performance of the system. System performance can also be affected by changes in system structure; for example the purchasing of new machines, the expansion of work space, and a change in the labor force.

Production planning involves an assessment of current system performance or an estimate of future performance under changing system structure and/or operating procedures. Specifically, it involves the design and evaluation of new facilities and machinery to meet future demand, and proposed operational procedures to increase system performance.

In this chapter we propose the use of network modeling for the design and analysis of production systems. We illustrate, by example, Q-GERT methods for obtaining performance measures under different sets of objectives and for diverse production configurations. The modeling of production systems is presented in this chapter at the conceptual level. The ideas, formulations, and network designs are presented in an abstract context and provide a foundation for the use of network modeling in production planning in general.

6.1.3 Introductory Examples

To introduce the use of Q-GERT concepts in production planning, we construct a Q-GERT model of a manufacturing process where the finished product is produced by one machine operation from one piece of raw material. The raw material, which we assume is an unfinished part, is delivered to the machine area. An operation is performed by the machine and the finished part leaves the machine area. Our interest is focused on the following three aspects of the system:

1. The arrival of unfinished parts to the machine area
2. The buildup of unfinished parts awaiting the service operation
3. The service operation

This is a single-resource queueing system. The parts to be processed are the items or *transactions* moving through the system. The machine is a fixed resource, which in Q-GERT is modeled as a *server*.†
The service activity is the machining operation. The buildup of parts awaiting service is modeled as a queue.

Following is a pictorial diagram of this one-machine center.

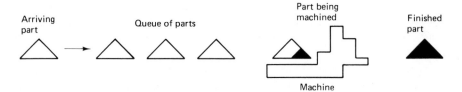

To build a Q-GERT network of this system, we start with the server. The service operation (the machining) is an activity and, hence, modeled by a branch. If the service activity is ongoing, that is, the

---

†In this chapter, transactions are usually parts to be processed and servers are usually machines that perform the processing. The reader should note that a transaction may be any physical or information item flowing through the system. Similarly, a server may represent any processing delay that requires an available resource. Servers may also be operators, such as inspectors and adjustors.

machine (server) is busy, arriving transactions (parts) must wait at a Q-node. Thus, we depict the machine area as follows:

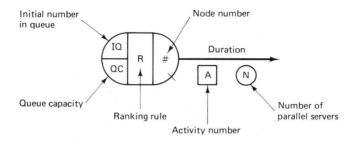

The branch (the service operation) is identified by an activity number A, a number of parallel, identical servers N, and a duration specification. In this example, there is only one machine and, hence, N would be set to 1. Since the machine time is an activity, any of the duration-time functions listed in Table 2-1 can be used to describe the time a part is in service. When the machine becomes available, a part is removed from the queue and another service activity begins. If a part arrives when the machine is busy, it waits by joining the queue. The queue is represented by the node whose number is specified by #. An initial number in the queue can be specified. Also specified is the capacity of the queue, QC, which is the largest number of parts that can wait for service at the Q-node. When an item arrives to a full queue, it will either *balk* or be *blocked*, as described in Section 2.5.2.

The arrival of parts can be modeled by causing successive releases of a source node. A branch representing the time between successive arrivals is used as shown here.

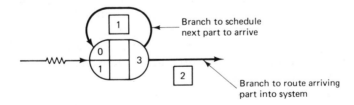

The squiggly line is used to denote a source node (a source node is released without an arriving transaction at the beginning of a run). In this case, the source node is identified as node 3 with zero transaction arrivals required for initial release (always the case for source nodes), and one transaction arrival required for subsequent releases. The time duration prescribed for activity 1 specifies the time between part arrivals.

The modeling of the departure of a part is accomplished by a node that has no branch emanating from it:

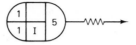

The node number for this sink node is 5. For both the first and subsequent releases of the node, a single incoming transaction is required. A squiggly line is used on the output side of the node to indicate that node 5 is a sink node. Specifying a number of transactions to arrive at sink nodes is one way to establish run termination conditions.

By combining the arrival, service, and departure elements, we have a network model for the machining system:

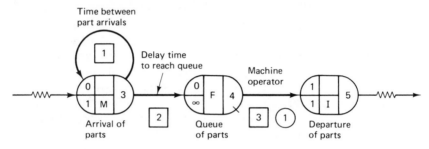

The network above models the processing of parts in the system. A part arrives at node 3. At its arrival time, the next arrival is scheduled to occur in an amount of time determined by the time duration of activity 1. The newly arrived part reaches the machine storage area (Q-node 4) after traversing activity 2. If the machine (service activity 3) is idle, the part enters service. Service time is determined by the duration specification for activity 3. If the activity is already ongoing, that is, the server is busy, the part joins the queue and awaits service.

Once service is completed, the part exits the system after releasing node 5. Sink node 5 has an interval statistics specification which indicates that observations on the interval of time for the part to go between a mark node and a statistics or sink node are to be collected. Marking is the act of associating the current time with a transaction as it passes through a node. All source nodes mark transactions at the time they enter the system. Hence, the interval or I-statistic in the network above represents the product flowtime; that is, each observation is for the time a part spends in the system.

As discussed previously, we are also interested in the number of parts processed per time period, the average time the machine is busy, the average time a part awaits the machine, and the average number of parts in the queue. The Q-GERT processor provides estimates of these system performance measures. The next section will address these measures in more detail. First, however, we will introduce complexity into the machining example to illustrate how the Q-GERT symbols can be arranged to reflect a change in system structure or operating policy.

Suppose that there were three machines in the example above. If all three of these machines operated identically then, as noted previously, the number of parallel servers could be specified as 3: a simple change in the network model. Often, however, machines that are not identical can be used to perform the same operations. For example, each may have a different operating speed. If more than one machine is available, a selection of which machine to schedule must be made. In this case, we use three server branches, one to represent each machine and we introduce an S-node in front of the servers. With multiple machines, we might employ multiple queues. S-nodes provide the capability of choosing from sets of parallel queues and servers. To illustrate, consider the situation depicted in the following schematic:

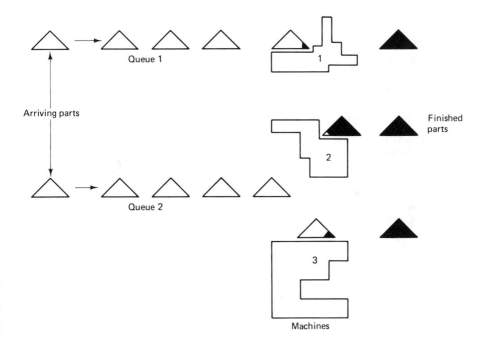

Here we have two arrival processes, two queues, and three servers. There are two types of decisions to be made in this situation. First, when a machine finishes processing a part, does the next part to be machined come from queue 1 or queue 2? Second, when a part arrives and more than 1 machine is available, to which machine do we assign the part? Such operating procedures can affect the total performance of the system. Q-GERT provides a means for modeling such operating decisions through the use of the S-node. A Q-GERT model of this manufacturing situation would look like this:

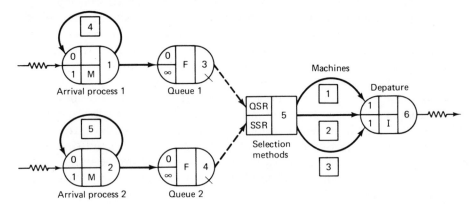

Source node 1 models arrival process 1. The interarrival time is determined by activity 4. Q-node 3 represents the first queue. Similarly, node 2 and activity 5 together represent the second arrival process, and Q-node 4 represents the second queue. Service activities 1, 2, and 3 represent the three machines, and the time specification (not shown) for each branch represents the operating characteristics of that machine.

The queue and server selection methods referred to above are modeled through the specification of selection rules for S-node 5. Q-GERT provides many options for Queue Selection Rules (QSR) and Server Selection Rules (SSR) as described in Tables 2-3 and 2-4. If a part arrives to either queue when one or more machines are idle, the S-node schedules the part for service by selecting one of the available machines according to the specified SSR. Similarly, when a machine completes service, the S-node takes a part from one of the queues in accordance with the QSR rule and routes the part to the machine.

All parts leave the system at node 6. The Q-GERT processor computes waiting times, time in the system, server utilization, and queue length statistics.

In subsequent sections, we make use of many of the Q-GERT concepts and symbols summarized in Chapter 2. Although we will review important Q-GERT features as we use them, reference to Chapter 2 for details of Q-GERT procedures is recommended. Before proceeding, this is a good time to refer to the sections on attributes and resources. Attributes are a means for distinguishing among items in the system. Each transaction flowing through the network has a specified set of attribute values. Attribute assignments are made at nodes using the standard functions that are also used in specifying activity durations. Through these procedures, an individual transaction can be identified by type, time of entry into the system, due date, and job priority. Attributes are used extensively throughout the remainder of this book.

Q-GERT resource concepts provide additional constructs for modeling service operations. With resources, complicated starting conditions for service operations can be specified. For example, after a resource is allocated, conditions can be tested for actually starting the service operation using branching operations. The resource approach also permits both the modeling of a sequence of activities by the same server and fluctuations in the number of resources available. The latter is modeled using ALTER nodes. Finally, resources are reallocated depending on where they are freed; hence, they can be moved to network segments based on current status information.

The decision to use a service activity or a resource to model a server is not an easy one. This flexibility included in Q-GERT avoids dictating a specific modeling solution. Several rules of thumb regarding the decision will become apparent as we discuss examples. For now, it is important to recognize the availability of both procedures. To illustrate the use of resources when modeling using Q-GERT, consider the one-server, single-queue network model introduced above. Letting the server be modeled as a resource instead of an activity results in the following network model:

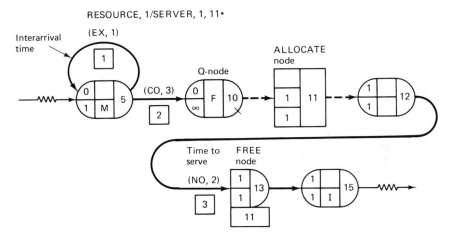

RESOURCE, 1/SERVER, 1, 11*

At ALLOCATE node 11, the server is allocated to a waiting transaction in Q-node 10. Activity 3 represents the time to perform the service operation. At FREE node 13, the server is freed and is allocated to waiting transactions at node 11. Clearly, this model of the one-server, single-queue system is more complex (three extra nodes) than the previous model that employed a service activity. However, resources can be used to expand the definition of service to include a set of branches between node 12 and node 13. In addition, the server resource could be removed from operation by altering the capacity of the resource through the use of ALTER nodes (see Section 2.6.3).

It is readily apparent that the Q-GERT symbols serve as powerful building blocks that can be assembled to model systems that contain structural and procedural complexities. We will deal with more examples of network features later in this chapter and in the following chapter. First, however, we will discuss performance measures in production planning and relate these measures to Q-GERT network analysis. Where possible, examples are utilized to clarify the significant points.

6.2 Q-GERT ESTIMATION OF PERFORMANCE MEASURES IN PRODUCTION PLANNING

In this section we discuss how the output from the Q-GERT processor can be used to estimate some of the commonly employed measures of system performance in production planning, such as throughput, lateness in meeting deadlines, resource utilization, and in-process inventory requirements.

6.2.1 Throughput

Throughput is the number of units produced during a time interval. It is an important performance measure for determining whether a system can meet expected demand. To estimate throughput, we need information on the number of transactions that departed the production system and the time span of the simulation. The Q-GERT processor maintains the variable NTC(NODE) as the number of transactions that pass through the node NODE. The variable for the current time during the simulation is TNOW. The time at which Q-GERT begins maintaining NTC($\cdot$) is TBEG. Therefore, at the end of an analysis run of the network, the throughput through any node of the network, NODE, is equal to TPUT=X/(TNOW-TBEG), where X=NTC(NODE). If the node NODE is the point of departure for all parts in the system, TPUT will represent system throughput. The value for this expression can be computed and conveniently outputted in user output routine UO. Since the value for throughput is a random variable, TPUT is only a single sample value. To obtain N samples of TPUT, N network runs should be made. In subroutine UO, the statement CALL COL(TPUT,1), included after TPUT is computed, will cause the program to observe TPUT after each run and automatically compute the average, standard deviation, standard deviation of the average, and the number of observations. User routine HIS can be used to obtain a frequency histogram of throughput. This histogram information permits the analyst to estimate the percentage of time that system throughput will be within a specified range.

It should be noted that if interval (I) statistics are collected at a node, the number of observations for this statistic will coincide with the number of transactions passing through the node. This information may be obtained without any user programming since I-statistics are obtained through an input specification.

Sometimes it is of interest to measure system throughput by the time between departures from the system. Throughput can be thought of as the inverse of the time between departures. Time between departures is useful if the output of the production system serves as input to another system, for example, a warehouse operation. This information can be obtained by specifying between-statistics for a node at the point of departure of transactions from the system.

Finally, we mention the case where a transaction represents a batch of items to be processed. Often, the size or volume of the batch is modeled as an attribute of the transaction. The number of units produced in this case is not the number of transactions passing through a node but the sum of the attribute values representing batch size. This running total of units processed can be maintained as a user variable UNITP, and updated in a user function which is called when a transaction departs the system. Suppose that attribute 1 represents batch size; then in function UF the code

$$UNITP = UNITP + GATRB(1)$$

would be used to update the user variable UNITP. The value of UNITP must be initialized to 0 at TBEG (subroutine UI could be used for this purpose if TBEG=0). UNITP and throughput can be recorded and printed in subroutine UO as described previously.

6.2.2 Meeting Due Dates

Typically, production managers strive to satisfy customer demand. One measure of a production system's performance in this regard is flowtime, the length of time a part spends in the system. Interval statistics are used to compute flowtime. Consider the single-machine system introduced earlier and redrawn here.

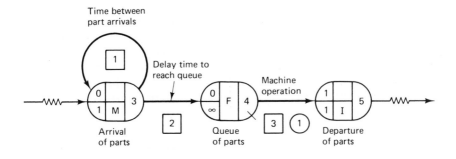

JOB-TIME

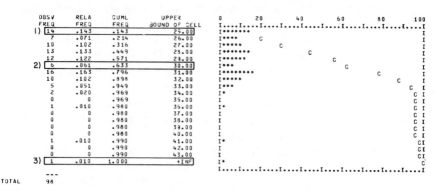

	OBSV FREQ	RELA FREQ	CUML FREQ	UPPER BOUND OF CELL
1)	14	.143	.143	25.00
	7	.071	.214	26.00
	10	.102	.316	27.00
	13	.133	.449	28.00
	12	.122	.571	29.00
2)	6	.061	.633	30.00
	16	.163	.796	31.00
	10	.102	.898	32.00
	5	.051	.949	33.00
	2	.020	.969	34.00
	0	0	.969	35.00
	1	.010	.980	36.00
	0	0	.980	37.00
	0	0	.980	38.00
	0	0	.980	39.00
	0	0	.980	40.00
	1	.010	.990	41.00
	0	0	.990	42.00
	0	0	.990	43.00
3)	1	.010	1.000	+INF

TOTAL   98

Interpretive statements:
1) 14 of the 98 jobs (0.143) were processed in less than or equal to 25 minutes.
2) 63.3% of the jobs were processed within 30 minutes.
3) one processing time was greater than 43 minutes.

Figure 6-2 Histogram of job times.

The interval statistics specification for node 5 causes the Q-GERT processor to observe the time interval required for a transaction to reach node 5 from node 3. Interval statistics can be used to observe the time lapse required to traverse any part of the system. In this case, the total time in the system is observed since no marking occurs between source node 3 and sink node 5. The Q-GERT processor computes the average, standard deviation, and related values for this time interval as well as a frequency histogram. The analyst can, therefore, estimate the proportion of jobs that exit in prescribed time intervals. An example of a histogram for I-statistics is shown in Figure 6-2. From this output, the analyst can estimate that:

1. 14.3% of all jobs will be processed in less than or equal to 25 minutes.
2. 63.3% of all jobs will be processed within 30 minutes.
3. 1% of all jobs will require more than 43 minutes.

Often, a job enters the system with a specified due date. We may want to compute the "lateness" of each job, that is, the time difference between when the job finished and when it was due. To accomplish this for the example above, we introduce the use of an attribute (in this case attribute 1) to represent a job's due date. For now we assume that all due dates are 40 time units from the date of arrival. We assign attribute 1 the value of TNOW+40 at source node 3. This is accomplished by the following user function:

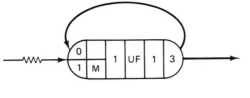

```
        FUNCTION UF(IFN)
        COMMON/QVAR/NDE,NFTBU(100),NREL(100),NRELP(100),NREL2(100),NRUN
       1NRUNS,NTC(100),PARAM(100,4),TBEG,TNOW
        GO TO (1,2) IFN
C****   SET ATTRIBUTE 1 TO CURRENT TIME + 40
   1    UF = TNOW + 40.
        RETURN
C****   RETURN A ZERO VALUE FOR USER FUNCTION 2
   2    UF = 0
        RETURN
        END
```

To take statistics on lateness, we need to subtract TNOW from attribute 1 when the transaction departs the system. If this value is negative, the job is late by the absolute value of the difference. If the value is positive, the job is early by this amount. To observe these values, we use subroutine COL in a user function called from sink node 5. We segregate our observations by assigning one statistics code to late jobs and another to early jobs. The FORTRAN programming in function UF to accomplish this is as follows:

```
   2    UF = 0
C****   XERLY = DUE DATE - DEPARTURE TIME
        XERLY=GATRB(1)-TNOW
        IF(XERLY.LT.0.) GO TO 10
C****   COLLECT EARLY STATISTICS
        CALL COL(XERLY,1)
        RETURN
C****   COLLECT LATE STATISTICS
  10    XLATE = - XERLY
        CALL COL(XLATE,2)
        RETURN
```

In this example, user-collected statistics with a code of 1 represents observations on early jobs. Code 2 represents observations on late jobs. Subroutine HIS could be used to obtain histograms of these observations.

The use of the user function for specifying due dates offers the analyst a great deal of flexibility. The due date need not be a simple constant number of time units into the future. Since the Q-GERT analyst can retrieve information on the current network status, including queue lengths [XNINQ(NODE)] and server status [ISTUS(NODE,NSERV)], a wide variety of due date specification policies can be modeled and evaluated.

6.2.3 Makespan

Another performance measure is makespan, which is the time to complete N jobs. Suppose that we wish to analyze the single-server system described above for 100 jobs and collect makespan statistics.

To accomplish this, node 6 would be added at the point of a transaction departure:

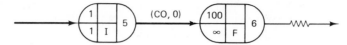

As before, interval statistics are prescribed for node 5 to estimate flowtime. At node 6, first-statistics (F-statistics) are specified to obtain the time of first release. Since the release of node 6 occurs after 100 transactions pass through it, F-statistics in this case describe the makespan for 100 jobs. The average, standard deviation, minimum, and maximum for makespan are computed over multiple runs. A histogram could also be obtained.

6.2.4 Server and Resource Utilization

Q-GERT can model machines by either service activities or by resources. A service activity restricts transaction flow like a resource but is passive, as it does not move through the network. A resource, on the other hand, can be allocated at more than one node in the network and is referred to as being active. Both active and passive resources are used to halt the flow of transactions until resources are available. Resource utilization is the fraction of time a resource is in use and is, typically, of interest to management. For instance, in the example above, we are interested in the utilization of the machine represented by server 3. Figure 6-3 contains illustrative output relating to server 3. A utilization figure is computed for each network run. For this illustration, 10 runs or observations were made. The average utilization over the 10 runs was 0.8416. Since each run is an independent observation of the utilization, we can utilize the central limit theorem to derive a confidence statement for the theoretical mean utilization. The standard deviation of the average (the standard deviation divided by the square root of number of observations) is 0.0534. The two σ-limits would then be (0.7348, 0.9484), and there is approximately a 95% chance that this interval contains the theoretical population mean. If a smaller confidence interval is desired, a larger number of runs should be made.

To obtain a frequency histogram for server utilization, the analyst can call the user histogram routine HIS in subroutine UO at the end of

		NO. PARALLEL	**AVERAGE SERVER UTILIZATION**						**EXTREME VALUES**	
				STD.	SD OF	NO. OF				MAX.
SERVER	LABEL	SERVERS	AVE.	DEV.	AVE	OBS.	MIN.	MAX.	MAX. IDLE	BUSY
									(TIME OR SERVERS)	
3	MACHINE	1	.8416	.1689	.0534	10.	.5986	1.0000	6.6469	28.0000

Figure 6-3 Server utilization output.

each run. Function TISS(NODE,NSERV) can be used to compute the server utilization at any time during the simulation.

Note that the output in Figure 6-3 also includes the minimum and maximum of the observed average utilizations. In addition, the maximum idle period over all runs (6.65 time units) and the maximum busy period over all runs (28 time units) is reported. If the number of parallel servers represented by a branch is greater than 1, the extreme values observed are the maximum number of servers that are concurrently idle and busy.

Consider now service activity 1, which ends at Q-node 3, which has a finite capacity of four transactions:

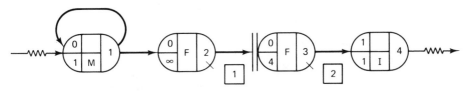

The vertical lines in front of Q-node 3 denote possible blocking of server 1. When Q-node 3 has four transactions in it when server 1 completes a service operation, server 1 cannot pass on the finished transaction nor can it start another service operation. In such a situation, we say that the server and the transaction are *blocked*. Thus, a server may be either idle, busy, or blocked. The blocked time per time unit (the time blocked divided by the total simulated time) is observed on each Q-GERT run. Outputted are the average blocked time per unit time, the standard deviation, the standard deviation of the average, and the minimum and maximum observations over all runs. The longest period blocked is also reported.

For active resources, each resource type has a maximum available number of units. Statistics are compiled on the number of resources in use (allocated to transactions) and available (not allocated to a transaction). An illustration of the computer output for active resources is shown in Figure 6-4.

6.2.5 In-Process Inventory Requirements

We have observed that as parts move through a production system, they queue up at different points in the system. This buildup may occur in machine areas, in temporary storage areas, and buffers for material handling equipment. The aggregate amount of raw material and unfinished parts in the system is known as in-process inventory. In order for the production system to meet demand, some level of in-process inventory is unavoidable. However, it is costly to have goods in any form in inventory because inventory represents a nonproductive use of capital. Hence, the production manager is continually faced with

AVERAGE RESOURCE UTILIZATION

RESOURCE	LABEL	AVE.	STD.DEV.	SD OF AVE	NO. OF OBS.	MIN.	MAX.	**NUMBER OF RESOURCES** MAX.
1	TRAINEE	.9467	.0205	.0065	10.	.9062	.9799	1.
2	MASTER	.9384	.0259	.0082	10.	.8801	.9659	1.
3	ADJUSTOR	.6420	.1912	.0605	10.	.3014	.8954	1.

AVERAGE RESOURCE AVAILABILITY

RESOURCE	LABEL	AVE.	STD.DEV.	SD OF AVE	NO. OF OBS.	MIN.	MAX.	**NUMBER OF RESOURCES** MAX.
1	TRAINEE	.0533	.0205	.0065	10.	.0201	.0938	1.
2	MASTER	.0616	.0259	.0082	10.	.0341	.1199	1.
3	ADJUSTOR	.3580	.1912	.0605	10.	.1046	.6986	1.

Figure 6-4 Resource utilization output.

the trade-off of keeping sufficient goods in the system to meet demand while maintaining low levels of inventory to keep such costs reasonable.

Another obvious problem with in-process inventory is that it requires space which is often limited. This problem is translated into a set of common questions such as:

1. How much space will we need for in-process inventory if we increase the production rate, design new facilities, or expand existing facilities?
2. How do changes in operating procedures affect in-process inventories?

The importance of measuring and controlling in-process inventory relates to the requirements for space, the number of dollars invested in work in progress, and the loss in production due to blocking.

In a Q-GERT model, the buildup of parts occurs at Q-nodes and statistics on Q-nodes relate to in-process inventory performance measures. The number of transactions in a Q-node is a time-persistent variable, an example of which is shown in Figure 6-5. The average number of transactions in the Q-node is obtained by averaging the number of transactions in the queue over time. For the data shown in Figure 6-5, the average number in the queue is 1.4167. As discussed in Chapter 5, for each run of the network, one sample value of the average number in a Q-node is obtained. Multiple runs are made to obtain estimates of the standard deviation of these average values. The Q-GERT processor records and outputs the average of the average values obtained over a set of runs and the standard deviation of these averages. Also printed are the minimum average and maximum average obtained

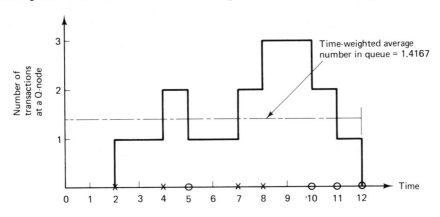

X   transaction arrival at Q-node

O   transaction removed from Q-node

Figure 6-5 Graphical portrayal of number of transactions at a Q-node and calculation of average number in queue.

NODE	LABEL	AVE.	STD. DEV.	SD OF AVE.	MIN.	MAX.	AVE. WAITING TIME AVE	SD	SD OF AVE	**NUMBER IN Q-NODE** MAX.
10	WS1-QUE	2.1062	0.1438	0.0455	1.8828	2.3279	2.0839	0.7892	0.2496	4.
15	WS2-QUE	1.5060	0.0557	0.0176	1.3919	1.5622	28.5087	15.3385	4.8505	2.

Figure 6-6 Sample Q-GERT output relating to a number of transactions in Q-nodes.

over a set of runs. An illustration of the Q-GERT output for the average number in two Q-nodes is shown in Figure 6-6.

The estimates of queue-length statistics are invaluable in gauging the storage space requirements of a proposed system or change to a system. Queue lengths are indicative of the space required in each storage area and as a group are a measure of total in-process inventory. Furthermore, knowledge of where excessive queue lengths occur in a proposed system aids in detecting and avoiding system bottlenecks. It is important to note that as with other network measures, queue length is a random variable. This randomness must be planned for adequately. Proper use of the estimate of the averages, standard deviations, and extreme values are helpful in this regard.

Often, a storage area consists of a finite space. In Q-GERT, this space limitation corresponds to a Q-node's capacity. When a Q-node has a finite capacity, we need to model what happens when an item arrives and the Q-node is full. In Q-GERT as in actual systems, either blocking or balking occurs. Blocking was discussed previously. Balking is the process of an item not entering the queue area because of lack of space. Q-GERT provides the opportunity to route a balked item to another node immediately. The network segment following this node will then determine the fate of the balked item. If this network segment is not included, the item is lost to the system. Balking is a consequence of space limitations and is, therefore, directly related to in-process inventory requirements.

The number of balkers from a Q-node is maintained for each run of a network. Clearly, the number of balkers is dependent on the length of the run. To normalize the outputs, the number of balkers per unit time is used as a measure of balking from a Q-node. That is, the number of balkers from each queue is divided by the length of the simulation run to obtain a balking rate for the run. An average and standard deviation over all runs of the balking rate is then computed together with the minimum and maximum balking rate observed on a run. An example of the outputs for the number of balkers per unit time averaged over 10 runs is shown in Figure 6-7 as 0.6235.

Before terminating the discussion of performance measures, it should be noted that some of the performance measures are related. For example, production managers know that, all else being equal, in-

NODE	LABEL	AVE.	STD. DEV.	SD OF AVE	NO. OF OBS.	MIN.	MAX.
10	WS1-QUE	.6235	.0823	.0260	10.	.4986	.7500

Figure 6-7 Sample Q-GERT output relating to number of transactions balking from Q-nodes.

process inventory increases if the time in the system for a job increases. This relationship can be derived mathematically from a version of Little's formula [192,195] for general queueing situations, which specifies that

$$\bar{N} = \bar{T} \times \bar{R}$$

where $\bar{N}$ is the average number in the system, $\bar{T}$ the average time in the system,† and $\bar{R}$ the average rate at which items arrive. Certainly, if $\bar{R}$ is held constant, an increase in $\bar{T}$ will increase $\bar{N}$. Another relationship is that the expected number of departures equals the expected number of arrivals in a stationary system. Relationships among system variables and measures are important but can be obscure and system specific. One of the tasks of an analyst is to ascertain the significant relationships between system inputs and outputs for the system under study. Q-GERT is an aid to uncovering such relationships.

6.3 SPECIFYING MACHINE TIMES AND OTHER SERVICE TIMES

The time duration of a service activity is modeled like other activity durations in Q-GERT. Because of the importance of service activities, however, we include a discussion of commonly used methods for defining service times. This discussion sets the stage for the example of the next section and provides supporting information for the material given in Chapters 7 and 8.

We begin by referring to server or machine 1 in the following network segment:

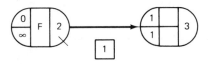

Q-node 2 represents the storage area for machine 1. Assume that the time duration of activity 1 represents the time to perform a given opera-

†This equation assumes that the time in the system for items not completely processed is the ending time of a run minus the items' arrival time.

tion on the machine. Typically, the time for this operation is observed in an actual system by a sampling process and the resulting data are characterized by a statistical distribution. Q-GERT users may incorporate this characterization within their Q-GERT models. As discussed in Chapter 2, the common statistical distributions are contained within Q-GERT to obtain sample distributions such as the normal (NO), uniform (UN), beta (BE or BP), triangular (TR), and gamma (GA). At times, it is necessary to hypothesize a distribution form. In such a case, the triangular or beta-PERT distribution provides a convenient way of characterizing service times because either can be specified in terms of an optimistic, pessimistic, and most likely value. When data are available, a distribution may be fit to the data. Programs to accomplish this are available [137,144] and a brief discussion of one of them is given in Section 20.4.

If it is desired to use data values from class frequencies or a histogram directly, function DPROB can be called in a user function prescribed for activity 1. For example, DPROB could be used to obtain service times defined as follows: machine 1 consumes 10 time units 30% of the time, 15 time units 45% of the time, and 20 time units 25% of the time. Probabilistic branching is an alternative method for specifying this service-time distribution, as follows:

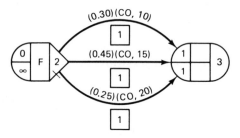

The use of probabilistic branching for service activities is restricted to a set of parallel, identical servers following a Q-node, whereas the use of DPROB can be made for servers following S-nodes as well as Q-nodes. In addition, for a large number of class frequencies, the use of DPROB can significantly decrease the number of activity descriptions required.

Frequently, the same machine performs different operations and the operation to be performed depends on the transaction entering service. The service-time information in such situations must be contained in the set of attributes associated with the transaction. Consider the case of two job types entering a machine area. Job type 1 requires an operation whose time is exponentially distributed with parameters from parameter set 4. Job type 2 requires an operation whose time is normally distributed with parameters as specified by parameter set 5. The following network segment can be used to model this situation:

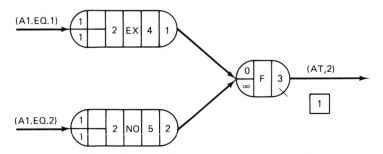

Attribute 1 is used to denote a job type. All job type 1 transactions are routed through node 1 according to the condition (A1.EQ.1). Similarly, job type 2 items are routed through node 2. Nodes 1 and 2 are used to assign operation times which are stored as attribute 2 and accessed later by the service activity in order to assign a job-dependent service time. Note that job type 1 items are assigned attribute 2 values through the specification (2,EX,4). Similarly, attribute 2 values for job type 2 items are assigned according to the notation (2,NO,5). The machine time, that is, the time for server 1 to perform service, is specified as (AT,2), which means that the service time is set equal to the value of attribute 2 of the transaction being served.

In the example above, ranking for Q-node 3 is specified as FIFO. By specifying the ranking procedure to be S/1, type 1 jobs would be given priority since attribute 1 is the job type. The specification S/2 would represent a shortest-processing-time job sequencing rule. If the actual service time is equal to the estimated service time plus a uniformly distributed sample, then it is required to rank transactions based on the estimates but to prescribe the actual time for the service activity. To model this, the following network segment would be employed:

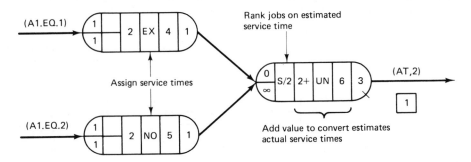

Upon arrival to Q-node 3, attribute 2 is the estimate of the processing time, and it is used to rank transactions in the Q-node. When a transaction is removed from the queue, the value assignment function of Q-node 3 is performed. This transforms attribute 2 from an estimated value to an actual value in accordance with the problem specification. If it is desirable to maintain attribute values for both the estimated and actual processing times, the value assignment at Q-node 3 could be specified as (3,AT,2), then (3+,UN,6). The service duration would then be specified as (AT,3).

6.3.1 Modeling Setup Operations

If service involves both a setup phase and a processing phase, then the use of the attribute specification for the service time is also appropriate. In this case the setup time is added to the processing time and stored as an attribute value. This attribute value is then prescribed for the service activity. When prescribing a service activity in this form, it is presumed that the server is busy during both setup and processing. Further, it is assumed that the next setup cannot be performed until the processing of the current job is completed. If a setup can be performed while processing is ongoing, the setup and processing operation should be modeled as a sequence of service activities. If only one additional setup can be performed during processing, then a Q-node with the blocking capability would separate the setup operation and the processing operation as shown in this network segment:

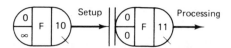

If it is desired to model the setup and processing operations as separate activities but to prohibit the start of another setup operation until processing is completed, the resource concepts of Q-GERT should be employed. The network segment for such a model is as follows:

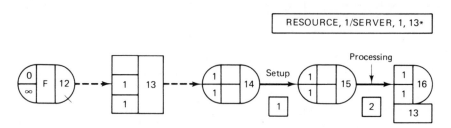

In this network segment, jobs wait for setup and processing at Q-node 12. When the server becomes available, he or she is allocated at ALLO-CATE node 13, and the transaction is moved from Q-node 12 to node 14. Setup and processing are then performed by activities 1 and 2.

FREE node 16 frees the server resource to perform another setup and specifies that the attempt to reallocate the resource be made at node 13. The transaction that was just processed is then routed from node 16.

The choice of modeling setup operations with resources or through the use of a single or sequential activities should be based on the problem being modeled. No general rules other than those given above are available.

6.3.2 User Functions for Machine Times

By prescribing that a service time is to be computed in a user function, any type of duration specification is made available. Within the user function, the analyst has access to information regarding a transaction's attributes, the current time, the status of servers and resources, the length of queues, and other network information. Hence, any functional relation can be prescribed for the service time.

To give an example, suppose that an S-node selected a server but the service time is to be a function of five quantities: job type as represented by attribute 1, the server selected, the number of ongoing service operations, the current number in a Q-node that precedes the S-node, and an associated batch size of the job as represented by attribute 2. We will illustrate the use of this information in specifying a service time for the following network segment:

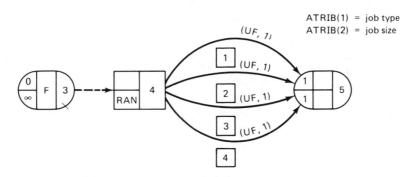

In this case, each of the four servers associated with S-node 4 has a service time defined by user function 1. This function is called at the time of service initiation. Within the user function, the analyst can retrieve attribute information of the transaction being scheduled for service through the use of the function GATRB(I). The statement A1=GATRB(1) defines A1 to be the value of attribute 1 for the current transaction. Hence, in this example, job type [GATRB(1)] and job size [GATRB(2)] are available. Since four servers utilize the same user function, the determination of the server number selected is made through the use of function NACTY(IDUM). To determine which service operations are currently ongoing, the function ISTUS(NODE,NSERV) is used with NODE equal to 4. The number of items in Q-node 3 is given by function XNINQ(3). With this information, the analyst can specify a service time as a function of the foregoing quantities.

Even more information is available. For example, the user has access to the capacity of different queues [function CAPQ(NODE)], the remaining service time of an ongoing operation [function REMST (NSERV)], the current unused queue capacity for a Q-node [function RCAPQ(NODE)], the number of transactions that have been routed through a given node [NTC(NODE)], the current transaction's mark time [function TMARK(I)], the time integrated number in a Q-node [function TINIQ(NODE)], and the utilization of a server [function TISS(NODE,NSERV)]. As discussed in Chapter 3, resource utilization information is also available [functions ICSRV(NRES) and TIRU (NRES)].

Within a user function, an analyst can draw a random sample from the standard distribution functions, put a transaction into the system, stop an ongoing server, extend an ongoing activity, halt an activity, or cause a nodal modification. Again, the reader is referred to Chapter 3 for more details on the use of these functions.

6.4 PLANNING FOR A MULTIPRODUCT, MULTILINE PRODUCTION SYSTEM

The basic concepts in modeling production systems have been introduced in this chapter. In this section, we describe an example of how one production plant was modeled and analyzed using a Q-GERT network simulation approach. The Q-GERT model and its output were used by decision makers in investigating improvements in system design, the procurement of new equipment, and the expansion of current facilities. The production line system described is based on a system that produces electronic components which was analyzed by Taylor et al. [198]. The material presented here is extracted from their paper.

The production system contains six separate line segments interrelated in such a way so as to produce two distinct products. Lines 1 and 3 produce subassembly A from inputs of component parts. These two lines are physically separated and have different input feeder systems. Lines 1 and 3 both contain two work stations, the first for subassembly preparation and the second for assembling the several components. Each station contains a number of parallel servers, and each station has capacity available for in-process queues. Although these two lines produce an identical subassembly unit and are similar in layout, service times vary between stations and between lines. The product of lines 1 and 3 is a subassembly unit which, when produced, moves to an in-process storage facility to be merged with subassembly B to produce the final product.

Line 2 produces subassembly B using three sequential work stations for drilling, assembling, and inspection. Since the unit produced on this line is of a more delicate and specialized nature, an inspection station is necessary. As units come from the inspection station, a proportion are rejected and scrapped, some of the units are reworked and sent back to the first station, and the remaining units not reworked or rejected are divided equally between two in-process storage stations. One of the in-process storage facilities feeds line 1 and merges with subassembly A for the subsequent production of product I. The other in-process storage facility for subassembly B combines with line 3 storage of subassembly A for the subsequent production of product II. For each of the three lines, conveyors transport the units from the final line station to the in-process storage areas.

The in-process storage facilities for lines 1 and 3 are limited to a maximum stock of 30 units. An additional centralized in-process storage system is designed as a backup system for both lines. When a stock level of 30 units is reached at either line, units are routed to the central in-process storage facility. When either the line 1 or line 3 in-process inventory falls below the 30-unit level, units are immediately transferred from the central facility to the line storage.

Subassemblies A and B from lines 1 and 2 are used to produce product I. The product I line contains three work stations, for merging the subassemblies, assembly, and inspection. After inspection, product I units are sent to a third production phase, rejected, or reworked. This same process takes place for the combination of subassemblies A and B from lines 2 and 3, resulting in product II. It should be emphasized that although the product I and product II lines are physically similar, they produce two unique and distinct products.

The final products are forwarded (by automatic conveyor) first to a cleaning station, then to a packaging station, and finally to inventory. Both product types are handled simultaneously at each of these stations. All work stations in the system have parallel servers and queues. Except for the time on the automated conveyors, server task times are considered as random variables.

Production planning for the three lines described above is a complex job. A network model was built to obtain the performance measures described in Section 6.2 related to throughput and bottlenecks in order to provide information for management analysis and decision making.

6.4.1 The Q-GERT Model

The Q-GERT model of the production line system is shown in Figure 6-8. Table 6-1 gives a description of network activities, including probabilities of occurrence, server task times and probability distributions, the number of parallel servers, and initial queue sizes. Each activity is identified by its start and end nodes.

Activity 10-10 represents the interarrival times of components that are the input to the system. Referring to Table 6-1, the interarrival times are exponentially distributed with a mean of 1.17 minutes. Upon arrival, the units move by conveyor (activity 10-11) to the first work station in 1 minute. Node 11 is a Q-node which represents component buildup prior to subassembly preparation in line 1. Initially, one unit is in this queue and there is no limit to the number in the queue at this station.

For activity 11-12, there are three identical parallel servers. The task times for each of these servers is normally distributed with a mean of 2.6 minutes and a standard deviation of 0.45 minute. Most of the remaining network activities and nodes are constructed similarly.

Node 19 has probabilistic branching to reflect the possibility of several alternative outcomes upon completion of the inspection activity. There is a 0.05 probability of rejection (branching from node 19 to 50), a 0.05 probability of subassembly rework (branching from node 19 to 20), and a 0.90 probability that the unit will be forwarded to in-process storage (since units sent to in-process inventory are equally divided between product lines I and II, branching probability values of 0.45 were assigned to branches 19-22 and 19-23, respectively). Activities 19-20, 19-22, and 19-23 are all conveyor operations.

Subassembly A and B units are merged from storage (Q-nodes 14 and 22, and 23 and 28) to form semifinished products as input to lines I and II, respectively. This merger is accomplished by "assembly" nodes 30 and 32, as there must be a unit of each subassembly available at the in-process queues for an assembly to take place.

Nodes 14 and 28 model the finite queues with capacities of 30 units previously described. When the maximum storage level is reached, all excess units balk to Q-node 31, the central storage facility. Units will remain at the central storage facility (Q-node 31) until either node 14 or 28 falls below the 30-unit level, at which time units are transferred from Q-node 31. This operation is achieved using S-node 29. The double line prior to S-node 29 indicates that it can be blocked, and it operates in the following manner. If Q-nodes 14 and 28 are both filled to capacity of 30 units, S-node 29 blocks units from leaving Q-node 31. If either Q-node 14 or 28 has fewer than 30 units in it, the S-node draws units from node 31 and transfers them to the unfilled Q-node. If

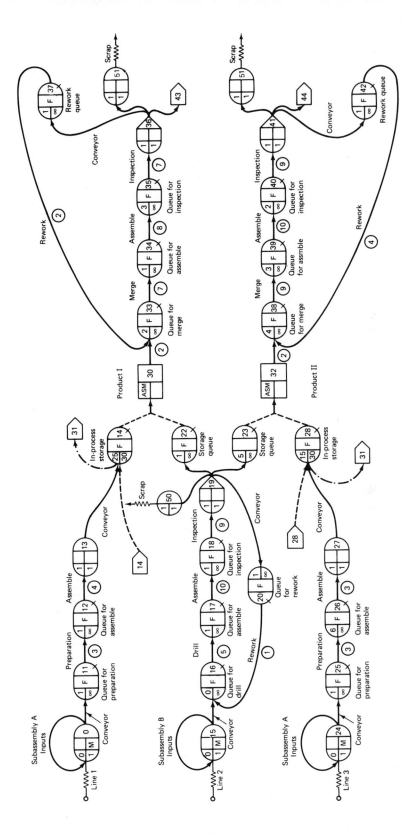

Figure 6-8 Q-GERT network of the production line system.

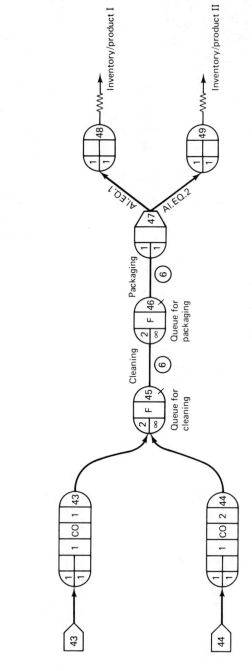

Figure 6-8 (Continued)

TABLE 6-1 Activity Descriptions

Activity (Nodes)	Activity Description	Probability of Occurrence	Server Task Times Minimum	Server Task Times Maximum	μ	σ	Distribution	Number of Parallel Servers	Initial Queue Size
10-10	Line 1—Input	1.00	0.10	20.0	1.17		Exponential		
10-11	Conveyor A	1.00			1.00		Constant		
11-12	Preparation A	1.00	0.50	5.7	2.6	0.45	Normal	3	1
12-13	Assemble A	1.00	1.0	7.0	3.8	0.70	Normal	4	1
13-14	Storage conveyor A	1.00			1.0		Constant		
15-15	Line 2—input	1.00	0.10	20.0	0.65		Exponential		
15-16	Conveyor B	1.00			1.0		Constant		
16-17	Drill B	1.00	0.10	5.5	2.9	0.70	Normal	5	5
17-18	Assemble B	1.00	1.7	8.3	5.6	0.90	Normal	10	1
18-19	Inspection B	1.00	0.5	9.2	4.7	1.3	Normal	9	1
19-20	Rework conveyor	0.05			1.0		Constant		
20-16	Rework B	1.00	1.2	12.1	6.2	1.6	Normal	1	1
19-50	Reject/scrap	0.05			0		Constant		
19-22	Storage conveyor B	0.45			3.0		Constant		
19-23	Storage conveyor B	0.45			3.0		Constant		
24-24	Line 3—Input	1.00	0.10	20.0	1.35		Exponential		
24-25	Conveyor A	1.00			1.0		Constant		
25-26	Preparation A	1.00	0.10	6.2	3.2	1.0	Normal	3	1
26-27	Assemble A	1.00	0.50	7.3	3.8	0.9	Normal	3	5
27-28	Storage conveyor A	1.00			1.0		Constant		
14-31	In-process balk	1.00			0		Constant		25
28-31	In-process balk	1.00			0		Constant		15
31-29	Storage conveyor	1.00	0.50	3.0	1.5	0.2	Normal	1	30
29-14	To line 1	1.00			0		Constant		
29-28	To line 2	1.00			0		Constant		
14-30	Merge A/product I	1.00			0		Constant		25
22-30	Merge B/product I	1.00			0		Constant		1

TABLE 6-1 (Continued)

Activity (Nodes)	Activity Description	Probability of Occurrence	Server Task Times				Distribution	Number of Parallel Servers	Initial Queue Size
			Mini-mum	Maxi-mum	μ	σ			
23-32	Merge B/product II	1.00			0		Constant		6
28-32	Merge A/product II	1.00			0		Constant		15
30-33	Product I conveyor	1.00			1.5		Constant	2	
33-34	Merge I	1.00	2.5	11.7	7.1	1.0	Normal	7	2
34-35	Assemble I	1.00	1.5	15.0	8.2	2.1	Normal	8	1
35-36	Inspection I	1.00	1.0	14.0	7.5	2.0	Normal	7	4
36-37	Rework I conveyor	0.16			1.0		Constant		
37-33	Rework I	1.00	0.1	25.0	11.2	4.5	Normal	2	1
36-51	Reject I/scrap	0.10			0		Constant		
36-43	Attribute assignment 1	0.74			0		Constant		
43-45	Cleaning conveyor I	1.00			6.0		Constant		
32-38	Product II conveyor	1.00			1.0		Constant	2	
38-39	Merge II	1.00	0.5	18.0	9.1	2.6	Normal	9	4
39-40	Assemble II	1.00	0.01	22.0	10.1	4.2	Normal	10	3
40-41	Inspection II	1.00	0.01	20.0	9.0	3.0	Normal	9	2
41-42	Rework II conveyor	0.21			1.0		Constant		
42-38	Rework II	1.00	0.01	30.0	16.5	5.5	Normal	4	1
41-52	Reject II/scrap	0.08			0		Constant		
41-44	Attribute assignment 2	0.71			0		Constant		
44-45	Cleaning conveyor II	1.00			6.0		Constant		
45-46	Cleaning	1.00	0.01	10.0	4.2	1.6	Normal	6	2
46-47	Packaging	1.00	0.01	10.0	4.1	1.8	Normal	6	2
47-48	Inventory/product I	1.00			0		Constant		
47-49	Inventory/product II	1.00			0		Constant		

Source: Ref. 198.

both Q-nodes 14 and 28 are less than filled, S-node 29 sends units to the node with the smallest queue.

The second phase of the production process models the production of products I and II and is similar to the subassembly phase. Both product lines have inspection stations which classify units as scrap, rework required, and final product.

The third phase consists of merging both products into one line for cleaning, packaging, and final inventory. Products I and II are differentiated by assigning attribute values for each product at nodes 43 and 44. At node 47, conditional branching is used to separate the products.

6.4.2 Production Planning Outputs

The Q-GERT network was analyzed for 4800 minutes and 20 replications (runs) were performed. The production planning outputs for these runs are summarized in Table 6-2.

Taylor et al. also presented statistics on queue size, waiting times, and server utilizations for this model. However, the data in Table 6-2 provide sufficient information for production planning purposes. If the levels of output presented in Table 6-2 are not satisfactory to meet the needs of the firm, management can explore alternative strategies. For example, the addition of servers at various stations, the use of overtime and extra shifts, increased input arrival rates, and new machines can be tested to determine their viability for increasing production output. Each of these strategies is easily incorporated into the Q-GERT model.

In conjunction with planning production output, it may be necessary to analyze the quality control system of the production line. For example, the number of rejected units of products I and II given in Table 6-2 appears to be excessive. An increased quality reflected in lower rejection rates at nodes 36 and 41 and the corresponding increased output should be investigated. The Q-GERT model can be

TABLE 6-2 Production Planning Outputs

Performance Measure	Average	Standard Deviation
Throughput (units/hour)		
Product I	38.3	0.7
Product II	38.9	0.4
Product I scrap	5.1	0.4
Product II scrap	4.5	0.3
Subassembly B scrap	4.9	0.3
Storage bottlenecks		
Blocking percentage S-node 29	99	1.0
Balking percentage Q-node 14	13	2.0
Balking percentage Q-node 28	3	1.0

Source: Ref. 198.

tested to reflect such conditions and the results compared with the costs of the action. Additional details and evaluation of alternative designs are presented in the original paper [198].

6.5 SUMMARY

System performance for production planning has been categorized into measures of throughput, measures of ability to meet deadlines, measures of resource utilizations, and measures of in-process inventory. The procedures for obtaining these measures of performance from network models has been presented, including the factors that influence these performance measures. An example of the planning for a multiproduct, multiline production system is presented which illustrated the procedures for obtaining the performance measures. The example provides the basis for building network models for planning purposes and alludes to the types of analysis that would be useful when management is considering proposed expansion, new facilities, capital expenditures, and changes in resource levels.

6.6 EXERCISES

6-1 Given the data on the 20 jobs listed below, compute the following performance measures for a one-machine situation: throughput, lateness, tardiness, production rate, and makespan.

Job Number	Processing Time	Arrival Time	Due Date
1	7	0	10
2	4	0	10
3	10	0	15
4	6	3	25
5	5	3	30
6	7	3	35
7	3	6	40
8	10	6	45
9	2	6	50
10	5	12	55
11	9	12	60
12	1	12	65
13	6	16	70
14	3	16	75
15	6	16	80
16	2	20	85
17	4	20	90
18	3	20	95
19	10	25	100
20	7	25	100

6-2. Build network models of the following situations:

(a) Two products are stored in separate buffer areas to be processed by one of three machines. Product 1 can be processed using machine 1 or machine 2; product 2 can be processed using machine 2 or machine 3. When machine 2 is available, the operating policy is to select a type 1 product in preference to a type 2 product.

(b) Two products are stored in separate buffer areas to be processed by one of three machines. Product 1 can be processed by machines 1 and 2, and product 2 can be served by machines 1, 2, and 3. Machine 3 is to be used to serve product 2 only if machines 1 and 2 are not busy.

(c) The situation is the same as described in part (a) except that machine 2 should process product 2 before product 1 if the number of type 2 products waiting exceeds 5.

(d) Build an alternative model for the situations described in parts (a), (b), and (c). (*Hint:* If S-nodes were used, use ALLOCATE nodes. Alternatively, if ALLOCATE nodes were used, use S-nodes.)

6-3. Discuss methods by which jobs are assigned due dates in practice. Build Q-GERT networks for assigning due dates. Discuss methods by which due date assignment procedures may be included in an overall model of a production facility.

6-4. Discuss situations in which makespan is an important measure of a production system's performance.

6-5. Discuss how the performance measures associated with a production system can be used to influence management decision making regarding cost of alternatives, a design for system capacity, and the determination of operational requirements.

6-6. Design a user function to incorporate learning, fatigue, and other service characteristics so that these factors are included in the duration of the service time associated with a human–machine system.

6-7. Develop a Q-GERT network model of a multiproduct, multiline production system with which you are familiar. The purpose of the model is to perform an analysis similar to the one presented in Section 6.4.

7

Scheduling and Sequencing

7.1 INTRODUCTION

Scheduling is the process of determining the starting time of jobs and on which machines the jobs are to be performed. The scheduling process involves the following stages [1]:

1. Aggregate planning
2. Loading
3. Sequencing
4. Detailed scheduling

Aggregate planning is the activity of determining the overall level of output for a given time period and the level of resources to be deployed during the time period of interest. For example, a production manager's aggregate plan may call for producing 1000 units for the month of July using 10 machines and 20 workers. The aggregate plan does not specify starting times, the order of production, the machines to be used, or the workers to be employed.

The second stage in the scheduling process is called *loading*. Sometimes the term "shop loading" or "machine loading" is used. Loading is the action of allocating work to machine areas, and it establishes the load each machine center will carry under a given aggregate plan. A typical loading specification is "50 jobs of type 1 will be performed in work area B." Loading does not involve a specification of the order to perform jobs. The ordering of jobs is referred to as *sequencing* or "work dispatching." Sequencing implies establishing priorities for processing jobs at work centers. The term *job sequencing* refers to the determination of which job is to be performed next when a machine becomes available. The term *machine sequencing* is used for the process of determining which machine at a given work center is to be used next if more than one machine is idle.

The identification of start and finish dates for jobs at a work center is the final stage of scheduling and is called *detailed scheduling.* Detailed scheduling utilizes the determinations made during aggregate planning, loading, and sequencing and is often a direct consequence of these activities.

There are many different ways to schedule a production system [10,33]. The success of any scheduling process depends on whether it enables the production system to perform well with respect to the performance measures: throughput, meeting due dates, resource utilization, and in-process inventory. We have discussed how the output from Q-GERT models relates to these system performance measures. Now we will demonstrate how Q-GERT enables the analyst to incorporate into a model the important elements of the scheduling process. The use of Q-GERT to model different methods of aggregate planning, loading, sequencing, and detailed scheduling results in the direct evaluation of such methods. By evaluating, redesigning, and then reevaluating, better scheduling procedures can be designed, developed, and implemented.

7.2 AGGREGATE PLANNING BASED ON JOB ARRIVALS

The aggregate plan specifies the level of resources to be used and the amount of product to be produced. In Q-GERT, the level of resources is easily specified in terms of the number of servers, the number of resource types, and the availability of each resource type. The amount of product produced during a time period is usually related to the quantity of raw materials input to the system. This section describes the procedures of Q-GERT that relate to a specification of a given input of items to the system.

As an example, suppose that we specify that 50 items are to be produced and the aggregate planning period is to be 1000 time units. Through Q-GERT data input, the length of a simulation run can be specified; in this case, it would be 1000 time units. To specify that 50 transactions (items) enter the system at the beginning of the simulation run, the following node and branch can be used:

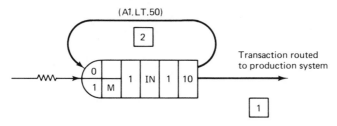

Source node 10 is released initially at the beginning of the simulation. At each release of the source node, an attribute assignment is made such that attribute 1 of the entering transaction is assigned a value according to the incremental function. The first transaction to enter the system, therefore, will have an attribute 1 value equal to 1, the second transaction will have an attribute 1 value equal to 2, and so on. In this way, a count of the total number of entering items is obtained. In addition, each item entering the system has a unique identification number.

The routing mechanism of node 10 permits us to stop the arrival process when this identification number reaches 50. The routing from source node 10 is conditional, take-all. This specification in combination with the condition on activity 2 controls the number of releases of node 10 and, hence, the number of entering items. Since the condition on activity 2 is (A1.LT.50), activity 2 will be rescheduled at each release of node 10 as long as the value of attribute 1 is less than 50. Activity 1 will always be initiated at a release of node 10 (the default condition). Hence, for the first release of the source node, both emanating activities are scheduled, resulting in one transaction entering the system. The second transaction enters the system when activity 2 releases node 1. Activity 2 is rescheduled at this point and the process continues for 49 more releases of node 10. The initial release of node 10, plus the 49 subsequent releases due to activity 2, cause 50 transactions to enter the system. After the fiftieth transaction, activity 2 will not be rescheduled; hence, releases of node 10 are stopped.

Specifying a zero duration for activity 2 causes all 50 transactions to enter the network at the beginning of a simulation run. If we desire to spread these transactions over the 1000 time units of the simulation, we could have specified an activity duration of 20 time units for activity 2. If we want 25 units to enter at time zero and 25 at time 500, any of the following subnetworks could be used:

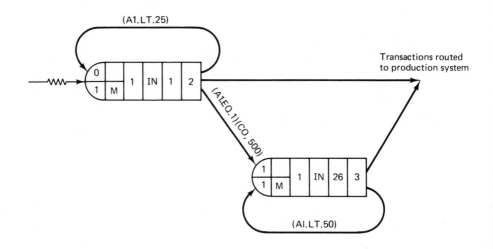

or, equivalently,

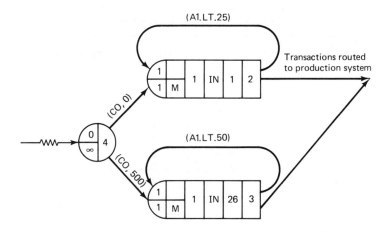

or, equivalently,

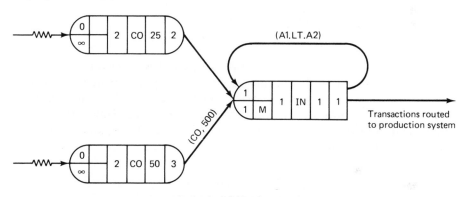

We mentioned above that the aggregate planning period corresponds to the length of the simulation run. This can be specified directly or can be modeled as an activity. Alternatively, a sequence of activities can be used for specifying the length of the planning period. This network segment could represent a nonconstant planning period, for example, until financing was obtained or until the first snowfall. Another common specification for determining the end of the planning period is to require a certain number of transactions to be produced by the system. This is controlled by requiring a specified number of releases for a sink node which represents the point of system departure for the finished product.

7.2.1 Poisson Arrivals

The foregoing discussion presented some of the fundamentals in specifying system arrivals. We will now detail more complicated procedures. Frequently, one is interested in modeling a Poisson arrival process. If units arrive individually and independently and the number of units that arrive after t time units is Poisson distributed with mean rate λ, the time between arrivals is exponentially distributed with a mean time between arrivals of $1/\lambda$. Hence, the following network segment represents a Poisson arrival process:

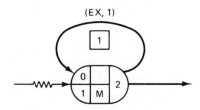

The time between arrivals is determined by an exponential distribution, where the parameter set number is 1.

7.2.2 Probabilistic Arrival Process

Combining branching mechanisms in Q-GERT permits the modeling of complex arrival processes. For example, consider an arrival mechanism in which the next arrival time is sampled from an exponential distribution 30% of the time but is a constant value 70% of the time. The Q-GERT model to portray this complex, mixed arrival distribution is as follows:

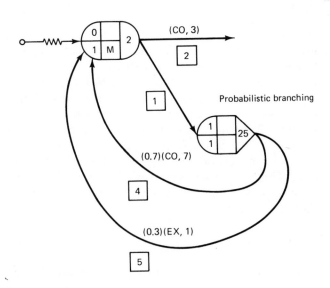

As another example of an arrival mechanism, consider the situation in which two transactions arrive to the system simultaneously 40% of the time. Sixty percent of the arrivals are single transactions. A Q-GERT representation would look like this:

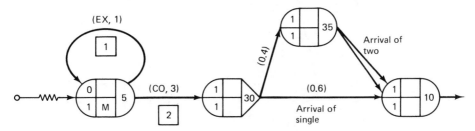

For this model, node 30 represents the decision as to whether one or two transactions should be routed to node 10. If one transaction is to be routed, the branch from node 30 to node 10 is taken and this occurs with probability 0.6. With probability 0.4, the transaction is routed to node 35. Node 35 has deterministic branching with two branches emanating from it. This creates two transactions and routes them both to node 10. The delay times associated with the four branches between nodes 30 and 10 are all zero.

7.2.3 Fixed Arrival Times

In some situations, a list of jobs defines the arrival pattern. There are several ways to do this. The list of jobs can be stored in a data base and accessed in chronological order every time a new interarrival time is needed. The data base access would be accomplished by using function UF to characterize the activity representing the interarrival time distribution. Simulations that employ fixed arrival times are sometimes referred to as trace-driven simulations.

7.2.4 Time-Dependent Arrival Process

Another commonly employed arrival mechanism involves changing the arrival process as a function of time or a function of activity completions within the network. Such arrival processes can be modeled by a switching mechanism involving the use of nodal modifications (see Section 2.7). Consider the situation in which transactions arrive to a system during the first 16 hours of operation, do not arrive during the next 8 hours, arrive during the next 16 hours, and so on. This arrival process, which is a function of the time of day, is modeled in Q-GERT in the following manner:

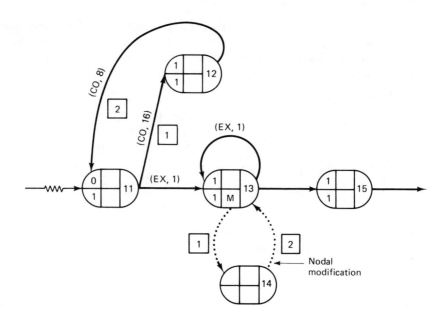

At source node 11, a transaction is set with an exponentially distributed delay to node 13. At the same time, a transaction is also sent to node 12 with a 16-hour time delay. This time delay, as modeled by the branch from node 11 to node 12, has been labeled as activity 1. The arrival process is modeled by node 13 and the branch from node 13 back to node 13 represents the time between arrivals. As shown, an exponentially distributed interarrival time is used. Transactions arriving at node 13 are routed to node 15 for further processing as long as activity 1 has not been completed. When activity 1 is completed, that is, after 16 hours, node 13 is removed from the network and transactions arriving at node 13 are routed to node 14. This nodal modification stops the arrival process, as no branching occurs from node 13 after activity 1 has been completed.

The completion of activity 1 also releases node 12; thus activity 2, which requires 8 hours, is started. When activity 2 is completed, node 14 is replaced by node 13 and node 11 is released. When node 11 is released, the activities represented by the branches from node 11 to node 13 and from node 11 to node 12 are started. Since node 13 is back in the network, branching from node 13 back to node 13 and from node 13 to node 15 is reinitiated. In this way, we have modeled the desired 16-hour-on, 8-hour-off schedule.

If the arrival process involves a different pattern during the 16-hour period, a feedback branch around node 14 could be included to represent the time between arrivals during this period. A series of arrival patterns can thus be modeled as a function of time. In addition, the activities that cause the arrival process to change need not be activities that represent clock time but can be activities that model system-related conditions.

We will mention one final commonly used arrival mechanism which involves putting a fixed number of items in the system initially. This was modeled previously through the use of conditional, take-all branching. It can also be modeled by taking advantage of the fact that Q-GERT schedules all servers at time zero if there are initial items in an associated queue. Consider the following network segment:

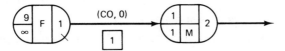

Since there are nine items initially in Q-node 1, server 1 is initially busy and activity 1 will be completed in zero time units. Node 2, therefore, receives a transaction at time zero and routes it into the system. Server 1 is immediately rescheduled and another item enters the system. In this way, 10 transactions enter the system at time zero. Node 2 is used to mark the transaction (all other attributes will be zero) and can be used to route these items in different ways using the probabilistic, attribute-based, or time-dependent concepts presented above.

7.3 LOADING

The loading of machine centers involves the routing of job transactions to queues of servers. This routing is accomplished through branching operations and queue selection procedures associated with S-nodes.

First, we describe loading through the use of branching operations. In loading, we are interested in routing a single transaction in one of several possible directions. This corresponds to either probabilistic branching or conditional, take-first branching. Probabilistic branching allows aggregate loading rules of the following type to be modeled. On the average, "10% of incoming items go to work center 1; 70% to work center 2; 20% to work center 3," as shown in this network segment:

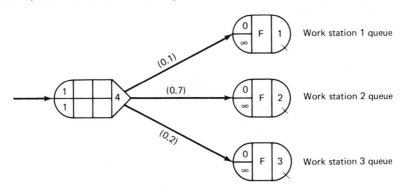

Probabilistic branching does not involve the assessment of the current network status or the use of a transaction's attribute values. To use this type of information, conditional routing is employed. Conditions can be specified as comparison statements involving the following:

1. The time at which routing is to occur
2. The time at which routing is to occur compared to an attribute value
3. The value of an attribute as compared to a specified value
4. The value of an attribute as compared with another attribute value
5. The release status of a specified node
6. The release status of a node specified as an attribute value

The first four types of conditions necessitate a comparison of values. In Q-GERT, comparisons may involve any of the following relational operators: LT, LE, EQ, NE, GT, and GE. The four types of comparisons used in conjunction with the six operators yields 24 possible combinations. Condition types 5 and 6 each can require a node to have been released or not. This adds four more combinations. Hence, 28 different possible specifications for conditional routing are possible (see Section 2.4.3). The following examples illustrate how conditional, take-first routing can be used to route transactions based on current network status or information contained in a transaction's attributes.

Suppose that we wish to route a transaction to one of three work stations as a function of the current simulation time. Machine center 1, represented by Q-node 1, is to receive transactions if the time in the system is less than or equal to 15 time units. Transactions that arrive after 15 time units but before 25 time units are to be routed to work station 2 (Q-node 2). All transactions arriving after 25 time units are to be routed to work station 3 (Q-node 3). The following network segment represents this routing specification:

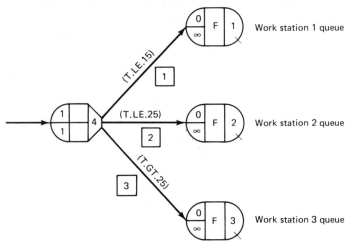

Only one branch from node 4 will be selected. The ordering of the branches is important since if TNOW is less than 25, two routing conditions are met. The first condition specified in the input list (in this case, TNOW.LE.15) will be selected. The ordering of activities for testing conditions is part of the Q-GERT data input.

Suppose that the routing of incoming transactions is to be based on part type and that part type is defined as attribute 1. In the following network segment, node 4 routes incoming transactions to work station 1 if attribute 1 is equal to 1, assuming that only three part types are defined.

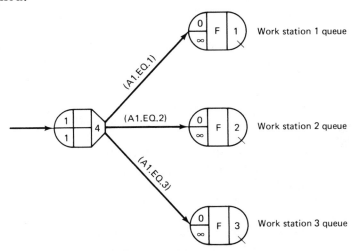

As another illustration, suppose that there are 20 different part types in the system and work station 1 is to process part types 1 and 2, work station 2 is to process part types 3 and 4, and work station 3 is to receive all other part types. The following network segment accomplishes this routing procedure:

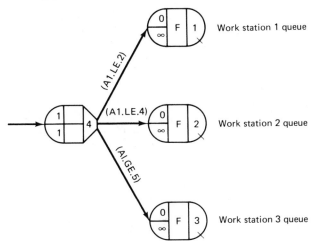

As mentioned above, conditional routing can also be a function of the nodal status in other parts of the network. Suppose that node 6 is a milestone which represents the time that parts will no longer be routed to work station 1. After the milestone is achieved, parts are to be routed to work station 2. The following network segment illustrates this type of conditional routing.

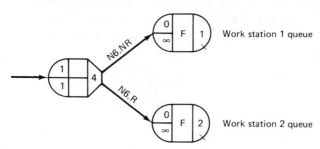

It is easy to see that the Q-GERT conditional routing logic provides the basis for modeling a wide variety of routing and loading procedures.

We now consider the routing of transactions based on current queue lengths at work stations. The motivation for selecting queues based on a function of their queue length is that it is often of interest to balance the work loads at different work stations. Queue selection methods can and do affect other performance measures of the production system.

Suppose that we desire to route transactions to one of a group of Q-nodes such that the selected Q-node has had, up to the current time, the smallest average number of transactions in it. To accomplish this special type of routing, we use the S-node. The queue selection method for accomplishing this routing is called SAV. The network segment for this routing method is as follows:

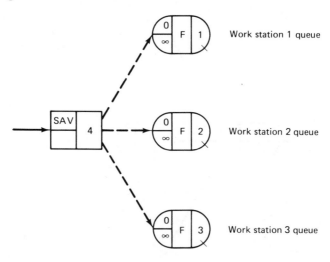

SAV stands for smallest average number of transactions to date and S-node 4 in the example above routes incoming transactions to Q-node 1, 2, or 3 based on this criterion. If we desire to route transactions to the Q-node with the smallest number of transactions currently waiting at the Q-node, Queue Selection Rule SNQ would be used. Another Queue Selection Rule, LWF, causes the routing of incoming transactions to the Q-node with its first transaction having the longest waiting time. This waiting time is computed as TNOW (current time) minus the transaction's mark time (the time it passed the last mark node or source node). If this mark time is the time the item entered the system, this rule reflects the total time in the system. If the mark time is not the time of entry into the system, the measure of interest will be the time since last marking.

It should be noted that an S-node always selects among available queues; that is, S-nodes do not consider routing transactions to Q-nodes that are full. If no queues are available, the S-node will cause transactions to balk or be blocked just like a Q-node.

Another important queue selection method is based on the amount of remaining unused capacity. Queue Selection Rule LRC selects a Q-node based on the largest remaining unused capacity and selection rule SRC selects a Q-node based on the smallest remaining unused capacity. If queues have a specific order of priority for receiving transactions, the Queue Selection Rule POR is used and the preferred order is given by the order of the Q-nodes on the S-node data input record. If a preferred order selection is specified, the S-node always examines the Q-nodes in the same sequence until it finds one that is not full. Cyclic priority is specified by using rule CYC. In this case, the S-node will choose the next available Q-node starting from the last Q-node that was selected. A random routing can also be specified. In this case, each available queue is given an equal chance of being selected. For example, if a selection is to be made from three Q-nodes and one is at capacity, a 0.5 probability is assigned to each of the two Q-nodes not at capacity.

To summarize, the Queue Selection Rules for an S-node preceding a group of parallel queues provide routing procedures based on the following quantities:

1. The average number of transactions in a queue to date (LAV,SAV)
2. The waiting time of a Q-node's first transaction where the waiting time is computed from its last time of marking (LWF,SWF)
3. The number of transactions currently in a Q-node (LNQ,SNQ)
4. The amount of unused capacity remaining in a Q-node (LRC, SRC)
5. A user-defined preferred order (POR)
6. A specified cyclic manner (CYC)

7. A probabilistic routing among available queues (RAN)
8. The number of balkers to date (LNB,SNB)

The Queue Selection Rules described above are listed in Table 2-3.

7.4 SEQUENCING

Sequencing decisions can be viewed from a machine or a job perspective. The former concerns a decision when a machine (server) completes an operation and the next job (transaction) is to be selected from a queue or queues. This is called *job sequencing*. The second type of sequencing decision involves selecting a machine (server) when more than one is available at the time an item arrives at a work station. This is called *machine sequencing*. Job and machine sequencing procedures are described in separate sections below.

7.4.1 Job Sequencing

Job sequencing involves the ordering of jobs for processing. Consider the following one-queue, single-server network segment:

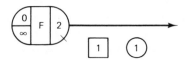

When server 1 completes service, the queue length of Q-node 2 is examined. If no items are in the queue, server 1 is made idle. Otherwise, the first item in the queue is removed and server 1 processes it. The ordered arrangement of items in Q-node 2 determines the job sequencing for the machine represented by server 1. This order in which items are arranged in a queue is controlled by the queue ranking procedure. Ranking may be either first-in, first-out (F or FIFO), last-in, first-out (L or LIFO), or attribute based. The F representing a FIFO ranking procedure means that items queue up in the order of their time of arrival to the queue and that priority is given to early arrivals. (The FIFO procedure is also referred to in the literature as FCFS or first-come, first-served.) Conversely, an L representing a LIFO ranking procedure gives priority to the last job that arrived at a queue. (The LIFO procedure is also referenced as LCFS or last-come, first served.)

Attribute-based ranking provides the means for ranking items on a variable other than time of arrival. For this procedure, priority is given to jobs according to the relative value of a specified attribute. To introduce attribute-based queue ranking, suppose that transactions representing parts with part type specified in attribute 2 arrive at a queue representing a work station's storage area. If the desired job sequence is to process part type 1 jobs before part type 2 jobs and part type 2 jobs before part type 3, a small-value-first rule on the part type attribute is specified, that is, S/2.

Should it be desired to reverse the foregoing sequencing order, that is, service large part type jobs first, the ranking rule B/2 would be used, that is, big-value-first based on attribute 2. Transactions can also be ranked based on their mark times by the specification S/M or B/M.

If two or more transactions have the same value for the ranking attribute, priority is given to early arrivals; that is, the tie-breaking rule is FIFO.

Since attribute assignments can be made prior to entry into Q-nodes and since the assigning functions can be of a general nature, attribute-based ranking provides the means for specifying a wide range of job sequencing rules. For example, consider a model of a one machine operation that receives two different part types. Suppose that it is desired to sequence jobs using a shortest-processing-time rule, that is, to give priority to jobs that have the smallest (estimated) processing time. To model this rule, we assign the processing time of a transaction prior to its entering the Q-node of the service operation. To illustrate, consider the following network, where attribute 1 represents the estimated service time and attribute 2 the part type. Transactions arrive at Q-node 3, where they are ranked small-value-first on attribute 1 (S/1). The interarrival time for part type 1 is represented by activity 1. Activity 2 represents the interarrival time for part type 2. The estimated processing times for parts 1 and 2 are 5 and 10, respectively.

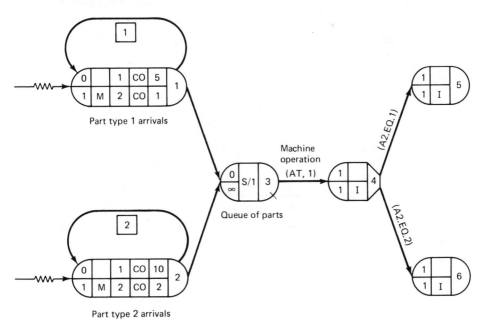

Note that node 4 collects time in the system statistics for both part types and then routes part type 1 to node 5 and part type 2 jobs to node 6 to obtain statistics by part type.

Suppose that we wish to rank jobs at Q-node 3 by part type first and then by processing time. One way to do this is to establish a ranking attribute, say attribute 5, to be defined as a function of the part type and processing-time attributes. The following function would define the job sequencing as "select among part type 1 first and part type 2 second and within each category give priority to the job with the shortest estimated processing time":

$$\text{attribute } 5 = 1000*\text{attribute } 2 + \text{attribute } 1$$

This can be implemented through the use of a user function assignment of attribute 5 at node 1 and 2 with the following specification:†
(5,UF,1). The following statement would be included in function UF:

$$\text{UF} = \text{GATRB}(2)*1000. + \text{GATRB}(1)$$

In this case, attribute 5 serves as a ranking index and the ranking rule at Q-node 3 would be changed to S/5. If large processing times are to be given priority after small values of job type, the statement should be

$$\text{UF} = \text{GATRB}(2)*1000. - \text{GATRB}(1)$$

With the flexibility inherent in function UF, a large variety of job sequencing rules can be modeled.

Table 7-1 lists 10 common job sequencing rules and the corresponding Q-GERT queue ranking procedure. We assume that each transaction is described by four attributes: (1) estimated processing time for the next operation, (2) due date, (3) number of remaining operations, and (4) estimated time for all remaining operations.

Table 7-1 includes rules regarding static slack and dynamic slack. Static slack is defined as the due date minus the current time. Since current time is subtracted from the due date of each job, ranking on due date or static slack results in the same job ordering. Variants of the static slack rule are rules based on the static slack divided by the operation's processing time (SS/PT), and the static slack divided by the number of remaining operations (SS/RO). To implement these rules in Q-GERT requires the definition of a ranking attribute (A5). For the SS/PT rule, the ranking attribute is defined as (A2-TNOW)/A1. Since TNOW is the current time and applies to each part that is awaiting processing, we can substitute an arbitrary constant and obtain the same ordering of part transactions without updating attribute 5; that is, we

---

†If job numbers are permitted to be multiples of 1000, attribute 3 can be defined simply through the assignments (5,AT,2) and then (5+,AT,1), where it is assumed that the assignment to attribute 2 was either 1000 or 2000.

TABLE 7-1   Q-GERT Representations of Common
Job Sequencing Rules

Sequencing Rule		Ranking Attribute[a]	Queue Ranking Rule
FIFO	First-in, first-out	—	F
LIFO	Last-in, first-out	—	L
SPT	Shortest processing time	A1	S/1
DD	Due date	A2	S/2
SS	Static slack	A2	S/2
SS/PT	Static slack/processing time	A5=(A2-1.)/A1	S/5
SS/RO	Static slack/number of remaining operations	A5=(A2-1.)/A3	S/5
DS	Dynamic slack	A5=A2-A4	S/5
DS/PT	Dynamic slack/ processing time	A5=(A2-A4)/A1	S/5
DS/RO	Dynamic slack/number of remaining operations	A5=(A2-A4)/A3	S/5

[a]Attribute 1 (A1) = estimated processing time for next operation; A2 = due date; A3 = number of remaining operations; A4 = estimated time for all remaining operations; A5 = ranking attribute if a function of above attributes is required.

define attribute 5 to be

$$A5 = (A2-1.0)/A1$$

for the SS/PT rule, and

$$A5 = (A2-1.0)/A3$$

for the SS/RO rule, where A3 is the number of remaining operations for the part. A3 must be updated for each transaction after every processing operation.

Dynamic slack is defined as the due date minus the estimated time needed for all remaining operations. To compute dynamic slack, an attribute must be updated after each operation to maintain the estimated time for all remaining operations. We use attribute 4 for this purpose.

Research has shown that the SPT rule is one of the best sequencing rules [33]. Its primary drawback is that lengthy jobs may be delayed in the system for long periods of time. To compensate for this, the SPT rule is often modified to form the *truncated SPT rule*. Under this rule, the SPT sequencing procedure is applied within two job categories. The job categories are set up depending on the value of slack, that is, the time remaining until the due date minus the remaining processing time on all remaining operations. If the slack is less than or

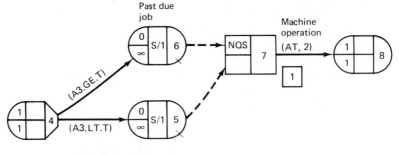

```
FUNCTION NQS(NODE)
COMMON/QVAR/NDE,NFTBU(100),NREL(100),NRELP(100),NREL2(100),NRUN,
1NRUNS,NTC(100),PARAM(100,4),TBEG,TNOW
DIMENSION ATT(3)
C**** IF Q-NODE 5 EMPTY, TRY Q-NODE 6
      IF (XNINQ(5).GT.0.0) GO TO 105
C**** IF Q-NODE 6 IS NOT EMPTY, NQS = 6
      IF (XNINQ(6).GT.0.0) GO TO 115
C**** NO TRANSACTION WAITING
      NQS = 0
      RETURN
  105 NQS = 5
C**** FIND FIRST TRANSACTION IN Q-NODE 5 WITH DUE DATE (ATRIB(3))
C**** LESS THAN TNOW
      NXACT = NFIND(TNOW,6,0,5,3)
      IF (NXACT.GT.0) GO TO 110
      IF (XNINQ(6).GT.0.0) GO TO 115
      RETURN
C**** PUT TRANSACTION PAST DUE IN Q-NODE 6
  110 CALL GETQ(NXACT,5,ATT,TIMEM)
      CALL PUTQ(6,ATT,TIMEM)
  115 NQS = 6
      RETURN
      END
```

Figure 7-1 Network segment and function NQS for modeling the truncated SPT rule: A1, estimate processing time; A2, actual processing time; A3, due date.

equal to zero, the job is given a high priority. Within each priority class, the jobs are ranked by smallest value of estimated processing time [48].

To model this situation, two Q-nodes will be placed before an S-node, as shown in Figure 7-1. Jobs that are late when they arrive to node 4 are routed directly in Q-node 6 based on conditional, take-first branching. Jobs not late are routed to Q-node 5. Jobs in both Q-nodes are ranked on the smallest value of the estimated processing time which has been prescribed for attribute 1.

S-node 7 is specified to have a user queue selection rule, NQS. In NQS, a selection between Q-nodes 6 and 5 is made and also a transaction may be transferred from Q-node 5 to Q-node 6 when a job becomes late. Function NQS for this situation is also shown in Figure 7-1.

Function NQS is called when the machine operation completes a job and S-node 7 is ready to select a transaction from one of the two Q-nodes preceding it. First, a test is made to determine if a job is waiting in Q-node 5 [XNINQ(5) > 0]. If not, Q-node 6 is examined. Q-node 6 is selected by setting NQS = 6 if there is a transaction in it [XNINQ(6) > 0]. If no jobs are waiting in Q-nodes 5 or 6, a value of zero is assigned to NQS to indicate that no transactions are waiting for the machine operation.

At statement 105, a tentative value for NQS is set equal to 5. A search of Q-node 5 is then performed using function NFIND to locate a transaction whose due date is past. If one is found, it will be the one with the shortest estimated processing time since the search starts at the beginning of the queue and transactions are ranked in Q-node 5 based on this attribute. The transaction is removed at statement 110 using subroutine GETQ (get transaction from queue). The transaction is placed in Q-node 6 using subroutine PUTQ (put transaction in queue). PUTQ will cause the transaction to be inserted in the queue in its proper position with respect to the ranking rule of the Q-node. After the transaction is inserted into Q-node 6, NQS is set to 6 so that a transaction will be removed from Q-node 6 for processing by the machine operation.

If no transactions are in Q-node 6 and one is not transferred, Q-node 5 is selected as the Q-node from which a transaction should be taken. This is accomplished by not branching to statements 110 or 115, which causes NQS to be returned with a value of 5 from function NQS.

The code presented above requires that the search operation find only the first transaction whose due date is past. If all transactions whose due date is past are desired to be stored in Q-node 6, repeated calls to function NFIND should be made.

We began this discussion of job sequencing by assuming a single queue before a server. When multiple queues of transactions precede a server (or group of servers), job sequencing is determined by both the selection of a queue and the selection of a job from that queue. To select a queue, we utilize an S-node in a look-backward mode. A queue selection rule is used to identify the Q-node that is on the input side of the S-node from which a transaction should be processed. For example, consider the following network segment:

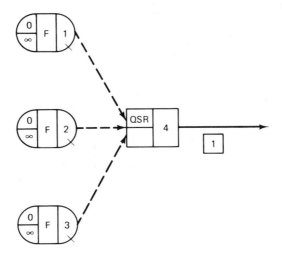

When server 1 completes service, a transaction is selected from either Q-node 1, 2, or 3 according to the queue selection rule. If all queues are empty, the server will become idle. If only one queue is nonempty, no queue choice exists, and a transaction is selected from the nonempty queue. When a choice does exist, however, any of the queue selection rules introduced previously (Table 2-3) can be used. Therefore, a choice can be made based on a specified order, a random order, a cyclic order, waiting time, current queue length, average queue length to date, and remaining capacity. One additional quantity that can be used in making a choice is the number of balkers to date. This measure was not appropriate when routing transactions to one of a set of queues because in that case any balking would occur from the S-node and not from one of the Q-nodes.

7.4.2 Machine Sequencing

Machine sequencing involves the determination of the order in which machines (work stations, resources, operators) should be used when a choice between or among machines exists. When each machine has a separate queue, routing jobs to the queues specifies an implied machine sequence.

In the network shown here conditional branching is used at node 8 to route transactions to service activity 1 or service activity 2:

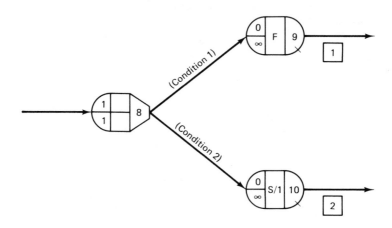

The conditions placed on the branches from node 8 to Q-node 9 and node 8 to Q-node 10 route transactions to machines. If both machines were idle, the conditions on the branches explicitly specify a machine selection procedure and, hence, can be classified as a machine sequencing vehicle. In this case, the machine sequencing is accomplished through the specifications of conditions on the branches following node 8.

A similar vehicle within Q-GERT is to use an S-node to select a Q-node/service activity combination to which a transaction should be routed. A network segment representing this situation looks like this:

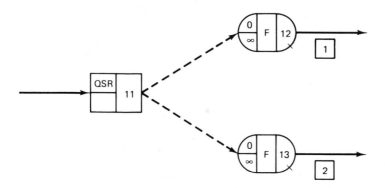

The queue selection rule at S-node 11 specifies the procedure for machine sequencing when both service activity 1 and service activity 2 are available.

A more direct machine sequencing procedure is the use of an S-node to select from among service activities emanating from it. This is shown here, where S-node 15, through the use of a server selection rule, SSR, selects among activities 1, 2, and 3.

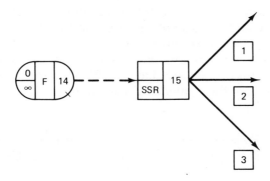

This network provides a general scheme for machine sequencing, since the user server selection (NSS) function can be specified and coded to select the machine to use next when a choice exists.

A more complex procedure involves a network segment with a

Q-node followed by two S-nodes, each of which can select from among parallel servers:

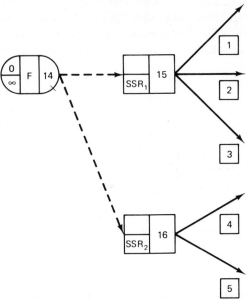

In this situation, SSR_1 at node 15 specifies the sequence for machines 1, 2, and 3 and SSR_2 at node 16 specifies the sequence for machines 4 and 5. On the QUE-input record the order of the S-node numbers indicates that the group of machines associated with S-node 15 are preferred to the group of machines associated with S-node 16. Thus, this network segment illustrates a two-level machine sequencing procedure.

A procedure similar to the one presented above is also available for sequencing resources. In the following network segment, the order in which ALLOCATE nodes are specified on the QUE-input record for Q-node 17 specifies the resource sequence to be used when a transaction arrives to Q-node 17 and both resources are available.

These illustrations show that Q-GERT provides extensive procedures for modeling the sequencing machines.

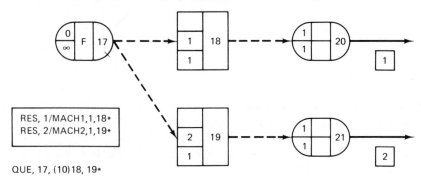

RES, 1/MACH1,1,18*
RES, 2/MACH2,1,19*

QUE, 17, (10)18, 19*

7.5 DETAILED SCHEDULING

The aggregate planning, loading, and sequencing aspects of scheduling provide information about jobs and work centers on a relative basis. The outputs from such analyses are: work center A should perform jobs 1, 3, and 7, and work center B should perform jobs 2, 4, 5, and 6; job 1 should be performed before job 3 at work center A. Detailed scheduling involves specifying start dates or completion dates for a list of jobs for each work center in the shop. Systems for detailed scheduling have been notoriously ineffectual. The main reason for the failure of detailed scheduling systems has been the lack of flexibility and adaptability when scheduling completion times for an interrelated set of jobs. In the past, a detailed schedule became obsolete as soon as new jobs arrived, unexpected machine delays occurred, or some disruption was experienced. Other causes for problems are inaccurate data and the absence of up-to-date progress information on individual jobs.

Recently, computers have been employed to perform detailed scheduling on an adaptive basis. Thus, instead of preparing a detailed schedule a week in advance, a daily or even job-by-job completion date specification is being performed. Such systems perform well as long as accurate records are kept, and the integrity of the data base supporting detailed scheduling is maintained. Without a concerted and continuous effort to maintain accurate data on current operations, any centralized, detailed scheduling system is doomed to failure.

The use of Q-GERT within a detailed scheduling system involves the writing of a user function at each node where a job transaction leaves a work center. In such a user function, a statement is included to record the job identifier, the work station, and the time the job transaction passed through the node. The time should be recorded in actual time units, which requires a translation of the Q-GERT variable TNOW to a date and specified hour. A subroutine to make this conversion has been written and requires as inputs a starting date, number of shifts worked per day, the start time of the shift, the length of a shift, the length and frequency of breaks, and the number of working days per week.

When all job times are constants, the completion dates for each job at each work center printed out by the foregoing procedure represents a detailed schedule. The detailed schedule is based on the aggregate planning, loading, and sequencing rules incorporated in the Q-GERT network. Changing any one of these planning procedures will result in a new detailed schedule. Through sorting procedures or by writing the completion dates to separate peripheral devices, the detailed schedule can be organized by chronological value, work center, and/or job number. By storing the values in a data base using SDL as discussed in Chapter 5, further analysis of the detailed schedule can be made [191]. If desired, Gantt charts for the schedule could be prepared automatically.

If machine times are random variables, any completion date is only one sample of the random variable describing the completion time. Detailed scheduling procedures have not been developed for this situation. A good research topic is the development of techniques for presenting detailed scheduling information at the shop floor when completion date, and hence start dates and slack values, are random variables. An estimate of the distribution of these random variables can be obtained by Q-GERT through the performance of multiple runs (this is done in a project scheduling environment in Chapter 18). A rule must then be used to translate the distribution information to a specific date. Possible rules are:

1. Use the expected date.
2. Use the date such that 95% of the completion times are less than the date selected.
3. Use the expected date plus two standard deviations.

The application of Q-GERT within detailed scheduling operations is a fertile research area.

7.6 EVALUATING THE EFFECTS OF RANDOM VARIATION ON SOLUTIONS OBTAINED BY ANALYTIC METHODS

Analytic methods have been developed to determine optimal solutions for special problem situations within production planning. Typically, the use of an analytic procedure involves linearity and deterministic assumptions. The use of analytic procedures can be considered as a first stage of problem solution whereby a first pass schedule or sequence is developed that is to be used for evaluation under more realistic conditions in which the linear and constant time assumptions are removed. Simulation procedures can be employed to evaluate the performance of the solution when such assumptions are relaxed. In this section this approach is used to evaluate proposed job sequences in a flow shop.

7.6.1 Johnson's Sequencing Role

Consider a shop consisting of two machines, where jobs are to be processed first on machine 1 and then on machine 2. The processing time for each job on both machines is known with certainty, although the times may be different for different jobs. The problem of sequencing jobs to minimize the total time for all jobs (makespan) is known as *Johnson's problem* since Johnson developed an optimal sequencing rule. The rule can be stated as follows [10]. Let t_{j1} represent the processing time on machine 1 for job j and let t_{j2} represent the processing time on machine 2 for job j. Let U be the set of jobs such that $t_{j1} < t_{j2}$, that is, $U = \{j \mid t_{j1} < t_{j2}\}$ and let $V = \{j \mid t_{j1} \geq t_{j2}\}$. If the elements of U are ordered with small values of t_{j1} first and the elements of V are ordered with large values of t_{j2} first, then an optimal sequence for performing the jobs on both machines is the ordered set U followed by the ordered set V.

We will now illustrate how this sequencing rule can be implemented in Q-GERT.† We will also indicate the procedure by which the Q-GERT model can be employed to evaluate the introduction of random processing times. The Q-GERT network and associated user function UF are shown in Figure 7-2.

For this example, 20 jobs are to be processed which are created at source node 1 with attribute 5 used as the job identifier. There is one user function which assigns values to attributes 1, 2, 3, and 4. Attributes 1 and 2 are the mean processing times for machines 1 and 2, respectively. All machine times are assumed to be normally distributed.†† The parameters for each job are input sequentially using the PAR input statements. Each job requires two parameter sets: the first for the processing time on machine 1, the second for the processing time on machine 2.

In function UF, the job number is retrieved from attribute 5 and is used to compute the position in the array PARAM, where the mean processing times are stored for the given job. Attributes 1 and 2 are assigned these mean values, which will be used in applying Johnson's rule. Attributes 3 and 4 are set equal to samples from normal distributions and represent the actual processing times used in the simulation. The statement CALL PUTAT(ATT) assigns the values of the attributes to the current transaction. This completes the description of function UF.

After the attribute assignments, the job is routed to either Q-node 2 or Q-node 3, depending on the relation of attribute 1 to attribute 2. Jobs in Q-node 2 are members of the set U and are ordered small-value-first based on attribute 1. Jobs in Q-node 3 are members of the set V and are ordered big-value-first based on attribute 2. The ordering of jobs in the Q-nodes takes place at time zero as no resources are allocated until all 20 jobs arrive. This is accomplished by having zero resources available initially as set in the resource block, which is (RES,1/MACH1,0,4*). Immediately after the twentieth transaction enters the system, the branch from node 1 to ALTER node 10

---

†It should be noted that any sequencing rule that orders all incoming jobs at time zero can be modeled by reading in the prescribed sequence in subroutine UI as discussed in Section 7.2.3. Another alternative is to use subroutine PTIN to put transactions into the system at the node of the first station in the prescribed sequence.

††To employ different distribution types for different jobs, a computed GO TO statement would be used in function UF.

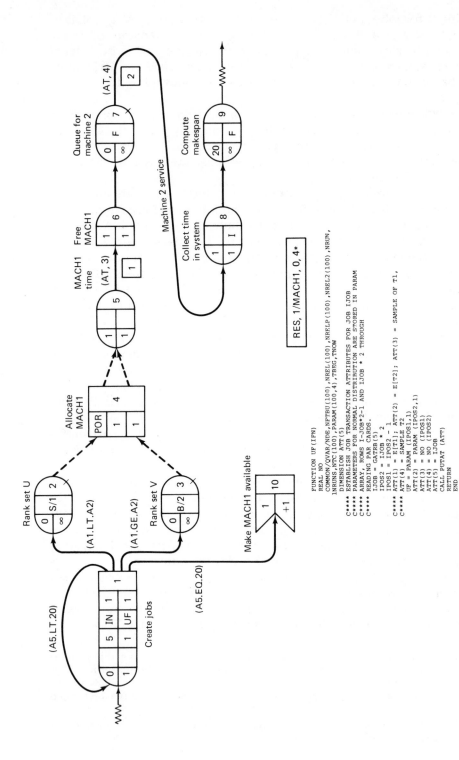

Figure 7-2 Q-GERT network and function UF for evaluating Johnson's sequencing rule.

with the condition (A5.EQ.20) is taken. ALTER node 10 increases by 1 the available number of units of resource type 1, which represents machine 1. Machine 1 is allocated at node 4, where a transaction from Q-node 2 or 3 is selected according to a preferred order. Specifying this order to be Q-node 2, then Q-node 3, on the SEL statement ensures that machine 1 will process the jobs according to Johnson's rule based on mean processing time.

The processing of a job on machine 1 is represented by activity 1, and requires a time equal to attribute 3 (the normal sample defined in function UF). FREE node 6 frees machine 1 (resource 1) and the next job is scheduled. After processing on machine 1, the job proceeds to machine 2. The time for the job on machine 2 is specified by attribute 4. Node 8 collects statistics on the flow time, that is, the time in the system. Node 9 requires that all 20 transactions reach it prior to its release. The time of release for node 9 is thus the makespan for a given run. First statistics are requested for node 9. By making multiple runs, statistics and a histogram for makespan over all runs are obtained.

7.6.2 Jackson's Sequencing Rule [88]

Jackson extended Johnson's problem, by considering the two-machine situation, where jobs may require the machines in either order and also may only require one of the two machines. Jobs that must start on machine 1 and then must go to machine 2 will be referred to as AB jobs. Jobs that must start on machine 2 and then be routed to machine 1 are referred to as BA jobs. The jobs to be processed only on machine 1 are called A jobs and those for machine 2 are called B jobs. Jackson has prescribed a rule to sequence the jobs optimally in this situation. The rule consists of two steps. The first step of the rule specifies that the following sequencing be performed:

1. Sequence AB jobs by Johnson's rule.
2. Sequence BA jobs by Johnson's rule.
3. Sequence A and B jobs in any order.

The second step of the rule states that machine 1 is to process all AB jobs first, all A jobs next, and BA jobs last. Machine 2 is to process all BA jobs first, all B jobs next, and AB jobs last.

The Q-GERT model for Jackson's rule is an extension of the previous network for Johnson's rule and is shown in Figure 7-3. Source node 1 generates jobs of type A and AB with job numbers ranging from 1 to 20. Five attribute values are assigned in function UF in a manner similar to that given in Figure 7-2. If a job is an A-type job, its processing time for machine 2 is specified as zero. As in the last section, the order of the PAR cards must correspond to the job number. Source node 11 generates jobs 21 to 40, which are type B and BA jobs. Type B

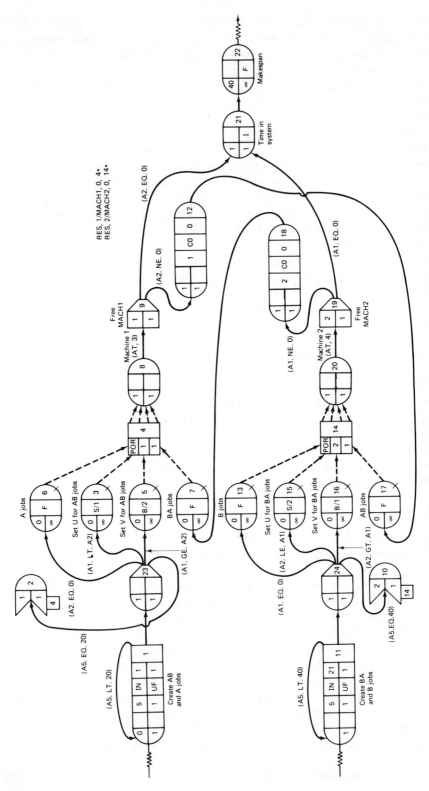

Figure 7-3 Q-GERT network model for evaluating Jackson's rule.

jobs are indicated by a zero value for processing on machine 1. As before, attributes 3 and 4 are sampled values for the actual machine times.

Q-nodes 3 and 5 order AB jobs according to Johnson's rule. Q-node 6 contains A jobs which can be identified by a zero value for attribute 2. (On input, the activity from node 23 to Q-node 6 is placed first so that this routing condition is the first one tested.) Similarly for machine 2, the input statement describing the branch to Q-node 13 from node 24 should be placed first to route B jobs to Q-node 13. Q-nodes 15 and 16 order BA jobs.

Resource 1 represents machine 1 and resource 2 represents machine 2. Both of these are initially unavailable as a capacity of zero is specified for both on the resource blocks. Node 2 makes machine 1 available when all AB and A jobs are ordered. Node 10 makes machine 2 available when BA and B jobs are ordered. When a job finishes at machine 1, node 9 routes the job out of the system if attribute 2 equals zero. If attribute 2 is not zero, the machine 2 operation must be performed and such jobs are routed to node 12 and then Q-node 17, where AB jobs wait for machine 2. Node 12 sets attribute 1 to zero so that when service is completed at machine 2, node 19 will route the job out of the system. Node 19 performs routing based on whether attribute 1 is zero or not. Thus, B jobs leave the system immediately after machine 2 finishes. However, BA jobs are routed to node 18, then Q-node 7. Node 18 sets attribute 2 to zero for BA jobs so that node 9 will cause these jobs to exit after machine 1 processing.

Jackson's rule is embodied in the queue selection rule of ALLO-CATE nodes 4 and 14. For machine 1, AB jobs are processed first (in Johnson order), A jobs next, and BA jobs last. For machine 2, BA jobs are processed first (in Johnson order), B jobs next, and AB jobs last. Node 21 provides statistics on flowtime and node 22 on makespan. Resource utilization statistics provide information on machine usage.

7.7 ASSEMBLY LINE BALANCING

An assembly line is a sequence of work stations where operators assemble units into subassemblies and finished products. Subassemblies are passed from work station to work station, usually on a conveyor. Typically, a production rate is specified for the entire line. For example, the line may have to produce 480 units in an 8-hour shift. This means that one unit must be produced each minute. Thus, the time interval from the completion of one finished part to the completion of the next is 1 minute. This time interval between completion of finished units is called the *cycle time*.

In this initial discussion we will assume a single operator at each work station. Each operator is assigned a set of tasks to perform on each unit that enters the work area. The completion of all tasks at all work stations results in a final assembled unit. Obviously, some tasks must be performed prior to other tasks. Nevertheless, there can be a great deal of flexibility in assigning tasks to operators at work stations. The objective in line balancing is to find the minimum number of groupings of tasks into stations so that (1) each station consumes no more time than the cycle time in completing assigned tasks, and (2) precedence relations among tasks are maintained.

The first constraint requires each unit to spend no more than the length of time equal to the cycle time at each station. The time it takes to perform all the tasks at a station for a given unit is called the station time. The cycle time minus the station time for station i is called the delay time for station i. The sum of all station delays is called the *balance delay*. It can be shown that the optimal grouping of tasks within stations results in a minimum balance delay. Thus a related problem is: Given a certain number of stations, task precedence relations, and the condition that the total station time not exceed the cycle time, assign tasks to stations to minimize cycle time (or balance delay).

Several approaches exist to line balancing [94,117]. These approaches assume constant task times. For a prescribed balancing scheme, Q-GERT can be used to simulate the assembly line to estimate delays and/or cycle times. In this way, balancing schemes can be evaluated in the face of random fluctuations of task times. Furthermore, once a Q-GERT network of an assembly line is constructed, it can be used to investigate alternative balancing strategies.

We illustrate by example the use of Q-GERT in evaluating line balancing strategies. Consider an assembly operation requiring nine tasks with constant task times as given in Figure 7-4. In Figure 7-4 both an activity network and a precedence diagram are given. The latter is used extensively in assembly line balancing studies and uses nodes to represent tasks and branches to indicate precedence relations among tasks. Hence, in Figure 7-4(b) we see that task 4 must be preceded by task 2 and task 3. Tasks 2 and 3 may be completed in any order but both must follow task 1. Similarly, task 8 must follow task 6 but tasks 6 and 8 start times are not dependent on tasks 5 and 7. However, task 4 must precede tasks 5, 6, and 7. Finally, task 9 cannot start until tasks 5, 7, and 8 are finished.

Table 7-2 gives an allocation of tasks to stations for this line balancing problem under the assumption of a cycle time of 14 time units. Tasks 1, 3, and 2 are assigned to station 1; tasks 4, 7, and 6 to station 2; and tasks 8, 5, and 9 to station 3. The station times are computed as the sum of station task times. The station delay is the cycle time minus the station time.

A Q-GERT network for this example is shown in Figure 7-5. Source node 1 represents the entry of units onto the assembly line. The time between releases of node 1 is controlled by activity 10 and is set

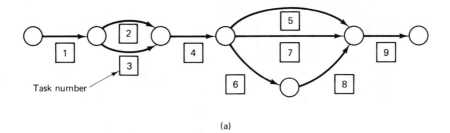

(a)

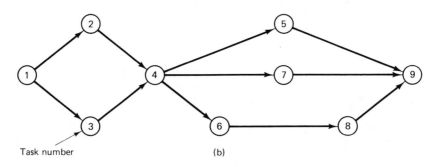

Task number   (b)

Task	Task time
1	5
2	3
3	4
4	5
5	1
6	4
7	5
8	4
9	6

Figure 7-4 Activity and precedence networks and task times for assembly line balancing example: (a) task on-branch network; (b) task on-node network.

TABLE 7-2 A Solution to the Assembly Line Balancing Problem

Station	Task	Task Time	Station Time	Station Delay[a]
1	1	5		
	3	4		
	2	3	12	2
2	4	5		
	7	5		
	6	4	14	0
3	8	4		
	5	1		
	9	6	11	3

[a]Cycle time is assumed to be 14.

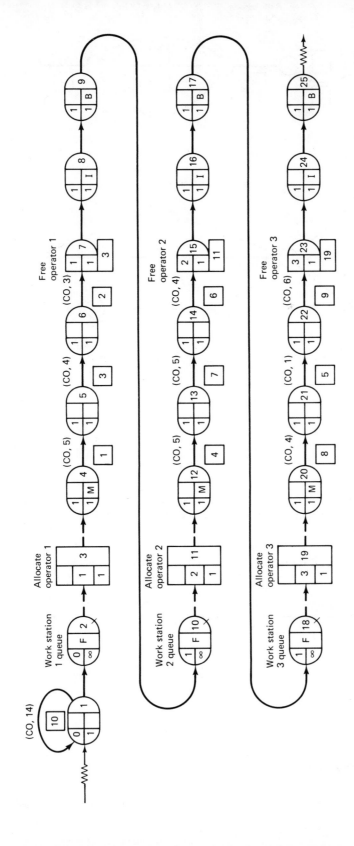

Figure 7-5 Q-GERT model of an assembly line balancing situation.

RES, 1/OP1, 1, 3*
RES, 2/OP2, 1, 11*
RES, 3/OP3, 1, 19*

equal to the cycle time, 14 time units. Nodes 2 through 9 represent the first work station, where tasks 1, 3, and 2 are performed. The activity numbers correspond to the task numbers. Activity times are shown as constants and are equal to the task times prescribed in Figure 7-5. Q-node 2 represents units waiting for the station 1 operator. A transaction will arrive from node 1 at time zero to be processed. The operator is modeled as a resource that is allocated at node 3. If a unit arrives at Q-node 2 and resource 1 is available, the transaction captures one unit of resource 1 and passes through node 4 to activity 1. The sequence of activities 1, 3, and 2 represents the tasks at station 1. Upon completion of task 2, node 7 frees the operator, who is either allocated from node 3 or becomes idle.

Each transaction is marked at node 4 and interval statistics are collected at node 8 which represent the station time for station 1. For the constant task times of this illustration, the station time will always be 12 for station 1. However, when the task times are random variables, the station time becomes a random variable and node 8 provides statistics on this quantity. The closer the station time is to the cycle time, the better the utilization of the work station. However, for random times higher utilization would result in higher probabilities of not completing all tasks in a cycle. The production rate at which the station is actually operating is revealed by the between-statistics of node 9.

The average number in Q-node 2 represents the backlog for the station, and resource utilization statistics for resource type 1 represents the usage and idle statistics for the operator.

The I-statistics do not take into account the waiting time at the queues between the stations. This could be done by changing the marking location. However, the current formulation permits the comparison of the station time with the cycle time, and the monitoring of any violation of the desired condition that the station time be less than the cycle time. The mean value for the I-statistics can be subtracted from the cycle time for an estimate of station delay. From the histograms obtained for nodes 8, 16, and 24, estimates of the probabilities that station times exceed the cycle time can be obtained. If statistics on station delay are desired, the delay for each transaction could be computed by a user function called from node 8. The delay would equal the cycle time (14) minus the quantity TNOW-TMARK(I), where TNOW is the time the unit reaches node 8 and TMARK(I) is the mark time for the transaction. User statistics would be employed to collect delay statistics through a call to subroutine COL. Furthermore, statistics could be segregated, according to whether the delay is positive or negative. Negative delay indicates a violation of the cycle time constraint. (In the model, we do not prohibit the violation of the constraint, as we are interested in evaluating system performance.)

To increase the number of operators at a station, the number of available resources is modified on the appropriate RESOURCE block.

To investigate other task assignments at a station requires changing only network branches and activity durations.

Before leaving the subject of assembly line balancing, it should be pointed out that the formulation above assumed that each task builds on the unit. Some operations normally involve combining units. To assemble transactions in Q-GERT, the ASM rule of S-nodes is used. If only a single transaction representing each unit can be available for assembly, a regular node can be used. These two options are shown here for the assembly of three units.

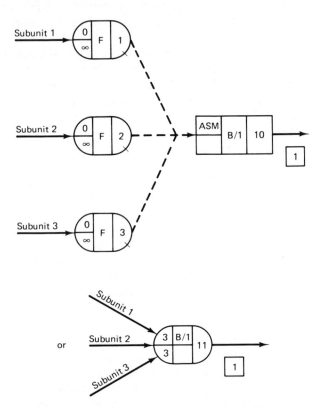

The difference in the network segments shown here is that regular node 11 does not require each subunit to be different. Thus, to use the regular node to perform this function, the modeler must be sure that the network prohibits two subunits of the same type from being assembled. Note that node 11 could be made a statistics node to collect delays due to assembly by specifying a D in the statistics field.

In the discussions above, the assembly activity, activity number 1, is represented by a single branch. By including complex network logic within the model for each work station, complex assembly line systems and line balancing schemes can be evaluated.

7.8 SUMMARY

This chapter has illustrated the complexity of scheduling and sequencing concepts. It has provided definitions of the different types of scheduling that are performed in a production context. The process of scheduling has been decomposed down to the level of Q-GERT elements which were then integrated in a network model of scheduling procedures. Building on these modeling concepts, the management scientist can explore the impact on the performance measures described in Chapter 6 of new procedures for aggregate planning, scheduling, sequencing, and assembly line balancing.

7.9 EXERCISES

7-1. Prepare a set of forms that can be used to portray the results (outputs) obtained from aggregate planning, loading, sequencing, and detailed scheduling. Define each output operationally and specify the inputs required to generate the values that would be inserted on your forms.

7-2. Prepare an aggregate plan for a computer center with which you are familiar.

7-3. Discuss how rules for job sequencing may influence the procedures used for machine sequencing.

7-4. Build a Q-GERT model to represent the arrival of two types of jobs. There are 1000 units of job type 1 and 500 units of job type 2 to be processed. Three operations are to be performed on type 1 jobs, with the machining times being exponentially distributed with a mean of 10. A due date for type 1 jobs is prescribed as 1.5 times the sum of the processing times, for its three operations. A type 2 job requires one operation, which may have to be repeated with probability 0.15. The time to perform the operation is normally distributed with a mean of 40 and a standard deviation of 5. For a type 2 job, a due date of 70 time units after its arrival is prescribed. In addition to building the Q-GERT model for the arrival of jobs, estimate (guess) the fraction of jobs of each type that will be late. Also estimate the makespan for this situation.

7-5. Describe the advantages and disadvantages associated with the following rules for loading jobs to queues:
   (a) Load the job to the queue that has had the smallest average number of transactions passing through it to date (SAV).
   (b) Load jobs to queues in a preferred order (POR).
   (c) Load jobs in a cyclic manner (CYC).
   (d) Load jobs to the area that has had the smallest number of balkers to date (SNB).

7-6. Develop a loading rule using function NQS which attempts to equalize the waiting time for jobs at work centers. Code FUNCTION NQS for the loading rule that you developed.

7-7. Test the job sequencing rules first-in, first-out (FIFO), last-in, first-out (LIFO), shortest processing time (SPT); smallest due date (DD); and smallest slack for the single-queue, single-server system under the following conditions:

(a) Exponential arrivals with mean 10; exponential service times with mean 8; due dates assigned as 20 units from arrival time.

(b) Same as part (a) with due dates equal to arrival time plus a sample from an exponential distribution with mean 20.

(c) Same as part (a) except for a constant interarrival time of 10.

(d) Same as part (a) except for a constant service time of 9.

7-8. Using the procedures described in Section 7.2.4, prepare for the arrival of the 20 jobs shown below, where each job is processed through three operations (A, B, and C) in the sequence given. Evaluate each of the rules specified in Table 7-1 for this particular job input stream.

Job Number	Arrival Time	Operation Sequence	Operation Times	Due Date
1	0	A, B, C	2, 3, 4	12
2	0	B, C, A	3, 4, 2	12
3	0	B, C, B	3, 3, 3	12
4	3	A, C, B	6, 1, 4	20
5	7	A, B, A	1, 3, 5	25
6	12	B, C, A	1, 2, 2	30
7	13	B, C, A	4, 1, 3	30
8	20	A, B, C	2, 3, 4	35
9	21	B, C, B	4, 3, 2	40
10	22	A, B, A	3, 1, 2	42
11	24	C, A, B	4, 1, 1	45
12	30	B, C, B	6, 3, 2	50
13	36	C, A, C	3, 4, 2	55
14	38	C, A, B	4, 1, 1	58
15	41	B, C, A	4, 1, 3	60
16	49	A, B, A	1, 3, 5	65
17	52	B, C, B	3, 3, 3	70
18	59	A, C, B	6, 1, 4	70
19	60	B, C, A	3, 4, 2	72
20	62	B, C, A	1, 2, 2	72

7-9. Given the following seven jobs, apply Johnson's rule to determine the sequencing of the jobs.

Job	Tooling	Production
A	6	9
B	8	6
C	8	7
D	1	3
E	5	4
F	16	9
G	11	16

Compare machine idle times if the jobs are done in alphabetical order against the sequence obtained using Johnson's rule. Assuming that the times given in the table above are normally distributed with a standard deviation equal to one-tenth of the mean, use Q-GERT to evaluate sequencing by Johnson's rule. Make statements concerning the probability that the makespan is less than prescribed values in this latter case.

7-10. Run the Q-GERT model shown in Figure 7-5 to obtain statistics that evaluate the proposed assignment of tasks to stations. Develop a new task assignment and evaluate it.

7-11. Change the duration specification for the activities in Figure 7-5 so that they are normally distributed with a mean equal to the constant value and a standard deviation equal to one-tenth of the mean value. The model is to be changed so that a job not completed within the cycle time is routed to an off-line station. Evaluate the proposed assignment of tasks to operators presented in Figure 7-5 by assessing the number of jobs that must be routed off-line.

7-12. Build a Q-GERT model for the following situation. Items flow through a paced assembly line. There are three stations on the assembly line and the service time at each station is exponentially distributed with a mean of 10. Items flow down the assembly line from server 1 to server 2 to server 3. A new unit is provided to server 1 every 15 time units. If any of the servers have not completed processing their current unit within 15 minutes, the unit is diverted to one or two off-line servers, who complete the remaining operations on the job diverted from the assembly line. One time unit is added to the remaining time of the operation that was not completed. Any following operations not performed are done by the off-line servers in an exponentially distributed time with a mean of 16. Draw the Q-GERT network to obtain statistics on the utilization of all servers, and the fraction of items diverted from each operation.

Embellishments:

(a) Assume that the assembly line is paced and that the movement of units can occur only at multiples of 15 minutes.

(b) Allow one unit to be stored between each assembly line server.

(c) If a server is available, route units back to the assembly line from the off-line servers.

8

Modeling Material Handling Systems

8.1 INTRODUCTION

The movement of material from place to place is an important aspect of producing a final product. In many situations, specialized material handling systems are required for the movement. As material handling equipment is a potential system bottleneck, it is typically modeled as a resource or service activity. In this chapter, methods for modeling different types of material handling systems are described. Specifically, we discuss conveyor systems, pipelines for continuous product flow, overhead cranes, and other vehicles on rails. In each case, emphasis is placed on incorporating within a Q-GERT model the specific material flow pattern peculiar to the system of interest. The modeling procedures permit the evaluation of throughput, time delays, and usage rates of the material handling equipment, as well as the production system it serves.

8.2 MODELING CONVEYOR SYSTEMS

Conveyors are important methods of transporting materials within a production system. Decision making may relate directly to the characteristics of the conveyor system, such as its capacity, or to the effect of the conveyor on the performance of the production at large.

We begin by considering a one-way conveyor moving between two points, a loading point and an unloading point. In loading a conveyor, there is a maximum amount of material that can be placed on the conveyor within a given time period. That is, once a unit of material has been loaded on a section of the conveyor, the loader must wait until the section of the conveyor moves forward. The length of time until another load can be put on the conveyor is a function of the conveyor speed. If a unit load occupies 50 centimeters of conveyor and the conveyor moves at a speed of 100 centimeters/minute, the wait time must be at least 0.5 minute. We refer to this time as the *one-unit move time*.

Another aspect of one-way conveyor transport is that the time intervals between departing unit loads from the conveyor are identical to the time intervals between placement of loads on the conveyor. This assumes that when the loading process terminates, the conveyor transports all material on the conveyor to the exit point.

With the above as background, we will model a conveyor using Q-GERT. At first, it appears that the conveyor is simply a service activity and can be modeled by the network segment shown here.

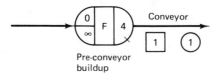

Q-node 4 models the buildup of material waiting to be loaded on to the conveyor. Server 1 is the conveyor and the time duration of server 1 is the time to traverse from an entry point to an exit point on the conveyor. This representation is inadequate, however, since it allows only a single unit load to occupy the conveyor. We might consider changing the specification for the number of parallel servers from 1 to N, where N represents the number of unit loads the conveyor can hold. But this would also be inadequate, in that loads cannot be placed on the conveyor simultaneously. Furthermore, we need to model the one-unit move time referred to earlier.[†] Following is a representation that accounts for the one-unit move time:[††]

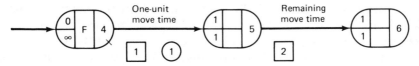

In this network segment, unit loads arrive at Q-node 4, but before entering the conveyor, a delay may occur depending on the availability of server 1. This service time represents the time for the conveyor to

---

[†]If this delay is not significant, a single Q-node with N parallel servers would approximate conveyor flow.

[††]Steven Duket of Pritsker & Associates performed the original modeling described in this section.

move one unit away from the loading area, that is, the one-unit move time. When a unit reaches node 5, it begins to traverse the remaining portion of the conveyor.

As an extension of this model, consider a situation in which excessive buildup may occur in the area where units exit the conveyor. If the conveyor cannot be unloaded when this occurs, all units on the conveyor become blocked as each load on the conveyor reaches a non-moving load in front of it. See formulation as modeled in (a), p. 179.

In this formulation, Q-node 8 represents the post-conveyor queue space. If a load arrives at the end of the conveyor when this space is saturated (here, saturation is 10 units), the load is blocked. That means that server 7 cannot pass on any further transactions until space becomes available in Q-node 8. This blocking process can affect the entire conveyor. Servers 2 through 6 process the units (in this case up to 5) between the first and the last conveyor positioning.† As units reach Q-node 7 they become blocked if server 7 is blocked. When all five of the middle units are blocked, the first unit may become blocked and a buildup may occur in Q-node 4. Unblocking occurs in the same order as blocking. Server 7 ensures that each unit exits at an interval not less than the one-unit move time.

As an alternative to the foregoing representation, we can visualize each conveyor segment as a separate unit and model the conveyor as in formulation (b) on the facing page.

The advantages of this representation are that conveyor movement is accurately modeled, additional entry or loading points are easily added, and conveyor shutdowns can be approximated by extending the duration of activity 7. This representation does have the disadvantage of requiring an activity and node for each conveyor unit.

Up to this point, our discussion has been concerned with unidirectional conveyors with a single entry and exit position. Some conveyors operate in a circular fashion and have a number of exit positions. To illustrate, consider the case of five servers stationed along a circular conveyor belt [154]. Items to be processed by the servers arrive at the conveyor belt with an interarrival time that is exponentially distributed with a mean of 1 minute. After being placed on the conveyor belt, it takes 2 minutes for the new arrivals to reach the first server. Service time for each server averages 3 minutes and is exponentially distributed. No storage space for items is provided before any server. If the first server is idle, the item is processed by that server. If the first server is busy when the item arrives, the item continues down the conveyor belt until it arrives at the second server. The delay time between servers is 1 minute. If an item encounters a situation in which all servers are busy, it is recycled to the first server with a time delay of 5 minutes.

---

†Parallel identical servers are not used because, owing to a technical restriction of the Q-GERT processor, they cannot be blocked.

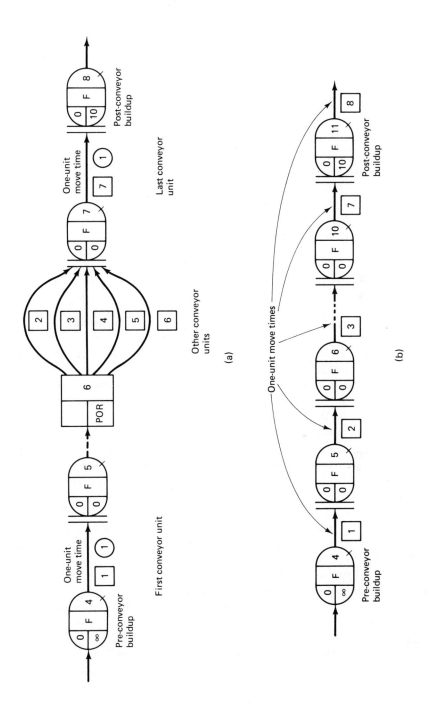

(a)

(b)

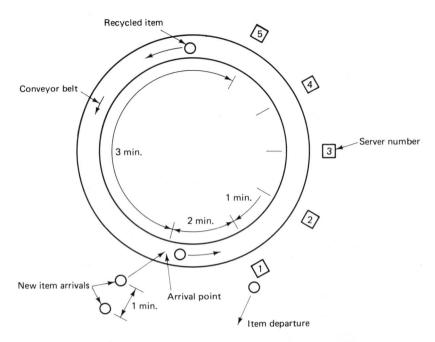

Figure 8-1 Schematic diagram of conveyor system.

At the completion of service for an item, the item is removed from the system. A diagram of the conveyor system is shown in Figure 8-1. We describe below a Q-GERT model designed to collect statistics on the system residence time for an item and the utilization of each server based on the processing of 200 items.

In this example, an item arrives and is transferred to the first server with a 2-minute time delay. The size of an item is small and the one-unit move time is considered insignificant. If the first server is free, the item is taken off the conveyor belt and service is initiated on it. If the first server is busy, the item must bypass the first server, that is, continue along the conveyor belt, and proceed to the second server. This decision as to whether the item will be processed by the first server can be modeled in Q-GERT using a Q-node with a zero queue capacity. If the server is idle, the item will flow through the Q-node directly to the server. However, if the server is busy, the item cannot stay at the Q-node because it has a zero capacity; hence, it will balk. In this situation, balking from the server means that the item continues down the conveyor belt toward the next server. The remainder of the Q-GERT model follows this pattern of attempting to gain access to a server through a Q-node with zero capacity and balking from the Q-node if the server is busy. The Q-GERT model for the conveyor system is shown in Figure 8-2.

Arrivals of items are modeled using source node 2 with a self-loop branch to represent the interarrival activity. Since it takes 2 minutes for

Production Planning   Part III

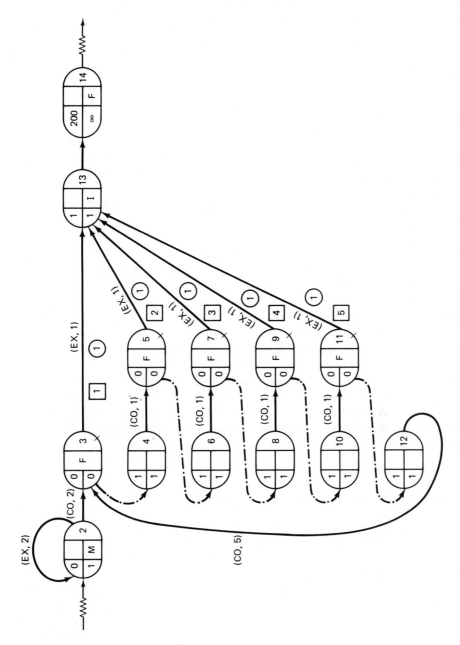

Figure 8-2 Q-GERT model of conveyor system.

the item to reach the first server, the branch from node 2 to Q-node 3 is given a 2-minute duration. Q-node 3 precedes server number 1 and has zero initial transactions in it and a capacity of zero. When a transaction arrives at Q-node 3 and server 1 is busy, the transaction balks to node 4. The branch from node 4 to Q-node 5 represents the item staying on the conveyor belt and moving to the next server. A 1-minute time delay is prescribed for the activity as represented by the branch from node 4 to Q-node 5.

When a transaction arrives at node 13 it has completed service and the time spent in the conveyor system by the item is collected. The item is then sent to node 14 to record that one more transaction has been processed by the conveyor system. Two hundred incoming transactions are required to release node 14, which is the sink node for the system. When node 14 is released, one run of the conveyor system will have been completed.

If an item balks from all Q-nodes, it reaches node 12. The activity from node 12 to node 3 represents the recycling of items, which requires 5 minutes. Starting at node 3, the processing of the item through the five-server conveyor system is repeated.

In this model, service activity 1 will be busier than service activity 2, which in turn will be busier than service activity 3, and so on. This occurs because arriving items attempt to gain access to servers in a prescribed order. One method for balancing the work load of the servers is to incorporate in-process storage areas prior to the servers. If larger storage areas are provided for servers with higher activity numbers, a balancing of the busy times of the servers can be made. More exotic systems could assign items upon their arrival to a particular server (centralized control) or make a decision at each server station as to whether the item should be routed to this server or remain on the conveyor belt (decentralized control). In-process storage and centralized and decentralized control procedures are easily incorporated into the network model.

8.3 CONTINUOUS PRODUCT FLOW THROUGH A PIPELINE

Continuous product flow, such as crude oil through a pipeline, can be represented in Q-GERT by visualizing the continuous flow as made up of blocks or batches that sequentially flow through the pipeline. With this transformation, pipeline flow seems analogous to conveyor transport. However, there is an important characteristic of pipeline flow that distinguishes it from conveyor flow. When input to a conveyor ceases, the output continues until the conveyor is empty. Furthermore, input to a conveyor does not cause an output from the conveyor. Thus, output from a conveyor can be obtained with or without input even if the conveyor is only half full. With pipeline flow, however, not only must the pipeline be full but there must also be an input to the pipeline before output is obtained. Units of material entering a pipeline "push" units ahead of them and if the pipeline is full, output is realized. Once input ceases, no output flows.

The key to modeling pipeline flow is to recognize that the characteristic of pipeline flow stated above is an *and* condition. When the pipeline is at capacity *and* there is an incoming unit of flow, the pipeline will produce one unit of flow as output.

One method of modeling this *and* condition is to have a server who is always busy and has a Q-node that has a capacity equal to the number of units required to fill the pipeline. When the Q-node is full *and* another arrival occurs, the arriving unit balks and can be considered as an output from the pipeline. The network segment that models this condition for a pipeline that can carry 10 units is shown below (the symbol ∞ is used to denote a large value). A capacity of nine is shown for Q-node 3, which gives a pipeline capacity of 10 as 1 unit is in service activity 1.

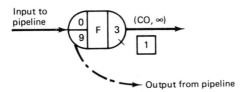

This model of pipeline flow has a serious drawback. The output from the pipeline is not the first arriving unit but the eleventh. If it is necessary to maintain attributes of the units flowing through the pipeline, the foregoing model is not adequate.

Following is another procedure for modeling pipeline flow, which maintains the proper ordering of transactions.

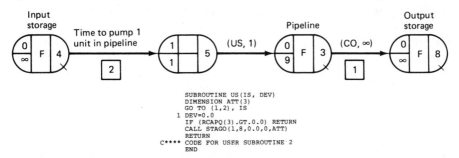

```
      SUBROUTINE US(IS, DEV)
      DIMENSION ATT(3)
      GO TO (1,2), IS
    1 DEV=0.0
      IF (RCAPQ(3).GT.0.0) RETURN
      CALL STAGO(1,8,0.0,0,ATT)
      RETURN
C**** CODE FOR USER SUBROUTINE 2
      END
```

In this network segment, a unit is pumped into the pipeline by the arrival of a transaction at node 5. The next activity is described by a user subroutine (US rather than UF is employed to show its use. UF could have been used). In US, statement 1 corresponds to user subroutine 1. The duration of the activity is set to zero in the user subroutine by equating DEV to 0 at statement 1. If the pipeline is full, a unit should be sent to node 8 representing the output from the pipeline. If the pipeline is not full, no output should be obtained. The computer code to accomplish this involves testing the remaining capacity of the pipeline, which for this model is the remaining capacity in Q-node 3. The remaining capacity is obtained from the function RCAPQ(3). When the remaining capacity is not greater than zero, activity 1 is stopped, and a transaction representing a unit is routed to output storage by a call to subroutine STAGO. Subroutine STAGO routes a unit from the pipeline to Q-node 8 and restarts activity 1 with the transaction that is next in line in Q-node 3. The unit that is arriving to the pipeline as represented by the transaction traversing the branch from node 5 to Q-node 3 will then have a space in Q-node 3; hence, it will be in the pipeline. By specifying a zero as the fourth argument in the call to subroutine STAGO, the attributes of the transaction that was in activity 1 are routed to Q-node 8, the output storage queue. In this manner, pipeline flow can be represented as a sequence of activities and Q-nodes, and the attributes of the units flowing through the pipeline are maintained in their proper order.

Note that if the system has a full pipeline initially, the initial number in Q-node 3 would be 9 and the test on remaining capacity would not be required. In this case, all completions of service activity 2 would cause a transaction to be sent immediately to Q-node 8.

8.4 MODELING OVERHEAD CRANES AND OTHER VEHICLES ON TRACKS

Many material handling systems involve vehicles that move on tracks. Examples of such systems are overhead cranes, transporter carts, and remotely controlled forklift trucks. From a modeling standpoint, these systems have common features, and therefore the Q-GERT modeling procedures are similar. For convenience, we refer only to the modeling of overhead cranes in this section, but it should be clear that other material handling systems that use tracks could be modeled in a similar fashion.

Consider the schematic drawing of an overhead crane system shown in Figure 8-3. There are two cranes on a T-shaped track. The dashed line shows the movement pattern for crane 1. This crane is used to transport material from input station 1 to output station 1 or 2. Crane 2, whose movement pattern is indicated by a dotted line, transports material from input station 2 to output station 2 or 3.

There are two interesting aspects to the modeling of this type of system. First, it is necessary to model the possible interference of the two cranes in reaching output station 2. Second, it is necessary to represent the differing travel times between input and output stations. We describe next how Q-GERT can be used to model this type of transport system.

The Q-GERT procedures for modeling a crane system are pre-

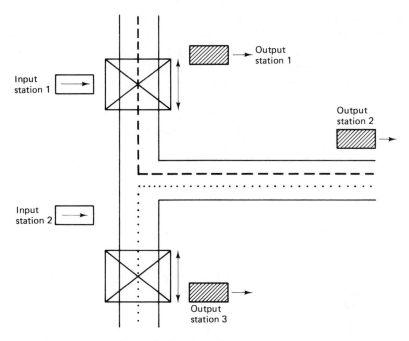

Figure 8-3 Schematic drawing of an overhead-crane system.

sented in stages, where each stage accounts for added features or difficulty. Typically, this is how models are developed. First, consider that crane interference is negligible and that travel times between stations need not be differentiated. Further assume that both input stations can be modeled in aggregate fashion by a single Q-node. We represent the output station by a Q-node and use an activity with parallel identical servers to represent the cranes. If attribute 1 represents a load's destination, we can utilize the following network segment:

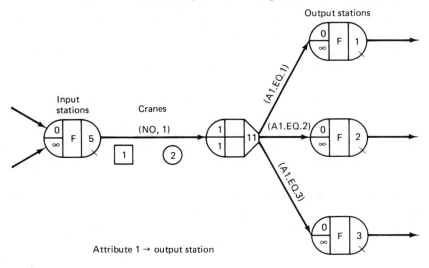

In this network segment, incoming transactions, which represent unit loads, arrive at Q-node 5. The two parallel servers associated with server 1 represent the two cranes. The travel time for each crane is described by a normal distribution (NO,1). When the transport operation is completed, that is, when the transaction arrives at node 4, the load is routed instantaneously according to the destination indicator, attribute 1, to station 1, 2, or 3, represented by Q-node 1, 2, or 3, respectively.

The assumptions of a single input queue and equal travel times are easily removed to yield the following network segment:

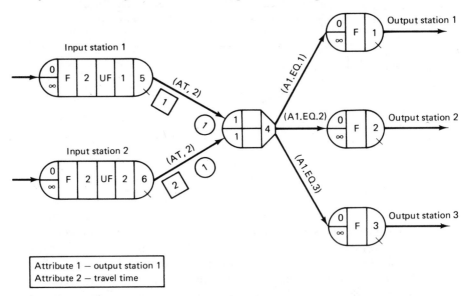

Attribute 1 — output station 1
Attribute 2 — travel time

In this illustration, Q-node 5 represents input station 1 and Q-node 6 represents input station 2. The attribute assignment at the Q-nodes defines attribute 2 as the travel time. User functions are used to determine travel times so that the starting location and the destination (represented by attribute 1) can be taken into account. Within function UF, user-defined distance tables and travel rates can be used to determine values of these travel times. Such tables could be established in subroutine UI.

In both of the formulations above the time to return to the input station is neglected. That is, once a server (crane) delivers the load, it becomes available for the next load. In actuality, the service operation consists of two activities: a delivery and a return. To represent this dual-stage service activity, we use the Q-GERT resource concepts as in Figure 8-4.

As before, Q-nodes 5 and 6 are the input stations and Q-nodes 1, 2, and 3 are the output stations. Attribute 2, defined at the input stations, is used to designate travel time. Resources 1 and 2 are used to represent cranes 1 and 2, respectively. ALLOCATE node 7 assigns

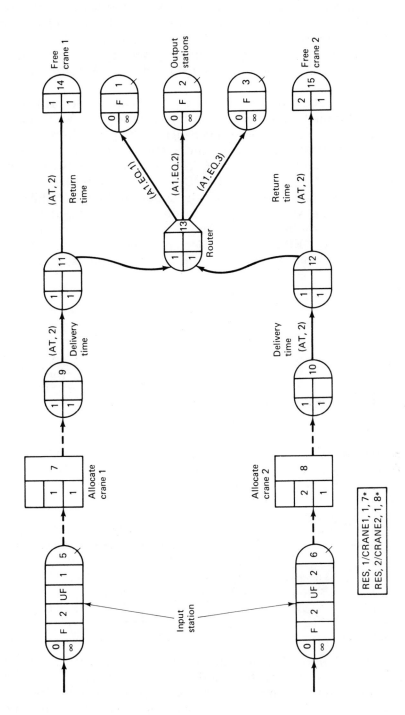

Figure 8-4 Q-GERT model of crane movements.

RES, 1/CRANE1, 1, 7*
RES, 2/CRANE2, 1, 8*

crane 1 to a load in Q-node 5 and routes the resulting transaction to node 9, where the delivery activity begins. All transactions reaching node 11 are instantaneously routed to their appropriate destination through node 13. In addition, a return-trip activity is scheduled. After the return trip, crane 1 becomes available when a transaction arrives at FREE node 14.

If the operation of the system allows items to be picked up at an output station for delivery to an input station, the modeling logic when a crane is freed needs to be changed. The general procedure for including alternative uses of a resource when it finishes a set of tasks is to incorporate additional ALLOCATE nodes in the network. For the situation alluded to above, an ALLOCATE node would be used to service items to be rerouted back to the input stations. In addition, an ALLOCATE node would be used to determine the input station to which the crane should be sent for its next forward movement. Following are the Q-GERT network elements that would be required to embellish the previous network with these added features.

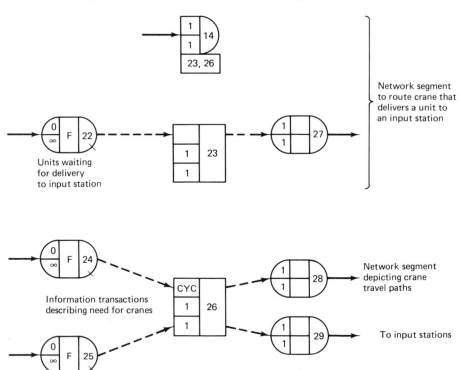

Network segment to route crane that delivers a unit to an input station

Units waiting for delivery to input station

Information transactions describing need for cranes

Network segment depicting crane travel paths

To input stations

At FREE node 14, one unit of crane 1 is allocated by polling ALLOCATE node 23 and then node 26. Preceding ALLOCATE node 23 are transactions waiting in Q-node 22 which are to be delivered to an input station. When a crane is allocated at node 23, the crane and the waiting unit are routed back to the input station through a network segment (not shown) starting at node 27. If no units are waiting at Q-node 22, an attempt is made to allocate the crane at node 26. Preceding node 26 are transactions in Q-nodes 24 and 25 which represent information about the needs of input stations regarding the use of cranes. Such transactions would be generated as units arrive to nodes 5 and 6 of the previous network segment. When a crane is allocated to return to an input station empty, the travel path to the input station would be depicted by the network segment starting at either node 28 or 29. Within the structure of the foregoing network segment, complex logical procedures regarding the disposition of a crane when it becomes free can be modeled.

The final concept illustrated in this section is the consideration of crane interference. Referring to the original crane schematic in Figure 8-3, note that both cranes utilize the same section of track to access output station 2. The key to accounting for crane interference is to model portions of the track that may be in conflict as a resource. To illustrate, consider the network in Figure 8-5. The network segments for the two cranes are similar, and we will limit discussion to the upper portion of the network, which models crane 1 movement.

First, observe that node 20 segregates loads by destination according to attribute 1. Loads destined for output station 1 wait for crane 1 (resource 1) at Q-node 5 and are routed to node 8 through node 7 when the crane becomes available. The queue selection rule for the ALLO-CATE node is important and permits evaluation of different priorities in selecting loads. A load destined for output station 1 travels to node 11 and then to Q-node 1. Node 11 also schedules the return trip and culminates in the freeing of crane 1 at node 14. Loads from input station 1 destined for output station 2, reside initially at Q-node 6 and are routed to Q-node 9 when crane 1 becomes available after traveling to the common track. Here, the loads must wait for resource 3, which represents the track in common with crane 2. Only when this track is available is travel to the destination permitted. The return trip is modeled in two segments; the first results in freeing the track (at node 13) and the second represents the time to go from the common track to input station 1, where the crane is freed (at node 14). Note that the common track cannot be used by crane 2 until crane 1 frees it at node 13.

8.5 SUMMARY

This chapter has illustrated how Q-GERT can be used to model the diverse special features and problems relating to material handling systems. The modeling representation for material handling equipment depends on the level of detail to be included in the model and the purpose for modeling. In applications of Q-GERT, material handling concepts are used extensively, as will be seen in Chapter 10.

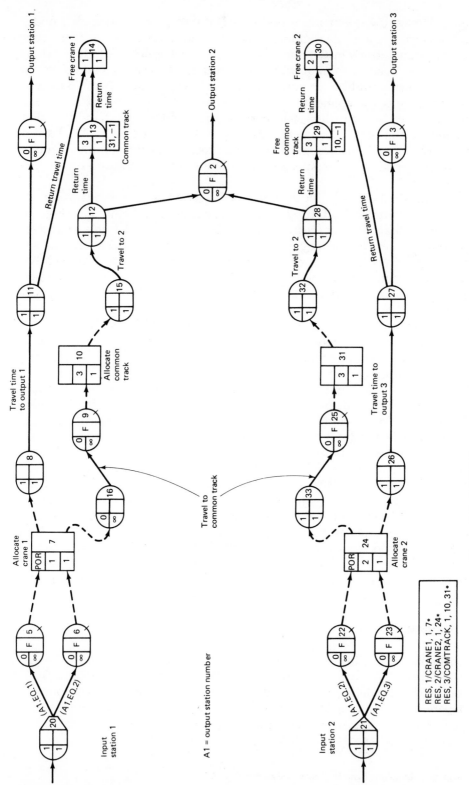

Figure 8-5 Q-GERT model of crane movements with interference.

8.6 EXERCISES

8-1. A conveyor system involves five servers stationed along a conveyor belt. Items to be processed by the servers arrive at the first server at a constant rate of four per minute. The service time by each server is 1 minute on the average and is exponentially distributed. Space for one item is provided before each server. At the end-of-service time, the item is removed from the system. The delay time to travel between servers on the conveyor is 1 minute. If an item cannot gain access to any of the servers, it is recycled to the first server, with a time delay of 5 minutes. Model this conveyor system to determine statistics on the time spent in the system by an item and the utilization of each server. Perform a simulation to obtain statistical estimates over a 500-minute period.

   Embellishments:
   (a) Repeat the simulation with a time delay of 2 minutes between servers. Is there an effect on the utilization of the servers because of a change in the time delay between servers, that is, the speed of the conveyor?
   (b) Evaluate the situation in which the last server has sufficient space for storage so that all items passing servers 1, 2, 3, and 4 are processed by server 5. Simulate this situation.
   (c) Assess the increased performance obtained by allowing a two-item buffer before each server. Based on the results of this study, specify how you would allocate 10 buffer spaces to the five servers.
   (d) Discuss how you would evaluate the trade-offs involved between reducing the number of servers in the conveyor system versus increasing the buffer size associated with each server.

8-2. For the conveyor system described in Exercise 8-1, a server number is assigned to an item at its arrival time. Build the Q-GERT models and obtain statistics using the Q-GERT processor for each of the following assignment procedures.
   (a) Random assignment of server numbers to items.
   (b) Assign server who has the smallest number in its queue.
   (c) Assign the server who has the lowest average utilization up to the time of arrival of the item.
   (d) Assign servers in a cyclic manner.
   (e) Assign to the first server who is idle when the item arrives.

8-3. For the conveyor system presented in Exercise 8-1, include within the Q-GERT model the logic that allows for decentralized decision making by deciding if a server should process an item when it arrives to a server station. Process the item at the station if:
   (a) The server is idle.
   (b) There is no server idle without recycling and space is available at the current service station.

8-4. Simulate the crane model given in Figure 8-5 to collect statistics on the throughput from each input station to each output station for the following data. The arrival rate to input station 1 is 4 units per hour, with 50% of the units to be sent to output station 1 and 50% to output station 2. The arrival rate to input station 2 is 2 units per hour, with every other unit to be sent to output station 2. The travel and return times (hours) from input stations to output stations are given in the following table.

| | | | Output Stations | |
| | | | Common | |
		1	Track[a]	3
	Travel to	0.12	0.05	—
1				
Return from	0.10	0.04	—
	Travel to	—	0.08	0.24
2				
Return from	—	0.06	0.22

[a] Each crane movement holds the common track an additional 0.1 hour.

Run the model assuming that all the times in the travel and return time matrix are constants. Repeat the analysis assuming that the times are normally distributed with a mean equal to the value given in the table and a standard deviation equal to one-tenth of the mean.

Embellishments:

(a) Evaluate the impact of giving priority to jobs that do not require the common track, that is, to jobs destined to output stations 1 and 3.

(b) Develop a procedure for investigating the impact of having two separate crane systems which do not require a common track, hence involve no interference. In this procedure, establish a cost structure to evaluate the potential savings due to reduction of interference time. Develop a Q-GERT model from which an assessment of this new system operation can be evaluated.

9

Production Planning – Special Topics

9.1 INTRODUCTION

Production planning is a broad field with many special topics. The purpose of this chapter is to explain a few of these topics in terms of network models. Our intention is to illustrate the flexibility available for both defining and using a network orientation.

The special topics of preemption of a service activity, machine maintenance and failure, queueing situations requiring both workers and machines, and job shop routing were selected for presentation. Models associated with these topics are frequently needed in applications. In addition, new modeling viewpoints are illustrated in the discussions. Only a cursory review of modeling inspection processes and work flow for batches of items is presented since these subjects are discussed elsewhere in the book in a different context.

9.2 PREEMPTING A SERVICE ACTIVITY

In planning production it is sometimes necessary to give priority to one class of jobs even to the extent of stopping the processing on one job in order to start a different type of job. Consider the situation where jobs of types 1 and 2 are processed by machine 1. The jobs are sequenced in a queue by giving priority to type 1 jobs. Furthermore, when a job of type 1 enters the work area and a job of type 2 is being machined, the machining is stopped and the type 2 job is returned to the queue so that the higher-priority job can be processed. The following network segment can be used to represent this situation.

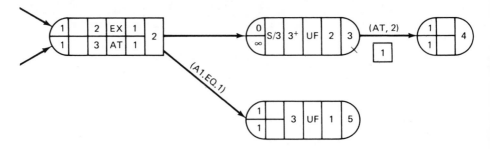

Legend:

ATRIB(1) = job type
ATRIB(2) = execution time
ATRIB(3) = queue ranking value

Both job types (attribute 1 represents job type) arrive at node 2, where a processing time value is assigned to attribute 2 for use later as the time specification for server 1. Attribute 3 is a value upon which queue ranking is based and is initially set equal to attribute 1 (job type). When a job is preempted, attribute 3 is set equal to 1.5 and the job is sent back to Q-node 3. Since Q-node 3 is ranked S/3, preempted jobs will be placed ahead of type 2 jobs but behind any type 1 jobs that might arrive.

To determine whether preempting is to occur, a check is made to see if server 1 is machining a job of type 2. This information must be maintained in a user-defined local variable which we name IJOB. This variable is initially set to 2 in UI and is updated each time a service is started on a job by a call to function UF from Q-node 3 with an argument of 2. This user function, which is called when a transaction enters service, sets IJOB to the job type being processed. At node 5, which is reached only for type 1 jobs, user function 1 is invoked. If the job type being processed (IJOB) is 1, no action is taken. If the server is busy with a job of type 2, subroutine STAGO is called† to stop the service and return the preempted transaction to Q-node 3 with attribute 2 equal to the remaining service time and attribute 3 equal to 1.5. It is important that the new job transaction arrive at Q-node 3 prior to releasing node 5 so that the new job transaction is at the front of the queue when preemption occurs. Since both activities emanating from node 2 have zero times, they will be completed in the same order in which they are started. Thus, it is important that the activity from node 2 to node 3 be first on the input statements or that an infinitesimal time

†The subroutine STAGO(NSERV,NODE,TIME,ICATT,ATT) causes server NSERV to stop processing a transaction and sends the transaction stopped to the node NODE with a delay of TIME. If ICATT is set to 1, the attributes of the transaction are changed to the user-specified vector ATT.

```
                           FUNCTION UF(IFN)
                           COMMON/UCOM1/IJOB,ATT(3)
                     C**** SET UF = 0.0 FOR EITHER USER FUNCTION
                           UF = 0.0
                           GO TO (1,2),IFN
                     C**** IF MACHINE IS PROCESSING
                     C**** A TYPE 1 JOB, DO NOT PREEMPT
                         1 IF (IJOB.EQ.1)RETURN
                     C**** PREEMPT JOB
                           ATT(1)=1
                           ATT(2)=REMST(1)
                           ATT(3)=1.5
                           CALL STAGO(1,3,0.0,1,ATT)
                           RETURN
                     C**** SET IJOB TO JOB TYPE BEING PROCESSED
```

Figure 9-1 Function UF(IFN) for preempting server example.

```
                         2 IJOB=GATRB(1)
                           RETURN
                           END
```

be assigned to the activity leading to node 5. The code for function UF(IFN) to accomplish these operations is shown in Figure 9-1. This code provides the basis for complex preemptions of service activities.

9.3 MODELING MACHINE MAINTENANCE AND FAILURE

Machine maintenance or failure changes the availability of a machine to process items. This selection describes how to model maintenance operations and machine failures by representing the machine as a resource.† Consider the one-machine queueing situation where the machine is modeled by a resource as in formulation (a) on p. 196. ALLOCATE node 11 allocates the machine to a transaction arriving or waiting at Q-node 10. Activity 1 represents the time to perform the service activity. At FREE node 13, the server is freed and is allocated to any waiting transactions at Q-node 10 by ALLOCATE node 11.

Now suppose that after every machining there is a 10% chance that the machine will require a 5-minute maintenance operation. We can model this situation by incorporating probabilistic branching in the network as in Figure (b). DETERMINISTIC branching is performed at node 19 following machine processing. One branch models the disposition of the job and the other the disposition of the machine. In the previous model, this was not required at node 13, as the machine was immediately available to process a waiting job. When maintenance operations may be required, we add probabilistic branching as shown at node 14. With probability 0.9, a transaction is sent immediately to node 13, where the machine is freed to be reallocated at node 11. Ten percent of the time a maintenance operation is performed which takes 5 minutes, as indicated by activity 2. This maintenance time on the machine makes it unavailable for processing during the 5-minute period.

This network representation accounts accurately for the added delays encountered due to machine maintenance. However, utilization statistics will not distinguish between maintenance time and processing time, as no differentiation between service and maintenance activities

†Pritsker [154] shows how server activity concepts can account for machine failure when augmented by user functions that use subroutines STAGO and PTIN.

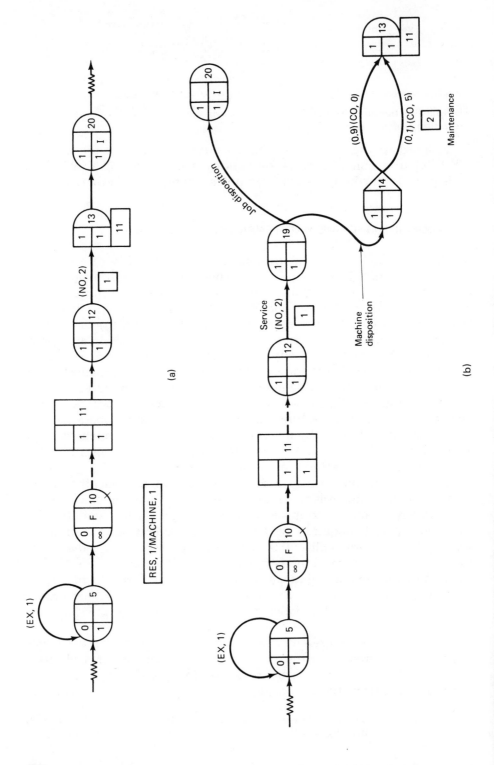

(a)

(b)

has been indicated. To make a differentiation, the maintenance time must not be considered as busy time for the machine. This is accomplished by decreasing resource availability prior to the 5-minute maintenance time through the use of an ALTER node. After maintenance, another ALTER node is used to indicate that the machine is operating again. Following is the network segment with these alter nodes added after node 14.

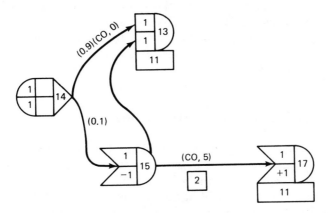

In this network segment, node 15 requests that the capacity of the machine be reduced by 1 when maintenance on the machine is to be performed. The branch from node 15 to FREE node 13 causes this reduction to occur, as altering occurs only when a machine is not in use. The freed machine is not made available, as the capacity change request made at ALTER node 15 is satisfied before a reallocation is made. The branch from node 15 to node 17 represents the 5-minute maintenance operation, after which the machine is put back into service by ALTER node 17.

In the examples above, maintenance is modeled as a probabilistic event following a service operation. Suppose that we desire to have maintenance occur periodically. The following disjoint network used in conjunction with the original network models a first maintenance operation at time 60, the length of maintenance as 5 time units, and the time until the next maintenance as 55 time units.

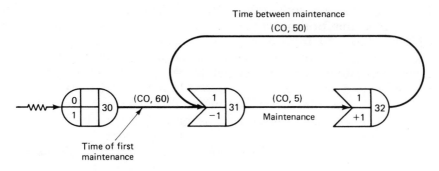

This model causes maintenance to be performed at the first opportunity following the completion of processing. If we were modeling failure, processing should be halted and repair action taken immediately. To model failures, the repair activity would have a duration as specified in a user function (UF), which calls subroutine HALTA to stop machine processing immediately. Subroutine PTIN would be used to route the transaction interrupted either back to the work queue or out of the system. Subroutine HALTA returns the remaining processing time for the job interrupted, and it can be used as an attribute in further processing of the interrupted job. As in the case of preempting jobs, attribute information and queue ranking procedures could be used to give priority to partially processed jobs.

9.4 LABOR-LIMITED QUEUEING SITUATIONS

In our discussion so far we have considered queueing situations where only one type of resource is in scarce supply. That is, we have modeled jobs arriving at work stations and awaiting one critical resource, machines. Any other resource that may be needed in the service operation has heretofore been assumed available. Suppose that labor is not always immediately available, as is the case when workers operate several machines at different locations. If labor is required for a machine operation but is currently unavailable, an idle machine will remain idle even though a job is waiting for it. This section shows how this situation can be modeled. The concepts presented are applicable to multiconstrained resource situations in general. For illustrative purposes, we restrict the discussion to labor-limited machine operations. Considerable research has been performed in this area [81,82,138].

There are two direct ways for modeling a service operation that requires multiple resource types. One involves the use of resource concepts; the second is the use of the ASM queue selection option of the S-node.

9.4.1 Resource Method

Consider a two-work station situation in which each work station has one machine. Both machines require a setup operation for each job and this setup is performed manually. A single operator is assigned the task of setting up the machines. The network shown in Figure 9-2 models this situation assuming that there is an equal likelihood that jobs are routed to either work station. Jobs for work station 1 arrive at Q-node 4 and jobs for work station 2 at Q-node 5. Resource 1 is machine 1, resource 2 is machine 2, resource 3 is the operator. All resources have a maximum capacity of 1. The network logic is the same at each station, and we will describe only the flow through work sta-

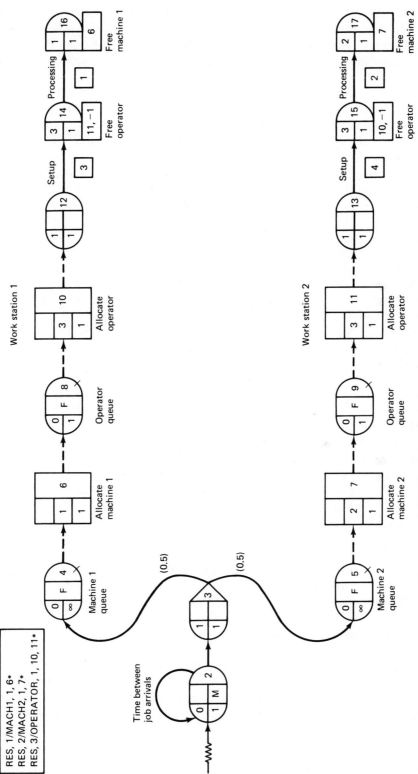

Figure 9-2 Q-GERT model of two work stations using a single operator.

tion 1. ALLOCATE node 6 allocates machine 1 to the first job in Q-node 4 if the one unit of resource 1 is not in use. Once this allocation is made, machine 1 is unavailable until freed (at node 16), which represents the completion of machining for that job. ALLOCATE node 10 attempts to allocate resource 3 (the operator) to the transaction representing a job–machine combination waiting in Q-node 8. If the operator is busy, the transaction waits in Q-node 8. If the operator is available, ALLOCATE node 10 routes the transaction to node 12 and activity 3, the setup for machine 1, is started. During the performance of activity 3, both machine 1 and the operator are in use. Hence, it is possible for jobs to build up in Q-node 4 awaiting machine 1. While this setup is ongoing, machining may be ongoing at work station 2 (activity 2) since this does not require the operator. However, setup (activity 4) at station 2 cannot be ongoing since there is only one operator (resource 3) and he or she is in use. Hence, during setup at station 1, jobs may accumulate at Q-nodes 4, 5, and 9.

When the setup at work station 1 is completed, activity 1 (machining) begins without delay. Also at this time, FREE node 14 frees the operator and ALLOCATE node 11 is interrogated to see if a setup at work station 2 can be started. There is no need to poll ALLOCATE node 10, as machine 1 is in use and a -1 ends the list under FREE node 14. If there were more than 2 stations, say n stations, the list of ALLOCATE nodes under a FREE node would contain $n - 1$ entries. The ordering of these nodes would be important since this would control the sequencing to be followed on the part of the operator when a choice of setup jobs exists. In the two-machine example, this choice does not exist.

After machining (activity 1), the job leaves station 1 and the machine (resource 1) is freed at node 16. ALLOCATE node 6 then checks to see if another job in Q-node 4 is waiting for a setup.

As mentioned previously, the logic at station 2 is similar. Through this use of resources, at most one setup will be ongoing at a time and jobs await setup by the operator before being processed. This added resource constraint will increase the idle time of the machines under heavy job loads and for this reason may be an important consideration. The reader should note that this example can easily be extended to situations involving additional stations, machines, and operators. Furthermore, additional types of critical resources can be modeled.

9.4.2 Modeling Labor Shifts

Another aspect of resource-constrained queueing situations involves a fluctuating supply of one or more resources. In one of the formulations given above, we used a disjoint network comprised of ALTER nodes to model changing machine availability. In a similar fashion, we can use the following network to represent a shift change for operators:

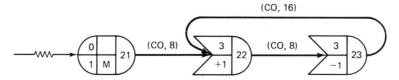

At time 8 we add one additional operator to the system by a transaction arrival to ALTER node 22. Resource 3 stays at this increased level for the next 8 time units. At node 23, we decrease the number by one and this capacity level persists for 16 time units, as modeled by the activity emanating from node 23.

9.4.3 S-node Method

The assembly (ASM) queue selection option of the S-node can also be used to model multiple-resource-constrained queueing situations. This approach recognizes that in a labor-constrained queueing situation, a job must be at the station, a machine must be available, *and* an operator must be available. It is this *and* logic that is represented by the S-node assembly (ASM) operation. An S-node with the ASM rule does not initiate service unless there is a transaction in each Q-node preceding the S-node. The network in Figure 9-3 represents a single-machine, single-operator situation modeled with the S-node having the ASM option. A transaction in a Q-node on the input side of the S-node satisfies one requirement for service to begin. A transaction in Q-node 1 represents an incoming job; in Q-node 2, a machine availability; and in Q-node 3, an available operator. We start with one transaction in Q-node 2 and one in Q-node 3. When a job transaction arrives at Q-node 1, S-node 4 assembles the three transactions and initiates service activity 1, which represents a setup. After setup, the operator becomes available and a transaction is routed from node 5 to Q-node 3 to represent operator availability. Whether this is physical movement or not is unimportant. The transaction in Q-node 3 represents an information signal indicating that the operator is available. Since a signal is not being sent back to Q-node 2 at this point, the machine is not available and the next setup cannot begin even if jobs are waiting in Q-node 1 and an idle operator exists in Q-node 3.

Node 5 also routes a transaction to Q-node 6. There is never any waiting at this Q-node since all delays occur prior to the S-node and all activities after the S-node proceed sequentially. The only reason a Q-node was included was to specify that activity 2 is a server and to ensure that utilization statistics on machine usage would be collected. After machining, node 7 routes the job transaction to other work areas

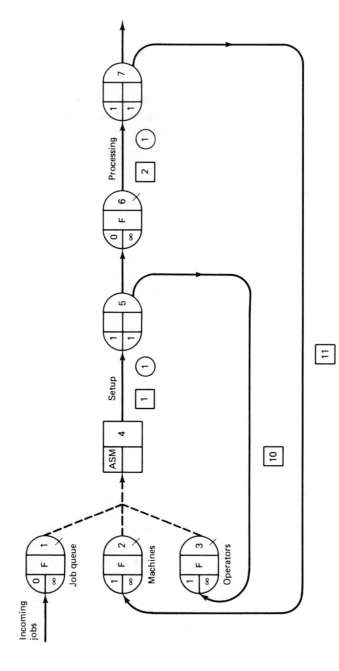

Figure 9-3 S-node approach to labor-constrained queueing situations.

(not shown) and also returns a transaction to Q-node 2 to represent the machine's availability.

Statistics on the number of transactions in Q-node 2 provide the fraction of time the machine is not being used for setup or machining. Similarly, the average number in Q-node 3 is the fraction of time the operator is idle. The fraction of time spent in setup is obtained from the average utilization of server 1, and the fraction of time spent machining is the average utilization of server 2.

Activities 10 and 11 represent the time to make the operator and machine available after setup and machining, respectively. This time can be zero or can be used to model post-processing delays. Post-processing delays may be complex and network segments may be necessary to model them.

One method of modeling shift changes for the operator is to define attribute 1 as the start time of the next shift. By using conditional branching at node 5, the operator return can be delayed if the condition (TNOW.GE.A1) is satisfied. In addition to delaying the operator when the condition is satisfied, the value of attribute 1 would need to be updated to the start time of the following shift.

The network presented in Figure 9-3 can be enhanced to model multiple machines and multiple operators by making appropriate changes to the initial queue lengths and queue capacities of Q-nodes 2 and 3, and the number of parallel servers prescribed for activities 1 and 2. For nonidentical operators, parallel branches emanating from S-node 4 would be employed. If nonidentical machines are to be modeled, an S-node would be required following Q-node 6.

A direct extension of the model in Figure 9-3 is the model presented in Figure 9-4, where the operator performs setup operations at two different work stations. In this case, Q-node 3 is associated with two S-nodes and there is a choice of which work station to go to if both are ready for setup. This choice is specified on input by indicating the order in which to poll the S-nodes associated with Q-node 3 when a transaction arrives at Q-node 3.

9.5 MODELING INSPECTION PROCESSES AND REWORK ACTIVITIES

An inspection activity may be performed after a machining operation, which results in some jobs being reworked or rejected. The results of inspection can be modeled by probabilistic branching, where the probabilities of acceptance, rework, and rejection are prescribed for branches following the inspection operation. To illustrate, consider the case of a single machine operation followed by an inspection process which is performed by either of two inspectors. Past data indicate that 5% of all

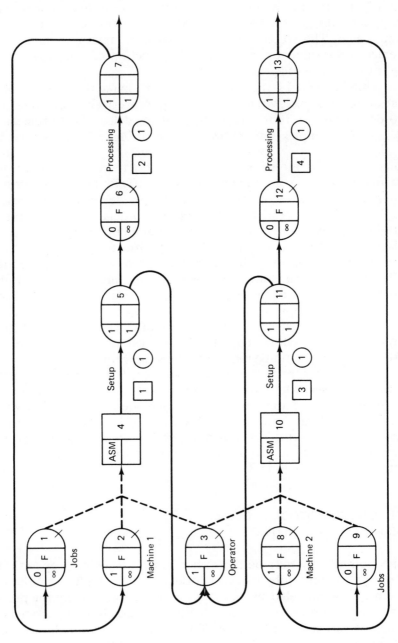

Figure 9-4 S-node approach to a labor-constrained, two-machine queueing situation.

jobs are rejected, 10% require reworking, and 85% are accepted. This situation is modeled by formulation (a) on p. 206. Work arrives at Q-node 2 and is sequenced in a FIFO manner. Machine processing is represented by server 1. Finished work awaiting inspection awaits at Q-node 3. Server branch 2 represents the two parallel inspectors. Branching from node 4 is probabilistic in accordance with the probabilities prescribed for the outcome of inspection. Accepted work is routed to node 6, rejected work is routed to node 5, and jobs to be reworked are routed back to Q-node 2.

Theoretically, a transaction can indefinitely loop from node 2 to 3 to 4 and then back to Q-node 2. However, on each loop there is only a 0.10 probability of returning to node 2. To limit the number of loops, attribute assignments can be used as formulation (b) on p. 206. Attribute 1 is used to represent the number of times a job has been machined. Attribute 1 is initially zero (set at source node 1) and then is increased by 1 (1+,CO,1) every time the transaction passes through Q-node 2. Node 7 is specified to perform conditional, take-first branching to limit the number of processing operations to 3. If the job fails inspection when attribute 1 equals 3, it is rejected by routing it from node 7 to node 5.

Note that by changing the queue ranking procedure of node 2 to B/1, we can give priority to jobs that need reworking. It may also be desirable to alter the machine time for reworked items. This can be accomplished by introducing attribute 2 as the machine time and prescribing (AT,2) as the time duration for server 1. Normal machine times can be established at source node 1 by assigning a value to attribute 2. Node 7 can be used to prescribe a value to attribute 2 when reworking is required.

Another embellishment is to modify the branching probabilities of node 4 based on the number of times the job has been reworked. This conditional probability may be modeled as shown on p. 207. Node 20 is used to determine which loop is in progress. Nodes 21, 22, and 23, with their associated branching probabilities, specify the chance of each inspection outcome for each possible loop value. An alternative method of representing this situation is to use attribute-based probabilistic branching (see Section 2.4.2) and to assign the probability values to attributes in a user function.

9.6 MODELING WORK FLOW IN BATCHES OR LOADS

In some models it is convenient to use a single transaction to represent a batch or a load of individual units. In modeling the flow of checks through a large bank, for example, where hundreds of thousands of

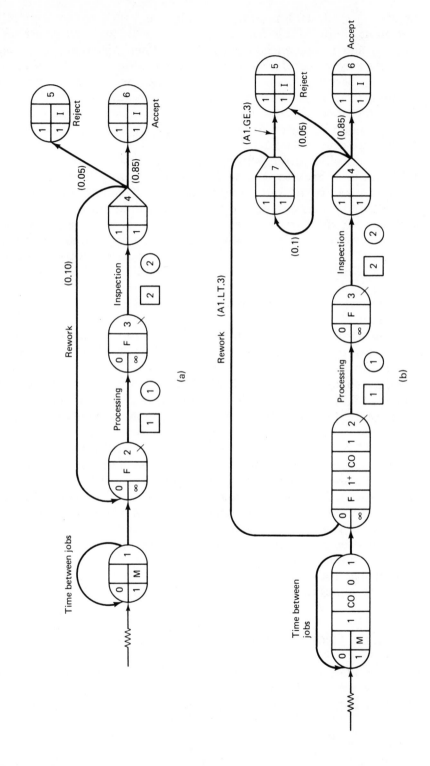

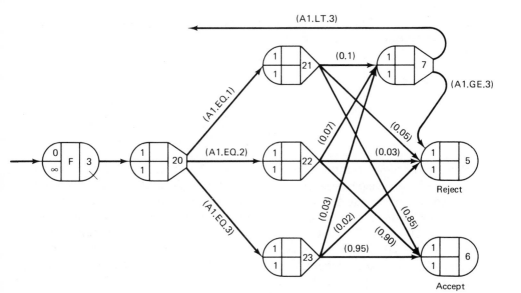

checks are processed each day, modeling batches of checks is a reasonable strategy. Although there is a reluctance to model situations at an aggregate level, it should be recognized that all models are abstractions of reality. It is not the one-to-one correspondence between system items and model transactions that should be of highest import but the timeliness and usefulness of the model in helping to make decisions and in comparing alternatives.

When a single transaction represents a batch of units, an attribute of the transaction is set equal to the size of the batch. Since batch size may vary, this attribute identification is important information that can be used in defining service times, routing, job loading, and job sequencing. When a transaction represents a batch, performance measures must take cognizance of different weights to be attached based on the batch size. In most cases, this can be accomplished by computing statistics on batch size as was done in the throughput analysis discussed in Section 6.2.1.

It is sometimes necessary to model the flow of individual units through a portion of the network, then accumulate units into loads, route the loads through other portions of the network, and finally disassemble loads into units again. This occurs with material handling models where individual items are assembled into pallet loads prior to transport and disassembled into individual items later. Q-GERT provides procedures for accumulating transactions into loads and breaking loads down into units. For example, if 10 unit transactions are to be accumulated into one load transaction, we can require 10 incoming transactions to release a node as shown here.

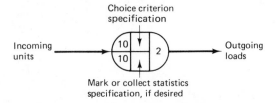

For this network segment, node 2 requires 10 incoming transactions for node release. Regardless of when each incoming unit arrives at node 2, a load departs node 2 only after each tenth arrival. An attribute assignment at node 2 could be performed if it were necessary to identify a load as 10 units. The attributes of the outgoing load will be taken from one of the 10 incoming units. The choice criterion for the node specifies the unit whose attributes are saved. The time the batch is created can be set by marking at node 2.

If incoming transactions represent loads of varying size and it is desired to accumulate these until a large load of a specified size is reached, we would employ a user function to perform the accumulation. To illustrate, assume that attribute 1 represents load size and that a resulting load size that equals or exceeds 100 is desired. The following network segment could be used.

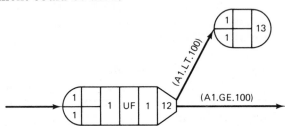

Branching from node 12 is conditional, take-first. The transaction is deleted from the system if the load requirement has not reached 100 by routing it to node 13. (Alternatively, no branch for this condition need be specified.) The second branch from node 12 represents the routing of an assembled load; that is, the branching condition of (A1.GE.100) is met.

In this network segment, the attribute assignment for node 12 is a user function (1,UF,1) which defines attribute 1 equal to the sum of incoming values for attribute 1. To do this, a local variable is maintained as the sum of previous attribute 1 values. The code for user function 1 is

```
1 TSUM=TSUM+GATRB(1)
  UF=TSUM
  IF(TSUM.GE.100.)TSUM=0.0
  RETURN
```

The variable TSUM should be initialized to zero in a DATA statement in subroutine UF. (If more than one run is to be performed, TSUM should be initialized in subroutine UI and put in a user COMMON block.) User function 1 begins by increasing TSUM by the current value for attribute 1 as obtained from GATRB(1). Attribute 1 of the current transaction will be equal to this value by the statement UF=TSUM. If TSUM is greater than or equal to 100, it is reset to zero after UF is prescribed. If exactly 100 unit loads are required, UF should be set to 100 when TSUM > 100 and TSUM reset to TSUM - 100.

The ASM option of the S-node can also be used to assemble transactions into loads. The use of this option for assembling transactions in assembly operations is discussed in Section 7.7. The reader is also referred to Section 2.5.3. MATCH nodes also provide specialized assembly logic since a MATCH node can be used to halt the flow of transactions until a group with the same attribute value is available. The MATCH node can then route all the transactions to an accumulate node for assembly.

Several procedures are also available to model disassembly. The basic method involves the use of deterministic routing. To generate five transactions from one incoming transaction, deterministic routing through five branches is used, as follows:

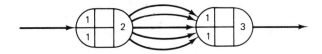

An alternative to using multiple branches is to use a user function and subroutine PTIN to put five units in the network. Another alternative is to employ attribute-based routing as shown in the following network segment.

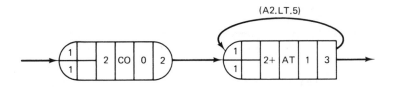

Each incoming transaction to node 2 is routed to node 3, where five transactions are generated.

A similar procedure is used to generate unit transactions from a batch transaction of varying size. If size is represented by attribute 1, we generate a transaction, decrease the value of attribute 1 by one, and continue until attribute 1 is no longer greater than zero. A network segment to do this is shown here.

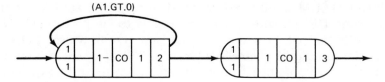

In this segment, each incoming load to node 2 generates A1 transactions. Each transaction is routed to node 3, where its batch size attribute is reset to one.

9.7 JOB SHOP ROUTING USING ROUTE SHEETS

In Chapter 6 we discussed the use of conditional, take-first routing as a loading mechanism and then showed how the use of the queue selection capability of the S-node extends the routing capability by taking into account Q-node status. In this section we illustrate how the conditional, take-first routing can be used to direct jobs through work stations based on a predetermined route sheet associated with each job. A route sheet specifies the sequence of work stations that a job is to visit.

Consider the job shop depicted in Figure 9-5, where a job's route sheet is depicted in a rectangle representing the job. Thus, the job first in queue (closest to the work stations) requires processing at station 2 and then at station 1. The second job requires processing at station 2 first, then at station 3. The third job is to be routed to all 3 stations in the order 1, 2, and 3.

In Q-GERT to follow the sequence specified by a route sheet, we make use of attribute information and conditional, take-first routing based on attribute value. We define the first attribute of a transaction as the next station on the route sheet and attribute 2 to be the number of the attribute which contains the next station to which the job is to be routed. Successive attributes correspond to the list of stations in their order of appearance on the route sheet. We use a zero to indicate

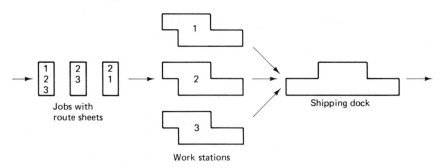

Figure 9-5 Schematic diagram of job route sheets in a work station environment.

the end of the list. Hence, the attributes of the transaction for job 1 of Figure 9-5 would initially be defined as follows:

Attribute 1 = 2   Next station
Attribute 2 = 3   Attribute number containing next station
Attribute 3 = 2 ⎫
Attribute 4 = 1 ⎬ Stations on route sheet
Attribute 5 = 0 ⎭

From these values and the definitions above we see that the next station to be visited is 2 (attribute 1). Attribute 3 contains this next station number as specified by attribute 2. Attributes 3, 4, and 5 correspond to the list of stations on the route sheet, with attribute 5 set to indicate that the job is to depart the system after processing is completed at the station specified by the previous attribute.

The Q-GERT network segment depicted in Figure 9-6 illustrates the routing of jobs using the attributes defined above. In this network, Q-node i is the queue for work station i and incoming transactions arrive at node 10. It is assumed that prior to this point, attribute assignments have been established in accordance with the route sheet. At node 10, the job is routed to the appropriate work station on the basis of attribute 1. After processing at the station, the job transaction is routed to node 11. A value assignment at node 11 changes the pointer to the next station on the route sheet by adding 1 to attribute 2 using the assignment (2+,CO,1). A second assignment at node 11 is (1,UF,1), which sets the value of attribute 1 equal to the value of the attribute whose number is represented by attribute 2. This is accomplished by the following statements in function UF:

```
1  I=GATRB(2)
   UF=GATRB(I)
   RETURN
```

The conditional routing from node 11 is based on attribute 1, which sends the job transaction to node 10 for rerouting to the next station if there is another station on the route sheet. Otherwise, the job transaction is routed to node 4, the sink node for jobs. In summary, after completion of processing at each station, the transaction is routed to node 11, attribute 2 is increased by 1, a new value for attribute 1 is obtained and routing is performed again. The process continues until each job is routed through its routing sequence and departs through node 4.

There are several ways to establish the routing sequence initially. If a set of jobs with a prescribed set of route sheets are to be modeled, subroutine UI should be used. The sequence of station numbers on each route sheet is input in this routine and stored in a user-defined array. To put the appropriate transactions into the system, the following net-

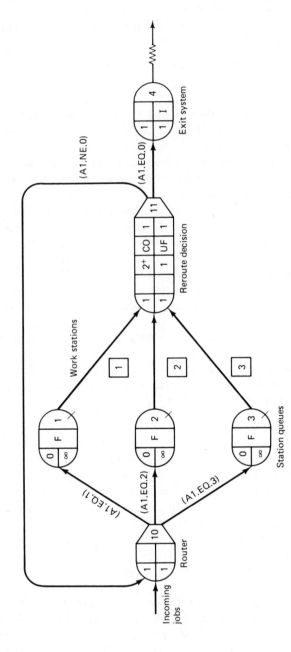

Figure 9-6 Work station routing of transactions using route sheets: A1, next work station.

work segment would be used:

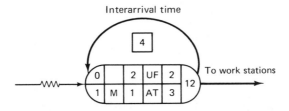

Attribute 2 is defined in function UF. In this user function, attributes 3, 4, and so on are defined as the stations numbers on the appropriate route sheet.† The route sheets would be read through a READ statement. These attribute assignments are made through the use of subroutine PUTAT. Activity 4 defines the time between creation of new jobs.

Sometimes it is desirable to generate arrivals with a route sheet specified in a probabilistic fashion. This could be performed in function UF with the use of function DRAND and subroutine PTIN, or through probabilistic routing. The latter has the advantage of providing a graphical representation and the disadvantage of requiring many nodes and branches for complex processes. An example of the use of a probabilistic-based routing model is shown in Figure 9-7. At node 12 a transaction is generated at time zero and after each completion of activity 10. Node 13 routes transactions probabilistically to nodes 14, 15, or 16. These nodes assign the first station number to attribute 3. Hence, there is a 30% chance that station 1 is first, a 40% chance that station 2 is first, and a 30% chance that station 3 is first. Probabilistic routing from nodes 14, 15, or 16 causes attribute 4 to be defined. Similarly, nodes 20, 21, and 22 define attribute 5 as the third station. Note that if station 3 is second on the route sheet, there is a 10% chance that a third station need not be visited. This scheme does not allow the same station to be prescribed for two sequential operations, although it is possible for the same station to be prescribed for the first and third routing positions. If this is not desirable, user functions or conditional routing can be incorporated to check for this condition and disallow it.

A more general method for generating a routing is to define an array P(I,J) that prescribes the probability of routing from station I to station J. Let the last column in the array represent an "exit" station. Define CP(I,J) to be $\Sigma_{k=1}^{J}$ P(I,k); that is, accumulate probabilities for each row. Random assignment to the first station can be done using function DRAND(ISTRM). If the station selected is I1, the second station is selected by using the transition probabilities contained in row I1. The code illustrating the writing of the user function for this procedure

---

†To avoid the use of an excessive number of attributes in the case of a large number of stations, the use of auxiliary attributes is recommended (see Section 3.13).

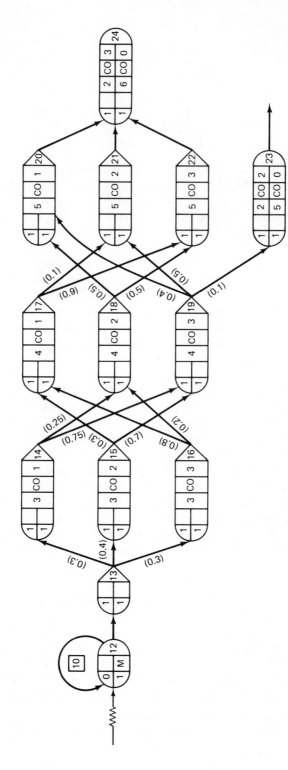

Figure 9-7 Probabilistic determination of work stations for a route sheet.

assuming N work stations (the Nth work station is for departure of units), at most M visits to work stations, and the cumulative probability that a work station is first on the route sheet is stored in FIRST(I) is shown below.

```
C**** USER FUNCTION CODE TO ROUTE A JOB TO AT MOST M WORK STATIONS
C**** N IS THE NUMBER OF DIFFERENT WORK STATIONS
C**** GENERATE A RANDOM NUMBER R
      R=DRAND(1)
C**** RANDOMLY SELECT FIRST STATION
      DO 10 I=1,N
      I1=I
      IF (R.LE.FIRST(I)) GO TO 20
   10 CONTINUE
C**** ATT(IN) IS THE NUMBER OF THE WORK STATION THAT IS IN THE IN^th
C**** POSITION ON THE ROUTE SHEET,
C**** IF ATT(IN)=0 ROUTE SPECIFICATION COMPLETED.
   20 ATT(1)=I1
      DO 30 IN=2,M
      IN1=IN
      R=DRAND(1)
      DO 40 J=1,N
      J1=J
      IF (R.LE.CP(I1,J)) GO TO 35
   40 CONTINUE
C**** I1 IS CURRENT STATION
C**** J1 IS NEXT STATION
   35 IF (J1.EQ.N) GO TO 50
      ATT(IN1)=J1
      I1=J1
   30 CONTINUE
      IN1=M+1
   50 ATT(IN) = 0.0
C**** STORE ATTRIBUTES WITH TRANSACTION OR USE AN AUXILIARY ATTRIBUTE
C**** ARRAY.
```

This code would be part of a user function called from the node at which a job transaction and its route sheet are created. In subroutine UI, it would be required to establish the arrays FIRST and CP.

9.8 SUMMARY

The network concepts presented in this chapter can be used in conjunction with standard production planning models for evaluation purposes. The example network segments provide the basis for the inclusion of special production planning topics. The material can be used within the modeling approach proposed in this book: start with basic models and add new features as they are required to meet the purpose of the project.

9.9 EXERCISES

9-1. Consider a system that has two job types, a single work station, and a rule that has type 1 jobs preempting type 2 jobs. Discuss the effects of preemption (a) on the average time for each job type to proceed through a work station, (b) on the utilization of a work station, and (c) on the time spent in a queue by all jobs.

9-2. Specify the changes required in function UF presented in Figure 9-1 if the job that is preempted is not given priority over other type 1 jobs in the queue, and if the preempted job must be restarted.

9-3. Write function UF for preempting a server when there are three categories of jobs. Jobs that are preempted are to be placed at the front of their job class and their processing time is to be equal to the remaining processing time plus 0.1. The function is to be written so that the new processing time is not permitted to exceed the original processing time.

9-4. Build a model of a single-machine situation where the machine requires maintenance. Assume that maintenance activities are represented as jobs and are given priority over regular jobs. Maintenance jobs, however, do not preempt regular jobs.

9-5. Build a model of a single-machine situation which requires that maintenance be performed after every 25 services are completed on the machine.

9-6. A company produces two types of electronic meters which are installed in residential buildings to measure power consumption. Meters A and B are designed for different voltage and amperage ranges. The meters consist of two subassemblies, labeled C and D, and two parts, labeled E and F. Meter A is assembled out of subassemblies C and D and 2 part E's. Meter B is assembled out of subassemblies C and D and one part E and one part F. Subassembly C consists of subassembly D and one part F. Subassembly D consists of one part E and one part F. The production process involves the building of parts E and F and their inspection. After the inspection, defective parts are removed from the line. Part E has a probability of 0.05 of being rejected, and the probability of part F being rejected is 0.04.

The basic parts E and F are maintained in inventory. They are assembled into subassemblies C and D, which are also inventoried. In addition, the final products, meters A and B, are inventoried. The processing time for all parts have been determined to be normally distributed (truncated). The mean, standard deviation, minimum value, and maximum value of these normal distributions are presented in the following table.

Item	Mean	Standard Deviation	Minimum Value	Maximum Value
A	5.0	0.25	0	10
B	8.0	1.00	0	20
C	6.0	1.00	0	10
D	4.0	1.00	0	10
E	2.0	0.25	0	10
F	1.2	0.50	0	10

Develop a Q-GERT model to answer the following questions [85]:

(a) Given 50 units in initial inventory for parts E and F and 50 subassemblies C and D, how long does each process need to operate, on the average, to produce an order for 100 units of meters A and B? (Assume that no ending inventory is desired.)

(b) What is the production lead time required on the average to complete the scheduled orders of meters A and B?

(c) What percent of the time is each of the processes idle due to the lack of preprocess inventories?

(d) Is there sufficient production capacity to meet the order requirements in 1000 time units? Indicate which operations may be potential bottlenecks. How many units of each part are required to satisfy the order?

9-7. Describe how the S-node method for modeling labor limited queues allows for the direct reassignment of operators to different activities.

9-8. Modify the network presented in Figure 9-4 so that there is a duplicate of machine 1 that is always available for processing jobs.

9-9. Modify the second model presented in Section 9.5 so that after each rework operation, the probability of requiring rework decreases by 0.02 and the probability of passing inspection increases by 0.02.

9-10. (From Ref. 171) A production shop is comprised of six different groups of machines. Each group consists of a number of identical machines of a given kind, as indicated below.

Machine Group Number	Types of Machines in Group	Number of Machines in Group
1	Casting units	14
2	Lathes	5
3	Planers	4
4	Drill presses	8
5	Shapers	16
6	Polishing machines	4

Three different types of jobs move through the production shop. These job types are designated as type 1, type 2, and type 3. Each job type requires that operations be performed at specified kinds of machines in a specified sequence. All operation times are exponentially distributed. The visitation sequences and average operation times are shown in the following table.

Job Type	Total Number of Machines to Be Visited	Machine Visitation Sequence	Mean Operation Time (minutes)
1	4	Casting unit	125
		Planer	35
		Lathe	20
		Polishing machine	60
2	3	Shaper	105
		Drill press	90
		Lathe	65
3	5	Casting unit	235
		Shaper	250
		Drill press	50
		Planer	30
		Polishing machine	25

Jobs arrive at the shop with exponential interarrival times with a mean of 9.6 minutes. Twenty-four percent of the jobs in this stream are of type 1, 44% are of type 2, and the rest are of type 3. The type of arriving job is independent of the job type of the preceding arrival. Build a Q-GERT model that simulates the operation of the production shop for five separate 40-hour weeks to obtain:

(a) The distribution of job residence time in the shop, as a function of job type
(b) The utilization of the machines
(c) Queue statistics for each machine group

Embellishments:

(a) Employ a shortest-processing-time rule for ordering jobs waiting before each machine group. Compare output values.
(b) Give priority to jobs on the basis of type. Job type 3 is to have the highest priority, then type 2 and then type 1 jobs.
(c) Change the average job interarrival time to 9 minutes and evaluate system performance.
(d) Develop a cost structure for this problem that would enable you to specify how to spend $100,000 for new machines.

10

Production Planning – Applications

10.1 INTRODUCTION

Chapters 6 through 9 presented the general concepts and procedures in production planning. This chapter describes the application of network modeling to ongoing business operations and decisions. Five industrial studies that used Q-GERT to evaluate decision alternatives in production planning are presented. The industries involved are the steel, heavy machinery, oil, banking, and insurance industries. This diversity of industries was selected to illustrate the commonality of the planning problems across a spectrum of companies. Indeed, it is the commonality of management decision making that accounts for the wide application of network techniques in general and Q-GERT in particular. Close attention should be paid to the common considerations in each case study and the way in which these common system features are represented in Q-GERT.

Each study is discussed on two levels. The first level allows the reader to absorb the general system description and management concerns without involvement in the technical aspects of the model. The use of the output from the model is also presented with this objective in mind. The second level permits an analyst to see how specific system features were modeled using the Q-GERT network logic. The reader on this level should strive to understand the correspondence between the logic underlying the system being analyzed and the general Q-GERT network logic used to model the system. In addition, we indicate the correspondence between the desired system performance measures and the output provided by the Q-GERT processor.

The models described in this chapter have been abstracted from actual case studies with only the essential and novel elements presented. For additional details, the literature cited should be consulted.

10.2 EVALUATING CAPITAL EXPENDITURE
IN THE STEEL INDUSTRY

In the steel industry, as in most industries, capital expenditures are made in new facilities and equipment for the purpose of increasing the rate of production or throughput of a given facility. It is rare that a planned investment is known to meet with certainty new output requirements. Modeling has played a significant role in evaluating proposed capital expenditures by predicting their impact on productive capacity.

This section describes a Q-GERT study of a capital expenditure to be made by a major steel company.† The expenditure is for a new facility that would upgrade the quality of current production as well as increase throughput. From among several alternative production designs, the company desired to choose the one with the lowest cost that would be able to meet throughput and quality requirements. An alternative was selected and a Q-GERT model of the proposed system was built. Management specified a desired throughput level and the model was used to estimate the probability that this level of production could be met.

10.2.1 The System and Management Concerns

A schematic drawing of the proposed system is shown in Figure 10-1. Heated steel parts enter the system in the upper left corner of the figure. The first operation to be performed is rolling. Through a conveyor line transfer, the material is moved to a cooling area. Cranes then transfer the steel parts to another roller line, where a processing operation is performed. After processing, the individual steel parts are accumulated into loads and enter an overhead-crane material handling and storage system. Each load goes through a preliminary inspection process at station B. If the load fails the inspection, it waits for crane 1 to move it to station A. Rejects are removed from this station. If a load passes the initial inspection, it waits for a crane to move it to station C. Either crane 1 or crane 2 can perform this move. At station C the load is stored as it awaits a second inspection process. If a load passes

---

†In the interest of confidentiality, the model described herein has been simplified and hypothetical values employed.

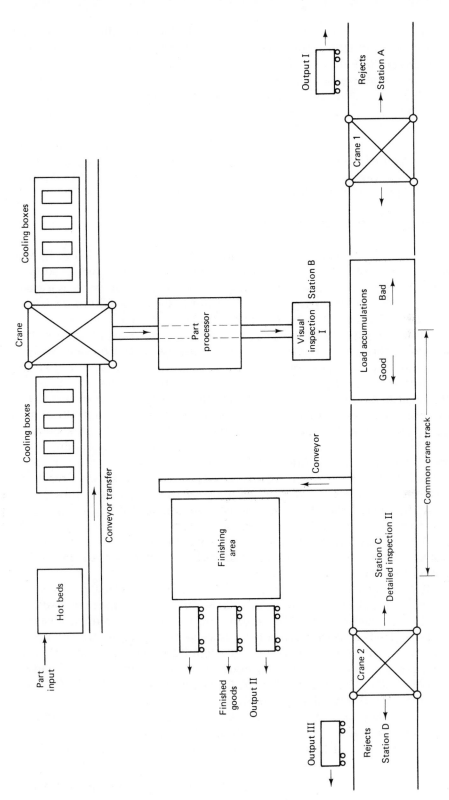

Figure 10-1 Schematic diagram for steel industry example.

this inspection, it is automatically moved along a roller line to the finishing area. Rejects are moved by crane 2 to station D, where a roller line removes them.

Management was concerned that delays due to crane interference along the track between stations B and C might prevent the system from achieving the required throughput. For this reason, an alternative crane system was designed and only the overhead-crane subsystem was modeled. A delivery rate was specified for steel entering the load accumulation center from the processing operation. The question posed was: What throughput can be expected from station C for the specified input rate and proposed design of the crane system?

10.2.2 The Q-GERT Model

A Q-GERT model of the system is shown in Figure 10-2. In the network, resources 1 and 2 are used to model cranes 1 and 2, respectively. Resource 3 is used to represent the portion of track between stations B and C which is common to both cranes. Inspection decisions are modeled by probabilistic routing at nodes 2 and 19.

Source node 1 and activity 10 represent the output of the part processor operation and thus provide the inputs to the model. Node 2 accumulates this output into loads of 10 units each by requiring 10 incoming transactions for release. Following the release of node 2, probabilistic routing of a load to Q-node 3 or Q-node 8 occurs. This represents the first inspection process. It is estimated that 5% of the loads will be rejected at this inspection and 95% will be accepted. Rejected loads wait in Q-node 3 for crane 1 to become available. When it does, the branch to node 6 is taken representing the time for crane 1 to deliver the load to station A. Node 6 collects statistics on the time between load arrivals to give an estimate of the throughput rate at station A. In Figure 10-2 this variable is labeled as output I. The activity from node 6 to node 7 represents the return trip of crane 1 to station B from station A. At the end of this trip, the crane is freed and ALLOCATE nodes 4 and 11 are checked, in that order, to determine the next task for crane 1.

Returning to the branching from node 2, loads that pass inspection at station B are routed to Q-node 8. Since these loads are destined for station C, the portion of track common to both cranes must be available prior to transport. A resource is used to represent this common track, as described in Chapter 8. ALLOCATE node 9 allocates this resource and places the load into Q-node 10. At this point the load can be moved by either crane 1 or crane 2. Consider crane 1 first. ALLOCATE node 11 tests the availability of this resource. If crane 1 is available, the load travels to station C and reaches node 14 in the network. At this point, two activities are initiated. First, the crane travels back to station B. On arrival at station B, the common portion of track is freed

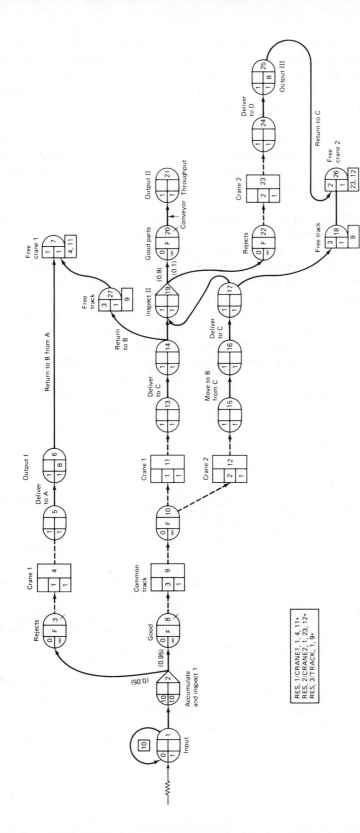

Figure 10-2 Q-GERT model of overhead-crane system.

(node 27) and the crane becomes available at station B (node 7). Second, the newly delivered load at station C is inspected. The outcome of the inspection is determined by node 19. As mentioned above, this load could also have been carried to station C by crane 2. This process is modeled by nodes 12, 15, 16, and 17. In the latter case, node 18 frees the track used by crane 2 and node 26 frees crane 2.

Rejects from the second inspection reside in Q-node 22, where they await crane 2 for transfer to station D. Node 25 collects statistics on this variable, which is labeled output III in Figure 10-2. After a return to station C, node 26 frees crane 2. Loads that pass the second inspection enter Q-node 20 and are removed from station C using a roller line. The number of loads reaching node 21 is a critical statistic of the model since it represents the throughput of finished product. Since node 21 represents the point of departure for finished product, the number of transactions passing through this node (maintained as the variable NTC(21)) is used to collect throughput statistics, as discussed in Section 6.2.1. The length of each run is specified on input as 1000 time units. (A figure suggested by management as a reasonable test period.) At the end of each network run, the variable NTC(21) represents the throughput of finished product for the 1000 time units. In subroutine UO, user statistical routines COL and HIS are used to collect observations on NTC(21) for the purpose of computing statistics and a histogram on system throughput. The following code is included in subroutine UO and executed after each network run.

```
SUBROUTINE UO
COMMON/QVAR/NDE,NFTBU(100),NREL(100),NRELP(100),NREL2(100),NRUN,
1NRUNS,NTC(100),PARAM(100,4),TBEG,TNOW
X=NTC(21)
CALL COL(X,1)
CALL HIS(X,1)
RETURN
END
```

By including this code, the computation of statistics and the printing of a histogram on NTC(21) and therefore system throughput is provided automatically on the Q-GERT output.

The sequencing of crane operations in this model is important and requires careful and precise specification. In Figure 10-2, the sequencing is specified by which Q-nodes are associated with which ALLOCATE nodes and by the order in which the ALLOCATE nodes are listed under each FREE node. For example, when crane 1 returns to station B at node 7, ALLOCATE node 4 is polled first and then node 11 is checked to see if the crane can be assigned. This means that crane 1 will be kept busy with loads between stations A and B as long as rejected loads are waiting at Q-node 3. An alternative operating procedure would be to combine ALLOCATE nodes 4 and 11 and employ a Queue Selection Rule to select from Q-nodes 3 and 10. Similarly, when crane 2 is freed at node 26, its disposition is controlled by the interrogation of ALLOCATE node 23 and then ALLOCATE node 12.

Hence, crane 2 is modeled to travel between stations C and D unless there are no rejected loads at station C.

10.2.3 Model Output and Use

Table 10-1 provides a summary of the output obtained from the model presented in Figure 10-2. Throughput statistics for finished product are obtained through user statistics as discussed above. Between-statistics give estimates of the rate at which rejects are delivered to stations A and D. This information is useful in determining the rate at which the interfacing roller lines must be able to remove units from the system. In-process inventory statistics are provided by the Q-node statistics for nodes 3, 8, 20, and 22. Resource utilization statistics provide estimates for the fraction of time each crane and the common track portion are in use.

An illustrative histogram representing throughput after 1000 hours is shown in Figure 10-3. This output is for 100 runs. Note that 5% of the time, throughput was less than 10,000 loads in 1000 hours. If we assume that management required a throughput of 10,000 loads in

TABLE 10-1 Summary of Performance Measures Computed
by the Model in Figure 10-2

Performance Measure	Q-GERT Statistic
Throughput of finished product (output II)	Statistics provided by user COLlect statistics on user variable 1 (NTC(21)); frequency distribution provided by HIStogram number 1
Rate of rejected loads delivered to station A (output I)	Between-statistics for node 6
Rate of rejected loads delivered to station D (output III)	Between-statistics for node 25
In-process inventory of inspection I rejects at station B	Q-node statistics for node 3
In-process inventory of inspection I accepted loads at station B	Q-node statistics for node 8
In-process inventory of inspection II rejects at station C	Q-node statistics for node 22
In-process inventory of inspection II accepted loads at station C	Q-node statistics for node 20
Utilization of crane 1	Resource statistics for resource 1
Utilization of crane 2	Resource statistics for resource 2
Utilization of track between stations B and C	Resource statistics for resource 3

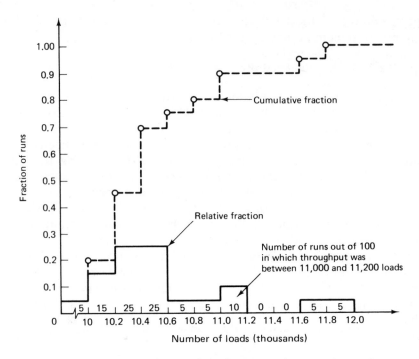

Figure 10-3 Example of throughput histogram for 100 observations.

1000 hours, we can estimate that 95% of the time this requirement will be met. The histogram shows that 5% of the time the throughput during this time period will be in the range of 9800 to 10,000 loads. The use of the outputs from the Q-GERT processor enabled decision makers working in conjunction with systems analysts to evaluate proposed capital expenditures for this production system.

10.3 ANALYZING COMPUTERIZED MANUFACTURING SYSTEMS

More and more industries are considering the automation of their manufacturing processes. A computerized manufacturing system (CMS) consists of machine tools, material handling equipment, and storage facilities that are integrated and controlled by a computer. Among the potential benefits of a CMS are lower labor costs, less setup time, decreased in-process inventory, increased machining accuracy, and increased production rates. The capital expenditures involved are great, however, and for this reason it is essential that the system be designed and operated efficiently. Q-GERT simulation models have been used to analyze these systems and have been useful in their evaluation and design [77,118,166]. This section presents a Q-GERT model of a

CMS. The model presented illustrates the important concepts required to analyze a CMS without encumbering the discussion with extensive details of the system's operation and the actual size of the installation modeled.

10.3.1 The System and Management Concerns

Figure 10-4 illustrates a schematic diagram for a proposed CMS. Parts to be processed arrive at the load/unload area. All parts after loading travel through the system on special pallets. Pallets are a constraining resource of the system since parts must wait if all pallets are in use. Six pallets are used in the proposed design. The parts are loaded manually onto the pallets. Manual assistance is always considered available in both loading and unloading. Once loaded, the pallets are ready to travel to one of the three machines. This transport is accomplished automatically by the material handling system, consisting of two computer-controlled carts. It is assumed that all parts can be machined by any of the three machines. Following each machine operation, a pallet must be transported to an area for part inspection. After inspection, the pallet requires a cart for transport back to the load/unload area. After unloading, the part leaves the system and the pallet is available for reuse. An important operational consideration is that a machine cannot service the next pallet until one of the carts has removed the current pallet from the machining area. The same constraint applies to the inspection station. Thus, a machine may be busy, idle, or blocked.

The following are the types of questions that are addressed in the

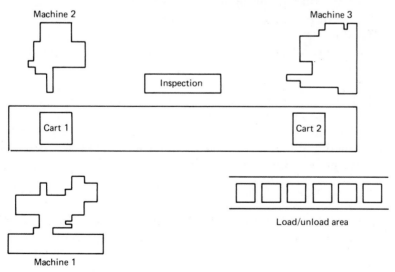

Figure 10-4 Schematic diagram of computerized manufacturing system.

analysis of the operation of computer manufacturing systems:

1. What is the production rate and throughput of the system?
2. What is the utilization of each machine, that is, the percentage of time busy?
3. How often is each machine prevented (blocked) from working because a cart is unavailable? because a part is unavailable (idle time)?
4. What is the utilization of each cart?
5. What is the in-process inventory; that is, how many parts wait for pallets, how many pallets wait for carts, and how many pallets wait for machines?

Answers to these questions provide the basis for evaluating the effectiveness of a CMS.

In addition, questions regarding the capability of the CMS to accommodate changes in system configuration and operational procedures are posed. The following are examples of such questions regarding potential ways to improve the CMS:

1. What effect does adding more carts have on production rate or machine utilization?
2. How does the system perform under different part arrival patterns?
3. What is the effect of increasing the number of pallets?
4. What is the productive capacity of the system; that is, at what production rate are more machines required?
5. Can new dispatching methods increase the production rate? What method is best?
6. What is the effect of employing a different material handling system?

The following section describes a Q-GERT model designed to represent the CMS described above and to account for the managerial concerns. The model is abstracted from Q-GERT studies dealing with the Sundstrand CMS in operation at Caterpillar Tractor [166] and a Kearney and Trecher CMS in use at Ingersol-Rand [77].

10.3.2 The Q-GERT Model

Figure 10-5 contains a Q-GERT model for the CMS presented in Figure 10-4. The arrival of parts to the system is represented by source node 4. Entering transactions are marked here so that interval statistics can be obtained when they depart the system. If a pallet is not available when a part arrives, it waits in Q-node 5. Pallets are modeled as a resource, as there are only six of them and they are in use during the

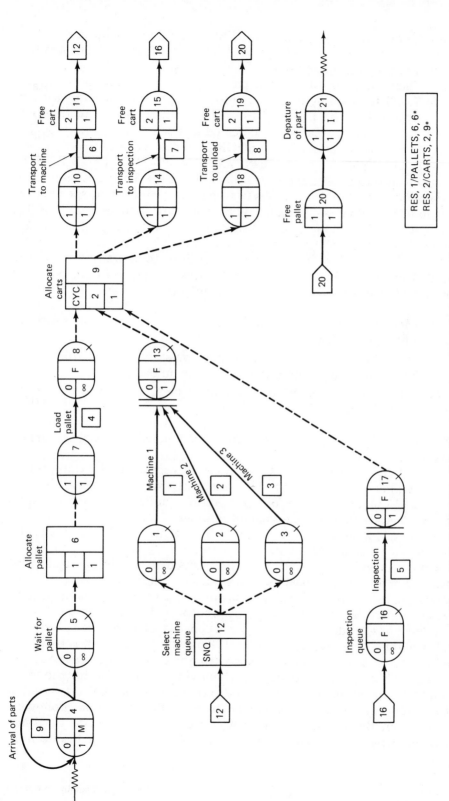

Figure 10-5 Q-GERT model of a computerized manufacturing system.

entire processing of a part. The RESOURCE block indicates that resource 1 represents pallets, that there are six pallets available, and that they are allocated at node 6.

When a part is allocated a pallet, the part transaction is sent to node 7 and the loading of a part onto the pallet is modeled by activity 4. After loading, the part and the pallet wait for a cart to transport them to a machine. Carts are allocated at node 9. Resource type 2 is used to represent carts. The RESOURCE block specifies that two carts are available. For this model, carts are only allocated at node 9 and all transportation by carts is decided upon at node 9. The decision rule for allocating carts to transactions waiting for transport is specified as cyclic (CYC). Preceding ALLOCATE node 9 are Q-nodes 8, 13, and 17. Transactions in Q-node 8 are waiting for transport to a machine. Transactions in Q-node 13 are waiting for transport to the inspection operation, and transactions in Q-node 17 are waiting to be transported to the unload operation. By specifying a CYC queue selection rule, carts will be allocated when possible in the following order:

1. Following a transport to a machine, a cart will be used for transporting to inspection.
2. Following a transport to the inspection station, a cart will be used for transporting from inspection to the unload area.
3. Following a transport to the unload area, a cart will be used to transport a loaded pallet to the machine area.

If a transaction is not waiting in any of the queues, the cart resource is made idle.

Activity 6 from node 10 to node 11 represents the transport of a loaded pallet to a machine. Following the transport, the cart is freed at node 11 and is available for reallocation at node 9. The part is routed to the Q-node that has the smallest number of parts in it by S-node 12. Machines 1, 2, and 3 are represented by activities 1, 2, and 3, and the queues of these machines are represented by Q-nodes 1, 2, and 3. Following a machining operation, it is presumed that only one pallet and part from any of the machines may wait on the track for a cart. Thus, the logic is set up to block any machine that completes its operations when a part is still waiting to be transported to inspection. This is modeled at Q-node 13 by specifying a capacity of 1 and the blocking of all machines when Q-node 13 is at its capacity. When a cart is freed and allocated to the movement of parts from machines, the transaction in Q-node 13 is routed to node 14, which is the start node for the transport to inspection. At node 15, the cart is freed and the part is routed to Q-node 16, where, if necessary, it waits for inspection. Following inspection, the part attempts to wait for a cart at Q-node 17. Again only one part may wait for a cart and if a second part has been inspected, it blocks the inspection station until a cart transports a part from the inspection area. The transport of the inspected part to the unload area is accomplished by activity 8, after which the cart is freed. Next, the pallet is freed, that is, one unit of resource type 1 is made available. The part leaves the system at sink node 21, where interval statistics are collected. This provides information on time in the system for each part. By dividing the number of observations at node 21 by the total simulated time period, an estimate of the production rate can be obtained. Following a discussion of model output and potential uses of this model, procedures for embellishing this model are given.

10.3.3 Model Output and Use

Table 10-2 summarizes the Q-GERT output statistics that correspond to the desired performance measures. The time parts spend in the system is collected at node 21 through the specification of interval statistics. As mentioned above, the production rate can be computed from this statistic. An alternative way to measure the production rate is to compute it from the time between departures from the system. This can be accomplished by adding a statistics node after node 21 and requesting between-statistics.

Machine utilization estimates are derived from the utilization outputs for servers 1, 2, and 3. Blocking statistics for these servers represent the fraction of time the machines were neither busy nor idle but were delayed from continuing work because a cart was unavailable. The uti-

TABLE 10-2 Summary of System Performance Measures Computed by Q-GERT Model

Performance Measure	Q-GERT Statistic
Time parts spend in the system	I-statistics for node 21
Production rate	Number of observations for node 21 divided by length of simulation
Machine utilization	Busy- and idle-time statistics for servers 1, 2, and 3
Time a machine is prevented (blocked) from operating because a cart is unavailable	Blocking statistics for servers 1, 2, and 3
Usage of material handling system	Busy and availability statistics for resource 2
In-process inventory	
Machine area	Queue statistics for nodes 1, 2, and 3
Load/unload area	Queue statistics for nodes 5, 8, 13, and 17
Inspection station	Queue statistics for node 16

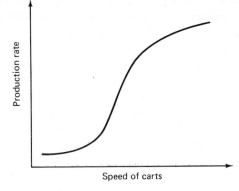

Figure 10-6 Relationship between material handling speed and production rate.

lization of resource 2 represents the usage of the material handling system. The in-process inventory estimates are obtained from statistics on the number of transactions in Q-nodes 1, 2, 3, 5, 8, 13, 16, and 17.

Runner and Leimkuhler [166] used Q-GERT to investigate several operating and design parameters for a Sunstrand system installed at Caterpillar. One of these involved determining the relationship between production rate and the speed of the material handling system. In the model in Figure 10-5, cart speed is related to the time for production activities 6, 7, and 8. By varying this speed for several runs, a graph like the one depicted in Figure 10-6 can be obtained. From such experiments, a trade-off evaluation can be made between a high-speed transport system and a desired level of production. In this case, a diminishing rate of return is observed at high speeds.

Similarly, the relationship between the number of transport pallets and production rate can be obtained. In the Q-GERT model, this involves simply changing the capacity of resource type 1 (pallets). Figure 10-7 characterizes the output observed for this potential design change.

Other operating procedures can be readily assessed. For example, an increase in the number of machines involves associating additional

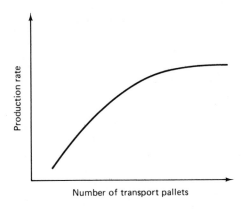

Figure 10-7 Relationship between number of pallets and production rate.

Q-nodes with S-node 12. By changing the queue selection rule for S-node 12, the effects of dispatching procedures for the carts can be investigated.

To add more carts to the system, the capacity of resource 2 is increased. In fact, a useful way to determine the number of carts needed to avoid delays is to assign a large number of carts in one run. The Q-GERT processor automatically computes the maximum units of a resource ever in use, which would correspond to the maximum carts needed to avoid all delays due to material handling requirements.

Another use made of the model was to determine the sensitivity of system performance due to variation in the arrival pattern as specified at source node 4. This permitted evaluation of the system under different forecasted needs and allowed estimates of the capacity of the system to be made.

10.3.4 Embellishments to the Computerized Manufacturing Q-GERT Model

There are many ways in which the Q-GERT model of Figure 10-5 can be extended. Standard parameter changes can be investigated for availability (pallets and carts); in-process buffer sizes as represented by the Q-nodes, service times characteristics, and number of servers. In this section we concentrate on possible procedural modifications.

Suppose that no room is provided at the inspection station for an inspected unit to wait for a cart. At first glance, it appears that Q-node 17 should be changed to have a zero capacity. This would cause the inspector to be blocked if a cart was not immediately available when inspection was completed on a part. However, once this occurred, allocation of a cart could never occur to inspected parts, as no transactions would be in Q-node 17. This would result in no additional inspection of parts because of the blocking. To model this situation, we should define the inspector as a resource and change the network portion of Figure 10-5 that involves inspection to the network segment on p. 234.

Q-node 16 still holds the parts to be inspected. Instead of modeling the inspection as a service activity, we now employ an inspector resource, which is allocated at node 26. The inspection activity is represented by the branch from node 27 to Q-node 17. This inspection will be performed only when an inspector resource is allocated to a part. Following inspection, inspected parts wait for a cart to be allocated in Q-node 17. In this network segment, no capacity restriction on Q-node 17 is required nor is blocking of the inspection activity needed (since it is a nonservice activity, it is not allowed). Only one inspected part can reside at Q-node 17 because only one inspector resource is available and it is not freed until the part is removed from Q-node 17,

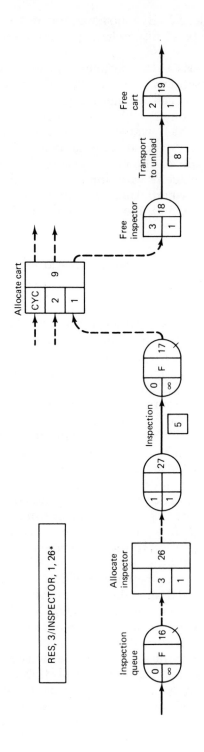

which occurs at FREE node 18. When ALLOCATE node 9 allocates a cart to inspected parts, the part and cart are routed to FREE node 18, where the inspector is freed. The inspector can then be reallocated at ALLOCATE node 26 and another part can be inspected. The inspected part that was allocated a cart is then transported to the unload area as indicated by activity 8. The remainder of the network shown in Figure 10-5 is unchanged.

We now investigate the procedures for allocating carts to transactions waiting before ALLOCATE node 9 of the original model. A first embellishment would be to represent parts waiting at each machine by a separate Q-node. This is shown here, where one machine part can wait for a cart while another part is being machined.

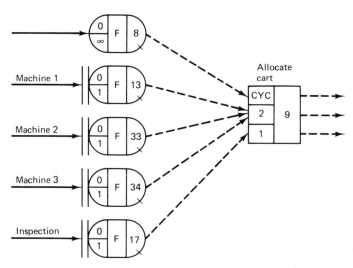

By providing a queue for the output of each machine, a more detailed allocation procedure can be modeled. In this case, a CYC queue selection rule is used whereby Q-nodes 8, 13, 33, 34, and 17 are polled in order. If a cart was last allocated to a machined part from machine 1, the next cart that is freed will look for a transaction starting in Q-node 33. This differs from the original model in that after transporting a machined part, the next transport operation would involve an inspected part if one was waiting. In the network segment above, the deaggregation of the queue for machined parts allows for a greater polling of queues of machined parts.

The cart allocation procedure can be embellished further by allocating carts at two ALLOCATE nodes. This possibility is indicated below, where one ALLOCATE node is used for transporting parts to machines and from inspection and a separate ALLOCATE node for transporting machined parts to inspection. By having two ALLOCATE nodes, an order can be prescribed at FREE nodes for specifying the ALLOCATE node that should be polled when reallocating a cart. An illustration of this is shown in the following network segment.

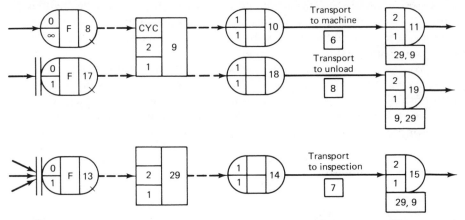

In this network segment, when a cart is freed after transporting a part to a machine at node 11, the cart will first attempt to transport a machined part to inspection by polling ALLOCATE node 29. If no machined parts are ready to be transported, an attempt will be made to transport an inspected part to the unload area. This assumes that no inspected part was transported by a cart during the use of the cart freed at node 11. The latter condition results since the CYC rule employed at ALLOCATE node 9 starts looking at queues from the last queue from which a transaction was taken. Thus, the specification at the FREE node states which ALLOCATE nodes to poll and the queue selection rule at the ALLOCATE node prescribes the order for interrogating the Q-nodes preceding the ALLOCATE node.

When a cart is freed after transporting an inspected part to the unload area, an attempt to transport a new part to a machine or to transport another inspected part to the unload area is attempted. This specification at FREE node 19 is accomplished by examining ALLOCATE node 9 first. If the cart is not required for either of these operations, it will be allocated if possible to the transport of a machined part at ALLOCATE node 29. At FREE node 15, the reallocation of a cart is prescribed to consider machined parts first and then new or inspected parts.

The procedure for reallocating carts can be further extended by providing separate ALLOCATE nodes for each type of transport required. When this is done, a separate order for polling the ALLOCATE nodes can be prescribed following each type of transport. The embellishments described above are only a small sample of the potential use of Q-GERT for modeling computerized manufacturing systems.

10.4 CAPACITY PLANNING FOR AN OIL DISTRIBUTION SYSTEM

In recent years the production of crude oil in the United States has declined and the importation of foreign crude has increased. The processing of foreign crude significantly affects crude distribution and storage facilities in two respects: (1) large volumes (tankerloads) arrive at irregular intervals, and (2) wide ranges in the quality of crude require additional segregations at pipeline stations and refineries.

The increased levels of crude runs and foreign imports have strained the facilities for handling the crude oil, especially the crude tankage at the refineries and pipeline stations. By the mid-1970s it had become apparent that additional crude tankage would be highly desirable, but it was not obvious where the additional tankage should be located and how much additional tankage could be justified on an economic basis.

This section describes a Q-GERT study conducted for a large oil company that assessed the capacity requirements of a crude oil distribution system consisting of pipelines, wells, tankers, and pumping stations [11].

10.4.1 The System and Management Concerns

Figure 10-8 contains a schematic drawing of the crude oil distribution system. The circles represent storage areas. Storage areas exist at pumping stations, docks, and refineries. Pipelines connect the storage areas and provide the link between the various system inputs and outputs. There are two forms of input to the pipeline. First, tankers arrive at docks and deliver crude to the pipeline. This form of input is not continuous, but rather is turned on and off as a function of the arrival of tankers. Another form of input is the delivery of crude oil to the system by the wells. This is a continuous input into the system. Once crude enters the pipeline from any of the input sources, it flows continuously through the system. As shown, crude may flow to a pumping station and reside in a storage facility before being pumped to the next destination. Each pumping station redirects flow to other stations or to refineries. The goal of the distribution system is to deliver crude oil to the refineries, and therefore the amount of crude delivered represents a system output. A complication to be considered is that the distribution system is designed to transport crude oil of different types and it is necessary to model the flow of each type of crude oil.

The objective of the project is to determine whether the proposed storage capacity is adequate. If it is not, the amount and location of the needed storage is to be determined. Management desires that the system be analyzed under a variety of input conditions, as specified by pro-

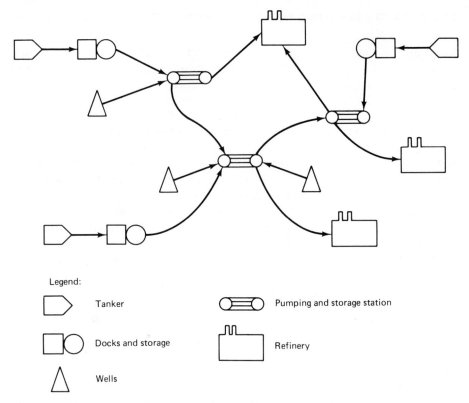

Legend:

⬠ Tanker

▭◯ Docks and storage

△ Wells

◯▭◯ Pumping and storage station

🏭 Refinery

Figure 10-8 Schematic diagram of a crude oil distribution system.

jected ranges of values for the tanker and well inputs. New storage capacity requirements for combinations of input values are to be determined.

10.4.2 The Q-GERT Model[†]

Crude oil flow is transferred between locations in batch units, where one unit represents 5000 barrels of crude. The tanker and well input are modeled as discrete arrivals using procedures similar to those discussed in Section 7.2. Continuous pipeline flow is modeled as discussed in Section 8.3. Identification of crude oil type is maintained by an attribute value and the storage areas are represented by Q-nodes. The maximum capacity of each Q-node is set to the capacity of the proposed storage tank. Balking in the model corresponds to an overflow. By measuring the overflows, a determination of new storage capacity

[†]The Q-GERT model for this study was developed by Steven D. Duket, D. Brent Bandy, Brad Overturf, and Jerome Sabuda [11]. The material presented in this section is a highly abstracted and simplified version of their Q-GERT model.

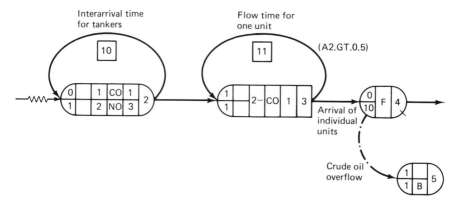

Figure 10-9 Q-GERT representation of tanker arrivals: attribute 1: crude oil type; attribute 2: number of units.

requirements can be made. In this section we discuss the important model features of tanker input, well input, pipeline flow, and crude oil overflow.

Figure 10-9 shows the Q-GERT representation of the arrival of tankers loaded with crude oil. Source node 2 and activity 10 control the arrival of tanker loads at a given dock. Two attribute assignments are made to describe each arriving tanker load. Attribute 1 is the crude type. At node 2, the crude type is 1. Attribute 2 is the load size in units of 5000 barrels. In this model, load size is modeled as a normally distributed random variable.

Loads enter the system at source node 2 and are routed to node 3. The purpose of node 3 is to divide the tanker load into units and place a transaction representing one unit into storage at Q-node 4. Since the number of units is represented by attribute 2, this is accomplished by decrementing the value of attribute 2 by 1 and creating a transaction after each decrement until attribute 2 is less than an arbitrary fraction, say 0.5. This decrement function is accomplished by the value assignment $(2-,CO,1)$ at node 3. Activity 11 is taken conditionally as long as $A2.GT.0.5$. The time duration of activity 11 is set equal to the time to unload one unit. Activity 12 represents the arrival of units to the dock storage area, which is represented by Q-node 4. The capacity of Q-node 4 is set at 10, which means that the storage at this dock is limited to 50,000 barrels. If storage for more than 50,000 barrels is required at this location, balking from Q-node 4 will occur. The number of units that overflow (balk) per time unit is reported by the Q-GERT processor. Units that balk from Q-node 4 are routed to node 5, where between-statistics are maintained to provide information on the time between spillage of individual units. Hence, balking statistics and between-statistics are used to measure overflow.

The above representation of the unloading dock assumes that

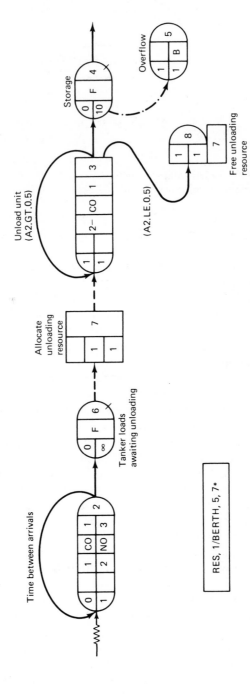

Figure 10-10 Q-GERT representation of tanker arrivals when unloading resources are limited.

resources are always available for unloading tankers at the time of their arrival. Examples of dock resources are docking berths, unloading equipment, and personnel. When resources cannot be assumed to be available, the representation in Figure 10-10 is used. In this example we incorporate the constraint that there are only five docking berths. As before, source node 2 controls tanker arrivals, node 3 performs the unloading operation, Q-node 4 represents storage, and node 5 computes overflow statistics. Before unloading begins at node 3, however, an unloading resource, represented by resource type 1, must be available. Tankers wait in Q-node 6 until the resource is available. ALLOCATE node 7 allocates one unit of the resource to the tanker. Node 3 then performs unloading. The maximum number of tankers that can be unloaded simultaneously is equal to the maximum number of available resources (berths), which is specified as 5 in the RES block. After unloading is completed for each tanker, the branch to node 8 is taken and the docking berth is freed. In this way, unloading delays due to resource constraints are modeled. In the actual project, multiple resource requirements were modeled by including multiple resource types, ALLOCATE nodes, and FREE nodes.

The representation of the unloading dock given in Figure 10-10 can be embellished to account for dock shutdowns due to shifts or tides or failure by incorporating ALTER nodes in disjoint subnetworks.

Consider now the modeling of the continuous flow of crude oil into the system from a well. Modeling this flow involves the creation of a transaction representing 5000 barrels based on the time to pump this amount out of the well. This is shown in Figure 10-11, where node 12 creates transactions representing one unit, and the duration of activity 20 is the pumping time for 5000 barrels. The storage tank is represented by Q-node 14 and node 15 is used to compute overflow statistics. As before, attribute 1 represents the crude oil type and attribute 2 represents the load size, which in this case is 1 since unit loads come from the well.

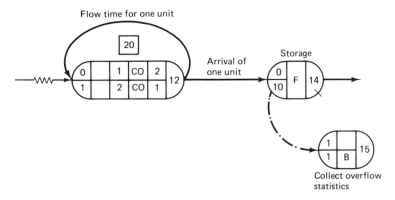

Figure 10-11 Continuous crude flow from wells.

To model continuous pipeline flow, we have selected one of the methods discussed in Section 8.3, and it is presented in Figure 10-12. Node 16 is used to route crude of different types to different storage areas. Tanker loads for crude type 1 are stored at Q-node 4, which represents dock storage. Q-node 10 represents the pipeline segment between dock storage (Q-node 4) and one of the pumping station storage tanks (Q-node 13). If there are any units in dock storage, service activity 1 pumps a unit into the pipeline. A user function (UF,1) is used to set this flowtime because in the actual problem some special processing was required. In the user function, a check on the remaining pipeline capacity (RCAPQ(10)) is made. If this is zero, that is, if the pipeline is full, a transaction is sent immediately to node 6 through the use of subroutine PTIN. ALTER node 6 increases resource type 1 by one. Resource 1 serves as a switch which is initially set to zero (off). The control of the switch is done solely by node 6. In this way, units leave the pipeline (Q-node 10) only when the pipeline is full (the switch is on) and a unit is being pumped out of dock storage into the pipeline. The first unit in the pipeline is pumped out of the pipeline through activity 22 and into the station storage area (Q-node 13).

The network segments given in Figures 10-9 through 10-12 form the basic elements of the distribution system. These segments can be connected to represent the entire distribution system depicted in Figure 10-8. The actual model of the proposed system consisted of over 100 nodes. The modeling concepts presented above capture the significant aspects of the network model. However, extensive user function code was employed to portray actual refinery demand and crude oil routing and mixing. The refinery demand established the type of crude oil required, which, in turn, was an input to the decision as to which tank should serve as an input to a pipeline. Of course, a decision of this type is required for each pipeline, and it was necessary to consider such decisions simultaneously.

10.4.3 Model Output and Use

The important outputs for this study are the balking statistics, average values in storage tanks (Q-nodes), and between-statistics that characterize the overflow at storage areas. The model was run under various input conditions concerning estimates of tanker arrivals and well production. Essentially, the model converted these inputs into storage usage and requirements. The ideal situation is to have no overflow, which corresponds to no balking. For most runs, however, overflow was obtained at several storage areas. In some runs, new routing rules could alleviate the overflows. In other situations it was necessary to add new storage tanks. In this way, capacity requirements were designed and evaluated for various input conditions. Discussions of model

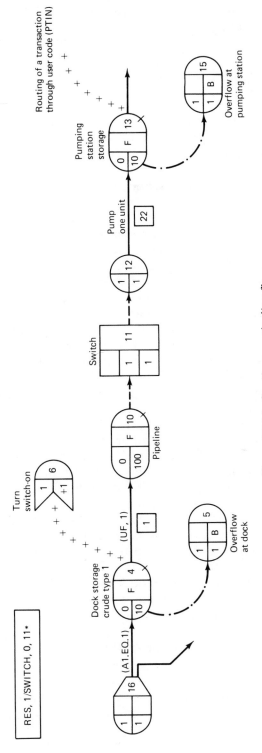

Figure 10-12 Continuous pipeline flow.

243

validation and output results for a sample problem are reported by Bandy and Duket [11].

10.5 ANALYZING A CHECK PROCESSING FACILITY OF A MAJOR BANK

Over a million checks and other account transactions arrive each day at a central New York bank from its regional branches. The need to process this large volume of items has turned large banks into huge data processing facilities. This section describes one such facility and a Q-GERT study that was performed to evaluate check processing procedures.

10.5.1 The System and Management Concerns

Figure 10-13 is a schematic diagram of a check processing facility. Checks and other items arrive in batches from regional branches and from other departments within the bank. Although deliveries to the bank occur at regular hours, there are delivery delays within the bank in getting the checks to different departments. The information from each batch of checks that arrives is entered on a computer tape. These tapes are sent to a tape processing department. While the tapes are being processed, the checks are audited. The auditing function is performed only during daytime shifts, whereas the other departments operate on a 24-hour basis. After auditing, the checks are matched against the computer tape released from the tape processing department. This matching and verification process involves a delay called the verification delay. After the delay the checks are moved to a machine room, where operators feed them into one of four machines for automatic debit and credit transfers. This computerized machining operation represents the final processing stage for the checks at the facility.

A study of the system was initiated by bank management for two reasons. First, new regional banks were opening and the work load of the facility was expected to increase by 20%. Second, it was desirable for personnel reasons to do all auditing during a single 8-hour shift (current auditing was performed on two shifts). Management posed questions relating to the effects due to the proposed changes on the following performance measures:

1. The time a batch spends in the system
2. The rate at which batches are processed

Both of these measures provide for a quantitative assessment of "customer–bank" relations. Of significant import is that if a check is

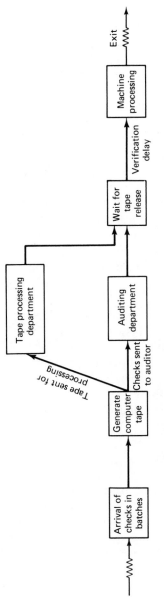

Figure 10-13 Schematic diagram of check processing facility.

processed before a specific time, it can become part of a bank's float, which, in turn, determines the lending capability of the bank.

Preliminary analysis and opinion indicated that the machine processing operation was the current bottleneck of the system and that ways to increase the efficiency of this last stage of the process needed to be investigated to accommodate the expected increase in work load. However, sufficient uncertainty regarding this opinion and the need for quantitative analysis led to the development of a Q-GERT model to answer management's concerns. The model is presented in the next section in simplified form in the interest of confidentiality and ease of presentation.

10.5.2 The Q-GERT Model

Figure 10-14 contains a network model of the check processing facility. Nodes 1, 2, and 3 represent the arrival of batches of checks to the system. Two attributes were assigned to each batch for identification purposes. Attribute 1 represents the type of item arriving (the actual study involved over 30 classifications of bank items). Attribute 2 represents the number of items in the batch, that is, the volume of the batch. The volume is a random variable. Thus, the size of arriving batches is characterized by a density function. Arrivals of each type of check occur at regular intervals during the day as follows: type 1 arrive at 8, type 2 arrive at 14 (2 P.M.), and type 3 arrive at 20 (8 P.M.). These regular intervals are modeled by the activities emanating from source node 20. For each type of check, there is a delay in delivery to the facility. These delays are represented by activities 5, 6, and 7. At node 4, two additional attribute assignments are made. For each batch, a unique identifying number is assigned to attribute 3. This assignment is necessary to match the check batch with the computer tape of the batch. This assignment to attribute 3 is accomplished through the use of the incremental function (3,IN,1). A batch priority value is assigned to attribute 4 using user function 1. A user function was employed so that different batch priority algorithms could be evaluated.

Deterministic routing is performed from node 4 and transactions with identical attribute sets are routed to nodes 11 and 5. Activity 10 represents the time for tape processing. After processing, released tapes are routed to Q-node 11. Tapes wait in Q-node 11 until the corresponding batch goes through auditing. This waiting for a transaction with a particular attribute value is controlled by MATCH node 12.

The batch of checks is processed starting at Q-node 5: note that auditing (activity 11) is begun when both an item is in Q-node 5 and a transaction is in Q-node 6, where Q-node 6 represents the availability of the auditor. This *and* logic is controlled by the assembly queue selection rule (ASM) of S-node 7. When auditing is completed at node 9, the auditor transaction must traverse activity 8 or 9 in order to return to Q-node 6 and permit the next batch to be audited. It is this

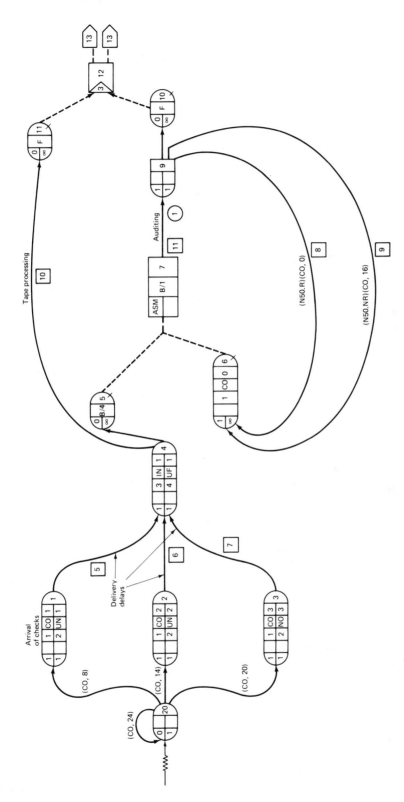

Figure 10-14 Q-GERT model of a check processing facility: A1: check type; A2: volume of batch; A3: batch number; A4: batch priority.

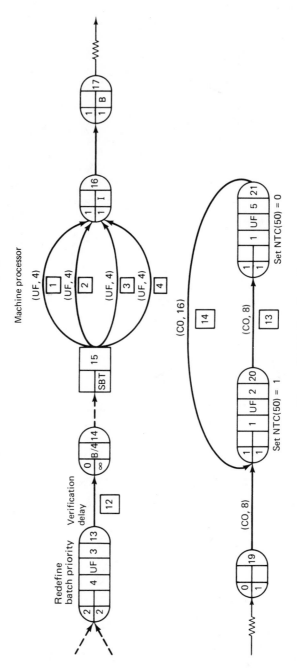

Figure 10-14 (Continued)

loop that permits the modeling of the auditor shift. Auditing is permitted only when the auditor is in Q-node 6; therefore, by controlling the time to return to Q-node 6, we can model different shift policies. In this model, the release of node 50, a dummy (nonexistent) node, controls the time for the auditor to return. In a disjoint network, NTC(50) is set to 1 to indicate that node 50 has been released (auditor working) and then to 0 to indicate the auditor is not working. This approach illustrates the control of conditional branching using the NTC array.

Q-node 5 is ranked big-value-first on attribute 4 (B/4), where attribute 4 is assigned at node 4 in user function 1. Attribute 4 can be thought of as an index with higher values of the index receiving greater priority. By setting the index as a function of a batch's size, type, and time of arrival, different sequencing rules were incorporated into the model. Additional auditors are modeled by changing the initial number in Q-node 6 and the number of parallel servers prescribed for activity 11.

At S-node 7, two transactions are assembled, and a choice of which set of attributes to maintain for the assembled transaction must be specified. Since the attributes of the batch of checks should be kept, the choice specification, B/1, is used and attribute 1 of the transaction representing the auditor is set to zero at Q-node 6.

When both the tape and auditing functions are finished for a specified batch number, a match occurs at node 12. This match is based on attribute 3, the batch number. Both transactions are then routed to node 13. Two transaction arrivals are required to release node 13, where the tape and batch are merged into a single transaction. Since the identity of the tape equals that of the batch, the choice of the attribute set to maintain is not relevant. At node 13, attribute 4 is redefined to be the batch priority index for ranking work in Q-node 14. Activity 12 is a verification task which ensures that there is a proper association between tape and batch information.

Server activities 1, 2, 3, and 4 represent each of the four processing machines. The service time is a user function, so that it can be determined as a function of the batch type and size (attributes 1 and 2). Parallel server branches had to be employed since each machine has a different operating speed. S-node 15 selects among available machines using the rule: choose the machine that has had the smallest busy time to date (SBT). By varying this selection rule and the priority ranking in the queue, different machine sequencing procedures were modeled and evaluated.

Nodes 16 and 17 are statistics nodes and are used to collect the departure statistics for each batch leaving the system. Interval statistics from node 16 provide information about the time in the system. Between-statistics from node 17 yield information about the frequency of batches leaving the system. A nodal trace for node 17 illustrated sample times of departure of batches. Subroutine TIM was called with the batch size attribute (attribute 2) as an argument to obtain a time-weighted average of the volume of batch processing.

The control of the auditor shifts is depicted by nodes 20 and 21 and the emanating activities. The branch from node 19 to 20 represents the time until the first shift. At node 20, user function 2 is employed to set NTC(50) to 1, which indicates a working shift. After 8 hours, node 21 is released and user function 5 is invoked, in which NTC(50) is set to 0 to indicate a nonworking shift. To make a change in shift policy, one need only change the duration of activity 13 to the length of the new working shift and activity 14 to the length of the nonworking time.

10.5.3 Model Output and Use

The main performance measures of interest for this application are (1) the total time it takes to process a batch of work, (2) the rate at which batches depart the system, and (3) the utilization of the four machines. Estimates of these quantities are obtained from the Q-GERT model from (1) the interval statistics for node 16, (2) the between-statistics for node 17, and (3) the utilization of servers 1, 2, 3, and 4.

This model was used to investigate sequencing methods to improve the utilization of the four machines by varying the batch priority rule defined at node 13 through user function 3. The effect of the different rules was measured in terms of the effect on the time a batch spends in the system. The effect on the system of projected additional work load was observed by increasing the arrival rates of batches. The effect of the batch priority rules was further measured in light of this increase in work load.

The model was also used to evaluate personnel shift changes in the auditing department. Management was interested in the effect of proposed shift changes on the time to process work. The model was run

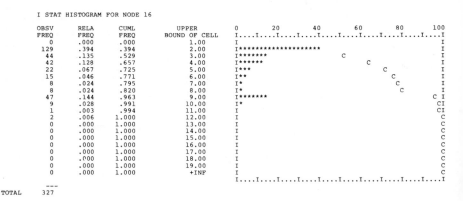

Figure 10-15 Histogram for time to process work.

under the case of the new shift change policy. An example histogram for the time to process batches under this situation is shown in Figure 10-15. From this histogram it is observed that under the new shift policy 82% of the work was processed within 8 hours. Fifty-two percent of the work was processed within 3 hours. Management was encouraged by these estimates and instituted the proposed one-shift operation.

10.6 WORK FLOW ANALYSIS IN A REGIONAL SERVICE OFFICE OF A PROPERTY AND CASUALTY INSURANCE COMPANY

Q-GERT has been used to evaluate operating procedures within a regional office of a large property and casualty insurance company which processed various types of claims, endorsements, and new business items [107]. The office can be viewed in terms of paper flow through 14 distinct operating units, or departments, including a centralized computer-based information system. Over 150 personnel are involved in the processing of hundreds of transactions each day. The office is a complex queueing situation which was modeled using Q-GERT to identify the bottlenecks in the work flow and to assist in investigating the effects of selected managerial decisions.

Management was concerned about the effect of projected business increases on the quality of service provided the claimants. New operating procedures had been designed and an evaluation of the new design was needed. The following specific and general questions were posed by management:

What will personnel requirements be at this regional office in the future?
How should proposed service centers in other areas be designed or operated to maximize service and effectiveness?

10.6.1 The System and Management Concerns

The regional service center involves a paper work flow system that contains many interface points with a computer-based information system. The service center handles six basic work flows, each of which involves many decision-making points, and record-keeping activities. A preliminary analysis indicated that the computerized information system appeared to be a critical component in the system and that only four of the six work flows interfaced with the information system. These four work flows are endorsements, new business, internal changes, and claims. A brief description of each of the work flows is given below.

The endorsement work flow consists of activities that are concerned with making adjustments to existing insurance policies. For example, the paperwork required to change the amount of liability coverage on an insured automobile would be classified as an endorsement. The endorsement work flow begins with a policyholder or an agent contacting the regional service office by telephone or mail and requesting that a change be made to a policy. After the initial processing, the request for a change in existing coverage undergoes a thorough review to determine the feasibility of the requested policy change. If acceptable, the endorsement is keyed into the computer system and the change is made on the customer's policy. This activity involves communication with a central computing system in another city. When computer processing is completed, a document is produced and mailed out to the policyholder. If the endorsement is rejected, a letter is sent to the customer citing the reason the endorsement could not be made.

The new business work flow involves processing requests of potential customers for automobile or home insurance coverage. The new business work flow contains a comprehensive underwriting review procedure.

The work flow related to internal changes includes updates in record-keeping classifications and the correction of administrative errors. These changes are initiated in the policy services unit, the underwriting unit, or the verification and assembly unit. The flow from these departments is to the computer system for processing. Eventually, a document is produced which is added to the policyholder's file.

The claims work flow begins with the policyholder initiating a claim action by telephone or through the mail. After initial records are filled out, a claims reserve is set by a claims representative. Both a manual and a computerized file are set up on the claim to store incoming information. These files are periodically updated as more information is obtained. When the claim is settled, payment is sent out and the file is closed.

An overview of the system is presented in Figure 10-16. Although the exact work flows are not drawn, the overview illustrates how the office accommodates all four work flows and the number of personnel involved in processing the paper flows.

A Q-GERT model was developed to estimate the consequences of specific actions contemplated or anticipated by management. These actions involved:

1. Changes in the volumes of the type of work processed by the regional service office.
2. Changes in priority rules for the processing of work in an operating unit.
3. Changes in the work flow paths
4. Reallocation of personnel among the different departments
5. Changes in processing times for specific items due to the introduction of training programs

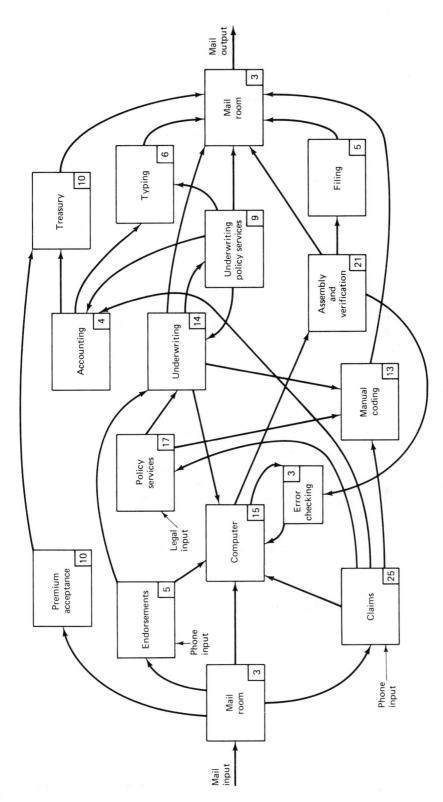

Figure 10-16 Diagram of work flow through the regional service office. Number in box indicates the number of personnel in the department.

10.6.2 The Q-GERT Model

The Q-GERT model consists of over 250 nodes and 500 branches; hence, only the basic model components can be presented in this book. An understanding of these basic components will provide sufficient insight to understand the development of the entire network model.

Because of the large volume of paperwork flow, batches of work rather than single items were modeled. The transactions flowing through the network are batches of 100 items of work classified as endorsements, new business, internal changes, or claims. The attributes of a transaction are listed in Table 10-3.

Source nodes generate arrivals of each type of work to the system and assign a value to attribute 1 to establish the work type and to attribute 5 to provide a unique batch number. Each department has a queue of work to be processed and a set of servers corresponding to the personnel in the department. The flow paths through the network depend on work type. Routing of work through the system is controlled by branching based on the route tag (attribute 2), that is, where in the network the work came from. This allows different transactions to enter a department and be properly differentiated when they exit a department. Service times and work priorities are a function of the work type.

Figure 10-17 shows the Q-GERT representation of the underwriting department. To simplify the graphic presentation, only the processing of new business and endorsements is shown in the figure. When a batch representing new business arrives at node 156 from the policy services department, it is assigned a new route tag (attribute 2). Upon emerging from the department at node 14, transactions are routed based on attribute 2. Node 8 similarly tags a transaction from the endorsement unit before it enters the underwriting department. Nodes 156 and 8 also assign to attribute 3, the time required for the underwriters to process this particular work. This value is used by the service branches emanating from S-node 17 and 18. Node 156 assigns the service time according to a beta distribution (BE) using parameter set 4. Node 8 assigns attribute 3 according to a normal distribution (NO) using parameter set 5.

TABLE 10-3 Attributes of a Transaction

Attribute Number	Definition
1	Paperwork type code with 1 = endorsement, 2 = new business, 3 = internal change, and 4 = claim
2	Route tag, that is, the node number last visited by the transaction
3	Next service time
4	Priority value for next work queue
5	Unique batch number

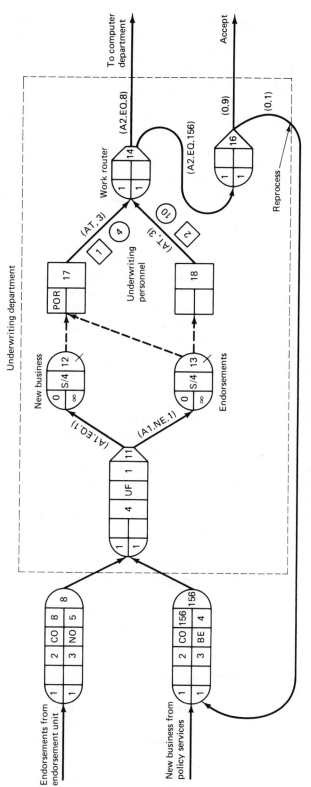

Figure 10-17 Q-GERT representation of underwriting department.

Q-node 12 represents the stack of unprocessed new business, and Q-node 13 represents unprocessed endorsements. All work is ranked on attribute 4, which is assigned to all incoming transactions by a user function (UF) at node 11. This function uses the time the transaction entered the system [TMARK(I)] and the work type (attribute 1) to assign a priority value. Small values are used to indicate a high priority. Different procedures for ranking work can be modeled by modifying user function 1.

Service activities 1 and 2 represent the underwriters and indicate that there are 14 underwriters in the department arranged in two groups. Four highly trained underwriters, represented by activity 1, handle new business primarily, but they can work on endorsements. Preference on the part of these underwriters is given to new business, as indicated by the POR queue selection rule for S-node 17. The other 10 underwriters do not have sufficient experience to work on new business and are used exclusively for endorsement work.

Each type of work performed by the personnel is established by a separate entry point (node) to the department. The time to perform the service is equal to the transaction's third attribute value which is set at the entry node, so that service time is a function of both the type of work and the routing of the work.

To summarize, endorsements that come to underwriting wait in accordance with a prescribed priority in Q-node 13 until they can be processed by one of the 14 underwriters in the department. After processing, endorsements are routed to the computer department by node 14. New business transactions arrive to node 156 and wait in Q-node 12 to be processed by the same underwriting personnel. New business is routed to node 16, where probabilistic branching is used. Ninety percent of the time a new business transaction is sent to the next department. Ten percent of the time it is rerouted to node 156 for additional processing by the underwriters. This is similar to the inspection process described in Section 9.5. As discussed in Section 9.5, this situation could be embellished to have service times and reprocessing probabilities that reflect the number of reworkings. In addition, excessive reworking of a new business application could be avoided by keeping track of the number of times a transaction is reprocessed.

The other departments and work flow of the regional service center were modeled in a fashion similar to the underwriting department. All the departments are connected through entry and exit nodes as illustrated, with the routing to and from a department based on the work flow specifications.

One additional network modeling feature deserves mention. In the computer department, claim information is recorded in a data base while the actual claim is processed concurrently in the policy service unit. The claim is not allowed to proceed to other departments until both operations are performed. To model this, a duplicate transaction is created and sent to policy services prior to entry into the computer department. A MATCH node is used to control the flow of the two transactions. After a match is made, they are merged back into a single transaction. The matching attribute is attribute 5, the unique batch number. The network concepts for modeling this matching are analogous to those presented in the bank check processing model (see Figure 10-14).

10.6.3 Model Output and Use

The network representing the operation of the regional service office was simulated for a one-month period using data compiled from an on-site study. The Q-GERT output provided the following type of information:

1. Statistics on personnel utilization for personnel in each department (server statistics)
2. Statistics on work congestion: the average number of items waiting to be processed in each department (Q-node statistics)
3. Statistics and histograms on work flow time (interval statistics from sink nodes). This information was further categorized by:
   a. The time to process accepted endorsements
   b. The time to process rejected endorsements
   c. The time to process accepted new business
   d. The time to process rejected new business
   e. The time to process internal changes
   f. The time for internal changes to reach the premium acceptance department

Using the model, an analysis was performed which provided the basis for the following statements:

1. The projected new business work load caused a significant degradation in system throughput.
2. Different work priorities could be used to decrease the time required to serve new customers.
3. Personnel utilization was improved by reallocation based on in-process work loads.
4. The number and type of new positions that were needed to provide a given level of service under a projected increased work load was determined.

Quantitative estimates of each improvement were provided to management.

Another use of the model was to measure the impact of training programs on the efficiency of personnel. The effect of training programs is readily quantifiable, as it is modeled by a decrease in service times. Hence, runs of the model with these new service times evaluated the training programs. In fact, service time can be incorporated in the model as a function of learning (using a learning curve). This and other information obtained from the model enabled management to plan better the operation of the proposed new service centers as well as to redesign the existing centers. In summary, the network approach provided the basis for the systems analysis required to probe, formulate, convey, and study this work flow problem.

10.7 SUMMARY

Five applications involving the use of Q-GERT models are presented in this chapter. The highlights of each application in terms of objectives, Q-GERT modeling concepts, and model uses are described. By building network models, the common features of seemingly diverse applications are uncovered. Such similarities or analogs are indicative of the role of experience in approaching and resolving system-type problems. Throughout the chapter, emphasis has been placed on modeling, performance measures, and problem resolution.

10.8 EXERCISES

10-1. For each of the performance measures listed in Table 10-1, specify the anticipated changes due to the following elemental modifications to the overhead-crane model presented in Figure 10-2. Develop a qualitative relationship between the output measure (where appropriate) assuming each elemental change is made independent of other changes.
   (a) An increase in the input rate by decreasing the time specifications for activity 10
   (b) An increase in the probability of rejection from inspection station I
   (c) An increase in the time to return from station B to station A for crane 1
   (d) An increase in the length of the common track
   (e) A decrease in the number of unit transactions that can be handled concurrently by a crane
   (f) An increase in the acceptance probability at inspection station II

10-2. Given the system throughput histogram as shown in Figure 10-3, specify activity times on the Q-GERT model of Figure 10-2 that could produce such output. Run the Q-GERT model under your hypothesized activity times. Statistically compare the output results with the histogram presented in Figure 10-3.

10-3. Modify the model of the computerized manufacturing system (Figure 10-5) so that the movement of the cart to the machine involves bringing a new part to the machine and removing a processed part. The only time a cart will load or unload a machine is when it cannot perform both operations for lack of a part or machine availability.

10-4. Explain the qualitative relationship depicted by the curves in Figures 10-6 and 10-7 between production rate and the independent variables: material handling speed and number of pallets.

10-5. Write subroutine UO to produce a stylized summary report of the statistics described in Table 10-2. The summary report should only present averages and should be presentable to management.

10-6. Develop a new network symbol to represent a pipeline and discuss how it could be used in a network modeling language.

10-7. Discuss the similarities of the case studies on check processing and work flow analysis in an insurance company. Specify the requirements of a network language for modeling systems of paperwork flow.

10-8. Define a situation for which production planning in a plant is required.
   (a) Draw a schematic of the production system.
   (b) Define the performance measures necessary to accomplish production planning.
   (c) Develop the Q-GERT network to obtain the performance measures.
   (d) Run the Q-GERT processor to obtain the performance measures.
   (e) Evaluate various production plans using the computer program.

10-9. A chemical plant has been designed to produce two grades of a liquid product [163]. The location of the plant dictates the use of rail traffic as the primary method of product distribution, and business considerations require a highly reliable distribution system. The company distributes to the following five consumers: two packaging units, an export terminal, a redistribution terminal, and an outside customer. The physical facilities required at the production site are storage tanks and a tank car fleet for each product grade, a tank car loading rack, and a marshaling yard. New storage and unloading rack facilities are also required at the export terminal and the redistribution terminal. In addition, product receiving and storage facilities at the two packaging units may require upgrading to be capable of handling the new product flows. The major activities of the distribution network to be modeled are described below.

The production unit makes two product grades, which are stored in separate tanks. Upon arrival of an empty tank car, product is removed from the appropriate tank and loaded into the empty car. A consumer demand causes a train of full cars to be assembled and shipped. The train travels to its destination, is disassembled, and the cars are unloaded into a storage tank which supplies the consuming unit. The empty cars are assembled into a train and returned to the production unit for reuse.

Build an aggregate (qualitative) network model to determine the size of storage and rack facilities and the tank car fleet sizes required to meet the project objectives. The primary measures of effectiveness of the distribution system are the frequency and the duration of both the stockouts at the consumer locations and shutdowns due to high inventory at the production unit. Additional statistics to be collected are rack utilization, the number of surplus cars, the required marshaling yard capacity, and the delays at the consumers' unloading facilities. Discuss how different alternative designs would be represented in the model.

Embellishment: Hypothesize data values and evaluate alternative design strategies.

10-10. A bank uses a distributed data processing network to support its nationwide on-line banking operations. This highly complex, interactive network is controlled by two distributive computing facility centers. These two centers are the focal points of the bank's data communications network. Information is transmitted between these two centers and the bank's branch offices by means of communications channels. Teller access to these channels is regulated by programmable control units, located in each branch office. At the branch offices, teller transaction terminals are used to service customers through the communications network.

The bank has a concern about the functional and physical expansion of the communications network. Long delays in response to teller requests could seriously jeopardize customer services. The bank, having an acute interest in customer satisfaction, needs to determine the inherent limitations and performance characteristics of this system before making any managerial decision regarding its expansion. Develop a modeling strategy that will help bank management analyze this complex, on-line, computer communications system. Specify performance measures for evaluating strategies.

IV

Logistics and Inventory Control

11

Logistics Systems Analysis

11.1 INTRODUCTION

A logistics system consists of a collection of personnel and machines organized to procure, store, and transport material or people. A logistics system may exist in one facility, such as an airport terminal, or it may be a collection of facilities, such as the network of air force bases. In this chapter we introduce the basic concerns in the analysis of logistics systems through simple examples that describe a network approach to logistics system analysis. Sections are included that define common performance measures, and Q-GERT calculation procedures to obtain these measures. In addition, special Q-GERT topics in logistics are identified and Q-GERT applications of logistics analysis are presented.

A logistics system has characteristics similar to a production system where the processing operations are replaced by the transport of goods from one location to another. With this orientation, many of the concepts and procedures described in Chapters 6 and 7 are applicable. However, when modeling logistics processes, consideration is usually given to the effects of reliability, maintainability, maintenance planning, support, and test equipment in addition to the normal elements of supply and transportation. In fact, integrated logistics support (ILS) not only includes the elements listed above, but defines facilities, personnel and training, technical data, funding, and management information as part of the logistics system. A logistics analysis could include the modeling of any of the elements of an ILS, and we illustrate Q-GERT procedures for modeling such elements. A prime advocate of Q-GERT analysis of logistics systems is Lt. Col. R. E. Mortenson and the material presented in the next sections is based on his applications [135].

11.2 TYPICAL LOGISTICS PROCESSES

Figure 11-1 depicts a simplified support process for an air transportation system. When a piece of equipment fails on an aircraft, a diagnostic process is initiated which results in the removal of the component that caused the equipment to fail (the "faulty box"). The faulty box becomes an input to a repair process which may involve a transport or move activity. The box eventually arrives at a repair facility to be fixed. To fix the box requires tools, test equipment, and a repairman. The unavailability of any of these resources may cause the box to wait. When all the required resources are available, the box is fixed. Following another transport activity, it becomes a spare. When another box of the same type fails, the repaired box that became a spare is installed and a logistics cycle is completed.

There are many performance aspects associated with the simplified support process described above. Operational questions relate to the aircraft and its readiness. Factors that affect the operational readiness (OR) are the number of spares available, the cycle time for repairing a spare, the failure rate associated with the equipment, and the level of maintenance support on the flight line. These latter quantities are a function of how the logistics support system operates and how we measure its performance. Support system performance can be considered in terms of its cost, efficiency, and utilization.

To introduce logistics systems analysis, a baseline Q-GERT model of the aircraft support system presented in Figure 11-1 will be developed. The Q-GERT model is shown in Figure 11-2. Activity 1 represents the time between equipment failures. The branch from node 1 to node 2 represents the time to the first failure. The branch from node 2 to node 3 represents the time to discover the box that failed. After discovery, the aircraft must wait for a specialist to remove the failed box, which is modeled by Q-node 3. The removal of the box is modeled as activity 3, which shows that any of four support personnel are capable of removing a failed box. If all four are busy, the box waits at Q-node 3. After removal, the box moves from node 4 to node 5, which represents the travel time to the repair shop. The branch from node 4 to node 10 (activity 7) represents the time to order a spare. Thus, at node 4, two transactions have been created. The transaction routed to node 5 represents the faulty box. The transaction routed to node 10 represents the aircraft.

Following the upper path, we see that the box waits for one unit of a test station at Q-node 5. When a test station is available,

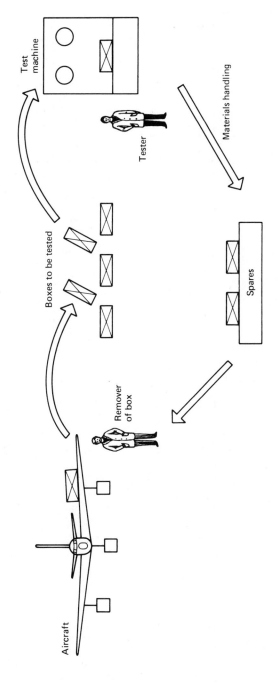

Figure 11-1 Simplified aircraft support system.

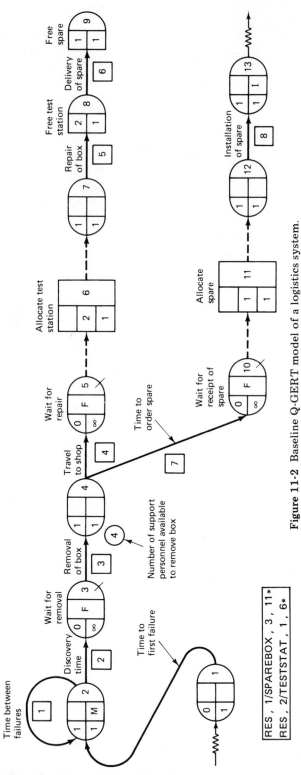

Figure 11-2 Baseline Q-GERT model of a logistics system.

ALLOCATE node 6 assigns the box to the test station and moves the box to node 7. The box is repaired with a repair time that is associated with the activity between nodes 7 and 8 (activity 5). At FREE node 8, the test station is made available for repairing other faulty boxes. Activity 6, from node 8 to node 9, represents the time required to deliver the spare. The availability of the spare is modeled through FREE node 9, which makes one unit of resource 1 (SPAREBOX) available. The resource block given in the legend of Figure 11-2 indicates that three spare boxes are available initially and they are allocated at ALLOCATE node 11.

Returning now to the aircraft, we see that the aircraft waits for a spare at Q-node 10 and, when one becomes available, it is allocated to the aircraft. The installation of the spare is modeled by the activity from node 12 to node 13 (activity 8). At node 13, the aircraft becomes operational. At node 13, the time that the aircraft is out of commission is collected, which, in this case, is the time from when a failure was detected until the time the aircraft is operationally ready. Other performance measures associated with the model in Figure 11-2 include the availability of spares (resource 1), the utilization of the test station (resource 2), the utilization of support personnel to remove failed boxes (activity 3), and the various waiting times associated with the resources and servers.

The model of Figure 11-2, although simple, does present a baseline model for understanding logistics systems. In the following sections, changes will be made to various elements of the baseline model to indicate how other functions associated with an integrated logistics support system may be modeled.

11.3 RELIABILITY

In the baseline model, failure of boxes is represented by one activity and a combined failure rate for boxes was used. This assumes that a box is a generic piece of equipment for which there was a set of spares. To include reliability aspects of different subsystems, multiple failure generation nodes and activities would be incorporated in the model, as illustrated in Figure 11-3 for three boxes. This essentially requires a node and branch similar to node 2 and activity 1 that operate in parallel and provide input to Q-node 3. An attribute would be used to identify the failed subsystem. A resource block representing a spare for each type of subsystem failure would also be required. Although additional nodes, branches, and resources are required to model the reliability of subsystems, the structure of the baseline Q-GERT model presented in Figure 11-2 is unchanged. Q-GERT networks which include these reliability concepts have been built at the Air Force Test and Evaluation Center (AFTEC) to study the combined reliability of the B52 bomber and Air Launch Cruise Missiles (ALCM).

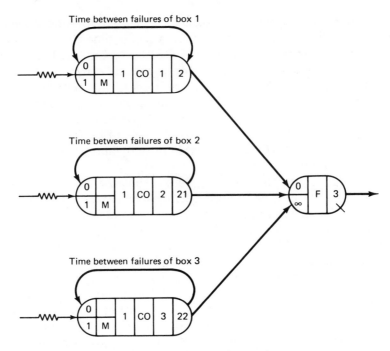

Figure 11-3 Modeling failures for equipment types.

11.4 MAINTAINABILITY

Maintainability relates to the detection, discovery, removal, and replacement operations associated with failures. Each of these activities can be modeled in as much detail as necessary to portray the system under study. In the baseline model, the activities associated with maintainability are activities 2, 3, 5, and 8. These operations are modeled at an aggregate level in Figure 11-2. The detailed tasks associated with each of these operations could be inserted directly in the network. The level of detail depends both on the use to be made of the model and the extent to which independence can be assumed among maintenance activities. If independence holds, separate analyses for each operation using a detailed Q-GERT network of tasks could be made to obtain the distribution of the time to perform an operation. The desirability and feasibility of such a decomposition of the problem is normally contingent upon the dependence between the waiting time required and the failure time associated with the aircraft equipment.

An important issue with regard to maintainability is the use of resources for detection and discovery operations when a false alarm is issued. Since false alarms are common when built-in test features are designed into the system, another input node should be included when built-in testing is employed. Figure 11-4 illustrates inclusion of false alarms into the logistics network model. In Figure 11-4, detection of

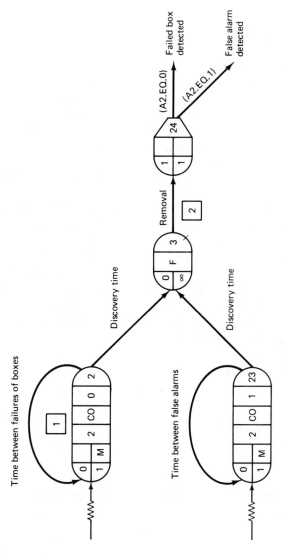

Figure 11-4 Modeling false alarms.

false alarms is assumed after a box is removed. A more complex model would involve the detection of false alarms after later activities and include a probability of detection using probabilistic branching. Probabilistic branching can also be used to model incorrect detection and categorization, that is, classifying a failure as a false alarm, and vice versa.

11.5 MAINTENANCE PLANNING

Maintenance planning involves decisions regarding the number of personnel associated with maintenance activities, the type of organizational structure for maintenance (in place, shop, or depot repair), and the complete spectrum of production and scheduling problems addressed in Chapters 6 and 7. To study staffing questions associated with maintenance planning, the network segment shown in Figure 11-5 can be used. In this figure, failures are generated for different boxes. Based on probabilistic branching at node 33, a classification of the type of repair action required is made. In Figure 11-5, it is seen that 10% of the failures are classified as "could not duplicate" (CND). For CNDs, the only maintenance actions required are associated with the discovery activities. Twenty percent of the indicated failures are for "repair in place," which requires personnel to be available on the flight line but eliminates the need for supply or transportation operations. In 70% of the indicated failures, a box is removed, and the operations described in Figure 11-2 are performed. For models of this type, the effect of personnel availability as a function of the probabilities associated with failure actions can be assessed.

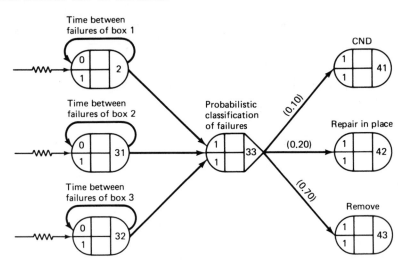

Figure 11-5 Model to investigate maintenance organizational structures.

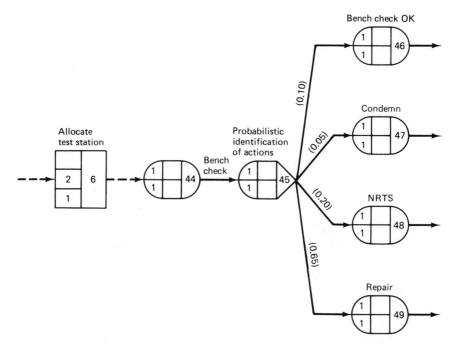

Figure 11-6 Model to assess effects of bench checks on maintenance manpower use.

Another example of maintenance planning is shown in Figure 11-6, where shop repair actions following the removal of a box are illustrated. The activities after removal involve the classification of the failed box with regard to its potential disposition. Probabilistic branching at node 45 results in the following possible courses of action:

1. The failed unit checks out satisfactory and the unit is deemed acceptable as a spare without further action (bench check OK).
2. The unit is not good enough to repair and it is condemned. This action reduces the number of spares available in the system or could institute a reorder for more units of this type (see Section 11.6).
3. The unit is classified as "not repairable this station" (NRTS) and a routing of the unit to another station is made.
4. The unit is routed through the repair operations performed at this station.

Through the classification above, the routing of failed units can be determined, and staff loading at the shop level can be evaluated.

11.6 SUPPLY

Effects of adding or deleting spares to the baseline model can be investigated directly by changing the number of resources available on the RESOURCE block. Another way of capturing the effect of spares is to include an inventory model within the logistics system. Thus, as items are condemned or classified as "not repairable this station" (NRTS), levels could be checked and additional spares introduced into the system after delays are incurred for ordering, producing, and transportation activities. Inventory or wholesale supply (which is covered in detail in Chapter 13) is an integral part of maintenance planning. Figure 11-7 illustrates the procedures for including a depot inventory control system within the logistics model. The significant feature of this model is the allocation of spare parts at ALLOCATE node 56 and the receipt of new parts at FREE node 62. The reorder point is set at node 61 and when five failures occur, node 61 is released and an order for five new spares is initiated (activity 9).

Another procedure for including spares production in the model is to include a production subnetwork in which the operations associated with producing spares is included. A model of this type has been developed for the Tennessee Valley Authority in which the production of equipment for nuclear facilities was modeled in order to determine the construction time for new nuclear reactor facilities.

11.7 TRANSPORTATION

Transportation activities associated with logistics support are easily modeled in Q-GERT by branches representing transportation times. Different types of transportation activities can be included. Thus, a branch in a Q-GERT network could represent the flying of the aircraft, the transportation of spare parts and failed units, or the movement of personnel. In some models, it has been found that the movement of personnel or resources to a work site is significant. For example, the time to transport personnel to a remote site that houses communications equipment or intercontinental ballistic missles can be larger than the actual repair time.

11.8 PERSONNEL AND TRAINING

As was discussed in the baseline model, crew sizes are modeled as the number of parallel servers or the number of resources available. Separate resources can be used to represent different skill levels of people and different types of people. By requiring multiple resources to do a job, different crew makeups can be modeled. Multiple resource require-

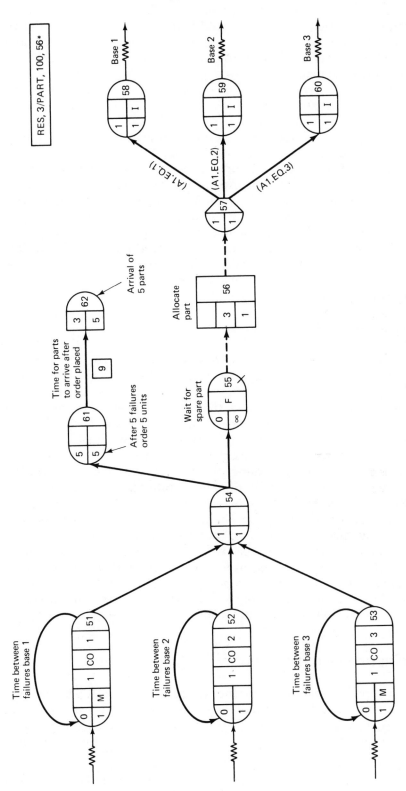

Figure 11-7 Spares reordering subnetwork.

ments can be specified by a series of ALLOCATE nodes or by using an S-node with the assembly (ASM) selection rule. For complex multiple resource requirements, subroutine ALLOC can be used to decide if an allocation should be made.

The training of personnel can be represented by a disjoint network which produces new repairmen which alters (increases) the capacity of the personnel resource due to training. Learning effects can be included in the activity times by making network modifications as a function of the current time of the number of repairs completed. An interesting use of Q-GERT has been proposed for studying job performance aids. A job performance aid, such as a maintenance manual or directory, can be thought of as adding tasks to the maintenance person's job. However, by performing tasks associated with looking-up or checking procedures, the actual time to perform the maintenance task is reduced. Trade-offs can then be made using models with an increased number of tasks but with a reduced time for the main task. In this way, improvements through the use of job performance aids can be evaluated.

11.9 SUPPORT AND TEST EQUIPMENT

Detailed models that incorporate activities relating to support and test equipment have been developed [44,208]. These models break out the specific functions associated with support and test equipment and model these functions by separate activities. Specifically, two models of the EF-111A test stations have been completed. These models include activities representing independent failures of line replaceable units (LRU), statistics on spare LRU usage, and failures of the test stations. An advanced model includes the capacity to change the configuration of individual test stations by defining separate test bays as resources. An analysis was performed to determine the impact of changes in test station configuration to the changes in the individual bays. The evaluation was made in terms of both projected spare LRU usage and the time the various resources were in use. A recent development relative to the F-16 automated intermediate shop (AIS) includes some of the organizational-level maintenance action breakout that was shown in Figure 11-5. It has been proposed to use this F-16 AIS model to study the effects of scheduling rules associated with test station outputs.

11.10 LOGISTICS FACILITIES ANALYSIS

Aerial ports receive cargo from trucks, rail, and aircraft. The cargo is unloaded, inspected, documented, sorted into aircraft loads, packaged, and moved through the terminal. The packaged cargo is then loaded onto aircraft and flown to specified destinations. During this processing, the cargo is frequently set aside in temporary storage areas. Thus, the system can be viewed as a large queueing network where cargo arrives by different methods and is routed by various material handling systems through different storage queues. This system has multiple resource constraints in that special crews, forklifts, conveyors, towline carts, and other equipment are needed for the service operations.

Q-GERT has been used extensively to analyze the logistics involved in Air Force base operations [7,8,108,113]. McNamee [111] was first to note the need for a network analysis in the design of port facilities and he showed how Q-GERT can be used to determine design requirements for new facilities as well as to evaluate suggestions for redesign of existing facilities. Auterio [7] defined the role for network analysis within the Military Airlift Command as a means for managers of the airlift system to measure the productive capacity and effectiveness of aerial port cargo processing. He further identified the need to determine the effects of fluctuating demands for cargo on airlift system performance and posed the following common managerial questions:

1. Is it worthwhile to introduce new material handling equipment at a given port? If so, what are the desirable equipment specifications?
2. How many aircraft can the air terminal handle simultaneously for different demands loads?
3. During contingencies, when demand activity is increased, what is the maximum performance that can be attained? What kind of additional resources would be necessary to improve performance?

In the next section, we describe a model abstracted from projects performed by Duket, Wortman, and Auterio for the Military Airlift Command that answered these types of questions [7,45].

11.11 ANALYZING THE LOGISTICS SYSTEM AT DOVER AIR FORCE BASE

Figure 11-8 depicts a schematic of the Dover Air Terminal.† Trucks arrive with cargo to one of three unloading docks. If a dock is not available, a queue of trucks forms. An unloading crew utilizes forklifts to unload truck cargo, to sort it by destination, and to place the sorted cargo units into carts.

A cart towline system then transports carts of cargo units to one of two storage areas (based on destination), where cargo units are accu-

†In the interest of confidentiality and ease of presentation, hypothetical data and a simplified version of the actual model are employed. In particular, document handling, which is a large part of the logistics system, is not included. Also, the features of logistics analysis previously discussed in this chapter are not included since examples of network modeling of such operations have been demonstrated.

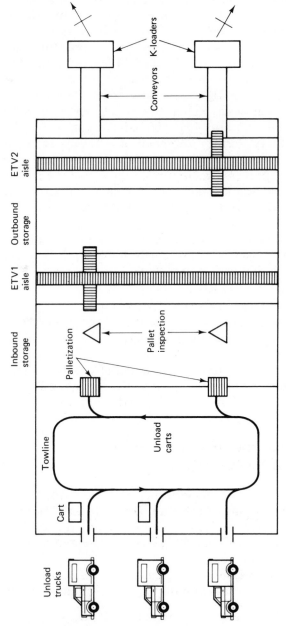

Figure 11-8 Schematic of air terminal.

mulated into pallet loads. In this example it is assumed that cargo for only two destinations is generated and that segregation of cargo in the storage areas is not required. When an entire pallet load is accumulated, the cargo is palletized and inspected at a palletization station. Inspection may result in minor adjustments and rework to the pallet formation. A material handling machine called an Elevating Transfer Vehicle (ETV) transports pallets from the palletization stations to an outbound storage area. At different points in time, a decision manager, called a load planner, determines if an aircraft load should be formed. At this time, a second ETV transfers individual pallets for the aircraft load to one of the two conveyor lines leading to a transport vehicle known as a K-loader. Ramp crews utilize the K-loaders to load the aircraft and the aircraft departs the system.

Different types of aircraft arrive at the base and await cargo loading by the K-loaders. In this example, we will consider only two aircraft classifications, large and small. Large aircraft are capable of carrying 36 pallet loads and travel to destination 2; small aircraft have a capacity of 18 pallet loads and travel to destination 1.

The actual study considered further complexities for carriers and cargo which are briefly mentioned here but are not included in the example. In the actual system, cargo is received also by rail and by air. Aircraft are unloaded and the same resources are utilized to transport the cargo from the planes to inbound storage areas through a depalletization process. Cargo can also be moved out of the system by truck or rail. Three additional cargo types were included and defined as explosive cargo, special handling cargo, and outsized cargo. Each cargo type involved the use of special facilities in addition to competing for the resources described above. Documentation processing is also an important part of the system that is not included in this abstracted example. Details of the actual study are included in the literature [45].

The managers of the aerial port were interested in port performance under different cargo flow conditions. Port performance was defined in terms of throughput, equipment and labor utilization, and the time aircraft were delayed on the ground.

By varying cargo input and measuring throughput, the model provides a means for determining the peak port throughput, that is, port capacity. The model also permits the identification of system bottlenecks and suggested alternatives to improve port operations. Alternatives would be evaluated by analyzing the revised model.

11.11.1 The Q-GERT Model

Figure 11-9 shows the Q-GERT model of the system described above. Source node 1 and activity 10 control the arrival of trucks to the dock area. Attribute 1 is used to indicate the number of cargo units on a truck. The attribute assignment (1,CO,40) at node 1 establishes the

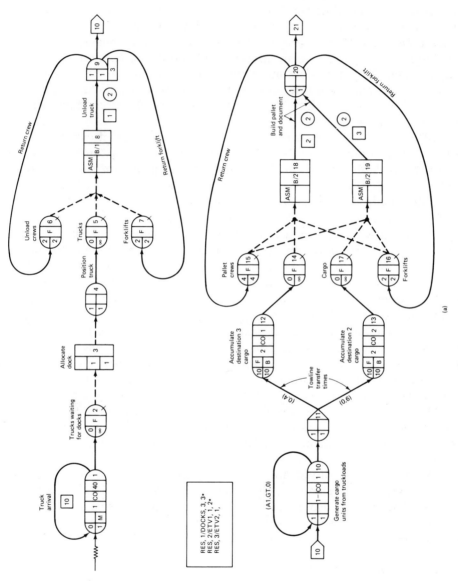

Figure 11-9 Q-GERT model of an air terminal.

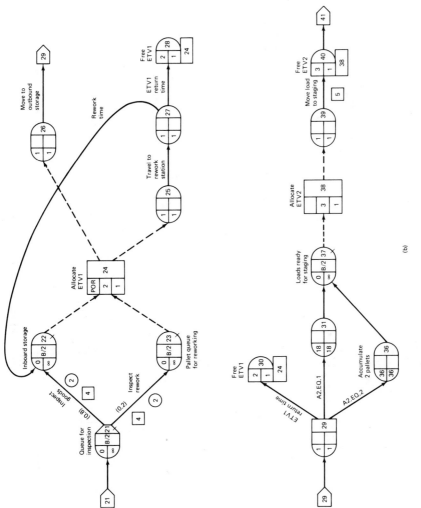

Figure 11-9 (Continued)

(b)

279

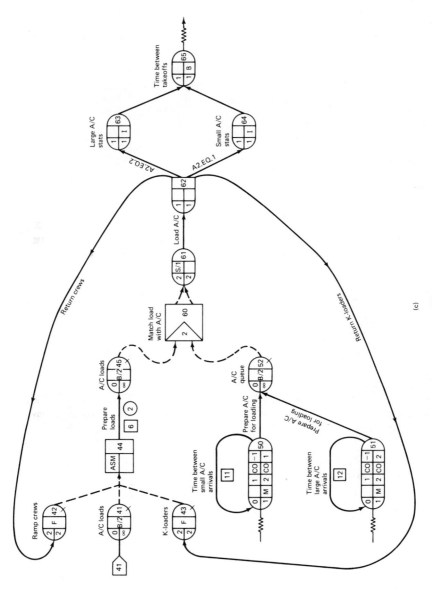

Figure 11-9 (Continued)

(c)

load size to be 40. (Again, this is a simplified representation of the actual model which differentiated types of trucks and assigned truck load sizes in a probabilistic fashion based on truck type.) Source node 50 [Figure 11-9(c)] and activity 11 model the arrival of small aircraft. Source node 51 and activity 12 model the arrival of large aircraft. An aircraft is loaded when a match between load size (or destination) and aircraft type occurs at MATCH node 52. Loaded aircraft depart the system at sink node 65, where statistics on the times between departures (takeoffs) are observed. The mean time between departure is inversely related to throughput rate.

A detailed description of cargo flow through the aerial port beginning with the arrival of trucks will now be given. When trucks arrive, they wait for an available unloading dock. Three docks are modeled and are represented as resource 1. Trucks wait for an available dock in Q-node 2 and are allocated docks by ALLOCATE node 3. The activity from node 4 to node 5 represents the delay due to positioning the truck at the unloading dock.

The configuration of nodes 5, 6, 7, 8, and 9 model the unloading operation. The actual unloading is modeled by service activity 1. This is a resource-constrained queueing process in that an unloading crew and a forklift must be available prior to unloading (see Section 9.4 for alternative methods of modeling resource limited queueing situations). Q-node 5 represents trucks waiting for unloading. Q-nodes 6 and 7 represent available crews and forklifts, respectively. The assembly (ASM) queue selection rule of S-node 8 specifies that a transaction must be in Q-nodes 5, 6, *and* 7 before server 1 begins service. The values for Q-nodes 6 and 7 indicate that two crews and two forklifts are available initially.

Server 1 represents parallel unloading operations. The number of busy servers corresponds to the number of trucks being unloaded. The maximum number of busy servers will never exceed the minimum number of available crews or forklifts. That is, at most two trucks will be unloaded simultaneously. FREE node 9 frees a dock, that is, one unit of resource 1. The branches to nodes 6 and 7 return the crew and forklift used during unloading to their availability queues.

Node 10 is used to generate cargo units into the system at each truck unloading. The attribute assignment at node 10 decreases attribute 1 by one through the specification (1–,CO,1). The loop around node 10 reschedules a release of node 10 if attribute 1 is greater than zero. The branch to node 11 is taken at each release of node 10. Therefore, each truck transaction that reaches node 9 causes 40 (original value of attribute 1 set at source node 1) transactions to arrive at node 11.

The cargo units are next sorted according to their final destination. Probabilistic branching at node 11 specifies that 40% of the cargo units are for destination 1 and 60% are for destination 2, with the classification done on a random basis. The activities from node 11 to node 12 and from node 11 to node 13 represent the time for cargo to traverse the cart towline system. Although it is possible to model this subsystem in more detail, for example, to include it as a resource, this was not considered necessary by the analysts of the system.

Nodes 12 and 13 represent the accumulation of cargo units into pallet loads. A pallet load is a grouping of cargo units that will eventually be placed on a pallet. The number of incoming transactions required for the release of these nodes is 10, indicating that 10 units comprise a pallet load. These nodes also assign the destination number to attribute 2, and are used to collect statistics on the time between pallet load accumulations. When sufficient cargo for a pallet load is accumulated, a transaction is sent to either Q-node 14 or 17 depending on cargo destination. To build and document pallets by either service activity 2 or 3 requires both a pallet crew and forklift. Nodes 14, 15, 16, 17, 18, and 19 illustrate the use of multiple S-nodes for assembling transactions. This is a resource-constrained service operation similar to the one discussed above for truck unloading. Q-node 15 represents available "pallet crews" of which there are 4, initially. Q-node 16 represents available forklifts of which there are 2, initially. For this model, Q-nodes 15 and 16 reference both S-nodes 19 and 18 in that order. This ordering specifies that a pallet transaction in Q-node 17 is to be assembled before a pallet transaction in Q-node 14, when both a forklift and a pallet crew become available.

After pallet building, pallet inspection takes place. Pallets waiting for inspection reside in Q-node 21. Only one inspection occurs at a time, but the length of the inspection time is chosen in a probabilistic manner. Eighty percent of the pallets have been built correctly and a normal inspection time is incurred. For 20% of the pallets, the inspection is more detailed and corrective action is required. Good pallets wait in Q-node 22 and pallets requiring rework are placed in Q-node 23.

After inspection, a pallet requires ETV1 in order for it to be moved. Q-nodes 22 and 23 are associated with ALLOCATE node 24. Pallets to be reworked are routed to node 25. The activity from node 25 to 27 is the time to move the pallet to the rework area. For the purposes of this illustration, the availability of a rework crew is assumed. The activity from node 27 to Q-node 22 represents the rework time for the pallet. The activity from node 27 to 28 represents the return time for ETV1. Following this activity, ETV1 is freed and will be reallocated at node 24. Pallets passing inspection wait for ETV1 at Q-node 22. When available, ETV1 moves the pallets to outbound storage. In the outbound area, transactions represent loads. For destination 1 cargo, small aircraft are used, and 18 pallets correspond to a load. A load for destination 2 employs large aircraft that can carry 36 pallets. Conditional, take-all branching from node 29 is used to return ETV1 after a travel activity at FREE node 30 and to route the pallet. The pallet is routed to node 31 if it is for destination 1 or to node 36, where 36 pallets are accumulated into a load for destination 2.

Loads ready for staging wait at Q-node 37 with loads for destination 2 given priority. For aircraft loads to be moved to final staging requires the use of ETV2 as shown at ALLOCATE node 38. The time to move the load to staging (activity 5) was made a function of the type of load (attribute 2). No queue selection rule is given at node 38, as only a single Q-node precedes the allocation of ETV2. If more complex decision making is desired with respect to the processing of loads for large aircraft and small aircraft, separate queues could be placed before ALLOCATE node 38 and a queue selection rule used to decide whether loads for large aircraft or small aircraft should be processed next.† The activity between nodes 39 and 40 represents the delay associated with moving the load to final staging. At FREE node 40, one unit of resource 3 (ETV2) is made available.

At Q-node 41, the aircraft loads are available and it is required to have the ramp crew and a K-loader available to prepare the load. Nodes 41, 42, 43, 44, and 45 again represent a labor-limited queueing situation as previously described and the concepts involved should be clear from the Q-GERT network.

The aircraft arrival process is represented by source nodes 50 and 51. The aircraft ready for loading wait in Q-node 52. Large aircraft loads are matched with loads for destination 2 and small aircraft loads with loads for destination 1 by employing a MATCH node (node 60) and matching on attribute 2, which has been set equal to 1 for small aircraft and destination 1 loads and to 2 for large aircraft and destination 2 loads. When a match occurs, a plane to be loaded emanates from node 61. At node 61, the SAVE criterion for attributes is specified as S/1, a small value of attribute 1. This saves the attributes of the aircraft as a negative value for attribute 1 is assigned at node 50 and 51. Thus, the mark time associated with aircraft arrivals is maintained when transactions are accumulated at node 61. To load the aircraft requires the ramp crew and the K-loader, and these are returned following the loading of the aircraft by the branches returning to Q-nodes 42 and 43. If a large aircraft is loaded, a branch to node 63 is taken so that statistics on the time large aircraft are at the terminal can be collected. A similar function is performed at node 64 for small aircraft. The time between takeoffs is collected using between-statistics as node 65. This completes the description of the Q-GERT network that models the movement of material through an air terminal.

†Load planning decisions at a terminal are varied and complex. In one situation, a user function was employed to test the type of aircraft currently on the ground. In addition, it is possible to schedule an aircraft to land given a load is ready. The reader should note that modeling aircraft as resources would facilitate these embellishments.

11.11.2 Model Output and Use

For the actual terminal port studied, there were extensive statistical summaries obtained for many quantities. To illustrate the diversity of outputs obtained, Table 11-1 lists the complete set of output variables obtained from the actual application. The footnoted entries signify that the output variable was not included in the abstracted version of the model that was presented in this chapter. As can be seen from the output variables listed, the primary portion omitted from the abstracted

TABLE 11-1 Output from Q-GERT Model
of an Air Terminal

1. Quantity and frequency of input to the facility
   1.1 Truck and aircraft arrivals
   1.2 Cargo pieces and shipments received
   1.3 Transshipments[a]
   1.4 Missions scheduled
   1.5 Advance notification documents[a]
2. Quantity and frequency of facility production
   2.1 Total inbound aircraft loads
       (including documentation) handled
   2.2 Total outbound aircraft loads
       (including documentation) handled
   2.3 Pallet loads produced
   2.4 Pallet positions of unpalletizeable cargo[a]
   2.5 Reports to local authorities[a]
   2.6 Reports to headquarters and airlift authorities
3. Personnel/equipment requirements and busy times
   3.1 Receipt card runner[a]
   3.2 Load planning runner[a]
   3.3 Offloading crews[a]
   3.4 Onloading crews[a]
   3.5 Pallet buildup crews
   3.6 Forklifts for 15 locations[a]
   3.7 K-loaders/operators
   3.8 Customs inspectors[a]
   3.9 Documentation manual edits[a]
4. Terminal facility bottleneck indications
   4.1 Tally collections
   4.2 All cargo transfers
   4.3 Machine room preparation of advance
       receipt documents
   4.4 Load planning document preparation
   4.5 Ramp loading/unloading
   4.6 Truck dock unloading
   4.7 Pallet buildup/breakdown stations
   4.8 Load pulling and staging operations

[a]Outputs not available from abstracted example, and they represent quantities obtained from several Q-GERT models of air terminals.

model deals with documentation processing that must accompany any material processing.

One of the most important quantities associated with a cargo terminal is referred to as port saturation. *Port saturation* is defined as the total output level for which no additional output is obtained when there is an increase in inputs. The saturation values were obtained from the Q-GERT model by increasing cargo input rates and recording output rates from successive simulation runs.

Additional runs were made to determine the ability of the port to respond to emergency conditions. Of interest in this study was the amount of output that could be obtained in a 30-day period following the initiation of a decision to use the port at saturation levels. For this study, different initial conditions associated with inputs, pallet loads, and aircraft availability were specified, and the output as a function of increased input levels to the port was investigated.

Resource studies were also made using the port model. At one of the terminals (not Dover), it was determined that the primary constraint involved documentation processing prior to load planning activities. When these constraints were removed in the model, saturation capacity increased by an average eight aircraft loads per day and the secondary constraint became the forklift distribution. The removal of the forklift constraint resulted in an additional 1.5 aircraft loads being processed [7].

11.12 SUMMARY

A framework for studying logistics systems problems using network models has been presented in this chapter. In particular, the concepts of reliability, maintainability, maintenance planning, supply, transportation, personnel and training, and support and test equipment were discussed in terms of Q-GERT modeling capabilities. An example showing how Q-GERT can be used for logistics facilities analysis has been presented with reference to an abstracted model of the activities and logic involved in moving material through Dover Air Force Base.

11.13 EXERCISES

11-1. For the baseline model of a logistics system, develop qualitative relationships between the following performance measures and system elements:
   (a) The time to replenish a spare and the time to order a spare
   (b) The time to replenish a spare and the number of support personnel available to remove a box
   (c) The number of aircraft waiting for repair and the time to install a spare
   (d) The time an aircraft is out of commission to the number of support personnel available.

11-2. In the modeling of false alarms shown in Figure 11-4, embellish the network to model the misclassification of failures and false alarms.

11-3. Build a Q-GERT model to represent a system consisting of three parallel units which fails only when all three units fail.

11-4 Combine the various submodels presented in this chapter into an integrated model of a logistics system. Discuss the impacts of each submodel on total system performance and how a study could be performed to identify the critical subsystems in a total logistics system.

11-5. Discuss how regression analysis could be used to build a model that relates the Q-GERT output statistics to Q-GERT input values. Discuss the advantages and disadvantages of having a regression equation that models the Q-GERT model.

11-6. Cargo arrives at an air terminal in unit loads at the rate of two unit loads per minute. At the freight terminal there is no fixed schedule, and planes take off as soon as they can be loaded to capacity. Two types of planes are available for transporting cargo. There are three planes with a capacity of 80 unit loads and two planes that have a capacity of 140 unit loads. The round-trip time for any plane is normally distributed with a mean of 3 hours, a standard deviation of 1 hour, and minimum and maximum times of 2 and 4 hours, respectively. The loading policy of the terminal manager is to employ smaller planes whenever possible. Only when 140 unit loads are available will a plane of type 2 be employed. Develop a Q-GERT network to model this system to estimate the waiting time of unit loads and the utilization of the two types of planes over a 100-hour period.

Embellishments:

(a) Model failures in aircraft that occur with probability 0.1 after each flight. Repair time is 1.5 hours if a spare is available and 8 hours if no spare is available. Assume that spares are available 90% of the time.

(b) Modify the model for embellishment (a) by incorporating an inventory model for spare parts that keeps only one spare on line and which orders a spare every time one is used. The time to obtain a spare is 32 hours. Increase the simulation period for this model to 320 hours and evaluate system performance.

Reliability
and Quality Control

12.1 INTRODUCTION

The approach to system reliability problems follows directly from the basic concepts of systems analysis. Systems analysis is a procedure for studying a system by decomposing it into subsystems, analyzing the subsystems, and integrating the analyses into a total systems assessment.

In reliability evaluation, a system is decomposed into its component parts, analyses are done on the component parts to determine part reliability, and these part reliabilities are combined in a mathematical and logical fashion to obtain system reliability predictions. Networks and Q-GERT, in particular, also follow this systems analysis approach by providing elements (nodes and branches) for describing system components for which data are collected and then turned into system performance measures through the use of a network analyzer such as the Q-GERT processor. Thus, it seems natural that networks would be used in reliability analyses.

Many authors have used GERT for analyzing reliability situations. Skeith and Skinner have developed analytical procedures which employ Mellin transforms on GERT exclusive-or networks for special types of reliability problems. Whitehouse presents several approaches to reliability analysis using GERT [211,212]. The use of GERT IIIZ for reliability analysis has also been demonstrated [27,157].

Since reliability problems occur frequently, a specialized GERT IIIZ program was developed for analyzing the reliability of systems which includes both failure and repair. The program, called GRASP, was initially developed by Shulaker and Phillips and was finalized by Polito and Petersen [148]. The GRASP program has been used for complex reliability analysis for the Navy and at several steel corporations.

12.2 RELIABILITY DEFINITIONS

In an initial design of a system, operations or components are placed in series such that the failure of any component results in the failure of the system. To increase the working time of the system, the components are often replaced with subsystems consisting of parallel units, any one of which is capable of performing system operations. In this way, the failure of a unit does not result in the failure of the system. A reliability assessment requires the analysis of series, parallel, and combinations of series and parallel subsystems.

Definitions of reliability vary in the literature. The reason for this is that reliability can be considered in a static sense or in a dynamic sense. For a fixed time period, the reliability of a component can be considered as the probability that the component fails in the time period. This probability is the static reliability of the component performing satisfactorily during the lifetime of the system or the mission time for the system. Alternatively, we can define reliability in terms of the mean time to failure and consider repairing the component while a component in parallel performs the required operation. In this case, the reliability of the system is determined on a dynamic basis and depends on both failure distributions and repair distributions of operations being performed.

Q-GERT models to evaluate the static reliability of systems are straightforward. Models for determining the probability of the system working during a fixed mission time for three units in series and three units in parallel are shown in Figure 12-1. Node 11 represents system success and the probability of reaching node 11 reflects system reliability. When components are in series, all three components must work during the entire mission; hence, the three branches incident to node 11 must be completed in order to have system success. Thus the first release requirement, S, for node 11 is 3. If any of the components fail, node 12 would be released and a system failure would occur since for the first release requirement, R, for node 12 would be prescribed as 1. When components are in parallel, the values of S and R are reversed so that it only takes one activity incident to node 11 to achieve system success, and all three components must fail in order for node 12 to be released. For subsystems in series, the Q-GERT model of Figure 12-1 would be repeated for each subsystem with appropriate values of R and S inserted.

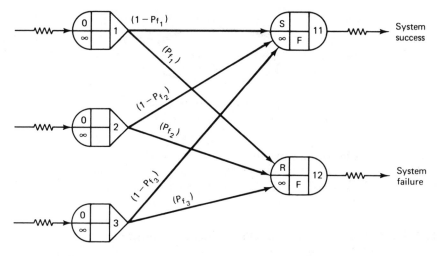

Figure 12-1 Static reliability for components in series and parallel. For components in series: S = 3, R = 1; for components in parallel: S = 1, R = 3; p_{f_i}, probability that component i fails during the mission time.

Let us now consider dynamic reliability assessment. In Figure 12-2, a Q-GERT model of three units in series is shown. Each unit is represented by an activity with the time to failure of a unit being the activity time. Since the units are in series, failure of any unit results in the failure of the system. Thus, we show the activities in parallel in the Q-GERT network of Figure 12-2, and the time to system failure is the time of the first component failure. Thus, only one release is required of node 3 for system failure to occur. Note that in modeling reliability in a dynamic fashion, it is not a question of whether the system will fail but when it will fail. The histogram associated with node 3 provides an estimate of the distribution of the time to failure. The probability of successful system operation up to time t is estimated by the fraction of runs on which the system time to failure is greater than t. Thus, the complementary value of the cumulative frequency is used to estimate system reliability.

In Figure 12-3, the Q-GERT network for three units in parallel is given. This network model is similar to the model of units in series presented in Figure 12-2. The only difference is the requirement for three

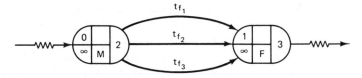

Figure 12-2 Q-GERT model to evaluate the reliability of three units in series: t_{f_i}, time to failure for component i.

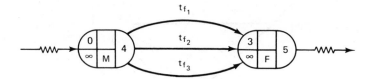

Figure 12-3 Q-GERT model to evaluate the reliability of three units in parallel: t_{f_i}, time to failure for component i.

activity completions at node 5. This specifies that all units must fail before the system fails. With this minor change, we have converted from a series system model to a parallel systems model.

12.3 RELIABILITY OF COMBINED PARALLEL–SERIES SYSTEMS [27,158]

To demonstrate the use of Q-GERT to model combined series and parallel systems, consider the following system configuration.

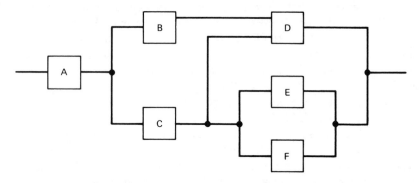

In this system, unit A is in series with a subsystem consisting of units B, C, D, E, and F. For the subsystem, unit B is in series with unit D and unit C is in series with both unit D and a subsystem consisting of units E and F in parallel.

The Q-GERT model to determine the time to system failure without component repair is shown in Figure 12-4. Node 15 represents system failure that can occur if activity 1 occurs or activity 7 occurs. Activity 7 occurs when the subsystem that is in series with unit A fails. The modeling of the subsystem is more complex in that it represents three parallel paths whose failure is modeled by nodes 11, 12, and 13. Node 11 will be released if either unit B or D fails, node 12 is released if unit D or C fails, and node 13 is released if unit C fails or both unit E and F fail. Figure 12-4 illustrates how Q-GERT portrays these potential failure paths.

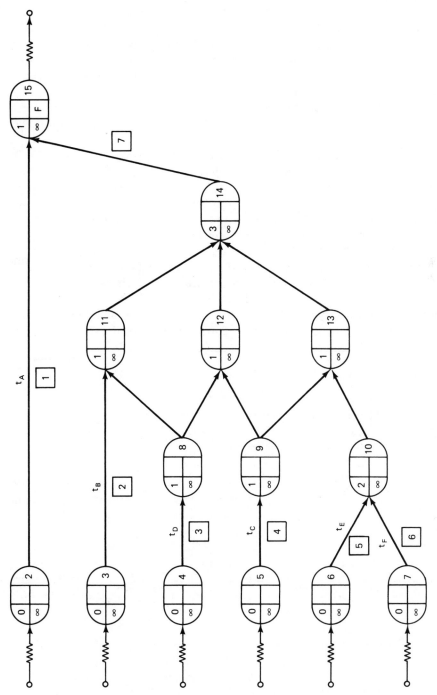

Figure 12-4 Q-GERT model of a combination of series–parallel units.

291

12.4 SYSTEM RELIABILITY WITH REPAIR

We now consider the case in which components can be repaired. If components are in series and every component is required for the system to work, our reliability assessment does not change due to the ability to repair the component because as soon as a component fails, the system fails. Thus, we restrict our attention to situations in which there are components in parallel.

When repair is possible, a unit can be in one of two states: operative or being repaired (nonoperative). Each state of a unit is modeled by an activity so that two activities are associated with a unit. Thus, modeling the unit's status creates no difficulty. Since the units are in parallel, it is necessary to indicate a system failure only when all units have a failed status; that is, all units are in the "being repaired" activity.

At first glance, to count the number of units being repaired appears to be best modeled by using network modifications. This is the case for two units in parallel which will be used to illustrate the modeling approach to this reliability problem. The network model is shown in Figure 12-5. Activity 1 represents the time to failure for unit 1 and activity 3 represents the repair time for unit 1. Activities 2 and 4 represent analogous states for unit 2. Following activity 3, activity 1 is started. When activity 1 is completed, node 22 is replaced in the network by node 4 through the use of a network modification. Thus, if

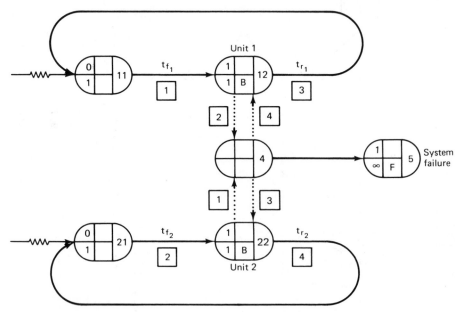

Figure 12-5 Q-GERT model to evaluate the reliability of two units in parallel with repair capability. Node ij represents component i and state of the system j, where $j = 1$ for working and $j = 2$ for being repaired: t_{f_i}, time to failure of component i; t_{r_i}, time to repair component i.

activity 2 is completed representing the failure of unit 2, a transaction arrives to node 4 and then to node 5 to indicate system failure. However, if activity 3 is completed prior to the failure of the second unit, the network is remodified, with node 4 being replaced by node 22. In summary, node 22 is taken out of the network when unit 1 fails and placed back into the network when unit 1 is operative. The same analysis applies to node 12 with reference to unit 2. By using these nodal modifications system failure for the two units in parallel when repair capability exists is modeled.

Although the repair process is shown by a single activity, it is clear that the activity could be replaced by a complicated Q-GERT network which involves the unit waiting for repairmen and potentially other types of resources.

The use of nodal modifications in Figure 12-5 essentially provides the counting process desired for the number of units that are in a failed or "being repaired" state. Typically in a Q-GERT network, a node is used for counting with its release requirement equal to the number defining a special state. Every time that a count is to be indexed, a signal would be sent to the node and the number of releases required would be decremented by one. With repair capability, such an approach is not feasible, as it is desirable to increase as well as decrease the number of release requirements associated with the node used for counting. The Q-GERT syntax does not have a direct mechanism for modeling the increase in the number of releases required at a node. As in previous situations, when the Q-GERT syntax does not provide sufficient capability to model the system in the manner desired, we resort to user functions.

Before presenting this user function, we digress to discuss the evolution of the model to be presented. In a draft paper by E. R. Clayton et al., a Q-GERT model of this situation was developed that involved several Q-nodes, a regular node, a MATCH node, and a disjoint network. Based on this model, we developed a network that required two nodes, two branches, and two user functions for each component in parallel and a single node to represent system failure. In this model, use was made of subroutine PTIN (put transaction into the network), which is probably the least pleasing graphically of the Q-GERT concepts. Ken Musselman of Pritsker & Associates, Inc., when reviewing this chapter developed an approach to the problem using resource concepts. After seeing the resource approach, we developed an approach based on Q-nodes and service activities that represented system failure by balking.

The gist of this digression is that models evolve over time and that they become simpler after they have gone through three or four stages of development. A similar observation has been made with regard to mathematical programming formulations [159]. To indicate this model development sequence, we present three of the modeling approaches to the system reliability problem.

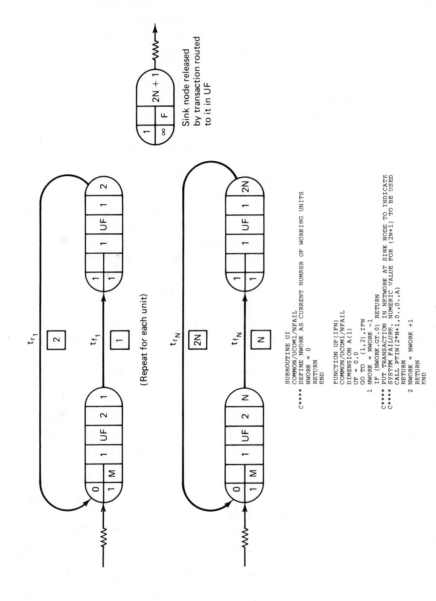

Figure 12-6 Q-GERT model and user function for system reliability assessment with repairs.

12.4.1 Counting in a User Function

Every time a unit fails, user function 1 will be called and the number of working units is decreased by 1. If the number of working units is zero, system failure occurs which will be accomplished by inserting a transaction into the network to arrive at a node representing system failure. Whenever a unit is repaired, user function 2 is called and the number of working units is increased by 1.

The Q-GERT network model, function UF, and subroutine UI for N units in parallel are shown in Figure 12-6. In this example, subroutine UI is employed to initialize the number of working units in parallel (NWORK) to zero. This initialization is performed in subroutine UI so that it is accomplished at the beginning of each run. Clearly, with the use of user functions, complex failure and repair operations can be modeled and information on the number of failures and the number of repairs can be obtained.

12.4.2 A Resource Approach

A resource approach to modeling system reliability when units are repairable involves defining operational units as a resource. Each time a unit fails and begins repair, the capacity of the resource is decreased by one. Following the failure of a unit, a check is made to see if the capacity of the resource has been reduced to zero. If this occurs, all units are in the failed state and a system failure has occurred.

The Q-GERT model of this situation, including function UF, is shown in Figure 12-7. In the Q-GERT model, conditional, take-all branching is used at node 1 to insert N units into the network. The capacity of the resource is increased by 1 at ALTER node 2. In the resource block, the capacity of the resource is initially set to zero. The failure time for each unit is specified in user function 1, which defines the duration for activity 1. All failure times are placed in one activity for compactness and to avoid the three-dot notation used in Figure 12-6 to indicate N parallel systems. When a unit fails, ALTER node 3 causes a decrease in the capacity of the units operating (resource 1) by 1. In user function 3, attribute 2 is set equal to the current capacity of resource 1. If attribute 2 equals 0, node 4 is released, which represents system failure. Otherwise, a repair is started with the repair time obtained from user function 2. When the repair is completed, the capacity of resource 1 is increased by 1. Within the framework of this model, the availability of resource 1 represents the number of units in an operative state. Thus, the statistics on the availability of resource 1 provide information on the average number of units working. This model illustrates an interesting use of resources, as they are never allocated.

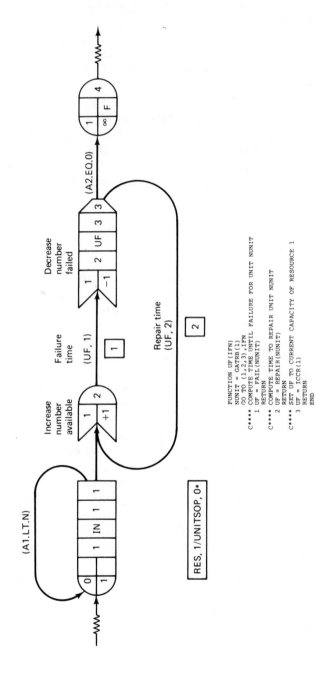

Figure 12-7 Q-GERT model using resources for system reliability assessment.

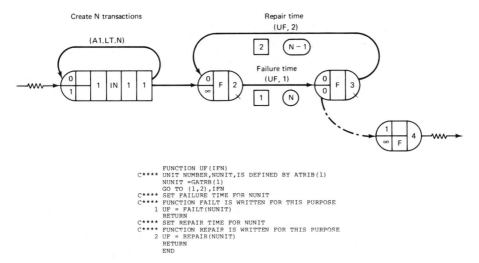

```
        FUNCTION UF(IFN)
C****   UNIT NUMBER,NUNIT,IS DEFINED BY ATRIB(1)
        NUNIT =GATRB(1)
        GO TO (1,2),IFN
C****   SET FAILURE TIME FOR NUNIT
C****   FUNCTION FAILT IS WRITTEN FOR THIS PURPOSE
     1  UF = FAILT(NUNIT)
        RETURN
C****   SET REPAIR TIME FOR NUNIT
C****   FUNCTION REPAIR IS WRITTEN FOR THIS PURPOSE
     2  UF = REPAIR(NUNIT)
        RETURN
        END
```

Figure 12-8 Q-GERT model using balking for system reliability assessment.

12.4.3 System Failure as a Balking Transaction

A third model for this system reliability problem is presented in Figure 12-8. The creation of the N components is accomplished at node 1 as before. Each of the components is placed in service activity 1, which models the unit's failure time. When a unit fails, it is placed in activity 2, which represents the repair operation. The number of concurrent repairs is restricted to $N - 1$. Thus, if a unit fails and there are $N - 1$ repairs ongoing, it is the Nth failure and a system failure has occurred. To detect this on the network, balking from Q-node 3 to node 4 is used. Thus, the time at which node 4 is released represents the time until system failure. The expected number of components operating is estimated from statistics on activity 1, and this is the reason for making node 2 a Q-node.

The presentation of three alternative methods of modeling the same problem illustrates the versatility of network modeling. In our opinion, there is not one best way to model a system and having the flexibility to model a system from different viewpoints is one of the great advantages of Q-GERT network concepts.

12.5 POWER STATION MAINTENANCE REPAIR EVALUATION[†]

As an example of reliability modeling using Q-GERT, consider a power station that requires three generators to be on-line at all times. Since all three generators must be operative to prevent a power system fail-

[†]This example was developed in conjunction with Robert Trent when he was associated with the Construction Evaluation and Research Laboratory (CERL) of the U.S. Army.

ure, company policy is to have one spare generator that can replace any generator that fails. In addition, it is company policy to start repair work immediately on a generator that has failed. The statistical characteristics describing the failure time t_f for each of the generators is assumed to be identical. However, the spare generator is not of the same quality as the on-line generators and its failure time is described by t_{f_s}. Let the time to repair a generator be given by the random variable t_r.

The Q-GERT network model of the power station generators to obtain statistics on time-to-system failure due to the simultaneous failure of two generators is shown in Figure 12-9. The three generators are created at source node 1 and placed into operation in activity 1, which represents the time until failure of a generator that is on-line. When a generator fails, node 5 is released, which causes the repair to start (activity 2) and the spare generator to be used (activity 3). If the spare generator fails before the completion of repair, that is, $t_{f_s} < t_r$, node 5 is released and the activity from node 5 to node 6 is taken. This indicates that the power station has become inoperative because one of the original generators failed and the spare failed before repair was accomplished.

If the generator is repaired prior to the failure of the spare generator, that is, $t_r < t_{f_s}$, activity 2 is completed before activity 3. This causes a transaction to pass through Q-node 2 and a generator to be put on-line again. At Q-node 2, a user function is employed to turn the spare generator off since it is no longer required once the failed generator is repaired and placed back on-line. The assumption being made here is that the spare generator is of lower quality than the on-line generators; hence, the spare generator should not be used except in emergency situations. To halt activity 3, subroutine HALTA is called in function UF as shown in Figure 12-9.

Statistics collected in this example are:

1. Between-statistics at node 5 to estimate the time between on-line generator failures
2. First-statistics at node 7 to estimate the time of failure for one on-line generator and the spare generator
3. First-statistics at node 4 to estimate the time of failure for the power station
4. Utilization of on-line generators on activity 1
5. Utilization of the repairperson on activity 2

These statistics can be used by management to answer the following types of questions:

Is power station reliability sufficient to meet customer requirements?

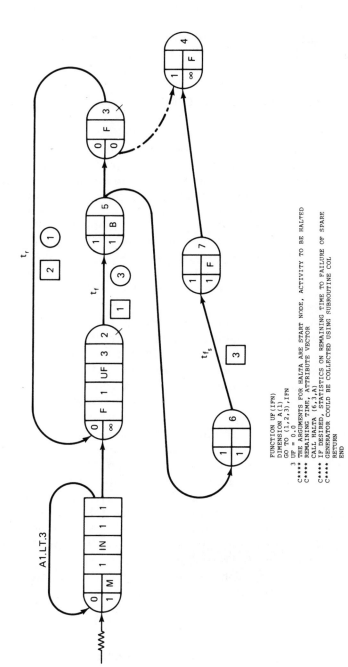

```
        FUNCTION UF(IFN)
        DIMENSION A(1)
        GO TO (1,2,3),IFN
      3 UF = 0.0
C****   THE ARGUMENTS FOR HALTA ARE START NODE, ACTIVITY TO BE HALTED
C****   REMAINING TIME, ATTRIBUTE VECTOR
        CALL HALTA (6,3,A)
C****   IF DESIRED, STATISTICS ON REMAINING TIME TO FAILURE OF SPARE
C****   GENERATOR COULD BE COLLECTED USING SUBROUTINE COL
        RETURN
        END
```

Figure 12-9 Q-GERT model of power station generator system.

299

Should a better spare generator be bought?

How many repairmen will be needed to fix failed generators?

The model presented can easily be modified to represent more generators, repairmen, and additional spare generators.

12.6 MODELING QUALITY CONTROL SAMPLING PLANS

Quality control sampling plans provide procedures for evaluating the quality of manufacturing lots. A properly designed quality control plan results in actions and methods improvements that can reduce the losses resulting from rejections, scrap, and rework. The investment in terms of time and cost for inspection typically yield high returns due to the avoidance of such losses and the gains obtained from an increased customer satisfaction with a quality product. As reported in Whitehouse [212], Fry, Powell, and Mullin studied Dodge's Continuous Sampling Plan, CSP-1, using GERT. Whitehouse [213] has used GERT to model diverse quality control systems and Whitehouse [212] and Skeith have developed network models of Military Standard 105D, which is a complex sampling plan.

Acceptance sampling plans are an integral part of quality control. The purpose of acceptance sampling is to determine a course of action rather than to estimate lot quality. The plan prescribes that a sample of size n be taken from the lot. If there are c or fewer defects in the sample, the lot should be accepted. From the acceptance sampling plan, the risk of accepting lots of a given quality can be estimated. In other words, acceptance sampling yields quality assurance.

To model acceptance sampling plans in Q-GERT, probabilistic branching is employed to specify whether an item is defective or not. A count is kept to determine whether the number of defects detected has reached the acceptance number. A count is also kept on the number of items inspected. If the count for defectives increases above the acceptance number before the count for the sample reaches the total sample size, the lot is rejected. Otherwise, the lot is accepted. Separate nodes represent the rejection and acceptance of the lot. By making multiple runs, estimates of the probabilities of accepting or rejecting a lot based on the sampling plan are made. In the next section, an example that demonstrates the use of Q-GERT to model a double sampling plan is given.

12.7 Q-GERT MODEL OF A DOUBLE SAMPLING PLAN

In a double sampling plan, a sample of size n_1 is taken first. If c_1 or fewer defective parts are detected, the lot is accepted based on this one sample size. If more than c_2 defective parts are detected, the lot is rejected. If more than c_1 but fewer than or equal to c_2 defective parts are discovered, another sample of size n_2 is examined. If more than c_3 parts are found defective, including those from the first sample, the lot is rejected; otherwise, it is accepted.

To evaluate the performance of this plan for various values of n_1, n_2, c_1, c_2, c_3, and a given probability of a defective item† p, the Q-GERT network given in Figure 12-10 is employed. In this example, testing times are omitted and only the number of parts tested is assessed. If times are added to the model, the total testing time required for the sampling plan can be determined. Similarly, the costs of these activities may be evaluated.

In Figure 12-10, activities 3 and 4 represent the testing and classification of a part. Activity 3 is selected with the probability $1 - p$ and activity 4 is selected with probability p. Thus, parts classified as defective cause node 3 to be released and parts classified as nondefective cause node 4 to be released. The network following node 4 is used to count the number of tests performed and to determine whether the lot should be accepted. The portion of the network following node 3 is used to count the number of parts classified as defective and to determine if the lot should be rejected. A branch from node 3 to node 4 is necessary since a test that classified a part as defective should also be counted toward the total number of parts inspected.

Node 5 counts the number of parts classified as defective and when that number is greater than c_1, activity 1 is taken. The number of the first release requirement for node 5 is $c_1' = c_1 + 1$. Activity 1 occurs when more than c_1 defective parts have been observed, and causes the network to be modified so that the lot cannot be accepted based on the first sample. This is accomplished by replacing node 7 with node 9 through a network modification. When this occurs, node 8 cannot be reached and, hence, we cannot accept the lot based on the first sample.

Following activity 1 is node 6, which is used to determine if the lot should be rejected on the first sample. c_2' inputs are required to release node 6, which represents the additional defective parts above c_1 required to reject the lot on the first sample; that is, $c_2' = c_2 - c_1 + 1$. If node 6 is released before the second sample is started, the lot is rejected. The second sample is started when node 7 is released, as it requires n_1 inputs to release it. If node 7 is released prior to the completion of activity 1, the lot would be accepted on the first sample.

The number of tests in the second sample is counted at node 10. The first completion of activity 2 removes node 5 from the network, as we no longer desire to reject the lot based on the first sample. In the model, the first completion of activity 2 modifies node 5 to node 12,

---

†If a lot fraction defective is estimated, the probability of classifying a part as defective will change slightly each time a part is tested. This would be included in the Q-GERT model using probabilistic branching based on attribute values.

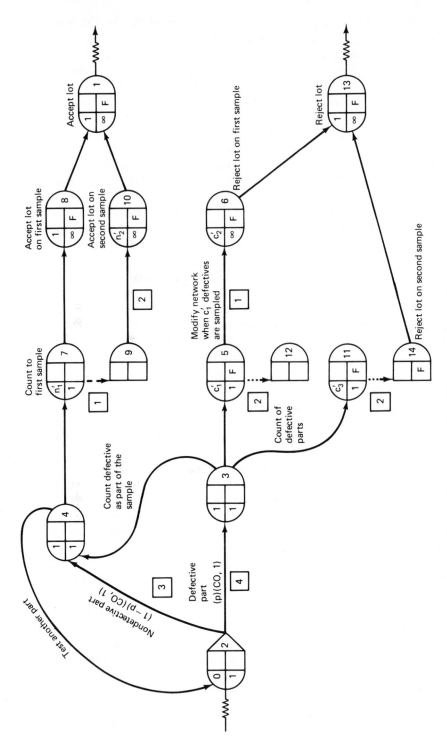

Figure 12-10 Q-GERT model of a double sampling plan: n_1, sample size 1; n_2, sample size 2; $n_2' = n_2 + 1$; c_1, acceptance number for n_1; $c_1' = c_1 + 1$; c_2, rejection number for n_1; $c_2' = c_2 - c_1 + 1$; c_3, acceptance number for n_2; $c_3' = c_3 + 1$; p, part fraction defective.

which is used only to stop transactions from reaching node 6. For node 10, $n'_2 = n_2 + 1$ inputs are required, as the last test of the first sample causes node 7 to be released and counts as one input to node 10.

Throughout the whole testing of parts in the sample, the number of defectives is counted at node 11. If this number becomes larger than c_3, the lot is rejected. However, if the second sample has not been started, no action is required, as the lot would be rejected based on the first sample. Thus, node 14 is inserted into the network when the second sample begins (activity 2) so that statistics on rejections on the second sample can be calculated. Statistics are also collected at nodes 8 and 10, which represent acceptance of the lot on the first and second samples, respectively. As mentioned above, statistics on nodes 6 and 14 represent rejection on the first and second samples, respectively. Nodes 1 and 13 are used to estimate total acceptance and rejection probabilities. The statistics collected are the number of tests performed until any one of the four outcomes listed above occurs.

The durations for activities 3 and 4 were defined as a single unit to represent a test. If testing times are known, these could be assigned to activities 3 and 4 and, if desired, could be made to depend on part classification. If testing times are added, the total testing time required for the sampling plan can be determined. Furthermore, the cost of these activities can then be evaluated and compared with the benefits of the sampling plan to determine the desirability of the plan.

12.7.1 Results for the Double Sampling Plan

The strategy in Table 12-1 was analyzed with the Q-GERT model of the double sampling plan.
The network was simulated for 1000 lots and the Q-GERT summary report shown in Figure 12-11 was obtained. From these results we see that the probability of acceptance (node 1) equals 0.235 and the probability of rejecting the lot (node 13) is 0.765. The results observed from OC curves [477] for this double sampling plan, where p is the lot frac-

TABLE 12-1 Strategy for Double Sampling Plan

Definition	Variable	Value
Acceptance number		
First sample	c_1	2
Second sample	c_3	6
Rejection number		
First sample	c_2	6
Sample size		
First sample	n_1	50
Second sample	n_2	100
Part fraction defective	p	0.08

GERT SIMULATION PROJECT DOUBLE SAMPL   BY PRITSKER
DATE 3/ 8/ 1982

FINAL RESULTS FOR 1000 SIMULATIONS

AVERAGE NODE STATISTICS

NODE	LABEL	PROBABILITY	AVE.	STD.DEV.	SD OF AVE	NO OF OBS.	MIN.	MAX.	STAT TYPE
13	REJ.LOT	.7650	76.7150	25.0082	.9042	765.	20.0000	149.0000	F
1	ACC.LOT	.2350	54.2553	20.2278	1.3195	235.	50.0000	150.0000	F
10	ACC.SEC.	.0100	150.0000	0	0	10.	150.0000	150.0000	F
8	ACC.FIR.	.2250	50.0000	0	0	225.	50.0000	50.0000	F
11	REJ.SEC.	.6510	82.7926	21.9068	.8586	651.	51.0000	149.0000	F
6	REJ.FIR.	.1140	42.0088	6.3196	.5919	114.	20.0000	50.0000	F
5	D.GT.C1	.7750	28.2697	11.5460	.4147	775.	3.0000	50.0000	F

Figure 12-11 Q-GERT outputs for double sampling plan.

tion defective, are 0.23 for the probability of acceptance and 0.77 for the probability of rejection. From these values it is seen that the Q-GERT model provides good estimates of these quantities (the standard deviation is approximately 0.0133 for a binominal variable with $p = 0.77$).

The Q-GERT model of the double sampling plan can be used to assess the worth of the plan, including the amount of testing that is required for either acceptance or rejection. From the output given in Figure 12-11 it is seen that the average number of tests to reject the lot is equal to 77, and the average number of tests to accept the lot is 54. Of great significance is the estimate that only 1% of the lots are accepted on the second sample. This indicates that the double sampling plan should be redesigned, as there is a strong motivation for rejecting the lot if it is not accepted on the first sample.

12.8 INCORPORATING MISCLASSIFICATION ERRORS IN THE SAMPLING PLAN

In an inspection process for maintaining high quality levels of manufactured parts, there is always the possibility of rejecting good units (Type I error) and/or accepting bad ones (Type II error). These considerations can be incorporated into the Q-GERT model. This section shows how the previously described model of a double sampling plan can be modified to consider these factors.

Node 2 and the branches from node 2 to nodes 3 and 4 in the double sampling plan of Figure 12-10 are removed from the network and replaced by the network section shown in Figure 12-12. The out-

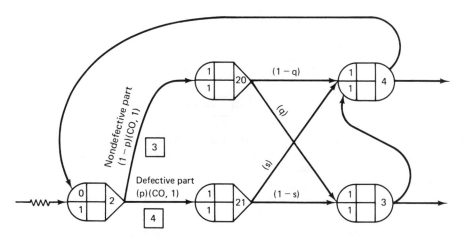

Figure 12-12 Adding part misclassification to the sampling plan network: p, fraction defective; q, probability of classifying a good part as defective; s, probability of classifying a defective part as good.

puts from node 3 and node 4 are as shown in the previous network. If a part is good, then with probability $1 - q$ it is classified as good, and with probability q it is classified as defective. If the part is defective, then with probability $1 - s$ it is classified as defective, and with probability s it is classified as good. Thus, misclassification is easily incorporated into the network model.

12.9 SUMMARY

Reliability and quality control are fundamental concepts of systems analysis. This chapter shows that Q-GERT networks are directly usable for incorporating reliability and quality control considerations in systems models. A network approach which is based on building system models from network elements parallels the reliability systems analysis approach of computing system reliability from component reliabilities. This chapter also gives an illustration of how Q-GERT models evolve and different models can be developed for the same system description.

12.10 EXERCISES

12-1. Develop a Q-GERT model to estimate the reliability of the following system configurations.

(a)

(b)

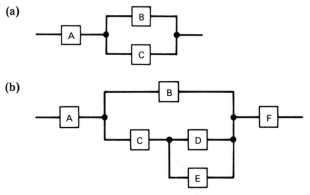

12-2. Given three components in series each of which has an exponentially distributed time to failure with a mean rate of λ, determine the distribution of the system time to failure.

12-3. Given three components in parallel each of which has an exponentially distributed time to failure with a mean rate of λ, determine the distribution of the time to failure.

12-4. In the model of the reliability of two units in parallel with repair capabilities (Figure 12-5), assume that the failure and repair times are exponentially distributed with a failure rate of 5 and a repair rate of 3. Using a table of random numbers, perform 10 runs manually to obtain the time to system failure.

Embellishment: For the system described in this example, compute the theoretical time to failure. (*Hint:* This is a three-state Markov process, with the states being zero failed systems, one failed system, and two failed systems.)

12-5. Discuss the advantages and disadvantages of the alternative models for assessing system reliability presented in Section 12.4. Describe why the function UF is needed in each approach.

12-6. Change the model of the power station maintenance and repair to include 10 generators on-line, three spares, and two repairmen.

12-7. Build a Q-GERT model for assessing the worth of MIL Standard 105D.

12-8. Explain the quality control principles involved in a double sampling plan to a manager using the Q-GERT network of Figure 12-10.

12-9. Build a Q-GERT model of a single sampling plan with which you are familiar.

12-10. Incorporate the double sampling plan of Figure 12-10 into a production system model and cause the production line to be shut down if two consecutive lots are rejected.

13

Inventory Control

13.1 INTRODUCTION

Inventory systems have been analyzed for many years and they continue to attract attention from practitioners and theoreticians in the industrial engineering and management science field. This interest is justified because of the potential cost savings from improved decision making in inventory situations. It has been demonstrated that solutions to inventory problems can be developed and improved through the use of quantitative methods. The number of studies on inventory situations is extensive.

All inventory systems involve the storage of items for future sale or use. Demands are imposed on an inventory by customers seeking supplies of the items. A company must establish an inventory policy that specifies (1) when an order for additional items should be placed, and (2) how many of the items should be ordered at each order time. The answers to these two questions depend on the revenues and costs associated with the inventory situation. Revenue is a function of the number of units sold and the selling price per unit. Costs are more complex and include ordering costs, inventory carrying charges (which may include an opportunity cost due to loss of the use of capital tied up in inventory), and stock-out costs. Stock-out costs can be considered as either the cost associated with a *backorder* (an order that is satisfied when inventory becomes available) or the cost associated with a *lost sale.*

Inventory theory deals with the determination of the best inventory policy. Equations have been developed for setting parameter values in specific situations. These equations, however, are based on restrictive assumptions in order to make an analysis tractable. Through network simulation such assumptions can be avoided. In this chapter we discuss the common concerns in inventory analysis and describe how network models are used to analyze inventory situations.

13.2 TERMINOLOGY

To introduce the terminology employed in inventory analysis, consider a single-commodity inventory system. The units of a commodity physically held in storage are collectively referred to as *stock-on-hand* or *inventory-on-hand*. The level of inventory-on-hand decreases when a customer's request or *demand* for stock is satisfied. Note that it is a demand that is important in inventory situations and not just a customer arrival. Inventory-on-hand increases when a shipment of goods (an order) arrives. An example graph of inventory-on-hand for a time period is shown in Figure 13-1. Initially, there are 3 units in stock. The arrow at time 1 indicates that a request for 1 unit of stock is made at time 1. This demand is satisfied since there is ample supply in stock. Hence, stock-on-hand drops to 2 at time 1. Another demand at time 2 causes a second decrease in stock. At this point an order is placed for 5 new units, as indicated by the letter O. The shipment is not received until three time units later, at time 5. This delay between the time of placing an order and the time of its receipt is called the *lead time*. The

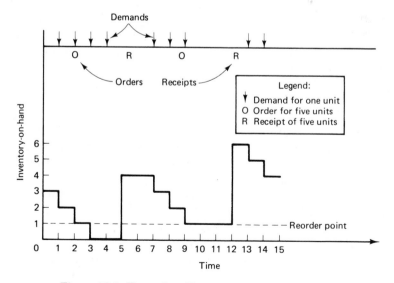

Figure 13-1 Example of inventory-on-hand changes.

lead time is important because stock outages occur during this interval. For example, at time 3 another demand depletes the stock. At time 4, a demand occurs but it cannot be satisfied. This is an example of a stock-out situation. Assuming that the customer agrees to wait until stock arrives, the request is entered on the books as a *backorder*. If the customer does not wait, a *lost sale* would result. In Figure 13-1, the stock-on-hand does not change when a backorder occurs. When the order is received at time 5, the backorder is satisfied and the number of units sent to inventory is only 4. In general, at the time of a receipt of an order, the stock level increases by the order value minus the number of current backorders. Continuing with the description of Figure 13-1, no demands occur at times 5 or 6. Demands do occur at times 7, 8, and 9. When inventory-on-hand reaches 1 at time 9, another order for 5 units is placed. As before, the order arrives 3 time units later. At time 12, the new shipment arrives, raising the stock level to 6.

The amount of inventory-on-hand at the time just prior to the addition of a newly arrived order is called the *safety stock*. The term "safety" is used because this quantity reveals how "safe" the company is from an undesirable stock-out situation. Safety stock at time 5 is zero and at time 12 is 1.

Another important system variable is *inventory position*. Inventory position is equal to inventory-on-hand, plus the number of units on order (the number due in), minus the number of units that have been backordered (the number due out). While inventory-on-hand represents the number of units physically available to be sold, inventory position represents the number of units that is or will be available to the company for potential sale. Inventory decisions regarding when to place an order and how much to order are normally based on the inventory position. The inventory position for the example in Figure 13-1 is shown in Figure 13-2. At times 1 and 2 there are no backorders or goods-on-order. Hence, inventory position equals inventory-on-hand. When an order is placed at time 2, however, the inventory position increases to 6 to reflect the fact that there are 5 units on order and 1 unit in stock. Here we see why inventory position is used as a decision variable as opposed to inventory-on-hand. If we review inventory-on-hand again at time 4 we might decide to order more units because inventory-on-hand is zero. If we had consulted our inventory position at time 4, however, we would not have placed an order since a shipment is due in. The inventory position reflects the number of units that we expect to have for future sale. Hence, the inventory position is decreased at time 4 when a demand is backordered. Also note that inventory position is increased only when an order is placed, not when a shipment is received.

In the discussion above, we did not specifically state how it was determined to place an order at times 2 and 9. Orders for more units can occur only at instants in time when the inventory position is reviewed. Two types of review policies are common in industry. Periodic

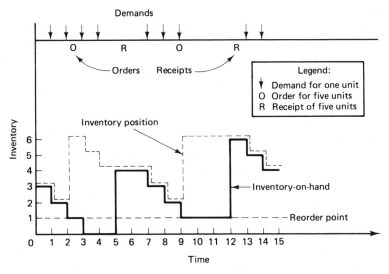

Figure 13-2 Graph of inventory-on-hand and inventory position.

reviewing involves establishing a time between reviews, TBR, and then measuring the inventory position every TBR time units. The measuring of inventory position may require the taking of a physical inventory and an examination of both the outstanding orders and the backorder file. A second type of review policy is to examine the inventory position at every demand instant. This type of review is referred to as a transaction reporting or continuous review policy.

13.3 INVENTORY COSTS
AND SYSTEM PERFORMANCE MEASURES

Associated with inventory situations are revenues and costs which are influenced by management policies and decisions. Through an examination of the costs, we will define the performance measures that are important to analyzing inventory systems. The costs associated with inventory include holding costs, stock-out costs, and costs of procedures such as reviewing and ordering.

The costs of holding inventory include such costs as insurance, taxes, breakage, pilferage, warehouse rental, and operational expenses. An additional cost is an opportunity cost since it costs money to have capital tied up in inventory. Typically, holding costs are expressed as a dollar cost per inventory dollar per time period. For example, a company could estimate that each dollar invested in inventory for a year incurs a holding cost of 30 cents. This cost typically includes interest charges on loans and lack of income from other uses of the monies. If an average stock level valued at $10,000 is maintained over one year, the holding cost would be $3000 for the year. To generalize, let HC represent holding cost per inventory dollar per time unit. Let CPU represent the cost for each unit in inventory and let ASV represent the average inventory-on-hand for a given time interval, T. Then the total holding cost incurred for the time interval T is given by HC × CPU × ASV × T. HC, CPU, and T are normally known or given values, and we can compute total holding costs if we estimate the average level of inventory-on-hand over time.

Although it costs money to keep goods in inventory, it also costs money to be without inventory. These costs are often difficult to measure since they include such factors as loss of customers' goodwill. We assume here, however, that some estimate can be made. Let CSL equal the cost of losing a sale and let TLS equal the total number of lost sales over a given time interval, then stock-out costs due to lost sales would equal CSL × TLS. If backorders are incurred, the cost due to backorders may be expressed as CPB × TB, where CPB is the estimated cost per backorder and TB is the total number of backorders. To include a cost for the time a customer is back-ordered, we use a cost per backorder per time unit backordered, CBPT, and ATB as the time-weighted average of the number of backorders. Over a given time interval, T, the total backorder cost would then be CPB × TB + CBPT × ATB × T.

One way to try to avoid stock-out situations is to review inventory and to order new shipments frequently. The degree to which this is advantageous is limited by the added holding costs for excess inventory as well as the cost attributed to the review procedure and the processing of an order. Let CPO and CPR represent the cost per order and the cost per review, respectively. If TO represents the total number of orders and TR the total number of reviews during a specified interval, CPO × TO represents the cost of ordering and CPR × TR equals the cost of reviewing.

The purpose of incurring all these costs is, of course, to have an inventory of goods that results in sales. Let TS equal the total sales, let CPU be the cost per unit, and let PPU equal the sale price per unit. Then the total revenues from sales is TS × (PPU − CPU).

Combining these cost and revenue figures, we can define a profit, P, for the inventory system in T time units as

$$P = TS \times (PPU - CPU) - (CPO \times TO + CPR \times TR + HC \times CPU \times ASV \times T + CSL \times TLS + CPB \times TB + CBPT \times ATB \times T)$$

where   TS = total sales in T
          PPU = price per unit
          CPU = cost per unit
          CPO = cost per order
           TO = total orders in T
          CPR = cost per review

TR = total reviews in T
HC = holding cost per inventory dollar per time unit
ASV = average inventory-on-hand in T
CSL = cost per lost sale
TLS = total lost sales in T
CPB = cost per backorder
CBPT = cost per backorder per time unit
TB = number of backorders in T
ATB = average number of backorders in T
T = time interval

When analyzing inventory systems, we assume knowledge of the coefficients PPU, CPU, CPO, CPR, HC, CSL, CPB, and CPBT. The analysis is used to estimate the following performance measures:

1. The level of inventory-on-hand over time and at receipt times (safety stock)
2. The number of backorders
3. The number of sales (satisfied demands)
4. The number of orders
5. The number of reviews
6. The number of lost sales

The profit equation developed above is only one method for evaluating inventory policies by combining the performance values. Sometimes it is not necessary to combine the measures. For example, a corporation could be most concerned about the loss of customers and use safety stock as the prime measure of performance even though safety stock is not part of the profit or cost calculations directly. In all cases, it is important to recognize that the system performance measures need to be analyzed if an inventory policy evaluation is to be performed. Later in this chapter, we will relate Q-GERT output to each of the performance measures. In the next section, we return to a discussion of inventory policy. With the introduction of performance measures and inventory costs, we can discuss how inventory policy affects system performance.

13.4 THE CENTRAL QUESTIONS: WHEN TO ORDER? HOW MUCH TO ORDER?

To avoid stock-out situations, large inventory levels should be maintained. However, the more inventory in storage, the larger the holding costs. If one countered this situation by ordering small amounts, frequent orders would be needed to avoid stock-out costs. But frequent orders are undesirable because of the cost of placing a large number of orders. Other factors, such as quantity discounts, also make small order quantities disadvantageous. Thus, there is a cost trade-off between placing frequent small orders and not-so-frequent large orders.

Inventory policies specify how often to order and how much to order. Typically, inventory policies are specified in one of two ways:

1. If the inventory position is less than a specified *reorder point*, R, order Q units.
2. If the inventory position is less than a specified reorder point, R, order up to a *stock control level* of SCL units.

Both of these policies use an ordering point based on inventory position and specify how much to order. Neither of the policies, however, specifies the actual time of ordering, which is dependent on when the inventory position is reviewed. As discussed in Section 13.2, two types of review procedures are common. A *periodic review* procedure specifies that a review is to be performed at equally spaced points in time, for example, every month. The transaction reporting or continuous review procedure involves examining the inventory position every time it decreases and requires keeping a running record of the inventory position.

Networks can be used to model the dynamic behavior of inventory situations to obtain estimates of the performance measures discussed above. Such models incorporate inventory policies as part of the network so that various strategies can be evaluated. Consistent with our approach to problem solving, we start with basic Q-GERT network models since they are easily embellished to include more complex inventory situations.

13.5 MODELING INVENTORY SYSTEMS HAVING BACKORDERS AND CONTINUOUS REVIEW POLICIES

The system to be considered involves a single-commodity inventory system with backorders. No lost sales are allowed and a continuous review procedure is used to monitor inventory position. When the inventory position decreases to a specified reorder point, R, an order for Q units is placed.

13.5.1 The Q-GERT Network

The Q-GERT model is shown in Figure 13-3. The demand for goods is modeled by source node 1. The self-loop around node 1 represents the time between demands. When a demand arrives at node 2, user function 1 is called to perform the review of inventory position.

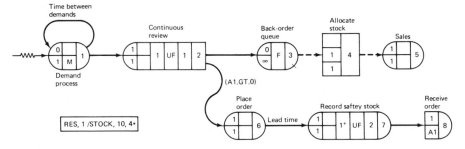

Figure 13-3 Q-GERT model of an inventory situation with backorders and continuous review.

The logic involved in the user function causes the following to occur at a demand time:

1. Inventory position is decreased.
2. Inventory position is compared against the reorder point.
3. If inventory position is less than or equal to the reorder point, an order for Q units is placed.

In user function 1, attribute 1 is set to zero if no order is made, or it is set to the amount ordered, Q, if an order is made. Conditional-take-all branching is used at node 2. Since no condition is specified for the branch to Q-node 3, this branch is always selected. Hence, all demands result in a transaction entering Q-node 3. Inventory-on-hand is modeled as resource 1 (labeled STOCK). The resource record specifies that 10 units are initially in stock (RES,1/STOCK,10,4*) and that stock when it is available is allocated to meet demands at ALLOCATE node 4. When a demand transaction reaches Q-node 3, a resource unit will be allocated to it if one is available, that is, if inventory-on-hand is greater than zero. When this occurs, the transaction is routed to node 5. A release of node 5 represents a sale. If stock is not available, the demand transaction waits in Q-node 3, and the transactions in Q-node 3 represent current backorders.

When a unit of stock is allocated, it becomes unavailable. Freeing resource units makes stock available again. The freeing of units of resource 1 occurs at node 8, which models a receipt of an order. An order is placed when user function 1 sets attribute 1 equal to Q and a transaction representing an order is routed to node 6. The activity from node 6 to node 7 represents the lead-time delay for an order and includes processing, shipping, and receiving delays. The release of node 7 represents the receipt of the order and the availability of the stock. At this node† we collect statistics on safety stock by observing the

---

†At node 7 we desire only to collect information and do not need to make an attribute assignment. This is accomplished by adding zero to a current attribute value; hence, the value assignment specification (1+,UF,2) at node 7.

```
SUBROUTINE UI
COMMON/UCOM1/POS,Q,R
POS=13.
Q=10.
R=3.
RETURN
END
```

Figure 13-4 Listing of subroutine UI.

status of resource 1, which represents the number of available stock units. Function ICSRA(1) returns this value, which is used in user function 2. User statistics subroutine COL and user histogram subroutine HIS are invoked to record this observation for future statistical reporting. A transaction arrival to node 8 causes Q units of resource 1 to be freed, where the value of Q is taken from attribute 1 (A1). This models an increase in stock by A1 units. If an order is received when transactions are backordered in Q-node 3, an allocation of units to the backorders is made. The number of units allocated is the lesser of the number of backorders and the number of units received.

User variables are defined for the inventory position, POS, the order quantity, Q, and the reorder point, R. These variables are included in user COMMON block, UCOM1. The variables are initialized in subroutine UI, which is presented in Figure 13-4. For this example, initial inventory position is set to 13, the reorder quantity to 10, and the reorder point to 3. The first executable statement in function UF sets UF to 0, as this is the normal value to be returned from both user functions (Figure 13-5). User function 1 is called when a demand occurs which results in a decrease in inventory position; that is, POS is decreased by one at statement 1. If POS is greater than the reorder point, R, no order is to be placed. Since UF was previously set to zero, routing from node 2 will not occur as attribute 1 is set to UF, which is zero. If POS is less than or equal to R, an order is placed. In this case, UF, and consequently attribute 1, is set to the reorder quantity, Q.

The code for user function 2 begins at statement 2. Its purpose is to collect statistics on the number of available resources of type 1 at the time an order is received, that is, the safety stock. The number of resources available is retrieved by the Q-GERT support function, ICSRA(1). User statistical and histogram subroutines COL and HIS are called to collect this value of safety stock. The use of COL and

```
       FUNCTION UF(IFN)
       COMMON/UCOM1/POS,Q,R
C**** SET UF TO ZERO AS THE STANDARD CASE
       UF = 0.0
       GO TO (1,2),IFN
C**** ANOTHER DEMAND. DECREASE INVENTORY POSITION BY ONE.
C**** INCREASE NUMBER OF REVIEWS BY 1.
     1 POS = POS-1.
C**** CHECK POSITION AGAINST REORDER POINT
       IF (POS.GT.R) RETURN
C**** PLACE ORDER FOR Q UNITS
       UF = Q
       POS = POS + Q
    10 RETURN
C**** ANOTHER ORDER RECEIVED - COLLECT SAFETY STOCK STATISTICS
     2 X = ICSRA(1)
       CALL COL(X,1)
       CALL HIS(X,1)
       RETURN
       END
```

Figure 13-5 Listing of function UF for inventory example.

HIS causes the automatic computation and reporting of an average, standard deviation, and other statistics for the variable collected.

13.5.2 Summary of Modeling Concepts

This inventory example introduces most of the general Q-GERT concepts necessary to model inventory systems. The following list summarizes these concepts.

1. Demands are modeled as system arrivals. The arrival pattern can be varied to represent different demand processes.
2. Inventory-on-hand is modeled as a resource. When a demand arrives and the resource is available, a sale results. When a demand arrives and the resource is not available, a backorder results.
3. Backorders are maintained in a Q-node since backorders are demand transactions that wait for an available resource.
4. A receipt of an order results in freeing the inventory-on-hand resource by the number of units in the order. If backorders exist when a receipt occurs, the ALLOCATE node satisfies as many backorders as possible.
5. The lead time is represented by an activity time.
6. Inventory position is maintained as a user variable. Inventory position decreases when a demand occurs and increases by the order quantity when an order is placed.
7. A continuous review reporting procedure is modeled within a user function as a test on inventory position whenever a demand occurs. The order quantity and reorder point may be computed as a function of system status or initialized in subroutine UI. Orders are created by attribute assignment and routing logic.
8. Safety stock is obtained as the number of available resources at the time of the receipt of an order. User statistics subroutines are used to collect safety stock values.
9. Total sales, total reviews, and total orders equal the number of transactions that pass through nodes representing these functions. In Figure 13-1, the nodes representing sales, reviews, and orders are nodes 5, 2, and 6, respectively.

13.5.3 Q-GERT Assessment of Performance Measures, Costs, and Profits

The inventory performance measures discussed in Section 13-3 are directly obtainable from the Q-GERT output. The translation of these performance measures into inventory costs, revenues, and profits is accomplished using subroutine UO. In Table 13-1, each inventory performance measure is listed together with the relevant Q-GERT con-

TABLE 13-1 Q-GERT Outputs Corresponding to Performance Measures in Inventory Modeling

Performance Measure	Q-GERT Concept	Item in Example	Q-GERT Output
Inventory-on-hand	System resource	Resource type 1 labeled STOCK	Time-weighted average, standard deviation, standard deviation of average, minimum and maximum average, and maximum number
Number of backorders	Q-node	Q-node 3	Time-weighted average, standard deviation, standard deviation of average, minimum and maximum average, waiting-time statistics, and maximum number
Number of sales	Number of transactions passing through a node	Node 5, NTC(5)	Number of transactions passing through a node
Number of orders	Number of transactions passing through a node	Node 6, NTC(6)	Number of transactions passing through a node
Number of reviews	Number of transactions passing through a node	Node 2, NTC(2)	Number of transactions passing through a node
Safety stock	User statistics on number of available resource units representing inventory-on-hand	Use of subroutines COL and HIS with ICSRA(1) as the observed variable	Average, standard deviation, standard deviation of the average, number of observations, minimum and maximum, relative and cumulative frequency distributions
Number of lost sales	Number of transactions passing through a node		Number of transactions passing through a node

aNot included in previous example. See Figure 13-9, node 10.

cept, its manifestation in the example of Section 13.5.1, and its associated Q-GERT output.

The average inventory-on-hand corresponds to resource utilization. This average inventory-on-hand is computed at the end of each run so that a single value is obtained on a run. The average reported over multiple runs is the average of these average values over all runs. The standard deviation is an estimate of the variation within this set of observations and can be used to derive confidence intervals on the average inventory-on-hand. The Q-GERT processor also reports on the minimum and maximum average inventory-on-hand that is observed on any of the runs. In addition, the maximum number of units ever in stock in any run is reported.

Backorders wait for stock in a queue and backorder statistics correspond to average queue-length statistics. A time-weighted average number of backorders is computed at the end of each run and is considered as one observation. Multiple runs yield multiple observations. The standard deviation represents the variation over this set of multiple observations. A histogram of average backorders per run is an output option. Waiting-time statistics provide information on how long a backorder waits before it is satisfied.

In the Q-GERT model in Figure 13-3, a correspondence between number of sales, orders, and reviews and the number of passages of transactions through specified network nodes has been made. The Q-GERT processor maintains and prints the number of transaction passages through node NODE during the simulation as the variable NTC(NODE).

Through the use of the user subroutine COL, automatic output for safety stock statistics are obtained. Subroutine HIS provides a relative and cumulative frequency distribution of safety stock levels.

By combining the estimates for the performance measures, an average profit for a simulation run can be computed in subroutine UO. The Q-GERT processor calls subroutine UO at the end of each run. Subroutine UO for the basic inventory situation is listed in Figure 13-6. DATA statements are used to set the cost and price coefficients of the profit equation. The number of sales, orders, and reviews are set equal to their respective NTC(·) values. The quantity ATB*T equals the time-

```
      SUBROUTINE UO
      COMMON/QVAR/NDE,NFTBU(100),NREL(100),NRELP(100),NREL2(100),NRUN,
     1NRUNS,NTC(100),PARAM(100,4),TBEG,TNOW
      DATA PPU,CPU,CPBT,HC,CPO,CPR/75.,40.,10.,.004,25.,2./
C****
C**** PPU = PRICE/UNIT,  CPU = COST/UNIT,  CBPT = COST/BACKORDER/TIME
C**** HC = HOLDING COST/INVENTORY $/TIME UNIT,  CPO = COST/ORDER
C**** CPR = COST/REVIEW
C****
      TS = NTC(5)
      TO = NTC(6)
      TR = NTC(2)
      P = TS*(PPU-CPU)-(CPO*TO+CPR*TR+HC*CPU*TIRA(1)+CBPT*TINIQ(3))
      PPT = P/TNOW
      CALL COL(PPT,2)
      CALL HIS(PPT,2)
      RETURN
      END
```

Figure 13-6 Listing of subroutine UO.

integrated value of the number of backorders, that is, the time-integrated number of transactions in Q-node 3. The Q-GERT function for this value is TINIQ(3). The time-integrated value of inventory-on-hand ASV × T is the time-integrated value of resource usage for resource 1, TIRA(1). The estimated total profit, P, is computed using the previously derived profit equation assuming that the cost per backorder (CPB) is zero. A profit per unit time is computed by dividing P by TNOW. When subroutine UO is called, TNOW is the ending time for a run. Subroutines COL and HIS are called to collect the profit values over a set of runs. Other information can be reported by employing standard FORTRAN WRITE statements. Values of the performance measures for each run can be obtained by using the "E" specification for report type on the GEN record.

This example illustrates the ease of modeling a basic inventory problem with Q-GERT. Embellishing and altering the basic inventory situation involves minor adaptations and these are described in the following sections.

13.6 MODELING A PERIODIC REVIEW PROCEDURE AND A STOCK-CONTROL-LEVEL ORDERING POLICY

The network in Figure 13-7 is a Q-GERT model of an inventory situation in which a periodic review procedure is employed and an ordering policy based on a stock control level is used. The network is similar to the model given in Figure 13-3 except that a review does not occur after each demand at node 2 and, hence, ordering is not initiated from

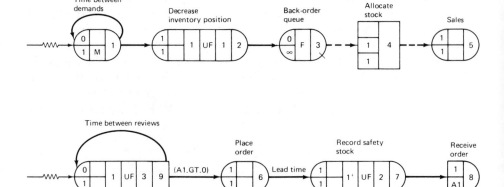

Figure 13-7 Q-GERT model of an inventory situation with backorders and periodic reviewing.

```
                                  FUNCTION UF(IFN)
                                  COMMON/UCOM1/POS,R,SCL
                                  UF=0.0
                                  GO TO (1,2,3),IFN
                            C**** USER FUNCTION 1
                                1 POS=POS-1.
                                  RETURN
                            C**** USER FUNCTION 2
                                2 X=ICSRA(1)
                                  CALL COL(X,1)
                                  CALL HIS(X,1)
                                  RETURN
                            C**** USER FUNCTION 3
                                3 IF (POS.GT.R) RETURN
                                  UF=SCL-POS
```
Figure 13-8 Function UF for net-
work in Figure 13-7.
```
                            C**** POS=POS+UF OR, EQUIVALENTLY POS=SCL
                                  POS=SCL
                                  RETURN
                                  END
```

it. In this model, node 2 is used solely to decrease inventory position by 1 when a demand occurs. Function UF, for this example, is shown in Figure 13-8. The only statement needed in user function 1 is POS= POS-1. User function 2 performs the function of collecting safety stock values as before. User function 3 has been added and models the periodic review process. Source node 9 initiates the first review and the self-loop activity around node 9 specifies the time between reviews. Hence, user function 3, called from node 9, provides the opportunity to test inventory position at periodic intervals. In the user function listed in Figure 13-8, inventory position, POS, is tested against the reorder point, R. If POS is greater than R, no action is taken. However if POS is less than or equal to R, an order is to be scheduled. Attribute 1, which represents the order quantity, is set equal to the difference between the stock control level, SCL, and the inventory position, POS. This is accomplished by setting UF=SCL–POS. SCL is a user variable contained in user COMMON and initialized in subroutine UI. In this way, the amount ordered always brings the inventory position up to SCL, that is, POS=SCL.

The branching from node 9 is dependent on attribute 1 and depends on whether an order is placed. The self-loop is always taken to schedule the next review. The branch to node 6 is taken only when an order is placed which occurs when attribute 1 is greater than zero. As in the previous model, node 6 initiates a lead-time delay, node 7 collects safety stock values, and node 8 increases the inventory-on-hand by the amount ordered (attribute 1). The performance measures and cost computations used in the model of Section 13.5 apply here except that reviews are represented by passages through node 9, not node 2. Hence, the number of reviews is NTC(9).

In the two models of inventory situations presented, standard rules for carrying out the inventory policies were used. Q-GERT models can be adapted to incorporate more advanced decision making. One possibility is to set the reorder point as an inverse function of the safety stock. Thus, if the average safety stock is small, the reorder point could be raised and if the average safety stock is large, a reduced value of the reorder point could be established. Another possibility is to make the amount ordered a function of the time since the last order was placed, the average number of backorders, and the average inventory-on-hand.

The complexity incorporated in a Q-GERT model for establishing the decision variables is limited only by the analyst's ability to conceptualize new strategies.

13.7 MODELING LOST SALES

In inventory systems, there are situations where a sale will not be made if the demand cannot be satisfied immediately. This occurs when backorders are not allowed to accumulate or when a customer decides to go elsewhere for a unit. In such cases, a sale is considered as lost. The model of this situation involves the use of a "backorder" queue that has a capacity of zero. A transaction that balks from the queue represents a lost sale. Such a model is shown in Figure 13-9 for the periodic review procedure. The main change is to Q-node 3, where the capacity is changed to zero and user function 1 is called. If a demand arrives at Q-node 3 and stock is not available (as determined by ALLOCATE node 4), the transaction balks to node 10. The number of transactions that reach node 10, NTC(10), represents the number of lost sales. This variable can be accessed in subroutine UO for inclusion in profit calculations.

User function 1 is now placed at Q-node 3 since POS is decreased by one only if a sale is made. Lost sales do not affect inventory position. The call to function UF at Q-node 3 occurs only if ALLOCATE node 4 allocates a unit to the transaction. Value assignments are not

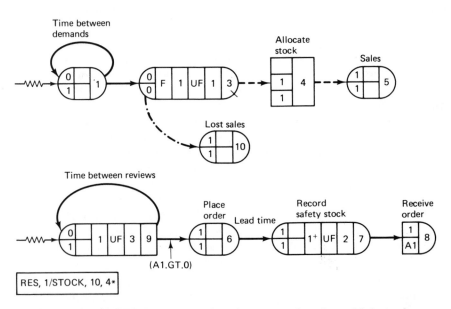

Figure 13-9 Q-GERT network of an inventory situation with lost sales and periodic reviewing.

made to a transaction that balks from a Q-node. Hence, inventory position is not affected by a lost sale.

As a further embellishment, suppose some backorders are allowed to accumulate before lost sales occur. For example, if four backorders are permitted before lost sales occur, the network model can be modified and statement 1 added to user function 1 given in Figure 13-8.

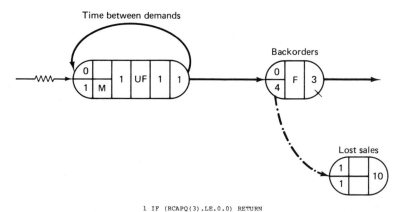

```
1 IF (RCAPQ(3).LE.0.0) RETURN
```

In this network segment, user function 1 is employed to check the remaining capacity of Q-node 3. The remaining capacity represents the difference between 4, the allowed number of backorders, and the current number of backorders. If no capacity is available, we have a lost sale, and the value of POS is not changed. After returning from user function 1, the new demand is routed to Q-node 3, from which it balks to node 10, since no space for it exists. In this manner, we obtain the lost sale.

Another way to specify lost sales is by introducing a probability that a customer will not backorder a unit. Suppose that 10% of the time customers decide not to backorder and a lost sale occurs. The following network segment represents this situation assuming that there is no limit on the number of backorders allowed.

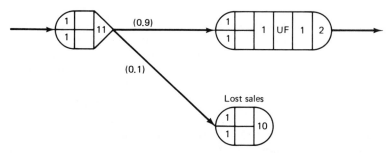

If we prescribe conditional branching for node 11, we can further embellish this lost sale decision. With a user function at node 11, an attribute value can be set based on the current system status. The attribute value is then used with conditional routing to specify when a sale is lost.

Sometimes a sale is lost because a demand waited too long in the backorder queue. To model this situation, consider the network on p. 325.

In this network, lost sales will occur if the current number of backorders exceeds four. Furthermore, before a transaction enters Q-node 3, its attribute 2 value is set equal to the current time, TNOW, at node 14. User function 4 accomplishes this by simply setting UF= TNOW. In this way, attribute 2 records the time of entry into the backorder queue. When the demand is satisfied, the transaction is routed to node 12, where attribute 2 is increased by a specified time interval, say 5 (2+,CO,5). By testing A2 against TNOW through the conditional routing of node 12, we can detect transactions that waited five time units or longer in the backorder queue. If TNOW is less than attribute 2, a sale results. If not, a lost sale results. In the latter case, the one unit of stock is freed by node 13. User function 5 is needed to increase the inventory position by one. In this model, it is assumed that the reneging of backordered customers is not known until an order is received, that is, until the customer is informed that his or her order has arrived.

13.8 USING SIMULATION TO IMPROVE INVENTORY CONTROL

Once a network model is built, the effect of changes to system performance due to changes in the component parts of the network can be measured. Both procedural changes in inventory policies and changes in the business environment are candidates for evaluation. Common changes in the business environment are:

1. A change in the demand for goods
2. A change in the cost of operation
3. A change in lead times

Although these types of changes may not be controllable, their effects can be anticipated. It may be critical, for example, to know the impact on inventory *before* a forecasted increase or decrease in demand occurs. Similarly, expected changes in operating costs and product lead times need to be assessed. A network approach provides a method for analyzing these types of changes as they involve simple modifications to the Q-GERT model. A change in a demand process can be as simple as a new data input for the self-loop around a source node or can be complex through the adding of nodes and branches to create special demand conditions. Examples of such changes are presented in Chapter 14. Cost changes are accounted for by adjusting the cost variables em-

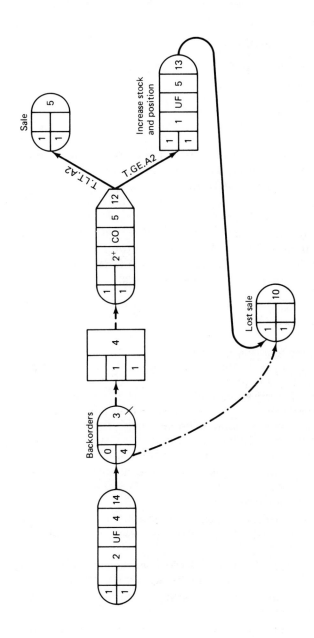

ployed in subroutine UO. Lead-time changes are controlled by activity branch specifications.

For a particular business operation, the procedural aspects of inventory systems can be evaluated and controlled by analyzing new values for:

1. The amount ordered
2. The level at which orders are to be placed
3. The review method

13.9 SUMMARY

Diverse inventory situations have been modeled in terms of Q-GERT networks in this chapter. The modeling of inventory control procedures involves the allocation of resource units to meet demands and decision logic to determine when resources are to be replenished. Complex situations are shown to be extensions of simple ones. Thus, the Q-GERT approach of combining elements into network models of systems facilitates the modeling and analysis of complex inventory situations. In addition, this chapter demonstrates Q-GERT models of procedures derived from control policy specifications.

13.10 EXERCISES

13-1. Discuss the following statements:
  (a) Orders to replenish inventory should be based on inventory position and not inventory-on-hand.
  (b) Safety stock is a measure of how well the reorder point is set.
  (c) Order quantity is more important than reorder point in determining the cost of keeping goods in inventory.
  (d) Relate the lead-time demand (the demand that occurs during the lead time) to the reorder point and safety stock values.

13-2. Discuss the differences between the continuous review and periodic review procedures with respect to the setting of order quantities, reorder point, back-orders, and stock control levels.

13-3. Perform a Q-GERT analysis for the model presented in Section 13.5 Attempt to increase the profit per week by resetting the values for the decision variables.

13-4. Develop a Q-GERT model in which an economic order quantity is used and price discounts are given for ordering in multiples of 100.

13-5. For the inventory model presented in Figure 13-7, collect statistics on the lead-time demand.

13-6. Show how the inventory model presented in Section 13.5 can be driven by demand data stored in a data base. Use an available data base (instructor prepared) or create a data base and run the inventory model for diverse policies.

14

More on Inventory Control

14.1 INTRODUCTION

The modeling of complex inventory control situations involves detailed descriptions of the demand process for single and multicommodity units. The major concern of this chapter involves the modeling of demands. Consideration is given to how to specify on a Q-GERT network the time between demands when the number of demands per unit time is given or explicit demand sequences are specified. Also discussed is the modeling approach for seasonal and bulk demands and the procedures for differentiating among different types of demands. The last section in this chapter presents a Q-GERT model for a two-commodity inventory system.

14.2 MODELING DEMAND PROCESSES

The modeling of the demand for a product or services is a complex subject. In this book we limit our discussion to characterizing data on demands and do not investigate the underlying processes that cause demands to occur. Demand data can be used directly or a distribution function can be used to characterize it. When used directly, a tacit assumption is made that the data observed are sufficient to portray the future situations of interest. Clearly, a demand data time series is only one history of what could have happened. By fitting a distribution function to the data, it is presumed that the data are representative of what could have occurred, and it is desired to capture all possible time histories.

Since modeling a demand process is similar to modeling an arrival process, the discussion in Section 7.2 on arrival processes in production systems is also relevant here. Before discussing special demand features in the following sections, some pertinent information relating to the modeling of demands is listed below.

1. If the time between demands is characterized by different distribution types, the next demand time is selected on a probabilistic basis.
2. If demand times are known, they should be read in as needed.
3. If a histogram is available that describes time between demands by a discrete probability distribution, function DPROB should be used to obtain the interdemand time.
4. If the demand distribution varies over time (for example, seasonal variations), or if demands for goods arrive in batches, or if demands have priorities, then functional specifications for these special features are required.

14.3 CHARACTERIZING THE INTERDEMAND TIME FROM DATA ON THE NUMBER OF DEMANDS

Frequently, demand data are in the form of a specified number of units demanded per time interval. For example, sales data may reveal that in any given week the number of units demanded is Poisson distributed with a mean of λ. When simulating, we need to know the time a demand occurs. This necessitates the conversion of the distribution of the number of units per time interval to a distribution of the time between demands. In this discussion we will refer to demand occurrences as events. In addition, the distribution of the number of events occurring in a given time interval will be referred to as the *distribution of counts*.

For the case where the distribution of counts is Poisson, converting to a distribution of the time between events is direct because the time between the events of a Poisson process with mean number per unit time λ is exponentially distributed with a mean time of $1/\lambda$.

With other distributions of counts, there is no direct transformation from the distribution of counts to the distribution of time between events. That is, more information than count data is required to model the time between events. If it is not feasible to obtain additional data, the modeler has several possibilities for making use of available data. For example, there is a version of the central limit theorem [61,62] that states that the distribution of the number counts in time interval t approaches the normal distribution with an expectation and variance of

$$E[N_t] = \frac{t}{\mu}$$

and

$$\text{var}[N_t] = \frac{t\sigma^2}{\mu^3}$$

where μ is the mean time between events and σ is the standard deviation of the time between events.

Pritsker and Pegden [157] discuss how this result can be used to verify assumptions about the distribution of the time between events given data on N_t. Our intent here is to use this result for another purpose. That is, we wish to start with $E[N_t]$ and $\text{var}[N_t]$ and estimate μ and σ. Although this is a convenient way to estimate μ and σ, we still cannot make a statement regarding the distribution of the time between events. Nevertheless, this is a method for approximating parameters for an assumed distribution. We can test the behavior of the assumed distribution using the network shown in Figure 14-1. The distribution for the time between events is specified as the time duration for activity 1. The network is simulated for t time units and n runs are made. Subroutine UO is called at the end of each run to observe the number of counts for each network run. For each run, NTC(2) represents one observation of N_t. Subroutines COL and HIS estimate statistics for N_t and provide a histogram of the observations. This information can then be compared to count distribution data using standard goodness-of-fit techniques. The between-statistic for node 2 permits the user to observe the experimental characteristics of the time between demands distribution specified for activity 1.

Another option is to assume a constant time between demands on a run but that the demands over all runs has the distribution of N_t. This

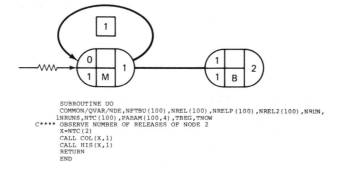

```
         SUBROUTINE UO
         COMMON/QVAR/NDE,NFTBU(100),NREL(100),NRELP(100),NREL2(100),NRUN,
        1NRUNS,NTC(100),PARAM(100,4),TBEG,TNOW
C****    OBSERVE NUMBER OF RELEASES OF NODE 2
         X=NTC(2)
         CALL COL(X,1)
         CALL HIS(X,1)
         RETURN
         END
```

Figure 14-1 Network for testing arrival distribution assumptions.

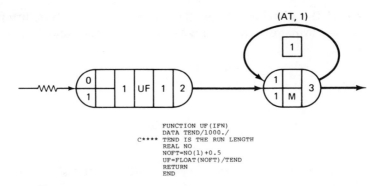

```
              FUNCTION UF(IFN)
              DATA TEND/1000./
         C**** TEND IS THE RUN LENGTH
              REAL NO
              NOFT=NO(1)+0.5
              UF=FLOAT(NOFT)/TEND
              RETURN
              END
```

Figure 14-2 Network for specifying time between demands, B, by sampling the number of counts, N_t.

is modeled by drawing a sample of N_t for a run and dividing the sample value by the stipulated length of a run. Since on each run a sample of N_t is drawn, the distribution of N_t over all runs is modeled. This scheme is illustrated in the network segment of Figure 14-2. On input, the user must specify the length, t, of the simulation and define it in a DATA statement. In the user function associated with source node 2, a sample from the known distribution for N_t is obtained and assigned to attribute 1. For the illustration, a normally distributed number of counts is assumed. The sample is obtained from function NO with parameters specified in parameter set 1. An integer value, NOFT, is obtained by rounding to the nearest integer. The constant time between demands is obtained by dividing by the length of the simulation, TEND, and set equal to UF, which is put in attribute 1. The self-loop around node 3, activity 1, uses this value as the time between demands to the system. Since attribute 1 equals the original sample for N_t divided by TEND, and since the network is simulated for TEND time units, the number of demands to the system will be the original sample value. Over n runs, the number of arrivals to the system will be characterized by the distribution for N_t. Since the distribution of N_t is not really dependent on the distribution we employed for the time between demands, this approach indicates the nonuniqueness of the interdemand time distribution for a specified distribution of the number of counts.

14.4 PREDETERMINED DEMAND SEQUENCES

As an alternative to characterizing demand data in functional form, it may be desirable to use a predetermined sequence of demands abstracted directly from purchasing records. This can be done using the following source node network segment:

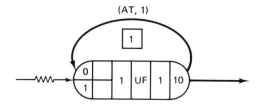

(AT, 1)

When source node 10 is released, user function 1 is called to define a value for attribute 1. This value is then used to define the duration of activity 1, the time until the next demand. Let us assume that the sequence consists of a list of demand times ordered by increasing time. This information may be read directly in function UF, and used as shown in the following statements assuming that the data have been placed on logical unit 10.

```
1  READ(10)X
   UF=X - TNOW
```

14.5 INTERDEMAND TIME DISTRIBUTIONS SPECIFIED BY A USER-DEFINED HISTOGRAM

In some cases, interdemand time data are characterized in form of a histogram. If it is not desirable or convenient to characterize this distribution by one of the standard distribution functions, the analyst can sample from the histogram directly. The user support function DPROB is used to obtain samples from cumulative distribution functions derived from histogram data.

Function DPROB(CPROB,VALUE,NVAL,ISTRM) obtains samples from a distribution function that is defined by the vectors CPROB and VALUE. CPROB(I) is the cumulative probability associated with VALUE(I). The number of values in the distribution function is specified by the value of the variable NVAL. ISTRM is the random number stream to be used when obtaining a sample from the vector VALUE.

When function DPROB is used in function UF, the user must define the vectors CPROB and VALUE. This can be accomplished in a DATA statement in function UF or in the initialization subroutine, UI. As an example of the use of DPROB, consider the probability mass function, PROB, and its associated distribution function, CP, shown in Table 14-1.

To obtain a sample from this distribution employing stream 2, the following statement would be used:

$$SAMP = DPROB(CP,VAL,6,2)$$

With the use of this statement, we expect 10% of the values of SAMP

TABLE 14-1 Example of the Use of DPROB

I	PROB(I)	CP(I)	VAL(I)
1	0.10	0.10	10
2	0.05	0.15	15
3	0.20	0.35	25
4	0.30	0.65	50
5	0.20	0.85	75
6	0.15	1.00	100

will be equal to 10, 5% will be equal to 15, 20% will be equal to 25, and so on.

14.6 SEASONAL DEMAND

Sometimes demand fluctuates over time, for example, by seasons. To model time-varying arrival patterns, the concept of network modification can be used. To illustrate, consider the following network segment.

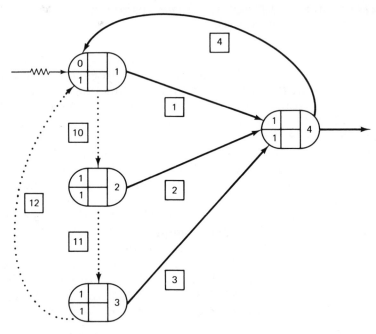

Activities 1, 2, and 3 represent a different interdemand time specification. Together they can be viewed as representing three different patterns based on a season. The pattern that is used depends on which activity is scheduled when activity 4 is completed. This in turn is controlled by network modifications, as indicated by the dotted lines between nodes 1 and 2 and between nodes 2 and 3. Node 2 replaces node

1 when activity 10 is completed. Node 3 replaces node 2 when activity 11 is completed and node 1 replaces node 3 when activity 12 is completed. Activities 10, 11, and 12 represent the length of each season and are modeled as a disjoint network as shown here.

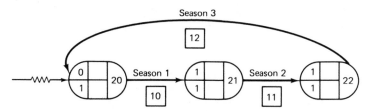

The length of a season could be modeled as a network and conditional branching based on node releases, NTC($\cdot$), could be incorporated in both the seasons network and the interdemand network to model complex time-dependent demand patterns.

14.7 DIFFERENTIATING AMONG DEMANDS

The modeling of the demand for units in inventory is similar to modeling customers who seek service. The characteristics described in Section 7.7 can be used in an analogous fashion for modeling demands. In particular, attribute values can be used for differentiating among demands for the same item. In this way, ranking of demands in Q-nodes can be specified by employing attribute-based queue ranking. In addition, different types of demands can be routed to distinct Q-nodes and queue selection rules can be assigned to S-nodes and ALLOCATE nodes to determine the Q-node from which demand transactions are to be satisfied.

14.8 BULK DEMANDS

Transactions can also be used to represent bulk or batch demands by employing an attribute that specifies the number of demands represented by the transaction. Satisfying of bulk demands then follows the procedures described for multiple arrivals associated with a single transaction. Also, the procedures for aggregating and disaggregating bulk demands are analogous to those described for bulk loads in Chapter 7.

14.9 MODELING MULTICOMMODITY INVENTORY SYSTEMS

The procedures for modeling multiple item or multicommodity inventory situations are a direct extension of the single-item model. We demonstrate the extensions for the two commodity case using the network given in Figure 14-3. The network in the upper half of the figure

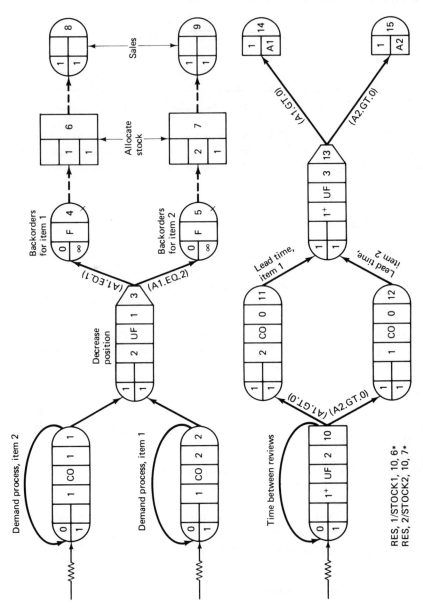

Figure 14-3 Q-GERT network for multicommodity inventory situation.

334

represents the demand, backorder, and stock components of the system. The network in the lower half of the figure represents a periodic review process.

Considering the upper network first. Source node 1 represents the demand for item 1 and source node 2 the demand for item 2. Attribute 1 is used to indicate item type. Hence, source node 1 assigns attribute 1 the value of 1 using the value assignment (1,CO,1); and source node 2 assigns attribute 1 the value of 2 using (1,CO,2). Node 3 decreases inventory position by calling user function 1 when a demand of either type occurs. Function UF is shown in Figure 14-4. The variables are indexed so that each item I has an inventory position, POS(I), reorder point, R(I), and stock control level, SCL(I). The variables are dimensioned to 2, the number of item types. In user function 1, I is set equal to the item type of the current demand which is obtained from attribute 1, that is, I=GATRB(1). The next statement causes the inventory position for type I to be decreased by 1.

Returning to the network in Figure 14-3, note that when the appropriate inventory position is decreased, a branch is made to one of the backorder Q-nodes. Item 1 demands go to Q-node 4 and item 2 demands go to Q-node 5. Resource 1 represents stock-on-hand for item 1, and resource 2 represents stock-on-hand for item 2. When an item 1 demand is satisfied, node 8 is released. When an item 2 demand is satisfield, node 9 is released. Hence, the number of releases of node 8 represents total item 1 sales, and the number of releases of node 9 represents total item 2 sales.

The review network includes a self-loop activity around source node 10 to specify the time between reviews. The conditional, take-all branching is set up so that the self-loop is always taken at each release of node 10 and other branches are taken if orders are placed. Attributes 1 and 2 represent order quantities for item 1 and 2, respectively. If attribute 1 is greater than zero, the branch to node 11 is taken. If attribute 2 is greater than zero, the branch to node 12 is taken. These attribute values are set in user function 2, which is called at each review time. Referring to Figure 14-4, we see that user function 2 performs a

```
      FUNCTION UF(IFN)
      COMMON/UCOM1/POS(2),R(2),SCL(2)
      UF=0.0
      GO TO (1,2,3), IFN
C**** DECREASE INVENTORY POSITION FOR ITEM I
    1 I=GATRB(1)
      POS(I)=POS(I)-1
      RETURN
C**** PERFORM REVIEW FOR ITEM I
    2 DO 10 I=1,2
      X=0.0
      IF (POS(I).GT.R(I)) GO TO 8
      X=SCL(I)-POS(I)
      POS(I)=POS(I)+X
    8 CALL PATRB(X,I)
   10 CONTINUE
C**** OBSERVE SAFETY STOCK FOR ITEM I
    3 DO 20 I=1,2
      IF (GATRB(I).EQ.0.) GO TO 20
      X=ICSRA(I)
      CALL COL(X,I)
      CALL HIS(X,I)
   20 CONTINUE
      RETURN
      END
```

Figure 14-4 Function UF for multi-commodity example.

review on each item. A DO loop is used to examine all items. The code shown here is general, although the range of the DO loop is only set for two item types. First, the proposed attribute value to set to 0.0 and then a test on the inventory position being greater than the re-order point is made. If it is, attribute 1 is assigned a 0.0 value by a call to subroutine PATRB(X,I). The next item type is then considered. If an order is to be placed, the order quantity, X, is set equal to SCL(I)-POS(I). The inventory position is increased by this quantity, and the appropriate attribute number is set equal to this quantity again by a call to PATRB(X,I). Note that the value assignment at node 10 specifies an addition to attribute 1. Since UF is always set to zero, user function 2 does not change the value of attribute 1.

Branching from node 10 is performed based on the values for at-tributes 1 and 2, the amounts to be ordered. Depending on the attri-bute values, either node 11 or node 12, both node 11 and 12, or neither node 11 nor node 12 will be released following a review. The total number of reviews performed corresponds to the number of releases of node 10. The number of orders of each type are represented by the number of releases of nodes 11 and 12.

The network allows for each order to have a different lead time. This is realistic if different suppliers furnish each item. All orders are re-ceived at node 13, where safety stock values are observed. At node 13, a test in user function 3 on which attributes are greater than zero indi-cates the item type for the order and which stock value is to be observed for safety stock statistics.

Branching from node 13 controls which FREE node is released. Routing to node 14 represents an order for item 1, while routing to node 15 represents an order for item 2. As can be seen, the modeling of multiple items closely parallels the single-item model.

The multicommodity model is also easy to embellish. For ex-ample, making the demand for item 2 dependent on the demand for item 1 can be modeled by adding a branch from node 1 to node 2. This branch would prescribe the delay time between a demand for item 1 and item 2. Another embellishment would be where the same supplier furnishes both order quantities. In this case, a single lead-time activity is required. To model this, an order is placed if attribute 1 or attribute 2 is greater than zero. If we use attribute 3 to be the sum of attributes 1 and 2, no order is placed only when attribute 3 is zero. In user func-tion 2, we add the following statement after statement 8:

```
UF=UF+X
```

In the network model, we change the value assignment at node 10 to (3,UF,2) and branch from node 10 based on attribute 3 as shown in Figure 14-5. In this modified model, an order that arrives to node 13 can contain units of item 1 and/or item 2 since both attribute 1 and

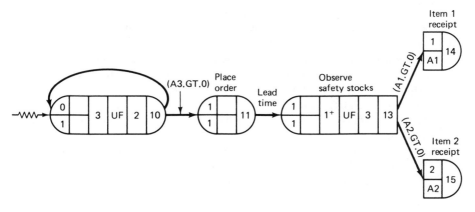

Figure 14-5 Network segment to model orders for multiple items.

attribute 2 could be greater than zero. In this case, routing from node 13 must be changed to conditional, take-all.

As mentioned previously, the two-commodity model can be easily generalized to the N-commodity case. Furthermore, the previously described lost sales logic, the continuous review procedure, and the complex demand processes can be incorporated for any or all of the item types. In addition, the profit calculations performed in subroutine UO can be adapted to account for item types individually or in an aggregate manner.

14.10 SUMMARY

The procedures for modeling inventory demand processes are similar to those for modeling job arrivals to production systems. The use of probabilistic and conditional branching together with nodal modifications facilitates the modeling of complex demand processes. A Q-GERT network model for a two-commodity inventory situation is presented which is not significantly different from the single-commodity model.

14.11 EXERCISES

14-1. Discuss the assumptions involved in using the following distributions as the interdemand time distribution: exponential, normal, lognormal, Erlang ($k = 2$), triangular, uniform.

14-2. Give three reasons for selecting a distribution type to represent interdemand times rather than using a histogram of the actual demand times experienced over the past year.

14-3. Modify the network for specifying the time between demands (Figure 14-4) so that the average obtained is used as the mean for an exponential distribution.

14-4. Use the concepts presented in Section 14.6 relating to seasonal demand to build a network model describing the sale of baseball bats.

14-5. Modify the inventory model presented in Section 13.6 to the situation in which the number of demands per demand instant is Poisson distributed with the mean of 3. Assume that if a value of zero is obtained as the Poisson sample that the customer does not place an order.

14-6. Build a general Q-GERT model for an inventory situation in which the demand distribution is characterized by a generalized Poisson distribution, a compound Poisson distribution, and a stuttering Poisson distribution. Provide operational definitions for these variants to the Poisson distribution.

14-7. Run the multicommodity inventory system as modeled in Section 14.9 and develop strategies for relating the inventory policies for the two-item system.

Network Decision Modeling and Project Planning

15

Decision and Risk Analysis

15.1 INTRODUCTION

In this chapter, networks are used to represent different types of decision and assessment processes. Various decision situations as modeled by the management scientist are presented in a single unified manner. A decision situation consists of a choice from a set of alternatives, A_i, in the face of uncertain future states, S_j. If the manager makes decision A_i and future state S_j happens, the outcome O_{ij} occurs. In making a choice of one of the alternatives, a decision maker either explicitly or implicitly assigns a value or values to the possible outcomes associated with the alternative. The values are defined by $V(O_{ij})$. He may also make a judgment about the possibility of future state S_j occurring. We define p_j as this probability. With this terminology, we can view decision making within the framework of the table presented in Figure 15-1.

The value associated with an outcome can be one or more performance measures. The performance measures may be known with certainty or only known probabilistically (distribution functions or moments of distribution functions). Common performance measures for outcomes are profit, cost, probability of bankruptcy, reliability, and probability of success.

Faced with a decision situation as presented in Figure 15-1, the manager needs a procedure for choosing an alternative. The selection of an alternative is referred to as a choice decision. Many principles of

Future state

	S_1	S_2	$\cdots$	S_F
	p_1	p_2	$\cdots$	p_F
A_1	O_{11}	O_{12}	$\cdots$	O_{1F}
A_2	O_{21}	O_{22}	$\cdots$	O_{2F}
$\vdots$	$\vdots$	$\vdots$		$\vdots$
A_C	O_{C1}	O_{C2}	$\cdots$	O_{CF}

Alternative

Figure 15-1 General decision framework: $V(O_{ij})$, value associated with outcome O_{ij}.

choice for selecting alternatives in light of diverse projected future states have been proposed. Examples of principles of choice are: select the alternative that has the highest expected value associated with the outcomes over all future states; select the alternative that maximizes the minimum value associated with any future state; select the alternative that has the highest expected value for the future state with the highest chance of occurring [132]. Note that the principles of choice take into account the occurrence or the "selection of a future state." This selection of a future state corresponds to a chance decision.

In discussing a decision situation, we have described only a single choice whose outcome was then determined through a chance decision. Sequential decision making involves the selection of a choice of an alternative, with the outcome being both the value associated with the outcome and a new decision situation. This can be thought of within the context of the decision framework presented in Figure 15-1 as each outcome consisting of a value(s) and a pointer to another decision table. Typically, we do not conceive of decision making as going on ad infinitum,† but that the final decision is one in which all the values of the outcomes can be specified in terms of the performance measures of interest; that is, no further pointers to decision tables are contained at the last decision stage.

It is in the area of sequential decision making that networks, and Q-GERT in particular, play an important descriptive and analysis role. In this chapter we present network models of sequential decision situations. Since decisions in many instances involve costs and profits directly rather than costs that are a function of activity duration, the next section describes the ramifications associated with replacing the time variable on the network with a cost variable. The remainder of this chapter describes decision trees, decision networks, risk assessment, and stochastic shortest-route analysis.

†When an infinite planning horizon is considered, little weight is given to the decisions that are to be made in the distant future.

15.2 THE USE OF COST IN PLACE OF TIME IN Q-GERT NETWORKS

In some network problems it is convenient to interpret an activity duration in terms of the cost of performing the activity. When employing cost in place of time in a Q-GERT network the same logical operations apply, but care is required when formulating a model to make sure that the concepts employed in Q-GERT are feasible. A few illustrations should be sufficient to indicate the benefits and potential pitfalls of a cost rather than a time orientation.

Activities in series model sums of activity costs. Following is a series of three activities.

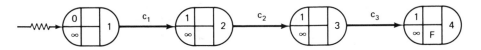

For each run of the network, a sample of the sum of the three costs $(c_1 + c_2 + c_3)$ is obtained by specifying the collection of first statistics at node 4. Any of the distribution functions to specify activity durations could be used to specify activity costs. A restriction when specifying costs is that a negative value cannot be associated with an activity. (This restriction also holds for the time specification for an activity.)

The minimum of a set of activity costs is modeled by activities in parallel with only a single release required to release the end node. This is shown for two activities.

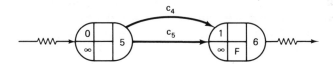

The maximum of a set of activity costs is also modeled by activities in parallel but with the number of release requirements equal to the number of activities in parallel. This is shown for two activities in parallel.

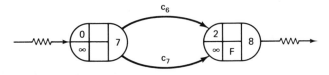

A weighted sum of costs is modeled by probabilistic routing. The following network models the selection of cost, c_8, with probability p_8 and the selection of cost c_9 with probability p_9.

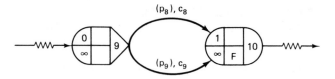

On any run, the cost to go from node 9 to node 10 will be either c_8 or c_9. If in N runs, c_8 occurs N_8 times and c_9 occurs N_9 times, then N_8/N and N_9/N are estimates of p_8 and p_9, respectively.

An average of costs can be modeled by having each activity release its end node and collecting ALL statistics at the end node. Following is the averaging of costs for two activities.

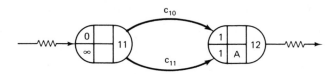

In this situation, the average on a run or on many runs will be taken over the number of times the end node is released.

A last illustration is for a queueing situation that is cost based.

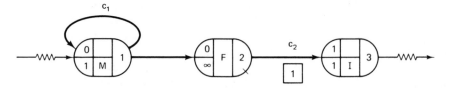

One interpretation of this network is that c_1 dollars must be expended before a next arrival to the network can occur. A cost is associated with service and a next service cannot be started until a cost of c_2 is expended on the transaction being served. In this case, interval statistics at node 3 represents the total service cost while a transaction is in the system. Clearly, care is needed when employing cost concepts directly on Q-GERT networks.

The standard procedure for including costs is to relate them to activity durations. By developing user functions in accordance with specified cost equations that are dependent on the activity durations, costs can be accumulated [129,158,208].

15.3 DECISION TREES

A decision tree has a special network form in which each node represents a decision point at which a selection is made of a single activity emanating from the node. Both chance and choice decisions are modeled in a decision tree. A chance decision corresponds to probabilistic

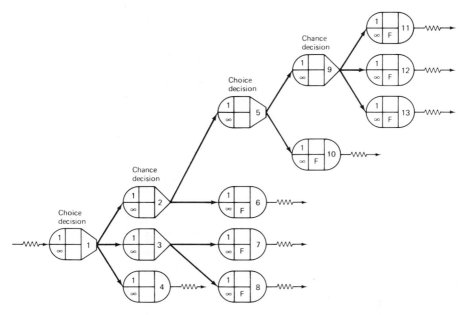

Figure 15-2 Q-GERT decision tree.

branching and a choice decision corresponds to conditional, take-first branching.

An important characteristic of a tree is that there is a unique path from the source node to any other node in the network. An illustration of a decision tree modeled in the Q-GERT syntax is shown in Figure 15-2. From the figure it is seen that a Q-GERT decision tree has the following properties: a single branch is incident to each node; every node can be released only once and requires a single input for its release; all branching is done either probabilistically or using conditional, take-first procedures; and no restriction on activity time is made. Multiple sink nodes are associated with the tree, with each sink node representing a different outcome since it can be reached by only one path.

A Q-GERT model portrays the time and/or cost to reach each sink node. For each branch emanating from a chance decision node, a probability of the branch being picked (the future state occurring) and the value for the outcome associated with the branch are specified. The end node for the branch represents the next decision point.

A special but often studied case of decision trees involves only chance decisions. Such trees are referred to as probabilistic decision trees, and they are modeled in Q-GERT by having all branching done probabilistically. The form of a probabilistic decision tree modeled in Q-GERT is given in Figure 15-3.

Activities are never performed concurrently in decision trees; that is, only a single activity is ever ongoing at a given time. Because of this simple structure, it is often possible to compute analytically the prob-

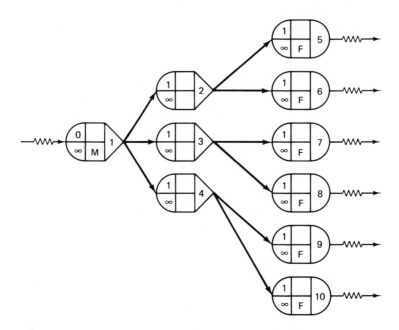

Figure 15-3 Probablistic decision tree.

abilities, release times, and costs associated with each sink node. For probabilistic decision trees involving no attribute assignments, the following statements can be made:

1. The probability of releasing a sink node is the product of the probabilities of the branches on the path leading to the sink node.
2. The time (cost) to reach a sink node is the sum of the time (cost) on the branches on the path leading to the sink node.

Q-GERT becomes an attractive tool for modeling decision tree processes when conditions as well as probabilities govern the branches to be taken. This will occur when the decision to be made at a node is not independent of the path to reach the node; that is, the current decision is not independent of previous decisions. The attribute assignment and conditional branching features of Q-GERT facilitate the representation of those decision tree processes for which analytic solutions are not readily available.

15.4 DECISION NETWORKS

Decision networks generalize decision trees by permitting more than one branch to be incident to a node and by allowing multiple source nodes. A decision structure is still present, as only a single branch is selected at each node. However, a decision network allows the possibility of different decision selections leading to the same outcome.

15.5 DECISION TREE MODEL
OF NEW PRODUCT INTRODUCTION

To illustrate decision tree analysis procedures, a network representation of the introduction of a new product will be presented. This example is an adaptation of a decision tree analysis presented by Hespos and Strassman [78], which is also discussed in Whitehouse [212]. The decision process involves sequential decisions regarding whether a product should be introduced regionally or nationally. First, a decision as to whether to market the product directly to a national market or to start regionally needs to be made. If initial marketing is done regionally, a second decision is required involving whether to remain regional or to go national based on the regional response observed. The Q-GERT network to model the situation is shown in Figure 15-4. The network model portrays the sequence of decisions to be made and not how to make the decisions, which would be a more difficult network modeling task.

The choice decision to be made by branching from node 1 selects initial marketing to be regional or national. If the product is introduced regionally, the branch to node 3 is taken. The output side of node 3 represents the chance decision that there will be a small regional demand (probability of 0.3) or a large regional demand (probability of 0.7). If a small regional demand occurs, node 4 is released. The return for regional marketing with a small demand is zero with probability 0.2, one with probability 0.5, and two with probability 0.3. The parallel branches† from node 4 to node 5 samples from this distribution probabilistically. No further decision making is involved when a small regional demand occurs.

When a large regional demand occurs, a choice decision to remain regional or go national is made at node 2. If the decision is to remain regional, node 6 is released followed by node 7. The release of node 7 occurs when the choice decisions are to introduce regionally and remain regional (REG-REG). If the decision at node 2 is to market nationally, node 8 is released and then node 9 is released. The return obtained from the choice to market nationally after introducing regionally is associated with node 9.

Note that the return based on the decision processes are represented by activity values (durations) in a manner similar to the costs described in Section 15.2. In Q-GERT, all such returns must be positive. If any negative returns are associated with the decisions, a translation of values must be made by the most negative value so that only positive values will be associated with the activities. When a translation

---

†The three parallel branches all describe the same activity and, hence, are allowed to be incident to a single node without violating the decision tree characteristics. Clearly, a single activity could be used to represent the three parallel branches.

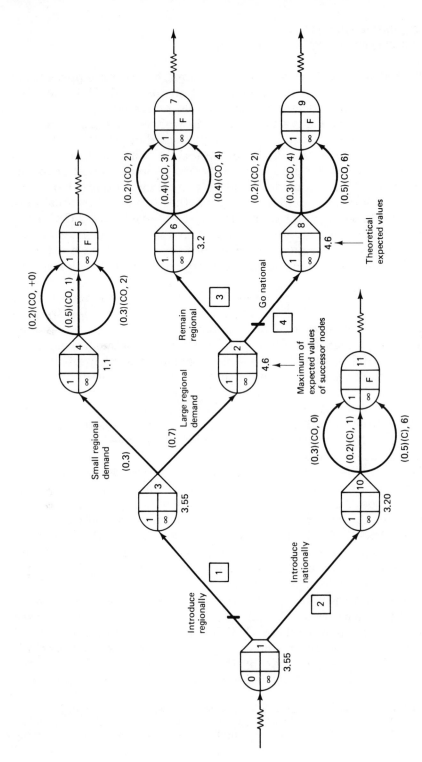

Figure 15-4 Q-GERT model of decision tree related to introducing a new product.

of values is made, the final result must be adjusted for each translation. Alternatively, user functions may be used to collect the cost or return statistics.

Before discussing the Q-GERT approach for this model, consider the standard method for evaluating the expected return from the decision network. The procedure starts at each sink node and computes the expected return associated with nodes whose emanating activities lead to the sink node. This process is repeated recursively until a choice decision node is encountered. At a choice decision node, the largest expected return associated with all nodes immediately following the choice decision node is determined. The largest of these expected values is then associated with the choice decision node, which assumes that the decision maker bases his or her choice on maximizing expected return. In this manner, expected returns for all nodes of the network can be obtained, and eventually an expected value is associated with the source node. The expected return for the source node is declared as the expected return for the decision tree. Since a selection for each choice decision node has been made in order to compute the expected return, it is a simple matter to trace from the source node through the network to identify each choice decision that should be made in order to maximize the expected return. Below each node in Figure 15-4, the expected return is given. A heavy vertical bar is shown on one activity following each choice decision node to indicate the choice that would be made using the maximum expected return criterion at each choice node.

We now examine the procedure for using Q-GERT to analyze the network. For a Q-GERT analysis, choice decisions are replaced with deterministic branching. This modification allows all paths in the decision tree to be activated so all possible choices can be assessed.

The outputs from the Q-GERT processor for 1000 simulations of the decision tree presented in Figure 15-4 with deterministic branching at nodes 1 and 2 are shown in Figure 15-5. The termination condition for a run was not specified, so each run ended after all activities had been completed.

From Figure 15-5 we see that each path in a decision tree is evaluated and estimates are provided of the probability of the path being selected and the average and standard deviation of the return. Each path represents a sequence of decisions or outcomes and a policy at the choice nodes. Thus, the values associated with node 5 are for the choice decision to introduce regionally followed by the chance outcome that a small regional demand occurs. The values associated with node 5 on the Q-GERT output correspond to the values associated with node 4 in a standard decision tree analysis. Similarly, the maximum of the values for nodes 7 and 9 would be associated with node 2. In this manner, the standard decision tree analysis could be performed using the Q-GERT outputs.

The procedures described above for the Q-GERT analysis parallel

```
                    GERT SIMULATION PROJECT DEC-TREE  BY PRITSKER
                            DATE  3/ 8/ 1982

                        **FINAL RESULTS FOR 1000 SIMULATIONS**

                              **AVERAGE NODE STATISTICS**

NODE   LABEL      PROBABILITY    AVE.    STD.DEV.   SD OF AVE   NO OF    MIN.      MAX.     STAT
                                                               OBS.                       TYPE

11     NATIONAL     1.0000      3.2400    2.8373      .0897    1000.      0       6.0000    F
 5     REGIONAL      .3060      1.0654     .6840      .0391     306.      0       2.0000    F
 7     REG-REG       .6940      3.1945     .7528      .0286     694.    2.0000    4.0000    F
 9     REG-NAT       .6940      4.5331     .5931      .0605     694.    2.0000    6.0000    F
```

Figure 15-5 Q-GERT output for new product introduction decision tree model.

those of a standard decision tree analysis. We provide this discussion to indicate how Q-GERT could be used in a standard decision tree framework. Q-GERT can be used more advantageously in decision analysis when the decision logic to be modeled is more complex. The Q-GERT syntax provides capabilities not available in decision trees through the use of conditional branching based on time, attribute values, and node realizations that can capture the significant aspects of the real decision process.

15.6 Q-GERT ANALYSIS OF NEW PRODUCT INTRODUCTION

The decision tree approach employs the criterion of largest expected value. This criterion does not take into account the distribution of returns associated with different decision policies. When a decision process is to be exercised once or only a few times, it is important to know the probability that the return may be small even if an optimal decision policy is employed. Q-GERT provides such information.

Decision alternatives can be viewed as competitors where the largest return from a decision policy is the winner of the competition. In a network form, this implies parallel paths leading to a node. The path with the largest return at the sink node constitutes the best policy. Viewed in this light, a sequence of decisions is represented by an inverted tree with many source nodes and a single sink node. The alternative decisions are represented by the activities that lead into a node and the activity that causes the node to be released is the choice to be made.

A Q-GERT model of the decision alternatives for the new product introduction example described in Section 15.5 is shown in Figure 15-6. The node numbers assigned in this network have been selected to agree, in the main, with those presented in Figure 15-4. Nodes 1 and 2 represent the choice decisions. The last activity to arrive at the node represents the desirable decision policy for a particular simulation run.† The selection of an alternative at a choice decision node is reflected in the number of times incoming activities release the node. When returns are equal for a set of alternative activities, an additional criterion is necessary to make the choice. For this example, we assume that it is preferred to go "national" if, at any time, the returns are equal. This is modeled in the Q-GERT network by assigning a small return ($\delta = 0.00001$) to those branches representing the "national" choice (activities 2 and 4). At each subsequent decision stage, δ is doubled to again break ties.

For each of the choice decision nodes, a user function is employed to record the number of the activity that released the node. The user

---

†If a minimization problem is being considered, the first release requirement for choice decision nodes 1 and 2 would be 1.

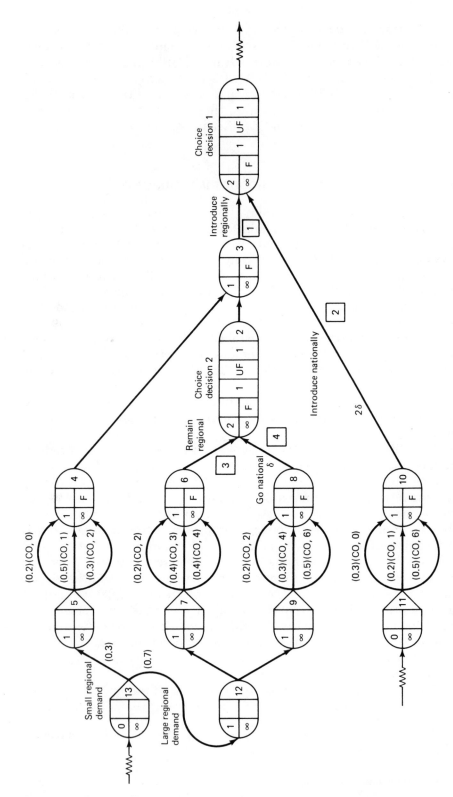

Figure 15-6 Q-GERT model of new product introduction decisions: $\delta = (CO, 0.00001)$.

```
FUNCTION UF(I)
COMMON/UCOM/COUNT(4)
DATA COUNT /4*0./
NA=NACTY(I)
COUNT(NA)=COUNT(NA)+1.
UF=0.
RETURN
END


SUBROUTINE UO
COMMON/UCOM/COUNT(4)
COMMON/QVAR/NDE,NFTBU(100),NREL(100),NRELP(100),NREL2(100),NRUN,
1NRUNS,NTC(100),PARAM(100,4),TBEG,TNOW
IF(NRUN.NE.NRUNS) RETURN
WRITE(6,2)
2 FORMAT(1H1///22X,4HBEST/5X,8HACTIVITY,7X,8HDECISION,7X,8HFRACTION/
16X,6HNUMBER,10X,5HCOUNT,10X,4HBEST//)
DO 10 NA=1,4
XCOUNT=COUNT(NA)/FLOAT(NRUNS)
WRITE(6,1) NA,COUNT(NA),XCOUNT
10 CONTINUE
1 FORMAT(I10,7X,F10.0,5X,F10.4)
RETURN
END
```

Figure 15-7 Function UF and subroutine UO for Q-GERT model of new product introduction.

function is shown in Figure 15-7, where function NACTY is used to determine the activity number, NA, that released the node. (Recall from Chapter 3 that the argument to NACTY is arbitrary.) The number of times that activity NA is the desirable choice is stored in COUNT (NA). Also given in Figure 15-7 is subroutine UO, where the values of COUNT and the fraction of times the activity is the desirable choice are printed.

The Q-GERT output reports for this example are shown in Figure 15-8.

In 1000 simulations of the new product introduction, a higher return was achieved 436 times if the product was introduced regionally, whereas in 564 runs, the optimal (or equivalent) decision was to introduce the product nationally. Thus, 56.4% of the time the better choice is to introduce the product nationally. There were 694 runs in which choice decision 2 was made and, in 573 of the runs, it was best to go national. This represents an 82.6% chance of obtaining a greater return when making the "go national" decision. These percentages are important, as they specify the fraction of time that the highest possible return was obtained.†

The statistics for the nodes of the network provide additional information. The values for nodes 4, 6, 8, and 10 provide estimates of the expected return, standard deviation, and minimum and maximum associated with each of the choice decisions. It is the expected value that the standard decision tree analyst uses when deciding to make a choice decision. Thus, for choice decision 2 to remain regional or to go national, the values of node 6 and node 8 would be compared and since the expected value for node 8 is higher (4.53 versus 3.19) the decision to go national would be made. From the analysis done in the

†A theoretical (complete enumeration) analysis of this model indicates that 16% of the time the returns are equal for choice decision 2 and 22.3% of the time the returns are equal for choice decision 1.

ACTIVITY NUMBER	BEST DECISION COUNT	FRACTION BEST
1	436.	.4360
2	564.	.5640
3	121.	.1210
4	573.	.5730

GERT SIMULATION PROJECT DEC-TREE-B BY PRITSKER
DATE 3/ 8/ 1982

FINAL RESULTS FOR 1000 SIMULATIONS

AVERAGE NODE STATISTICS

NODE	LABEL	PROBABILITY	AVE.	STD.DEV.	SD OF AVE	NO OF OBS.	MIN.	MAX.	STAT TYPE
1	CHOICE 1	1.0000	4.9010	1.7879	.0565	1000.	.0000	6.0000	F
8	GO NAT	.6940	3.5331	1.5931	.0605	694.	2.0000	6.0000	F
6	REM.REG	.6940	3.1945	.7528	.0286	694.	2.0000	4.0000	F
2	CHOICE 2	.6940	4.7882	1.2632	.0480	694.	2.0000	6.0000	F
4	SMALLREG	.3060	1.0654	.6840	.0391	306.	0	2.0000	F
10	INTRONAT	1.0000	3.2400	2.8373	.0897	1000.	0	6.0000	F
3	INTROREG	1.0000	3.6490	2.0484	.0648	1000.	0	6.0000	F

Figure 15-8 Outputs from Q-GERT model of new product introduction decisions.

preceding paragraph, we estimate the probability of this being the best possible decision as 0.826.

The statistics associated with node 2 provide the information that if the correct decision is always made, the expected return from choice decision 2 is 4.79 and the standard deviation of the return is 1.26. The statistics for node 3 provide the expected return if choice decision 1 was to introduce regionally and the correct choice decision 2 is always made. Note that this value is higher than the quantity (3.55) specified by Figure 15-4 since the correct decision at node 2 is presumed. For node 1, the largest possible average return is estimated for the new product introduction decisions. Thus, if the decision maker has complete information about each possible return, then, on the average, his or her return would be 4.90.

This example demonstrates key concepts associated with decision networks:

1. The incremental return from increased information can be quantified.
2. The expected return at a choice decision and the probability of making a correct choice are important variables in the decision process.
3. With discrete returns, equivalent choices (ties) can affect the percentage of times an alternative is selected.
4. The decision process can be broken down into understandable elements which lead to a comprehensive treatment of the choices available.

15.7 RISK ASSESSMENT

Risk is a performance measure that has been used to evaluate alternatives in a decision situation. *Risk* is usually defined as the product of the magnitude of an undesirable outcome† multiplied by the frequency of its occurrence. With this definition, risk is equal to the expected value of an undesirable outcome. A special case that is reported frequently in the literature defines the magnitude of an undesirable outcome as unity. This results in risk being defined as the probability of occurrence of an undesirable outcome.

Decision trees and decision networks are commonly used to perform risk analyses. In such situations, the sink nodes define the undesirable outcome associated with the risk. The probability of releasing the sink node is the desired estimate of risk.

When the magnitude of an undesirable outcome is defined, a user function can be employed with Q-GERT to obtain the product of the

†Standard terminology in risk analysis would refer to an undesirable event.

magnitude with the frequency of occurrence of the undesirable out-come. User-collected statistics are then used for computing statistical estimates over multiple runs. Alternatively, average value computations can be obtained using networks similar to those presented in Section 15.2, where a cost is given in place of the activity duration. If the risk analysis involves time delays as well as risk computations, a user func-tion for computing average risk is required.

In some risk analyses, the undesirable outcome is defined in terms of time. For example, an undesirable outcome might be the nondelivery of an item by April 15. As another example, the undesirable outcome could be the completion of a product development by a competitor before our product is developed. In these situations, risk is computed using Q-GERT by defining two disjoint networks, each having a sink node. In the network describing the product development, one sink node represents the desirable outcome. In the other network, the sink node represents the undesirable outcome. In multiple runs, the fraction of runs in which the undesirable sink node is reached represents the risk. If a value can be associated with this sink node, the product of the probability and the value can be formed and the generalized risk factor computed.

There is close association between risk analysis and project plan-ning since both are concerned with the probabilities and times associated with success and failure. The main difference is that a risk analysis is oriented toward an assessment of defined policies, whereas project planning is oriented to the development of plans and their assessment. Chapters 16 and 17 describe the use of Q-GERT for project planning.

15.8 STOCHASTIC SHORTEST-ROUTE ANALYSIS

A special type of decision problem that has received considerable atten-tion in the literature is the determination of the shortest route in a net-work. Many management science, operations research, and industrial engineering problems have been shown to be equivalent to defining the shortest path in a network [52]. When activity times or costs are deter-ministic (constants), the shortest path in the network can be found by finding the shortest path from the source node to an intermediate node and then finding the shortest path from the intermediate node to the sink node. By doing this for all intermediate nodes, an algorithm for finding the shortest path results [42,43].

When activity times are not deterministic, there is a probability associated with a path being optimal (shortest). These probabilities have been defined as optimality indices by Sigal, who has done the pioneering research in stochastic shortest-route problems [177,180,181]. Areas of application of stochastic shortest-route analysis are: equipment replace-ment, reliability, security and safeguards, stochastic maximal flow, and dynamic programming problems. In the following section, we demonstrate that Q-GERT can be used for analyzing stochastic shortest-route problems. Next, decision problems related to equipment replacement and security procedures are formulated as shortest-route problems.

15.9 Q-GERT APPROACH TO SHORTEST-ROUTE PROBLEMS

To model shortest-route problems with Q-GERT, networks are constructed using only the basic node type with the following specifications: a first release requirement of 1, a second release requirement of infinity, and deterministic branching. Nodes with these parameters allow only a single release of a node and, hence, only a single path to a node which is the shortest will be realized. By employing deterministic branching all activities emanating from the node are started, and all possible paths from the node are initiated. An activity that does not release a node cannot be on the shortest path and is removed from consideration. This is accomplished by specifying the second release requirement for every node as infinity.

First statistics are collected at a node in the network to estimate the shortest time to reach that node. Every trace of a run will present a shortest path for the network. If deterministic times are employed, a single run can be made and the trace will portray the path that is shortest. Should the activity times be characterized by random variables, the traces will also show the shortest path for each run, but different runs may have different shortest paths. To automatically obtain the probability that a given path is shortest (the optimality index), user functions are employed. The procedure for estimating path optimality indices is described in the next section.

15.10 ESTIMATING PATH OPTIMALITY INDICES

The use of Q-GERT in estimating path optimality indices will be illustrated by an example network. Consider the network in Figure 15-9. For convenience, all nodes have a user function with the user function number the same as the node number, as shown here, where N is the node number and also the function number for an attribute assignment.

The listing of Function UF(N) is shown in Figure 15-10 on page 359. Definitions of non-Q-GERT variables used in the program are in Table 15-1. Each call to UF passes the node number, N, which is the currently released node number. In UF, the activity number that released node N

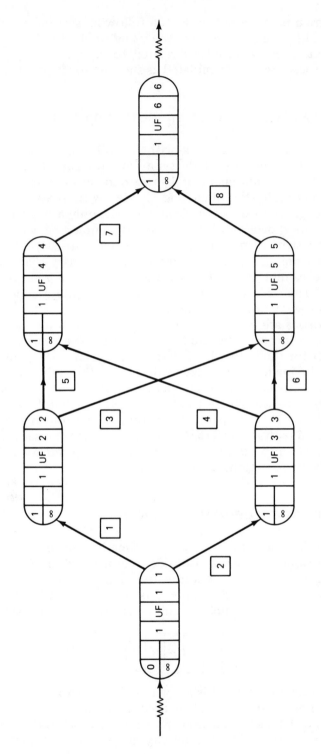

Figure 15-9 Example Q-GERT network for obtaining optimality indices.

TABLE 15-1 Non-Q-GERT Program Variables for Simulating Shortest-Route Problems

NNOD(N,1)	=	activity number of branch incident to node N which was completed on current run, before all other branches incident to node N (branch that caused the release of node N on the current run)
NNOD(N,2)	=	start node of activity NNOD(N,1)
IPATH(·)	=	list of activity sequences of unique paths encountered during simulation
COUNT(J)	=	number of times the jth path sequence in IPATH(·) was optimal during the simulation
NPATH	=	total number of paths in IPATH(·)

```
      FUNCTION UF(N)
      COMMON/QVAR/NDE,NFTBU(100),NREL(100),NRELP(100),NREL2(100),NRUN,
     1NRUNS,NTC(100),PARAM(100,4),TBEG,TNOW
      COMMON/UCOM1/NNOD(100,2),IPATH(1000),COUNT(100),NPATH
C**** RECORD ACTIVITY NUMBER OF BRANCH THAT RELEASED THIS NODE
      NNOD(N,1) = NACTY(IDUM)
C**** RECORD START NODE OF THIS ACTIVITY,STORED AS ATRIB(1)
      NNOD(N,2) = GATRB(1)
C**** SET UF TO CURRENT NODE SO EMANATING ACTIVITIES
C**** CARRY START NODE INFORMATION AS ATRIB(1)
      UF = N
      RETURN
      END
```

Figure 15-10 Layout of function UF(N).

is retrieved using function NATCY and is stored in NNOD(N,1). The variable NNOD(N,2) is used to record the start node of the activity that released node N. In this way, as the simulation progresses, NNOD contains information on the shortest route to each node for the current simulation experiment. The last statement of UF assigns UF to N so that attribute 1 of each emanating activity will record the start node of that activity.

When the sink node is released, which in this example is node 6, Q-GERT calls subroutine UO. Figure 15-11 contains a description of the logic used in this routine. The first step when a run is completed is

```
      SUBROUTINE UO

      COMMON/QVAR/NDE,NFTBU(100),NREL(100),NRELP(100),NREL2(100),NRUN
     1NRUNS,NTC(100),PARAM(100,4),TBEG,TNOW
C**** CODE TO DO THE FOLLOWING SHOULD BE INSERTED
C**** SINK NODE IS REACHED ONE MORE TIME
C**** WEAVE THROUGH NNOD( ) TO RETRIEVE SET OF
C**** ACTIVITIES WHICH REPRESENT SHORTEST PATH FOR THIS RUN
C**** CHECK IPATH( ) TO SEE IF THIS PATH
C**** SEQUENCE HAS BEEN ENCOUNTERED BEFORE.  IF NOT,
C**** RECORD THE SEQUENCE IN IPATH( ) AND INCREASE NPATH.
C**** DETERMINE THE RELATIVE PATH NUMBER, J, OF THIS
C**** PATH IN IPATH( ).  INCREASE COUNT(J) BY ONE
      COUNT(J) = COUNT(J) + 1.
C**** IF TOTAL NUMBER OF RUNS HAS NOT BEEN COMPLETED, RETURN.
C**** OTHERWISE COMPUTE AND PRINT PATH INDICES AND IPATH( ).
      IF (NRUN.LT.NRUNS)RETURN
      XRUNS = NRUNS
      DO 10 I = 1, NPATH
      XINDX = COUNT(I)/XRUNS
      WRITE(6,20) I, XINDX
   20 FORMAT(1X, 'INDEX OF PATH',I4,1X,'=',F10.7)
C**** WRITE NODES ON THIS PATH AS DETERMINED FROM IPATH
   10 CONTINUE
      RETURN
      END
```

Figure 15-11 Layout of subroutine UO.

TABLE 15-2 Sample Values of NNOD

N	NNOD(N,1)	NNOD(N,2)
1	0	0
2	1	1
3	2	1
4	5	2
5	3	2
6	7	4

to determine the activity sequence that represents the shortest path for this run. As stated above, this information is contained in the array NNOD. For example, suppose that the values of NNOD after the jth run were those in Table 15-2. Since node 6 is the sink node, the value of NNOD(6,1) indicates that activity 7 was the last activity on the shortest path. The start node of activity 7 is 4 [NNOD(6,2)=4]. Activity 5 released node 4 [NNOD(4,1)=5] and the start node of activity 5 is 2 [NNOD(4,2)=2]. Activity 1 released node 2 [NNOD(2,1)=1] and was the first activity on the shortest path since the source node for the network is node 1, and it is the start node for activity 1 [NNOD(2,2)=1]. Therefore, for this simulation, the shortest route is the path whose activities are 1, 5, and 7.

The next step in subroutine UO is to check the vector IPATH to see if the sequence of activities that represents the shortest path, that is, 1, 5, and 7, has been encountered on a previous run. If not, this sequence is recorded in IPATH and the number of unique paths observed, NPATH, is increased by one.† In either case, the counter variable COUNT(J), is increased by one to record that path J is the shortest path for this simulation run. The variable J corresponds to the relative location of this path in the vector IPATH. If the number of runs is less than the total number required, a RETURN is executed. If this is the last run, the path optimality indices are computed and reported. The optimality index for the Jth path is equal to COUNT(J)/XRUNS, where XRUNS is a real representation of NRUNS, the total number of runs. The array IPATH would also be printed to report the observed path sequences. Subroutine UI, called by Q-GERT prior to every run, is used to initialize NNOD as outlined in Figure 15-12.

This example demonstrates that Q-GERT enables a modeler to study stochastic shortest-route problems with a limited amount of computer programming. It permits a wide range of distribution types and standard network outputs are directly obtained. However, for simulating shortest-route problems, in general, special-purpose procedures are

---

†As an alternative to allowing the program to determine path sequences, the user can input (through subroutine UI) a select set of path sequences that are of interest. The Q-GERT model can then be used to record statistics on these paths, separately, and all others as a group.

```
SUBROUTINE UI
COMMON/QVAR/NDE,NFTBU(100),NREL(100),NRELP(100),NREL2(100),NRUN,
1NRUNS,NTC(100),PARAM(100,4),TBEG,TNOW
COMMON/UCOM1/NNOD(100,2),IPATH(1000),COUNT(100),NPATH
C**** INITIALIZE NNOD( , ) ON EACH RUN
C**** INITIALIZE COUNT( ) AND NPATH ON THE FIRST RUN
RETURN
END
```

Figure 15-12 General description of subroutine UI for stochastic shortest-route problems.

available to improve the efficiency of the simulation. A program that incorporates variance reduction techniques has been developed for this purpose [177].

15.11 STOCHASTIC SHORTEST-ROUTE ANALYSIS FOR EQUIPMENT REPLACEMENT

A problem commonly encountered by management is that of deciding how often to replace expensive equipment. As equipment ages, maintenance and operating costs increase. Although this cost could be reduced by frequently replacing existing equipment with new equipment, each replacement increases capital expenditures. Equipment replacement policies can be modeled as a network where each path represents the total cost of maintenance, operation, and capital outlay. Finding the shortest route through the network corresponds to selecting the policy that minimizes total cost.

As an illustration,† consider a company planning its equipment replacement during the next four years. Let c_{ij} be the cost of purchasing the equipment at the start of year i plus the cost of operating and maintaining the equipment until the start of year j. The network in Figure 15-13 represents the replacement options over the four-year planning horizon. Node i represents the start of year i. The arc ij represents the costs, c_{ij}, incurred from year i to year j and is the difference between the purchase price and the salvage value plus the sum of the operation and maintenance costs. By this construction, each path in the network represents a strategy of equipment replacement over the four-year planning horizon. For example, one option would be to replace the equipment at the start of each year at a total cost of $c_{12} + c_{23} + c_{34} + c_{45}$.

When the c_{ij} are known, a shortest-path algorithm can be used to find the minimum-cost solution. Here the c_{ij} are assumed to be independent random variables with known probability distributions, and the procedures described in the preceding section will be used to analyze this stochastic shortest-route problem.

The cost distributions for the example are given in Table 15-3. Although all the distributions used here are discrete, this is not a restric-

†This problem is adapted from a deterministic version of equipment replacement problems discussed by Phillips et al. [146].

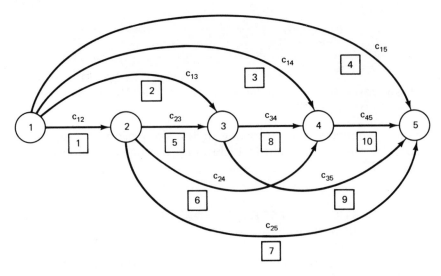

Figure 15-13 Network representing equipment replacement strategies.

tion, as any Q-GERT distribution type could be used. The objective of this stochastic version of equipment replacement problems is to select the replacement strategy that has the greatest probability of being the least-cost option.

The Q-GERT network for this problem is shown in Figure 15-14. Function UF, subroutine UO, and subroutine UI are shown in Figures 15-15, 15-16, and 15-17, respectively. The organization of these routines follows the description presented in Section 15.10. Most of the user variables were defined in Table 15-1. In this example, NSINK is the number of the sink node, IPATH is an array used to define the set of activities in the shortest path for the last run, and JPOS(J) is used to define the position in IPATH where path J's activity numbers are stored.

TABLE 15-3 Cost Distributions for the Network in Figure 15-13

Activity Number	Cost Variable	Distribution		
1	c_{12}	$(10, 1)$		
2	c_{13}	$(20, 1)$		
3	c_{14}	$(30, 1)$		
4	c_{15}	$(40, 1)$		
5	c_{23}	$(10, 0.5)$	$(12, 0.5)$	
6	c_{24}	$(18, 0.3)$	$(20, 0.3)$	$(22, 0.4)$
7	c_{25}	$(26, 0.2)$	$(35, 0.8)$	
8	c_{34}	$(9,\ \ 0.5)$	$(12, 0.5)$	
9	c_{35}	$(18, 0.2)$	$(20, 0.4)$	$(22, 0.4)$
10	c_{45}	$(9,\ \ 0.5)$	$(13, 0.5)$	

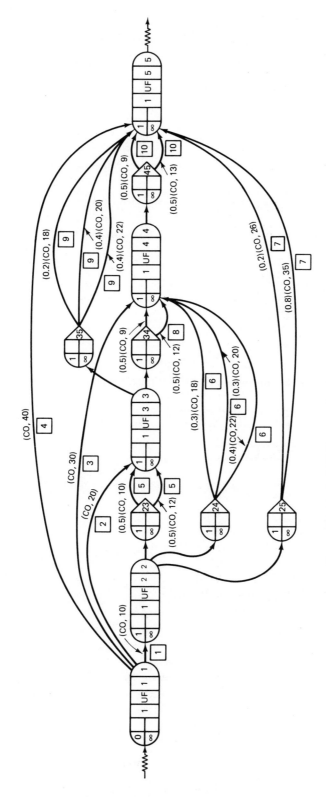

Figure 15-14 Q-GERT network of equipment replacement strategies.

```
      FUNCTION UF(N)
      COMMON/QVAR/NDE,NFTBU(100),NREL(100),NRELP(100),NREL2(100),
     1               NRUN,NRUNS,NTC(100),PARAM(100,4),TBEG,TNOW
      COMMON/UCOM/NNOD(5,2),IPATH(100),COUNT(20),JPOS(20),NSINK,NPATH,
     1               ILAST
C****
C**** RECORD ACTIVITY NUMBER OF BRANCH THAT RELEASED NODE
C****
      NNOD(N,1)=NACTY(IDUM)
C****
C**** RECORD START NODE OF ACTIVITY ,STORED AS ATRIB(1)
C****
      NNOD(N,2)=GATRB(1)
C****
C**** SET UF TO CURRENT NODE
C****
      UF=N
      RETURN
      END
```

Figure 15-15 Function UF for equipment replacement analysis.

```
      SUBROUTINE UI
      COMMON/QVAR/NDE,NFTBU(100),NREL(100),NRELP(100),NREL2(100),
     1               NRUN,NRUNS,NTC(100),PARAM(100,4),TBEG,TNOW
      COMMON/UCOM/NNOD(5,2),IPATH(100),COUNT(20),JPOS(20),NSINK,NPATH,
     1               ILAST
C****
C**** INITIALIZE NNODE(.,.) ON EACH RUN
C**** INITIALIZE COUNT,NPATH,IPATH AND JPOS ON FIRST RUN
C****
      IF(NRUN.NE.1)GO TO 30
      ILAST=0
      DO 20 I=1,20
      JPOS(I)=0
      COUNT(I)=0.
   20 CONTINUE
      DO 25 I=1,100
      IPATH(I)=0
   25 CONTINUE
      NSINK=5
      NPATH=0
   30 DO 40 I=1,NSINK
      NNOD(I,1)=0
      NNOD(I,2)=0
   40 CONTINUE
      RETURN
      END
```

Figure 15-16 Subroutine UI for equipment replacement analysis.

```
      SUBROUTINE UO
      COMMON/QVAR/NDE,NFTBU(100),NREL(100),NRELP(100),NREL2(100),
     1               NRUN,NRUNS,NTC(100),PARAM(100,4),TBEG,TNOW
      COMMON/UCOM/NNOD(5,2),IPATH(100),COUNT(20),JPOS(20),NSINK,NPATH,
     1               ILAST
C****
C**** SINK NODE IS REACHED ONE MORE TIME. WEAVE
C**** THROUGH NNOD(.,.) TO RETRIEVE SET OF ACTIVITIES
C**** WHICH REPRESENT SHORTEST PATH FOR THIS RUN AND
C**** STORE IN IPATH.
C****
      MACT=1
      INODE=NSINK
   10 IACT=NNOD(INODE,1)
      IF(IACT.LE.0)GO TO 15
      IPATH(MACT)=IACT
   15 INODE=NNOD(INODE,2)
      WRITE(6,115)NRUN,IACT,INODE
  115 FORMAT(5X,'NRUN=',I5,2X,'IACT=',I5,2X,'INODE=',I5)
      IF(INODE.EQ.0)GO TO 20
      MACT=MACT+1
      GO TO 10
C****
C**** CHECK IPATH(.) TO SEE IF THIS PATH SEQUENCE
C**** HAS BEEN ENCOUNTERED BEFORE.  IF NOT, RECORD
C**** SEQUENCE IN IPATH(.) AND INCREASE APPROPRIATE PATH.
C****
   20 IF(NPATH.GT.0)GO TO 40
      NPATH=1
      JPOS(NPATH)=1
      COUNT(NPATH)=1.
      INDX=MACT
      ILAST=INDX
      DO 30 I=1,MACT
      IPATH(I)=IPATH(INDX)
      INDX=INDX-1
   30 CONTINUE
      GO TO 80
   40 DO 50 J=1,NPATH
      INDX1=JPOS(J)-1
      INDX2=MACT
      DO 60 I=1,MACT
      INDX3=INDX1+I
      IF(IPATH(INDX3).NE.IPATH(INDX2))GO TO 50
      INDX2=INDX2-1
   60 CONTINUE
```

```
      COUNT(J)=COUNT(J)+1.
      GO TO 80
   50 CONTINUE
      NPATH=NPATH+1
      ILAST=ILAST+1
      IPATH(ILAST)=0
      JPOS(NPATH)=ILAST+1
      INDX2=MACT
      DO 70 I=1,MACT
      INDX3=ILAST+I
      IPATH(INDX3)=IPATH(INDX2)
      INDX2=INDX2-1
   70 CONTINUE
      COUNT(NPATH)=COUNT(NPATH)+1.
      ILAST=INDX3
C****
C**** IF TOTAL NUMBER OF RUNS HAS NOT BEEN COMPLETED,
C**** RETURN. OTHERWISE COMPUTE AND PRINT PATH INDICES
C**** AND IPATH(.)
C****
   80 IF(NRUN.LT.NRUNS)RETURN
      XRUNS=NRUNS
      DO 90 I=1,NPATH
      XINDX=COUNT(I)/XRUNS
      WRITE(6,100)I,XINDX
  100 FORMAT(1X,'INDEX OF PATH',I4,1X,'=',F10.7)
   90 CONTINUE
      DO 110 I=1,NPATH
      WRITE(6,120)I
  120 FORMAT(/6X,'ACTIVITIES ON PATH',I4//)
      INDX=JPOS(I)
  140 IF(IPATH(INDX).LE.0)GO TO 110
      WRITE(6,130)IPATH(INDX)
  130 FORMAT(6X,I4)
      INDX=INDX+1
      GO TO 140
  110 CONTINUE

      RETURN
      END
```

Figure 15-17 Subroutine UO for equipment replacement analysis.

TABLE 15-4 Summary of Outputs from 100 Runs of
Q-GERT Processor for Equipment Replacement Analysis

Path Number	Activities on Path	Optimality Index
1	(4)	0.38
2	(3, 10)	0.10
3	(2, 8, 10)	0.10
4	(1, 6, 10)	0.10
5	(1,7)	0.21
6	(2,9)	0.11
Average cost	38.34	
Standard deviation	1.57	
Minimum	36.00	
Maximum	40.00	

A summary of the output for this example is shown in Table 15-4. The optimality index for path 1 is the highest and shows that 38% of the time the least-cost strategy can be obtained by buying new equipment at the start of year 1 and keeping it for the entire four-year period. The second best strategy is to buy the equipment for one year and then to replace it after three years of operation. This policy has an estimated probability of 0.21 of being the optimal one.

15.12 SHORTEST-ROUTE ANALYSIS FOR SAFEGUARDS SYSTEM DESIGN

Researchers at Sandia Laboratories and Pritsker & Associates are currently applying shortest-route analysis to security procedures of nuclear facilities [86,177]. The network model consists of possible routes a saboteur could use to penetrate a site, access a target, and escape. The network arcs represent the time involved in traversing distances, removing obstacles, and performing other tasks involved in theft and escape. The primary research objective is to compare the thief's minimum time with the security force's response time. In addition, the identification of optimal routes of penetration provides information upon which to recommend policies regarding the nature and allocation of security procedures and expenditures.

To illustrate the general nature of the approaches to safeguards modeling, a simplified example is presented. Figure 15-18 represents a schematic drawing of potential routes of penetration by a saboteur entering a protected area. Walls of the building are shown by solid lines. Theft routes are shown by dotted lines. The target of the theft is located at point F. The thief, however, is not sure of the exact location of internal walls relative to point F. The thief's initial entry is at point

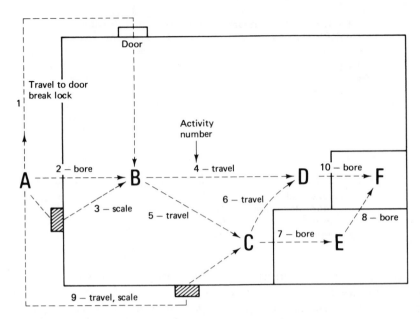

Figure 15-18 Schematic of possible penetration routes.

A, where he has four options to penetrate the first barrier resulting in his reaching interior point B or C. The options are:

1. Travel to one side of the structure where a door is located, break the lock and proceed to B.
2. Bore through the wall and arrive at B.
3. Scale the wall in the vicinity of B.
4. Move to another location to scale the wall and arrive at point C.

Since the thief is not certain of the exact location of F, when he arrives at C, he might decide to move to point D or to bore through the wall at C. If he bores through the wall at C, he will discover the mistake at point E and bore through another wall to reach F.

If the thief traveled through point B, he might travel directly to Point D or first go to C and then decide to try point D. At point D, he will bore through the wall to reach F.

The problem is to compute the probability that each route is the shortest. Also of interest in this problem is the distribution of the minimum time to reach the target. This distribution provides information on how long a safeguards system has to respond once a break-in has started.

The Q-GERT network for this example is shown in Figure 15-19. Estimates of the probability distributions of the activity times are given in Table 15-5. Statistics collected at node 6 provide an estimate of the

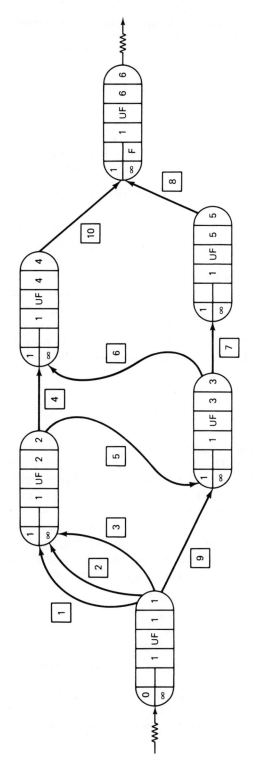

Figure 15-19 Q-GERT network for theft model.

TABLE 15-5 Probability Distributions of Theft Activity Times

Activity	Distribution		
1	(5, 0.2)	(7, 0.2)	(15, 0.6)
2	(15, 0.9)	(20, 0.1)	
3	(10, 0.5)	(20, 0.5)	
4	(5, 0.5)	(6, 0.5)	
5	(3, 0.3)	(4, 0.7)	
6	(4, 0.5)	(6, 0.5)	
7	(10, 0.4)	(20, 0.3)	(30, 0.3)
8	(10, 0.5)	(15, 0.5)	
9	(10, 0.5)	(15, 0.5)	
10	(20, 0.3)	(25, 0.6)	(30, 0.1)

minimum time distribution. The user function UF, subroutine UO, and subroutine UI are similar to the ones presented in the previous example and therefore are not shown.

Table 15-6 shows the output for this model. The three routes with high probabilities of being shortest are those with branch sequences (1,4,10), (9,7,8), and (9,6,10). The minimum time distribution assumes that a thief always chooses the optimal route. If the security detection system required over 44 time units to respond, it would fail 95% of the time according to the estimates provided in Table 15-6.

15.13 SUMMARY

This chapter presents advanced concepts with respect to decision modeling and risk analysis. The use of cost as the additive parameter instead of time is described. The methodology associated with decision trees, decision networks, and risk analysis is presented and examples are given where appropriate. The concept of a stochastic shortest route is described and the procedures by which Q-GERT can be used to analyze such problems are presented. Throughout the chapter examples are given which demonstrate the communication and analysis capabilities of a network approach to decision and risk analysis.

15.14 EXERCISES

15-1. Formulate the various principles of choice described in Section 15-1 in mathematical form.

Embellishment: If the outcome from an alternative-future state presented in Figure 15-1 is a pointer to another decision framework, show how the mathematical forms derived above would be altered.

TABLE 15-6 Output for Theft Model

Path	Activity Sequence				Optimality Index
1	1	5	7	8	0.1171
2	1	5	6	10	0.0000
3	1	4	10		0.3002
4	2	5	7	8	0.0000
5	2	5	6	10	0.0000
6	2	4	10		0.0380
7	3	5	7	8	0.0532
8	3	5	6	10	0.0000
9	3	4	10		0.1389
10	9	7	8		0.2324
11	9	6	10		0.2171

Minimum Time Distribution

Time	Frequency	Cumulative Frequency
28.0000	0.0120	0.0120
29.0000	0.0280	0.0400
30.0000	0.1100	0.1500
31.0000	0.0380	0.1880
32.0000	0.0240	0.2120
33.0000	0.0414	0.2534
34.0000	0.0766	0.3300
35.0000	0.1599	0.4900
36.0000	0.0840	0.5740
37.0000	0.0360	0.6100
38.0000	0.0432	0.6532
39.0000	0.0888	0.7420
40.0000	0.0938	0.8358
41.0000	0.0697	0.9055
42.0000	0.0045	0.9100
43.0000	0.0052	0.9152
44.0000	0.0353	0.9505
45.0000	0.0259	0.9764
46.0000	0.0169	0.9932
47.0000	0.0000	0.9932
48.0000	0.0000	0.9932
49.0000	0.0034	0.9966
50.0000	0.0023	0.9989
51.0000	0.0011	1.0000

15-2. Express the decision to buy a new piece of machinery in the decision framework presented in Figure 15-1, that is, provide specific definitions for each component of the decision framework.

15-3. Consulting firms are constantly bidding on contracts by preparing proposals. Define the alternatives and possible future states for a consulting firm with regard to the bidding to obtain a contract. Specify and discuss the principle of choice which you think is used by most consulting firms.

15-4. Build a Q-GERT network to estimate the distribution of the cost of performing three consecutive projects where the estimated costs for the first project are normally distributed with a mean of $10,000 and a standard deviation of $1000; the cost of the second project is exponentially distributed with a mean of $9,000; and the cost of the third project is triangularly distributed with a modal value of $16,000, a minimum of $12,000, and a maximum of $25,000.

15-5. Convert a decision situation with which you are familiar into a Q-GERT network model and run the model to obtain the values of the outcomes.

15-6. Explain in your own words the difference between the decision-making model presented in Figure 15-4 and the model representation shown in Figure 15-6.

15-7. An oil company needs to decide whether or not to drill at a given location before its option expires [212]. There are many uncertainties, such as cost of drilling and the value of the deposit. Records are available for other drillings in the area. More information can be obtained about the geophysical structure at the site by conducting a sounding. The following information is available. Drilling costs are estimated at $1,000,000 and might lead to payoffs (deposit values) which can be classified as

Big	$4,000,000
Moderate	2,000,000
Small	1,250,000

If a sounding is not taken, it is estimated that the probability of a big payoff is 20%, a moderate payoff is 50%, and a small payoff is 30%. A sounding costs $150,000 and the probabilities of the various sounding results are: big, 0.25; moderate, 0.50; and small, 0.25. From past experiences, the conditional probabilities of an actual result given a sounding result are as follows:

| | | Actual Result | | |
		Big	Moderate	Small
Sounding	Big	0.60	0.30	0.10
Result	Moderate	0.20	0.70	0.10
	Small	0.10	0.30	0.60

(a) Perform a standard decision tree analysis of the decision problem.
(b) Perform a Q-GERT analysis of the decision problem to obtain the distribution of payoffs.

15-8. The Soviet government is planning to transport waste from a nuclear plant from Vladivostok to Rostov [177,207]. The network shown here represents different routes between the two cities. There is an expense associated with each route due to the fact that precautionary action must be taken along each leg of the journey to avoid accidents or sabotage. This expense is not known with certainty and can only be estimated. The estimated expenses are shown in the accompanying table. Build a Q-GERT model to select the route that has the greatest probability of incurring the least cost.

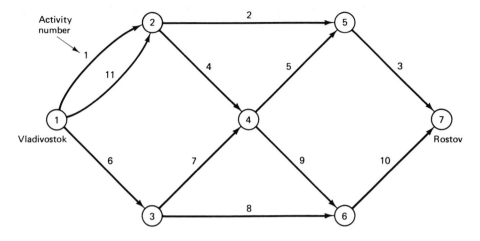

Branch	Distribution of Cost		
1	(10, 0.3)	(20, 0.3)	(30, 0.4)
2	(20, 0.6)	(40, 0.2)	(60, 0.2)
3	(30, 0.1)	(50, 0.9)	
4	(15, 0.5)	(20, 0.5)	
5	(40, 0.4)	(55, 0.6)	
6	(30, 0.9)	(40, 0.05)	(55, 0.05)
7	(10, 0.15)	(15, 0.75)	(20, 0.1)
8	(40, 0.5)	(60, 0.5)	
9	(30, 0.7)	(40, 0.3)	
10	(20, 0.75)	(40, 0.25)	
11	(15, 0.35)	(25, 0.65)	

16

Project Planning - Basic Concepts

16.1 INTRODUCTION

Larger and larger projects are being conceived, designed, and developed. As projects become larger, organizational and managerial problems increase. Individual efforts are no longer feasible and use must be made of integrated teams of workers, machines, and materials. This tendency toward larger projects results in the need for systems engineers and managers to plan, direct, and control the activities and resources allocated to the projects. A great deal of forethought is required to plan a large-scale endeavor. A major deterrent to good planning is the communication of ideas and concepts which are initially nebulous and possibly ill formed. Out of these concerns, graphical representations of projects for planning purposes have developed.

Many textbooks and monographs exist that describe the fundamentals of project planning and management [4,5,84,125,129,217]. Wiest [216] gives an excellent historical perspective of both the organizational and technical aspects involved in project planning. The Project Management Institute (PMI) is the professional society for individuals whose main field of interest is project planning. The project planning field has matured over the years and the use of project management techniques for the planning of construction projects, space vehicle developments, manufacturing systems, transportation conveyances, and the like is well documented.

The first techniques developed for project management were PERT (program evaluation and review technique) and CPM (critical path method). These network techniques provide a communication vehicle for describing large projects in a network form. However, the modeling versatility of these techniques is limited and their analysis procedures are inaccurate because of the many assumptions required when attempting to compute, analytically, measures of performance associated with project planning.

In this chapter, emphasis is placed on analyzing networks for project planning purposes and on demonstrating how Q-GERT eliminates the need for the modeling and analysis restrictions inherent in the PERT and CPM techniques.

16.1.1 Project Planning Terminology and Performance Measures

Although network models are discussed throughout this book, definitions of network terms in a project planning context are provided in this section to ensure that a project planning perspective is established. The fundamental concept in project planning is an activity. An activity is any portion of a project that requires time or resource elements such as labor, paperwork, and machines. Commonly used terms synonymous with activity are task and job. Typically, activities are graphically represented by branches. When activities are represented by branches, project planning models are referred to as activity-on-branch networks. When activities are represented by blocks or nodes, the models are referred to as activity-on-node networks or precedence diagrams. In activity-on-node networks, branches are used only to show the precedence between activities. (Q-GERT employs an activity-on-branch representation.)

In project planning, an event is an instantaneous point in time that marks the beginning or ending of an activity. In networks, nodes are used to represent events. Precedence between activities involves the specification that the ending event for one activity must occur before the starting event for another activity. A precedence relation is shown in network form by two activities in series separated by a node. The precedence activity is said to be incident to the node and the activity that requires the precedence activity is said to emanate from the node. Every activity emanating from a node has each activity incident to the node as a precedence activity.

The type of precedence described in the paragraph above is referred to as a direct or immediate precedence. Indirect precedence is modeled by having a sequence of activities, that is, a path segment. Thus, if activity 4 has activity 3 as a precedence activity and activity 3 has activity 2 as a precedence activity, activity 4 has activity 2 indirectly as a precedence activity. Such indirect precedence relations are inherent in a network model. Fundamentally, a network is a graphical representation of a project plan that shows the immediate and indirect precedence relations among all the activities defined for the project.

A list of all activities on a project is referred to as a work breakdown structure. The work breakdown structure organizes the activities in tabular form and defines the activities in terms of the time required to perform the activity, the cost of performing the activity, and any associated resources required to perform the activity. For advanced network modeling, a probability that the activity will need to be performed is included. Also, for advanced project planning models, the change in duration due to increased resources allocated to the activity are described. Following is a typical resource or cost versus activity duration curve, showing that shorter activity durations are obtained through increased resource or cost allocations.

Typical resources associated with an activity are workers, materials, machines, and money.

To illustrate project planning terminology, the following simplified network is presented.

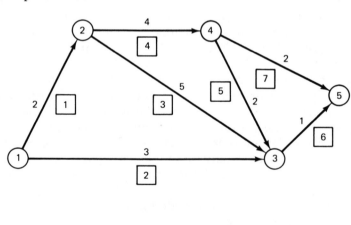

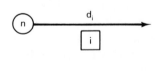

n	→	node number
i	→	activity number
d_i	→	duration of activity i

For this network there are five nodes and seven activities. Directly from the network it is seen that activity 1 must precede activities 3 and 4. Also, the precedence activities to activity 6 are activities 2, 3, and 5. Clearly, activities 1 and 4 must also precede activity 6 even though they are not incident to node 3. The event time associated with node 3 is the largest of the completion times of the activities incident to node 3. In this type of network, it is presumed that the number of release requirements for a node is equal to the number of incident activities.

Another way to display the project is to use a Gantt chart. In a Gantt chart each activity is displayed on a time line with the start time of an activity restricted to be after the completion of all precedence activities. The Gantt chart for the network above is as follows:

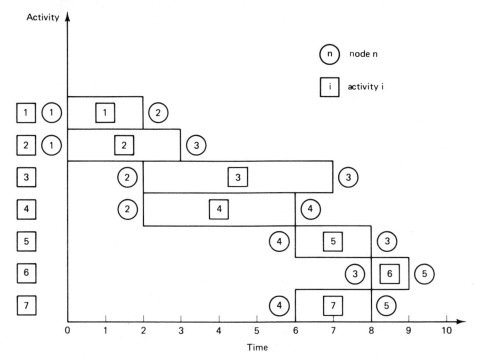

For convenience, the start and end node numbers have been placed on the Gantt chart in circles and the activity numbers have been shown in squares. The Gantt chart shows the time phasing of the activities but does not give a good display of precedence. From the Gantt chart, we see that the project duration is nine time units. Using this example, we will explain performance measures associated with project planning.

The project completion time is typically the most important measure of project success. The reason for this is that if the activity cost and resource usage are assumed as constant, the total project cost and resource use can be determined from information on the completion times of activities and the project. If cost and resource use are a function of when an activity is performed or how an activity is performed, additional performance measures associated with cost and resource usage need to be computed.

A measure of performance associated with an activity is the leeway available in starting the activity. From the Gantt chart, the start time of activity 7 can be delayed 1 time unit without increasing the project duration. This leeway is called slack or float in project planning. Different definitions of slack and the use of slack in project scheduling are discussed in Chapter 18.

A sequence of activities from the source node to the sink node is called a *path*. When activity durations are constants, there exists at least one path such that each activity on the path has no slack. Such a path is referred to as a *critical path*. The critical path method is a procedure for identifying a critical path and for computing slack times for activities not on the critical path. The PERT technique is used to perform a similar analysis.

In some project planning studies, significant events are defined which are referred to as *milestones*. A milestone is included on the network by a node and the time that the milestone occurs is also a measure of project performance.

16.2 GRAPHICAL REPRESENTATION OF PROJECTS

We introduce the graphical representation of projects with an example. Consider the network of a repair project shown in Figure 16-1. At the beginning of the project, three parallel activities can be performed that

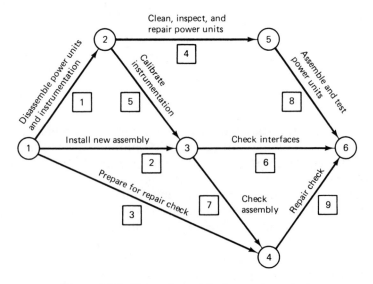

Figure 16-1 Network model of a repair project.

involve: the disassembly of power units and instrumentation $\boxed{1}$, the installation of a new assembly $\boxed{2}$, and the preparation for a repair check $\boxed{3}$. Cleaning, inspecting, and repairing the power units $\boxed{4}$ and calibrating the instrumentation $\boxed{5}$ can be done only after the power units and instrumentation have been disassembled. Thus, activities 4 and 5 must follow activity 1 in the network. Following the installation of the new assembly $\boxed{2}$ and after the instruments have been calibrated $\boxed{5}$, a check of interfaces $\boxed{6}$ and a check of the new assembly $\boxed{7}$ can be made. The repair check $\boxed{9}$ can be made after the assembly is checked $\boxed{7}$ and the preparation for the repair check $\boxed{3}$ have been completed. The assembly and test of power units $\boxed{8}$ can be performed following the cleaning and maintenance of the power units $\boxed{4}$. The project is considered completed when all nine activities are completed. Since activities 6, 8, and 9 have no successor activities, the completion of all three of these activities signifies the end of the project. This is indicated on the network by having activities 6, 8, and 9 incident to node 6, the sink node for the project.

One of the first steps in project planning is to construct a network as we have done for the example in Figure 16-1. Construction of the network requires the activities of the project to be defined and, typically, organized into work elements. This organization into work elements is called a work breakdown structure. The network is a graphical portrayal of the activities including precedence relations and provides a vehicle for communication during planning and analysis. The next step is to direct attention to the time durations of the activities. Data are collected† and each activity duration is quantitatively described. Frequently, a constant or a set of three values (most likely, optimistic, and pessimistic) is used for such a description. Guidelines for selecting an appropriate distribution function have been developed [137,154] and programs for fitting distributions to data sets are available (see Section 20.4).

We now translate the foregoing repair project description into Q-GERT terms. The resulting Q-GERT network is shown in Figure 16-2. Node 1, the source node, designates the initiation of the project. For this reason, the input specification of the node is $(0,\infty)$, which means that no incident activity completions are required for the first nodal release. Requirements for subsequent releases are irrelevant for all nodes of the network since each node is released only once in a given network realization.

Activities 1, 2, and 3 are scheduled at time 0 since they emanate from the source node. The time duration of each activity is assumed to be characterized by a triangular (TR) distribution.

---

†Early in the design process, the characterization of time durations may be subjectively determined by an analyst rather than by an analysis of data. This facilitates the modeling process and helps identify total data collection needs. However, characterizations established in this manner must be verified.

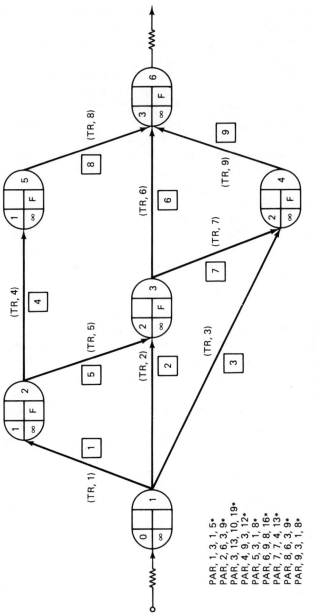

PAR, 1, 3, 1, 5*
PAR, 2, 6, 3, 9*
PAR, 3, 13, 10, 19*
PAR, 4, 9, 3, 12*
PAR, 5, 3, 1, 8*
PAR, 6, 9, 8, 16*
PAR, 7, 7, 4, 13*
PAR, 8, 6, 3, 9*
PAR, 9, 3, 1, 8*

Figure 16-2 Q-GERT network of repair project.

When activity 1 is completed, node 2 will be released since its input specification requires only one activity completion. Nodes 3 and 4, however, require two completions each. Therefore, activities 2 and 5 must be completed prior to the release of node 3 and, hence, prior to the initiation of activities 6 and 7. Node 4 will be released when both activities 3 and 7 are completed. Similarly, activity 8 will start when activity 4 is completed and node 6 will be released when the last of activities 6, 8, and 9 are completed. Node 6 is the sink node and its release corresponds to a network realization.

16.3 THE PROJECT COMPLETION-TIME DISTRIBUTION

One of the most important network measures in project planning is the project's duration time. Referring to our example network (Figure 16-2), the completion time of the project corresponds to the time that sink node 6 is released. Since each network activity is a random variable, the time each node is released is also a random variable. To compute statistics on node release times, the Q-GERT user specifies network nodes as statistics nodes with their time of first release (F) as the statistic of interest.

Figure 16-3 illustrates the Q-GERT output for 400 simulated observations of node 6. On the average, the project was completed in 20.8 days. The shortest completion time in 400 observations was 15.6, and the longest was 27.9. The standard deviation is 2.20 days. The standard deviation of the average time to complete the project is the standard deviation divided by the square root of the number of observations, that is, $2.20/\sqrt{400} = 0.11$ day. This indicates that with 95% confidence (two standard deviations from the average, assuming normality holds) the interval between 20.62 and 21.06 days includes the true mean project duration.

Referring to the histogram in Figure 16-3, we can make several interpretive statements about the project completion time as observed during the 400 network realizations. The far right column gives the upper bound of each cell in the histogram. Observed relative and cumulative frequencies for each cell are given in tabular form. Relative frequency is plotted with an asterisk. The letter "C" is used to plot cumulative frequency. Referring to the ninth cell of the histogram, we note that of the 400 network realizations, there are 26 project completion times greater than 18.5 but less than or equal to 19. The relative frequency of this observation is 0.065 or 6.5%. The cumulative frequency associated with 19 days is 0.212 or 21.2%. Based on this, we estimate the probability of the project being completed within 19 days as 0.212. The probability of the project taking more than 19 days is $1 - 0.212 = 0.788$. Other probability estimates can be made for any of the values listed in the histogram.

GERT SIMULATION PROJECT DEC-TREE-B   BY PRITSKER
DATE 3/ 8/ 1982

FINAL RESULTS FOR 400 SIMULATIONS

AVERAGE NODE STATISTICS

NODE	LABEL	PROBABILITY	AVE.	STD.DEV.	SD OF AVE	NO OF OBS.	MIN.	MAX.	STAT TYPE
6	PROJCOMP	1.000	20.8375	2.2017	.1101	400.	15.6401	27.9484	F

PROJCOMP

```
                                      UPPER
 OBSV    RELA    CUML     BOUND                0        20        40        60        80       100
 FREQ    FREQ    FREQ    OF CELL      I....I....I....I....I....I....I....I....I....I....I....I
   0      0       0      15.00        I                                                         I
   0      0       0      15.50        I                                                         I
   1    .002    .002     16.00        I                                                         I
   7    .017    .020     16.50        I*                                                        I
   4    .010    .030     17.00        IC                                                        I
   5    .012    .042     17.50        I*C                                                       I
  18    .045    .087     18.00        I**  C                                                    I
  24    .060    .147     18.50        I***   C                                                  I
1&2 26  .065    .212     19.00        I***       C                                              I
  26    .065    .277     19.50        I***        C                                             I
  36    .090    .367     20.00        I****         C                                           I
  39    .097    .465     20.50        I*****          C                                         I
  36    .090    .555     21.00        I*****           C                                        I
  27    .067    .622     21.50        I***               C                                      I
  34    .085    .707     22.00        I*****              C                                     I
  32    .080    .787     22.50        I*****                C                                   I
  19    .047    .835     23.00        I**                    C                                  I
  20    .050    .885     23.50        I**                      C                                I
 3 15   .037    .922     24.00        I****                      C                              I
  31    .077   1.000     +INF         I****                         C                           I
                                      I....I....I....I....I....I....I....I....I....I....I....I

 TOTAL
  400
```

Interpretive statements:

1. Probability of project completion by 19 time units = 0.212.
2. Probability of project taking more than 19 time units = 1 − 0.212 = 0.788.
3. Probability of project taking more than 24 time units = 1 − 0.922 = 0.078.

Figure 16-3 Statistics summary for node 6 and project completion-time distribution.

16.4 STATISTICS ON ACTIVITY START TIMES

As noted previously, the release of sink node 6 corresponds to the time of project completion. The release of any other network node corresponds to the start of the activities emanating from that node. The output for all the statistics nodes is shown in Figure 16-4. The statistics collected and the interpretive statements that can be made for each node are similar to those described above for sink node 6. These statistics provide valuable scheduling information on the probable start dates of the project's activities.

From the project network in Figure 16-2, the release of node 2 corresponds to the initiation of power unit cleaning [4] and instrumentation calibration [5]. The average start date is 3.0. The minimum start date is 1.2 and the latest is 4.9. Scheduling in the light of this uncertainty is difficult for a project manager. He or she must be prepared for change and have contingency plans ready. The degree of uncertainty in project planning is quantified by the start-time statistics presented in Figure 16-4. Further analysis of start times and finish times is presented in Chapter 18.

16.5 STATISTICS ON PROJECT INTERVALS

It is often of interest to estimate the time lapse between two project milestones. For example, in the repair project, suppose that we desired information on the elapsed time between the completion of the power unit disassembly [1] and the start of the repair check [9]. This time can be estimated through the use of interval statistics. We designate node 2 to be a mark node and node 4 to be a statistics node with I-statistics to be collected. This means that when activity 1 is completed (and node 2 is released), the time of this nodal release is "marked" or recorded internally. Every time STATISTICS node 4 is released, the time interval between the release of node 2 and the release of node 4 and the time node 2 was released is recorded for eventual statistics computation. Histograms will also be obtained if the cell width and upper limit of the first cell are specified for the STATISTICS node.

With regard to marking at a node, Q-GERT carries only one value as the mark time. Thus, only one reference node can be used at a time. For example, in the partial network shown in Figure 16-5, it is not possible to collect interval statistics from node 2 to node 4 and from node 3 to node 4. Even if a marking node is inserted prior to activity [7], it will not accomplish this goal, as a new mark time will erase any previously set mark time. To accomplish multiple interval statistics collection, user statistics routines should be used. First, the mark time is placed in the Jth attribute by setting ATRIB(J)=TNOW at the mark-

```
**FINAL RESULTS FOR 400 SIMULATIONS**

                    **AVERAGE NODE STATISTICS **

NODE  LABEL     PROBABILITY   AVE.     STD.DEV.  SD OF AVE   NO OF    MIN.      MAX.      STAT
                                                             OBS.                        TYPE

  6   PROJCOMP    1.0000     20.8375    2.2017     .1101     400.    15.6401   27.9484     F
  5   NODE-5      1.0000     11.0649    2.0095     .1005     400.     5.4002   15.6455     F
  4   NODE-4      1.0000     16.1214    2.0261     .1013     400.    11.2828   22.3419     F
  3   NODE-3      1.0000      7.4603    1.3917     .0696     400.     3.5281   12.0026     F
  2   NODE-2      1.0000      3.0277     .8164     .0408     400.     1.2196    4.9198     F
```

Figure 16-4 Final summary statistics for 400 simulation runs of repair project.

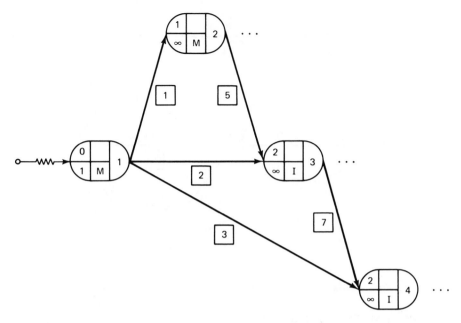

Figure 16-5 Illustration of marking and interval statistics collection.

ing node. The observed value is set to TNOW–ATRIB(J) at the statistics node and subroutine COL is called to record the observation.

It should also be noted that the choice criterion can affect the observation when collecting interval statistics in project networks. Referring again to Figure 16-5, the values collected at node 3 depend on the path taken to node 3. Table 16-1 gives the definition of the value collected at node 3 for each of the four possible specifications for the choice criterion at node 3. Clearly, care should be taken when modeling projects and collecting interval statistics.

TABLE 16-1 Definitions of Values Collected
at Node 3

Choice Criterion for Node 3	Value Collected at Node 3[a]
F (first)	t_5 if $t_1 + t_5 < t_2$
	t_2 if $t_1 + t_5 \geqslant t_2$
L (last)	t_5 if $t_1 + t_5 \geqslant t_2$
	t_2 if $t_1 + t_5 < t_2$
S/M (small value of mark time)	t_2
B/M (big value of mark time)	t_5

[a] t_i is the time to perform activity i.

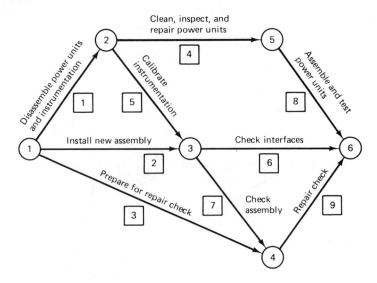

Figure 16-6 PERT network representation of repair project.

16.6 CRITICALITY INDICES

In a project network, activities on the critical path are denoted as *critical activities*. If any activity on the critical path is lengthened, the critical path is lengthened and the entire project is extended. Hence, from a project management standpoint the progress of critical activities should be monitored carefully to avoid delays in meeting project due dates. Alternatively, identification of these activities provides a means for evaluating which activities to expedite in order to expedite the total project.

The concept of a single critical path is an inadequate one for networks with random activity durations. The critical path and, hence, the set of critical activities may vary from network realization to network realization. Thus, the relative frequency, or probability, that an activity is on the critical path is important. This probability measure is called a *criticality index* [204].

In this section we use the repair project example to illustrate the computation of criticality indices using Q-GERT. For convenience the network in Figure 16-1 is presented again in Figure 16-6.

Consider that one run of the network has been made and that node 6 has been reached. The activity that caused node 6 to be released must be on the critical path as it caused the project to be completed. Thus, the *last* activity completed that is incident to node 6 (activity 6, 8, or 9) is on the critical path. If, when node 6 is released, the number of the activity causing this release is retained together with the start node for the activity, it will be possible to specify the critical activity as well as a prior node that is on the critical path. Suppose that activity

$\boxed{6}$ caused node 6 to be released. Then, on this run, activity $\boxed{6}$ would be critical and node 3 would be on the critical path.

Next, it would be necessary to trace back from node 3 to determine the activity that caused it to be released. Suppose that it was activity $\boxed{2}$. In this case, activity 2 would be critical on this run and its start node, node 1, would be on the critical path. Since node 1 is a source node, we need not trace back any further and the activities on the critical path for this run would be activities $\boxed{2}$ and $\boxed{6}$.

The procedure for tracing back through the network requires the storing of information as to which activity caused each node to be released. The start node of the activity is also stored as a potential node on the critical path. Thus, as the activities are performed and nodes are released, data are stored regarding potential critical activities and critical nodes. When the sink node is reached, the trace back through the network identifies the actual critical activities and critical nodes for the run of the network.

To accomplish the storing of potential critical nodes and critical activities, a user function will be prescribed for each nonsource node of the network. The user function number at a node will be the node number, that is, user function 2 will be called at node 2. The program insert for each user function will involve the recording of the last activity completed and the start node for that activity. The number of the last activity completed can be obtained by using the Q-GERT function NACTY, which returns the activity number of the last activity completed. The start node number of every activity will be assigned to attribute 1. The performance of the activity can be thought of as a transaction moving from the start node to the end node of the activity. At the source node, the source node number will be assigned to attribute 1. By using the choice criterion last at a node, the attributes of the transaction that released the node will be maintained. The user function at the node can then record the value of attribute 1. This value will be the start node number of the activity that was critical to the node. Also in the user function, the current node number will be placed in attribute 1 so that when branching occurs from the node, attribute 1 will contain the start node number for the activities emanating from the node.

16.7 EXAMPLE OF CRITICALITY INDEX ESTIMATION USING Q-GERT

The Q-GERT network model used to demonstrate how to obtain criticality indices is shown in Figure 16-7. The source node for the network is node 1. A value of 1 is assigned to attribute 1 using the specification (CO,1). Similarly at other nodes, the user function number and node number correspond. In the user function, attribute 1 is prescribed as the node where the assignment is being made.

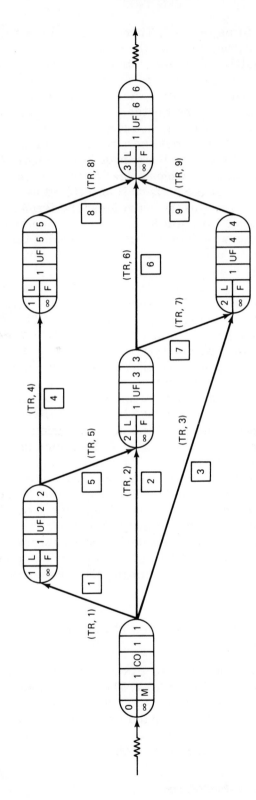

Figure 16-7 Q-GERT model for computing criticality indices.

```
      FUNCTION UF(NODEN)
      COMMON/UCOM1/NCACT(6),NCNOD(6)
C**** SET NCACT = ACTIVITY CRITICAL TO NODE NODEN
      NCACT(NODEN) = NACTY(1)
C**** SET NCNOD = START NODE OF CRITICAL ACTIVITY
      NCNOD(NODEN) = GATRB(1)
C**** SET ATTRIBUTE 1 BY SETTING UF EQUAL TO CURRENT NODE NUMBER
      UF = NODEN
      RETURN
      END
```

Figure 16-8 Function UF to maintain critical activities and nodes.

As was done previously for each node, the number of releases is set equal to the number of incoming branches. The choice criterion is specified as L so that the attributes of the last transaction arriving at the node are maintained. Statistics are kept on the first release time of the node on each run. When node 6 is released, one run of the project is completed.

The FORTRAN code for function UF is shown in Figure 16-8. User functions are prescribed for each node of the network, with the user function number equal to the node number, NODEN. The array NCACT(NODEN) is used to store the number of a critical activity to node NODEN. The array NCNOD(NODEN) is used to store the number of a critical node to node NODEN.

When a node is released, function UF is called and the activity number of the last activity completed is obtained from function NACTY. The statement NCACT(NODEN) = NACTY(1) stores this activity number as the critical activity to node NODEN. (The argument to NACTY of 1 was selected arbitrarily.) Since the attributes associated with the last arriving transaction are maintained, the statement (NCNOD(NODEN) = GATRB(1) causes function GATRB to obtain attribute 1 and store the value in NCNOD(NODEN) as the node that is critical to node NODEN. The last statement assigns the value of NODEN to UF. This statement causes attribute 1 of transactions that leave node NODEN to have an attribute 1 value equal to the node number. This completes the description of function UF.

When a run is completed, the Q-GERT processor calls subroutine UO. The FORTRAN listing of subroutine UO is shown in Figure 16-9.

```
      SUBROUTINE UO
      COMMON/QVAR/NDE,NFTBU(100),NREL(100),NRELP(100),NREL2(100),NRUN,
     1NRUNS,NTC(100),PARAM(100,4),TBEG,TNOW
      DIMENSION NUMC(9)
      COMMON/UCOM1/NCACT(6),NCNOD(6)
      DATA NUMC/9*0/
C**** LCA = LAST CRITICAL ACTIVITY
C**** LCN = LAST CRITICAL NODE
C**** NUMC(LCA) = COUNT OF TIMES ACTIVITY LCA IS CRITICAL
      LCN=6
  100 LCA=NCACT(LCN)
      NUMC(LCA)=NUMC(LCA)+1
      LCN=NCNOD(LCN)
C**** IF LCN=1, START NODE IS REACHED
      IF(LCN.NE.1) GO TO 100
      IF(NRUNS.GT.NRUN) RETURN
      XRUNS=NRUNS
      DO 200 I=1,9
      YCRIT=NUMC(I)
      YCRIT=YCRIT/XRUNS
      WRITE(6,300) I,YCRIT
  200 CONTINUE
  300 FORMAT(27X,35H THE CRITICALITY INDEX FOR ACTIVITY,I4,3HIS,F10.6)
      RETURN
      END
```

Figure 16-9 Subroutine UO, Example 10.

```
THE CRITICALITY INDEX FOR ACTIVITY   1  IS   .607500
THE CRITICALITY INDEX FOR ACTIVITY   2  IS   .197500
THE CRITICALITY INDEX FOR ACTIVITY   3  IS   .195000
THE CRITICALITY INDEX FOR ACTIVITY   4  IS   .120000
THE CRITICALITY INDEX FOR ACTIVITY   5  IS   .487500
THE CRITICALITY INDEX FOR ACTIVITY   6  IS   .275000
THE CRITICALITY INDEX FOR ACTIVITY   7  IS   .410000
THE CRITICALITY INDEX FOR ACTIVITY   8  IS   .120000
THE CRITICALITY INDEX FOR ACTIVITY   9  IS   .605000
```

Figure 16-10 Criticality indices for activities in the repair project.

First, the last critical node is established as the sink node for the network by the statement LCN = 6. At statement 100, the last critical activity, LCA, is the activity that is critical to the last critical node. The number of times this activity has been on a critical path is indexed by 1 by the statement NUMC(LCA) = NUMC(LCA) + 1. The start node of this last critical activity is established by the statement LCN = NCNOD(LCN). Note that the argument for the array NCNOD is LCN as critical nodes were stored with reference to subsequent nodes. Next, we test to see if the source node for the network has been reached. This will be the case if LCN is 1. If LCN is not 1, a transfer is made to statement 100 to continue the trace back process through the network. If LCN is 1, a test is made to see if all runs have been made by testing the number of runs to be made, NRUNS, against the current run number, NRUN. If all runs have not been made, a return is made to perform another run. If all runs have been made, the criticality index for each activity is computed as the number of runs on which the activity was deemed critical divided by the number of runs made. The activity number and its criticality index are then printed out.

The output of the criticality indices for each activity of the network is shown in Figure 16-10. The criticality index for activity 1 is 0.6075, which means that 60.75% of the time it was on the critical path. Based on this output, each activity can possibly be on the critical path. To decrease the project duration, the activities with the highest criticality indices should be examined for possible improvement. Improvement in these activities will not necessarily decrease project duration, as there is a (1 – criticality index) chance that the activity will not be on the critical path.

16.8 PROJECT COST ESTIMATION

Suppose that each activity in the repair project example had an associated cost consisting of a setup cost and variable cost that is related to the activity time. In this situation, it would be of interest to compute the total project cost. This total cost will be a random variable, as it depends on activity times which are modeled as random variables. We would like to obtain statistics and a histogram on project cost as well as project completion time. With cost statistics, we can formulate answers to the following management questions:

1. What is the expected project cost?
2. What is the cost range such that 95% of all possible project realizations are within this range?
3. What is the probability that the cost will exceed a specified number of dollars?

In Chapter 19, applications will be given that provide answers to these questions. In this chapter, we will only illustrate how to model cost considerations using the maintenance repair example. The network shown in Figure 16-11 is similar to the original network except that each activity time is described by the user function, UF. The activity number plus 10 is used as the function number for each call to UF. (This ID was selected to avoid conflict with user function numbers described in the previous section on criticality indices.) The user function is called at the beginning of each activity. It provides an opportunity to compute a setup cost for each activity and to add this value to a user-defined variable representing total cost. The time-dependent cost is determined by sampling from the activity's distribution function (triangular in this example) and multiplying the sample value by the variable cost prescribed for the activity.

The coding of UF to perform these computations is shown in Figure 16-12. Setup costs and variable costs are stored in the user-defined arrays SETC(IACT) and VARC(IACT), and total cost is maintained in the user variable TOTALC. These variables are initialized in subroutine UI, which is described below. As mentioned before, UF is called with an argument equal to the activity number plus 10. In the user function, IACT is established as the activity number. We assign an activity time to UF equal to a sample from the triangular distribution using the statement UF=TR(IACT). We also update the total project cost, TOTALC, which involves increasing TOTALC by the activity setup cost, SETC(IACT), and the time-dependent cost, VARC(IACT)*UF. This process is performed when each of the nine project activities is started.

When node 6 is released, the run terminates and subroutine UO is called. The code for subroutine UO is shown in Figure 16-13. In UO, a call is made to SUBROUTINE COL, which records the project cost, TOTALC as a single observation. Subroutine HIS is also called with TOTALC as an argument in order to produce a histogram of total project cost. With these two statements and some minor Q-GERT input specifications, the program will automatically provide the desired statistics and histogram for project cost.

Subroutine UI is called by the Q-GERT processor at the begin-

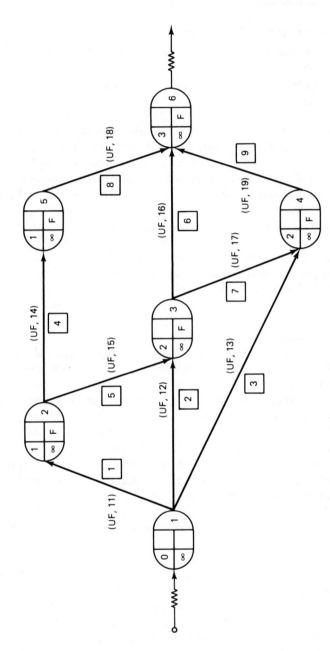

Figure 16-11 Q-GERT model for computing project costs.

```
        FUNCTION UF(I)
        COMMON/UCOM1/SETC(9),VARC(9),TOTALC
C****   COMPUTE TOTAL COST,TOTALC; UF IS ACTIVITY TIME (TRIANGULARLY
C****   DISTRIBUTED)
        IACT=I-10
        UF=TR(IACT)
        TOTALC=TOTALC+SETC(IACT)+VARC(IACT)*UF
        RETURN
        END
```

Figure 16-12 User function to collect activity costs in a project network.

```
        SUBROUTINE UO
        COMMON/UCOM1/SETC(9),VARC(9),TOTALC
        CALL COL(TOTALC,1)
        CALL HIS(TOTALC,1)
        RETURN
        END
```

Figure 16-13 User output to collect values of total costs in a project network.

```
        SUBROUTINE UI
        COMMON/QVAR/NDE,NFTBU(100),NREL(100),NRELP(100),NREL2(100),NRUN,
       1NRUNS,NTC(100),PARAM(100,4),TBEG,TNOW
        COMMON/UCOM1/SETC(9),VARC(9),TOTALC
C****   INITIALIZE TOTAL COST
        TOTALC=0.0
        IF(NRUN.GT.1)RETURN
C****   READ & PRINT SETUP & VARIABLE COSTS
        WRITE(6,101)
        DO 10 IACT=1,9
        READ(5,100)SETC(IACT),VARC(IACT)
        WRITE(6,102)SETC(IACT),VARC(IACT)
C****   CHANGE PARAMETERS FOR TRIANGULAR SAMPLING
        CALL CPTR(IACT)
    10  CONTINUE
        RETURN
   100  FORMAT(2F5.0)
   101  FORMAT(5X,'SETUP',5X,'VARIABLE'/6X,'COST',7X,'COST')
   102  FORMAT(F8.0,F12.0)
        END
```

Figure 16-14 Subroutine UI for cost model.

ning of each run. The coding for UI is shown in Figure 16-14. In UI, TOTALC is initialized to zero. If the current number of the network run (NRUN) is equal to one, we also read in and print out the activity cost values. This user input follows the normal Q-GERT input that describes the Q-GERT network elements.

One other statement requires discussion. Following the writing of the cost data, there is a call to subroutine CPTR(IACT), which changes the parameters for the triangular distribution for activity IACT. The parameters are read from PAR input cards as the mode, minimum, and maximum. Subroutine CPTR changes the values to facilitate obtaining samples from the triangular distribution (see Section 3.8). This change need only be done once.

16.9 SUMMARY

The terminology and performance measures used in project planning are presented in this chapter. The procedures for the modeling of a project in a network form are illustrated. Methods for estimating the project completion-time distribution, activity criticality indices, and project costs are described.

16.10 EXERCISES

16-1. For the repair project network shown in Figure 16-2, develop Gantt charts assuming that each activity time is the earliest time, the modal time, and the latest time. From these Gantt charts, specify the range of possible start times for each activity in the network.

16-2. Specify the effects on project completion time that you would anticipate if an exponential distribution were used in place of the triangular distribution for the example in Section 16.3. The mean of the exponential distribution should be set equal to the mean of the triangular distribution, that is, the average of the three parameters of the triangular distribution.

16-3. Employ Q-GERT to estimate the project completion time distribution and the criticality index for the following networks. Where feasible, use analytic techniques to develop the requested values. Compare the results with the PERT estimate for the project completion-time distribution.

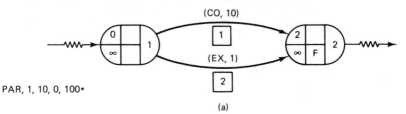

PAR, 1, 10, 0, 100∗

(a)

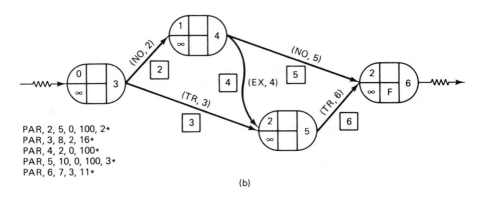

PAR, 2, 5, 0, 100, 2∗
PAR, 3, 8, 2, 16∗
PAR, 4, 2, 0, 100∗
PAR, 5, 10, 0, 100, 3∗
PAR, 6, 7, 3, 11∗

(b)

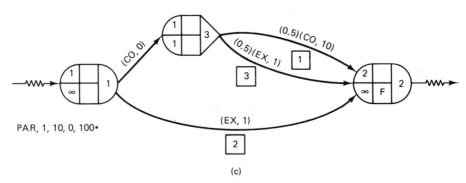

PAR, 1, 10, 0, 100∗

(c)

17

Project Planning – New Modeling Concepts

17.1 INTRODUCTION

Project managers are often faced with considerable project uncertainty and risks. These uncertainties can be due to external factors such as regulatory or government agency actions, financing difficulties, and weather. Internal factors that make project planning a nondeterministic activity are site location problems, design alternatives, unusual construction constraints, and construction change orders. In addition, there are technological considerations whose outcomes are not known with certainty, such as changing technology, contractor and subcontractor performance variability, and test, checkout, and rejects. Network modeling constructs have been developed to allow the modeling of uncertainty due to the factors noted above. In particular, Q-GERT provides the concepts of probabilistic and conditional branching, random activity times, network modification, and different nodal release requirements for this purpose. This represents a significant modeling improvement beyond the capabilities of PERT- and CPM-type networks. Detailed descriptions of new modeling and analysis concepts needed for project planning in the face of uncertainty are given by Wortman and Sigal [224] and Yancey and Musselman [226].

17.2 PERT SHORTCOMINGS AND Q-GERT CAPABILITIES

In Chapter 16, only a small subset of Q-GERT capabilities was used to develop a project network model. This was possible because PERT-type networks are constrained by the following list of modeling assumptions:

1. The number of activity completions required to release a node is equal to the number of branches ending at the node.
2. All branching is done on a deterministic basis.
3. No cycles (feedbacks) are allowed in the network.
4. Projects are always completed successfully as the concept of failure is nonexistent. Thus, a PERT/CPM analysis deals entirely with the time (or other additive variable) at which nodes of the network are realized.
5. No explicit storage or queueing concepts are present.

The following sections demonstrate the modeling flexibility available in Q-GERT to eliminate these modeling assumptions and the Q-GERT constructs that can be employed for planning purposes when uncertainty exists. A brief description of applied projects that have involved one or more of these constructs is provided in Section 17.7.

17.3 ACTIVITY FAILURE AND ITS RAMIFICATIONS

Often in project planning, one must account for the possibility that an activity ends unsuccessfully. Sometimes this outcome requires repetition of the failed activity; at other times it leads to project failure. Each of these cases and the repeated performance of an activity are important in planning projects.

17.3.1 Modeling Activity Failure

Suppose that in the repair project example presented in Chapter 16, the activity assemble and test power units, activity 8, had only an 80% chance of successful completion. Thus, 20% of the time, it is necessary to repeat the activity. The Q-GERT network shown in Figure 17-1 models this possibility. Node 7 has been inserted into the network and activity 8 terminates at node 7. Node 7 has probabilistic branching. Upon completion of activity 8, node 7 is released and only one activity will be scheduled from node 7. Twenty percent of the time activity 10 will be taken, which requires a one-unit delay before releasing node 5, which in turn restarts activity 8. Thus, activity 10 represents a decision to repeat activity 8. Note that activity 10 can cause subsequent releases of node 5; hence, the input specification for node 5 is (1,1). In this way, activity 8 will be repeated until activity 11 is taken, which is one of the inputs required for the release of node 6. Including activity failure and activity performance can increase the project completion time significantly.

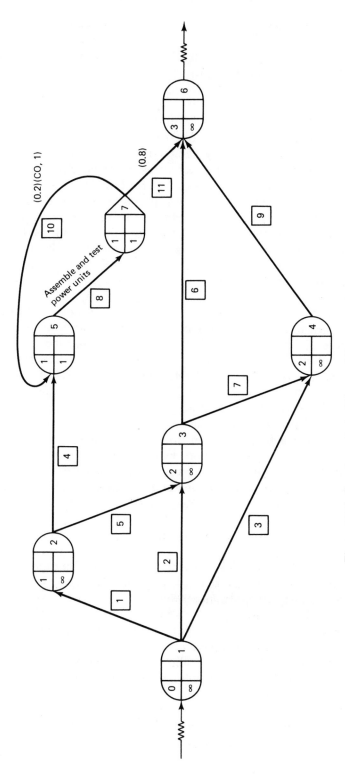

Figure 17-1 Repair project with possible repeated activity failure.

17.3.2 Project Failure

Another aspect of activity failure is that it may represent an inability to complete the project. In Figure 17-2, we present a Q-GERT model that models project failure which occurs when node 8 is released. Node 8 is released when activity 10 is selected; that is, the branching at node 7 probabilistically selects activity 10 and not activity 11. This selection of activity 10 would occur in 1 out of 5 runs on the average corresponding to the 0.20 probability assigned to activity 10. Project failure could also happen following other activities in the network.

In Figure 17-3, nodes have been inserted into the network following activities 4 and 6, which determine if the project fails based on the completion of these activities. The addition of node 9 and activities 12 and 13 are similar to the addition of node 7 and activities 10 and 11 described above. This addition shows how to model multiple locations where failure can occur probabilistically. The addition of node 10 with conditional, take-first branching models the decision process associated with project failure if activity 6 is not completed by time 100. Thus, at node 10, activity 14 is taken if activity 6 is not completed by time 100. Activity 14 causes node 8 to be released, which results in project failure.

The example presented in Figure 17-3 also illustrates the concept of multiple activities incident to a node (node 8) for which any activity completion causes the node to be released. This models the logical OR input specification for a node. If a 2 was specified for the first release requirement for node 8, we would be modeling a decision process in which two out of three of the failure conditions are required in order to declare the project a failure. When doing this, it is necessary to ensure that the project could be completed. For this example, this can be done by changing the first release requirement for node 6 from 3 to 2. Thus, if any two of the three branches leading to node 6 are completed, we have a project success; otherwise, the project fails.

17.3.3 Repeated Performance of an Activity

In Section 17.3.1 we described how to model the repetition of an activity. This concept can be extended so that the activity that is to be repeated has a diminishing or increasing chance of being repeated. This is accomplished by modifying the probabilities associated with a repetition and maintaining this probability as an attribute on which branching is based. Another mechanism for accomplishing this is to use an incremental function and only allow the repeating of the activity if an attribute value is less than a prescribed number of repetitions. This attribute value would be set using the incremental (IN) functional specification. An illustration of this branching concept is shown in Figure 17-4. In this network segment, activity 16 can only be selected two times, that is, when attribute 1 is 1 and attribute 1 is 2. When node

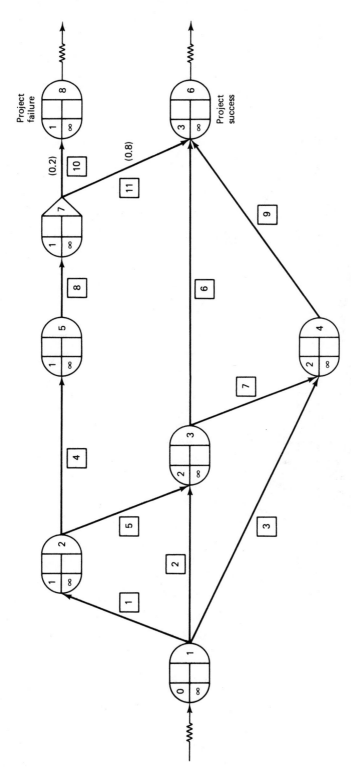

Figure 17-2 Repair project with possible project failure.

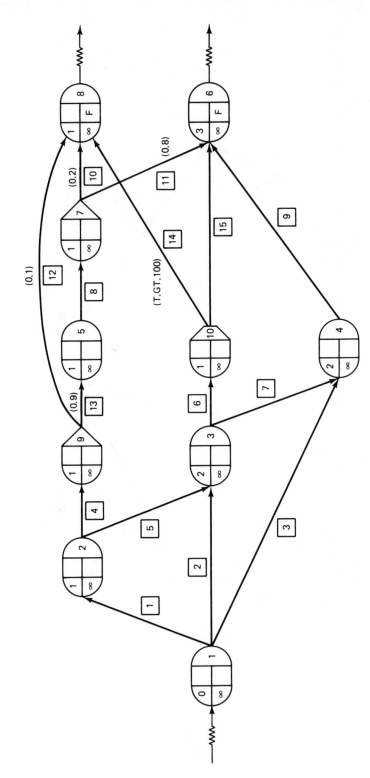

Figure 17-3 Q-GERT project network with multiple failure specifications.

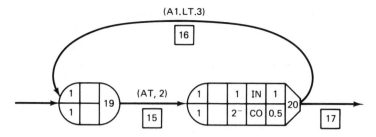

Figure 17-4 Limited activity repetitions with activity time modifications.

20 is released the third time, attribute 1 is set to 3 and the condition for activity 16 is not satisfied.

Also shown in Figure 17-4 is the changing of an activity time based on the number of repeats. At node 20, attribute 2 is decreased by 0.5 time unit each time a transaction passes through it. Attribute 2 defines the time for activity 15. Assuming that attribute 2 was set prior to the release of node 19, we see that the time to perform activity 15 is equal to attribute 2 for the first time; the original value of attribute 2 minus 0.5 for the second time; and the original attribute 2 minus 1 for the third time. More complex changes in activity times can be accomplished through the use of user functions which allow the modeling of learning effects, stress factors, and the like.

The concept of modifying activity times based on the number of activity repetitions can be generalized to model interdependent activity times for different activities. In the example above, a dependence has been inserted on the network with regard to the time to perform activity 15 based on previous performance times for activity 15. In an analogous way, other activities could be affected by the time to perform activity 15 through the incrementing or decrementing of the value of the attribute describing the time to perform activity 15 (in this case attribute 2) or through the assignment of a new attribute value, which is a function of attribute 2.

17.4 REPRESENTING DECISION LOGIC IN PROJECTS

Frequently, the occurrence of an event requires a decision as to which activity or set of activities to initiate from a group of candidate activities. In the planning process, normally we can only list the group of candidate activities and specify the criteria upon which the decision will be made. Since these criteria are normally related to time or the status of other network activities, we cannot predict with certainty the outcome of the scheduling decision. Q-GERT allows us to incorporate this decision logic in a network and account for its effect on our planning decisions through the use of conditional branching.

Consider an example where experiment I causes the project to fail if phase 1 fails twice. In Figure 17-5, we represent a decision process at node 18, the event identifying the occurrence of the second failure. The branching conditions are shown on the activities emanating from node 18. If time into the project is greater than 100 when node 18 is released, as specified by the notation (T.GT.100), the branch to node 17 is selected and the second failure leads to project failure. However, if time is less than or equal to 100 (T.LE.100), the branch to node 19 is selected and phase 1 is repeated for a third time. A third failure of phase 1 leads to project failure; a successful third attempt leads to the initiation of phase 2. Hence, we have represented a decision that is a function of time. We do not know how long it will take to reach node 18, but we do know that a successful performance of phase 1 must be initiated by time 100 if the project is to be considered successful. Conditional branching enables us to represent this decision logic and examine its effects on the planning process.

Decision logic at a node may be dependent on the status of other events. Consider Figure 17-6, where the decision on the second failure of phase 1 is modified to test the status of experiment II. If node 13 has been released, experiment II has been completed. In Figure 17-6, we specify that the branch to node 17 is to be selected if node 13 has been released (N13.R) by the time node 18 is released. The branch to node 19 is selected if node 13 has not been released (N13.NR). Hence, a third attempt of phase 1 is performed only if experiment II has not yet been completed when the second attempt failed.

Decision logic based on the status of other network activities is very important when planning for the potential impact of supporting technology that is being developed. For example, assume that node 50 in Figure 17-7 represents the successful development of a scientific procedure that would ensure the success of phase 1. Consequently, the branch from node 18 to node 17 will be selected if node 50 has not been released (N50.NR) by the time node 18 is released. If, however, node 50 has been released, the branch from node 18 to node 16 is taken. This activity corresponds to the application of the new technology. Since conditional branching can also be attribute-based, a modeler can incorporate additional complexity in the decision process by coding program inserts that describe decision-specific rules.

The use of conditional branching when coupled with attribute assignments using user functions provides extensive decision logic for modeling project failure and success conditions. Recall also that probabilistic branching can be based on attribute values, and hence, complex branching probabilities can be assigned and used to define the success or failure of an activity.

With the introduction of conditional and probabilistic branching in projects planning networks, there is a chance that some nodes in the network will not be released during a given run. For decision-making

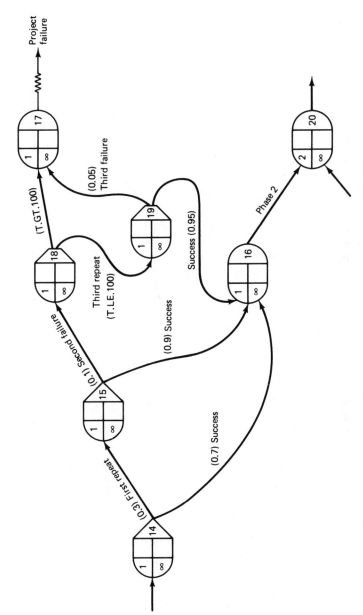

Figure 17-5 Network illustrating time-dependent decision logic at an event.

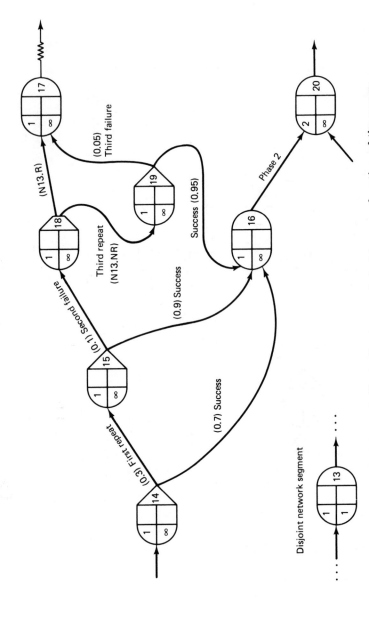

Figure 17-6 Network illustrating an event decision as a function of the occurrence of other events.

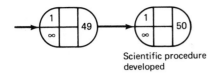

Scientific procedure
developed

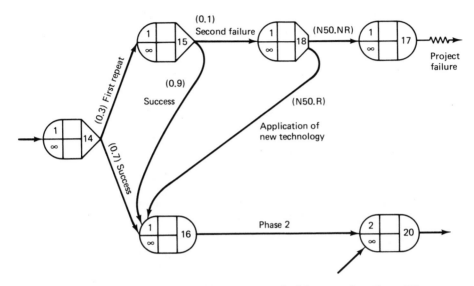

Figure 17-7 Network illustrating an event decision as a function of the completion of a separate network segment.

purposes, it may be important to have information concerning the probability that a node (milestone) will be reached. In the Q-GERT processor, the project is simulated many times (runs) and the proportion of runs in which a node is released is used to estimate the probability of releasing the node. It is computed as the fraction of the runs in which the node is released at least once, divided by the total number of runs. Note that a node could be released more than once in a run, but that the probability of nodal release is not affected by such multiple occurrences on a single run. The estimate of the probability of nodal release is printed on the Q-GERT Summary Report with other nodal statistics.

17.5 PROJECT MODIFICATION

Another important feature of Q-GERT is the ability to modify the network based on activity completions. Figure 17-8 illustrates this concept in a generic manner. At the beginning of phase II of a project, suppose it is decided that an increased rate of effort for phase III of a project is desirable. At node 30, the requisition process for obtaining added funds is shown in aggregate form as the subnetwork between

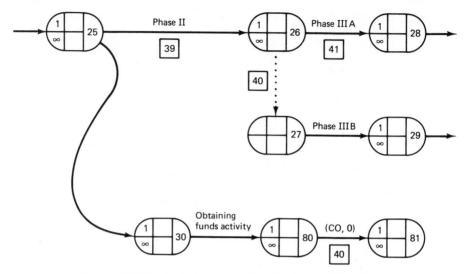

Figure 17-8 Project planning with adaptive modifications.

nodes 30 and 80. If added funds can be obtained prior to the completion of phase II, then phase III option A is performed under normal authorization for the added funds is not received prior to the termination of phase II, then phase III option A is performed under normal funding levels. The network model for this situation depicts the modification of node 26 to node 27 when activity 40 is completed. Thus, if activity 40 is completed before activity 39, node 27 will be in the network when phase II is completed. Otherwise, node 26 will be in the network and activity 41 will be started following the completion of activity 39.

The feature described in this section illustrates how Q-GERT can be used to include memory within a network model. This allows past performance to affect future performance and eliminates the need for Markovian assumptions that are associated with many network modeling techniques.

17.6 IMPLICATIONS OF PROJECT PLANNING IN THE FACE OF RISK AND UNCERTAINTY

Project planning when confronted with an uncertain future is a difficult process. It requires a management approach that establishes alternative plans that can be implemented based on the actual historical development of the project. By knowing in advance that specific uncertainties may occur and their possible impact on overall project performance, a project manager should be able to redirect a project when early warning signals indicate that a specified uncertain future is likely to occur. When uncertainty is considered, better choices of how to redirect a project activity to maintain low risk levels and required margins of safety can be included in project plans. This type of project planning requires a great deal of organization on the part of the project manager. The following steps are suggested when planning projects to take uncertainty into account:

1. Define the organizational responsibilities of technical and administrative managers.
2. Conduct training and indoctrination programs to acquaint all levels of project management with the potential alternative plans and the uncertainty associated with the plans.
3. Establish an implementation task team with the responsibility for network planning and status control that reports directly to the project manager.
4. Provide for periodic discussions and critiques of project plans and historical project activity.
5. Develop a definition of the project and alternative plans in terms of a work breakdown structure and work packages and require an agreement on the definitions used in the work breakdown structure.
6. Assign responsibility for reporting the performance for each work package of the work breakdown structure.
7. Assure that work packages and associated network plans clearly define work to be done before time estimating begins.
8. Assign primary responsibility for time estimation.
9. Require review of time estimates for any work packages involving any significant degree of uncertainty, and for those activities that have a high probability of being critical, verify the time estimates to a greater degree.
10. Establish updating procedures and due dates for control purposes.
11. Establish decision-making procedures for reallocation of resources and for decision making relative to alternative plans.

17.7 APPLICATIONS OF PROJECT PLANNING UNDER UNCERTAINTY

Brief descriptions of project planning under uncertainty using Q-GERT procedures are presented in this section. The general managerial concerns described in Section 17.6 are not included in the presentations, but it should be assumed that such concerns were taken into account. Emphasis is placed on the cause and need for considering the new modeling concepts described throughout this chapter.

17.7.1 The Assault Breaker Program

This project planning application description is extracted from a paper by Papageorgiou [141] in which the details of the network and simulation results are presented. The Assault Breaker Program [89] is a joint project between the Air Force and the Army and aims at the fulfillment of the goal of developing systems that could detect, locate, and strike enemy armor at ranges well beyond the forward edge of the battle area. Its concept includes a surveillance-strike system consisting of an airborne radar to sense second echelon armor and then guiding aircraft and/or air-to-surface missiles against that armor.

The objective of the Assault Breaker Program is to plan Air Force participation in a series of field technology demonstrations and to accomplish the development planning necessary to support a recommendation for full-scale engineering development.

Complexity and uncertainty are included in the Assault Breaker Program in that it is an accelerated program and the different segments have not followed the normal route of planning and development. For example, the radar and the control and communications segments will meet their first official milestone as a result of the current recommendation. Another complexity is the interagency character of the program that requires integration, coordination, and monitoring of the different aspects of the program and all the activities of the participating agencies. This complexity is indicated in the following paragraph [141].

> The Air Force has developed an airborne moving target indicator and synthetic aperture radar (Pave Mover) capable of locating armor and guiding munitions against the target. This is a segment of the Ground Target Attack Control System which aims at an integrated force management capability to manage and direct friendly forces against second echelon enemy forces. The other segments include the ground target attack control element that aims at real time operational control, weapon and target pairing, and aircraft and weapon guidance, the integration and interface segment that aims at incorporating this control center with existing and planned control and communications elements; and the aircraft/weapons interface segment that aims at developing the hardware that interfaces between the radar platform/aircraft and the weapons and direct attack aircraft. The Air Force has also developed air-to-surface munitions while the Army has developed a surface-to-surface missile which is interoperable with the Pave Mover radar.

A GERT network for the assault breaker program was developed. One of the major benefits derived from the application of GERT is the fact that the people involved were forced to organize their perceptions of the structure of the project and the interfacing of the activities in a systematic way. Although at the beginning the detailed structure of the project was nebulous in the minds of the people involved, they were forced through the networking process to think about it, clarify their perceptions, cross-verify them, and arrive at some kind of a consensus. As a result, the original draft of the network went through a number of revisions with each revision more closely approaching reality. The final draft of the network is presented by Papageorgiou [141].

A common feature of the network is that network modification was used to model the effect of tests on subsequent modifications of a component, and that the chance of further modifications of the component will be different than that before the first modification. Modeling concepts similar to those described in Section 17.5 were used for this project. Another part of the network required additional modifications based on the outcome from a field demonstration. The final network consisted of approximately 500 activities. Data were collected and the network was analyzed using a GERT simulation. The following is an extract from the conclusions section of the paper describing this planning project [141].

> GERT was applied as a demonstration in the planning of the Assault Breaker project, a cooperative effort between the Air Force and the Army, directed by the Air Force. The network model was developed and, on the basis of rough estimates of the relevant parameters, it was simulated using a prewritten software package. The benefits derived from this analysis were significant. The network development process itself helped the people involved with the project gain a better understanding of its structure and the interfacing of its component parts. The derived network can now serve as a basis for further refinements; briefings on the project of new staff or any people that have an involvement with the project; and further simulation for planning and control.
>
> The simulation showed the value of the derived output that can prove extremely helpful to the program director in planning the future course of the program, estimating the possibility of meeting deadlines, and systematically documenting proposed plans. Given the difficulties involved in estimating the values of the input parameters, sensitivity analysis can be carried out to test the sensitivity of the results to the accuracy of the data. Also, given the uncertainty that surrounds such programs, experimentation can be carried out by modifying the network and observing the effect of the modifications upon the plans.
>
> In view of the above benefits and usefulness of the GERT approach, it was recommended that it be adopted as a regular approach throughout the Air Force, the Army and the Navy, in planning major systems. It could also prove equally useful in the planning of R & D projects.

17.7.2 Project Networks Incorporating Improvement Curve Concepts

A GERT-based network approach for interactive project network analysis was developed by Wolfe et al. [221]. The concepts included in this GERT-based system included activity durations, which reflected improvement curve trends; storage limitation; alternative activities when bottlenecks occurred; probabilistic branching; and costs due to material shortages, personnel turnover, and other factors. The interactive capability provides a convenient means for inputting, formatting, and editing large data sets associated with planning the construction of large projects such as ships, aircraft, and turbines. Data base techniques were used for storing such information and to allow a multiple run capability in a manner analogous to that provided by SDL, as described in Chapter 5.

Wolfe et al. present an example of project planning of a ship fabrication and assembly project. They include an analysis of project completion time, resource utilization, and total costs. They conclude that such a GERT-based interactive computer system fulfills a growing need to incorporate uncertainty and advanced modeling concepts into project planning analysis.

17.7.3 Planning and Scheduling Overhauls of Ships

Overhauls of U.S. Navy ships are performed on the average every five years. With current force levels, this means that over 80 overhauls are going on each year. A regularly scheduled overhaul for a Navy ship can cost several hundred thousand dollars for a small tug or hundreds of millions of dollars for a large aircraft carrier. A regular overhaul consists primarily of the following eight types of activities: ripout; repair; shop tests; space preparation; installation of repaired equipment; in-place testing; systems testing; and sea trial testing. Each of these types of activities has nondeterministic times, may require that the activities be repeated, may require different resources and space, and, in general, require the type of modeling for uncertain conditions described in this chapter.

Johnston developed a Q-GERT model for analyzing regular overhauls of U.S. Navy ships [91]. Included in the Q-GERT model were resources and cost information. A detailed analysis of overhaul costs and time was performed, including a determination of criticality indices for the activities included in the overhaul. The Q-GERT model was developed to answer the following questions [91]:

How long does the overhaul take from start to completion? What is the extent of the variability, and what type of distribution does it generally follow?

How long does it take to achieve certain key overhaul events, such as the end of the dry dock period?

When should key events that require external observers/inspectors be scheduled?

How does failure of a critical inspection affect overhaul completion?

What key repair items are the most critical to timely overhaul completion and are worthy of increased attention?

What is the projected overhaul cost given the variability of the work package?

How are the shipyard resources (for example, dry docks and personnel) utilized in the course of the overhaul?

Johnston showed that it was necessary to include uncertainty in the planning and analysis of the regular overhaul process. He demonstrated how the outputs from the Q-GERT processor could be used to answer the foregoing questions and to improve decision making related to the scheduling and performance of regular overhauls.

17.8 SUMMARY

In this chapter project planning in the face of uncertainty is presented. The Q-GERT modeling concepts that support planning under uncertainty are described and network modeling procedures for such a purpose are presented. Application areas that employed such techniques are summarized. The need for including uncertainty in project planning is established.

17.9 EXERCISES

17-1. Give a possible rationale as to why the shortcomings listed for PERT/CPM in Section 17.2 were not of importance to its developers.

17-2. Reduce the network shown in Figure 17-1 to one that can be analyzed using PERT techniques. Describe how an analysis would be performed.

17-3. Analyze the network shown in Figure 17-2 by assessing the time to go from node 1 to node 8 and the time to go from node 1 to node 6. Make any assumptions you desire concerning the analysis procedure to be used in assessing the project completion times.

17-4. To illustrate the relationship between conditional branching and nodal modification, perform the following:
    (a) Convert the network in Figure 17-3 to one in which node 10 is replaced by node 11 when time exceeds 100 units.
    (b) Convert the network in Figure 17-8 to one that does not use nodal modification.
    (c) Describe a situation in which conditional branching cannot replace a nodal modification operation.

17-5. Discuss the differences between risk assessment and projects involving decision logic.

17-6. Write a paragraph that elaborates on the steps that were suggested in Section 17.6 for planning projects to take uncertainty into account.

17-7. Write a function UF that would incorporate improvement curve concepts into a project that was described by a Q-GERT network.

17-8. Discuss how a Q-GERT model can be used to answer the questions posed in Section 17.7 by Johnston in planning and scheduling the overhaul of ships.

18

Project Planning – Scheduling and Resources

18.1 INTRODUCTION

This chapter extends the basic concepts associated with project planning through the introduction of activities whose times are random variables and whose performance requires resources. Activity durations are important when establishing schedules for the beginning of activities and for determining times associated with the achievement of nodes. In project planning, specialized terminology has evolved which facilitates the determination of these quantities. In Sections 18.2 and 18.3, scheduling terminology and scheduling computations for constant activity durations are presented. This is followed by sections that describe the scheduling procedures when activity durations are random variables. Included in these sections are criteria for judging the criticality of an activity with respect to meeting its scheduled start and end times. The last sections of the chapter are devoted to project planning when resources are limited.

18.2 SCHEDULING TERMINOLOGY

In scheduling the activities of a project, it has been found that certain quantities associated with nodes and activities provide helpful information. For example, the earliest time an activity can start provides information that restricts the time horizon associated with the starting of an activity. The early start time, abbreviated ES, for an activity is equal to

410

the realization time of the node that immediately precedes the activity. Another quantity of interest is the early finish, EF, time for an activity, which is the sum of ES and the activity duration. When all activity durations are constants, all early start times and early finish times can be computed from the precedence relations depicted on the network. The early start times of activities emanating from source nodes are assumed as zero. These activities' early finish time is then equal to their duration. The early start times for other activities are equal to the release time of the node from which they emanate. The release time is the largest of the early finish times of the activities incident to the node. When a project has a single sink node, the largest early finish time of an activity incident to the sink node of the network is then the anticipated project duration. This process for computing the project duration is called the *forward pass*.

Assuming that it is desirable to finish the project as early as possible, the project duration as computed above also represents the latest finish, LF, time for all activities leading into the sink node. Starting with the latest finish time, a late start, LS, time can be calculated by subtracting the activity duration from the late finish time. Consider now a start node of an activity that leads to the sink node. The smallest of the late start times of the activities emanating from this node defines the latest release time for the node that does not result in a delay for the project.

This latest time for a node release is then specified as the late finish time for all activities leading into the node. Given the late finish time, the late start time for each of these activities can be computed. This process is the *backward pass* through the network and continues until all source nodes are reached.

After making both the forward pass and backward pass, the amount of slack or float associated with an activity for scheduling purposes can be estimated. There are at least four methods for defining slack, with the two most commonly used slack values being free slack and total slack.†

Free slack (FS) is the amount of time that an activity started as early as possible can be delayed before it affects the start time of activities emanating from the end node of the activity. This type of slack is local in that a decrease in the amount of slack may not directly affect the total project duration. The computation for free slack is the earliest release time for the end node of the activity minus the activity's early finish time.

---

†Two other slack values are interference slack and safety slack. *Interference slack* assumes that all predecessor activities are delayed to their latest start times while succeeding activities are started as early as possible. This type of slack represents the most stringent constraint on the scheduling of activities. *Safety slack* is defined as the amount of time an activity start can be delayed without delaying the start of successor activities, assuming that all predecessors start as late as possible.

A slack value that does directly affect the total project duration is referred to as *total slack* (TS). Total slack for an activity is defined as the difference between the late finish time and the early finish time for the activity. If the activity takes additional time units above the total slack, the project will be delayed as the latest release time for the end node for the activity will be increased.

18.3 SCHEDULING COMPUTATIONS

The following nomenclature will be used in the formulas that describe the various scheduling computations and in the graphical diagrams.

t_j = mean duration for activity j
ES_j = earliest start time for activity j
EF_j = earliest finish time for activity j
LS_j = latest start time for activity j
LF_j = latest finish time for activity j
TE_n = earliest release time for node n
TL_n = latest release time for node n
TS_j = total slack for activity j
FS_j = free slack for activity j
$s(j)$ = start node number for activity j
$e(j)$ = end node number for activity j

The computations required for the forward pass are:

1. $TE_{source} = 0$
2. $ES_j = TE_{s(j)}$
3. $EF_j = ES_j + t_j$
4. $TE_{e(j)}$ = largest of the EF_j values for all activities whose end node is $e(j)$

The backward-pass computations are:

5. $TL_{sink} = TE_{sink}$
6. $LF_j = TL_{e(j)}$
7. $LS_j = LF_j - t_j$
8. $TL_{s(j)}$ = smallest of LS_j values for all activities whose start node is $s(j)$

The computations for total slack and free slack are:

9. $FS_j = TE_{e(j)} - EF_j$
10. $TS_j = LF_j - EF_j = LS_j - ES_j$

TABLE 18-1 Scheduling Computations Based on Expected Values

| Activity | | | | | | Total Activity | Activity Free |
Number, j	Expected Duration, t_j	Early Start, ES_j	Late Start, LS_j	Early Finish, EF_j	Late Finish, LF_j	Slack, TS_j	Slack, FS_j
1	3	0	0	3	3	0	0
2	6	0	1	6	7	1	1
3	14	0	1	14	15	1	1
4	8	3	5	11	13	2	0
5	4	3	3	7	7	0	0
6	11	7	8	18	19	1	1
7	8	7	7	15	15	0	0
8	6	11	13	17	19	2	2
9	4	15	15	19	19	0	0

The computations associated with the scheduling algorithm given above are shown on the diagram† of Figure 18-1. A table showing the values for each activity is given in Table 18-1. As long as each activity time is assumed to have a constant value, the algorithm for making these computations is straightforward.

18.4 Q-GERT APPROACH TO SCHEDULING COMPUTATIONS

When Q-GERT is used to simulate a PERT network, the forward-pass computations are made for every run of the network. The node release times are the $TE_{s(j)}$ values for each node which define the early start times for each activity whose start node is j, that is, $ES_j = TE_{s(j)}$. Since the expected value of the sum of two random variables is the sum of their expected values, the expected activity duration, t_j, can be added to the average ES_j to estimate the average early finish time, EF_j, for an activity. Of course, the sample activity duration values could be used, but by using the expected activity durations directly less variation exists in the early finish time estimates.

Q-GERT does not automatically store the information to make the backward pass required to compute the late start, late finish, and slack values. The user functions necessary to make these computations are presented in the next section. Before presenting the user functions, a direct approach is presented which, although involving hand computations, does illustrate the underlying procedures involved in performing the scheduling computations.

The backward computations involve the analysis of the network starting at the sink node and proceeding toward the source node. This can be accomplished with Q-GERT by redefining the network such that

†Moder and Phillips [125] refer to the type of network given in Figure 18-1 as a space diagram. As can be seen, it contains a large amount of information which may be confusing to a manager or a decision maker.

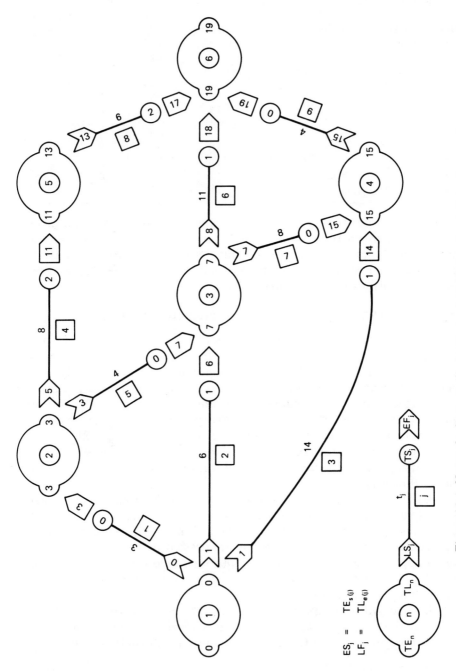

Figure 18-1 Network diagram illustrating scheduling computations for repairman problem.

the sink node is the source node and reversing the direction of each activity, that is, make the end node of the activity its start node and the start node of the activity its end node. A forward simulation of this "reverse" network provides the information required to make the backward-pass computations for the original network. The node realization times in this reverse network after subtraction from the project duration represent the TL_n values for the network nodes. The latest start and latest finish times can be obtained by subtracting the node realization times from the project duration as computed during the forward pass. In order to have the same time durations for each run of the network, a separate stream number is used to generate the durations for each activity. This avoids having to store the activity durations for the backward pass. Although this step is not necessary, as statistical variation in the activity durations is to be expected when employing Q-GERT, the use of the same random stream decreases the variability of the results.

The outputs from running the backward pass using Q-GERT are shown in Figure 18-2 for triangularly-distributed activity durations as specified in Figure 16-2. Combining these values with those presented in Figure 16-4, we can prepare Table 18-2, where unbiased estimates of the expected values for the quantities have been obtained.

In Table 18-2, the standard deviation of the activity times is obtained by making the computations required for the triangular distribution associated with each activity.† The early start time for each activity is obtained as the node release time estimated by the simulation of the original network (Figure 16-4). The early finish time is computed as the early start time plus the expected duration. The late finish time for an activity is obtained from the backward pass which was performed through a simulation of the reverse network (Figure 18-2). Late start times are computed by subtracting the expected activity duration from the late finish times. The computation of total activity slack and activity free slack are made using the equations given previously.

Comparing the values of start and finish times presented in Tables 18-1 and 18-2, it is seen that all values are larger when using the Q-GERT outputs. This is to be expected since the scheduling computations based on expected values can be proven to be optimistic. Thus, even for the small network associated with the repairman problem, improved scheduling for start and end dates can be made based on refined estimates of the start and finish times.

Additional information regarding start and finish times can be obtained. The Q-GERT output provides the standard deviation for the

†The variance for a triangularly distributed random variable with parameters a, m, and b is

$$\sigma^2 = \frac{a(a - m) + b(b - a) + m(m - b)}{18}$$

GERT SIMULATION PROJECT RETRO—NET-6B   BY PRITSKER
DATE 3/ 8/ 1982

FINAL RESULTS FOR 400 SIMULATIONS

AVERAGE NODE STATISTICS

NODE	LABEL	PROBABILITY	AVE.	STD.DEV.	SD OF AVE	NO OF OBS.	MIN.	MAX.	STAT TYPE
1	PROJCOMP	1.0000	20.8375	2.2017	.1101	400.	15.6401	27.9484	F
5	NODE-5	1.0000	5.9979	1.1923	.0596	400.	3.0613	8.6351	F
4	NODE-4	1.0000	3.9898	1.5003	.0750	400.	1.2446	7.8448	F
3	NODE-3	1.0000	12.8595	2.1112	.1056	400.	8.5695	19.0634	F
2	NODE-2	1.0000	17.2527	2.3492	.1175	400.	11.0764	26.0247	F

Figure 18-2 Simulation results for "reverse" repairman network.

TABLE 18-2 Scheduling Computations Based on Q-GERT Outputs

| Activity | | | | Averages | | | | | |
Number j	Expected Duration, t_j	Standard Deviation, σ_j	Early Start, ES_j	Late Start, LS_j	Early Finish, EF_j	Late Finish, LF_j	Total Slack, TS_j	Free Slack, FS_j
1	3	0.816	0	0.58	3	3.58	0.58	0.03
2	6	1.225	0	1.99	6	7.99	1.99	1.46
3	14	1.871	0	2.85	14	16.85	2.85	2.12
4	8	1.871	3.03	6.84	11.03	14.84	3.81	0
5	4	1.472	3.03	3.98	7.03	7.98	0.95	0.43
6	11	1.764	7.46	9.84	18.46	20.84	2.38	2.38
7	8	1.871	7.46	8.85	15.46	16.85	1.39	0.66
8	6	1.225	11.06	13.84	17.06	20.84	3.78	3.78
9	4	1.472	16.12	16.84	20.12	20.84	0.72	0.72

TABLE 18-3 Variance and Standard Deviation Estimates for Start and Finish Times

Number j	Activity Variation		Early Start, ES_j		Late Start, LS_j		Early Finish, EF_j		Late Finish, LF_j	
	σ_j^2	σ_j	s_j^2	s_j	s_j^2	s_j	s_j^2	s_j	s_j^2	s_j
1	0.667	0.816	0	0	6.185	2.487	0.667	0.816	5.518	2.349
2	1.500	1.225	0	0	5.956	2.410	1.500	1.225	4.456	2.111
3	3.500	1.871	0	0	5.750	2.400	3.500	1.871	2.250	1.500
4	3.500	1.871	0.667	0.816	4.921	2.218	4.167	2.041	1.421	1.192
5	2.167	1.472	0.667	0.816	6.623	2.574	2.834	1.683	4.456	2.111
6	3.111	1.764	1.937	1.392	7.960	2.821	4.048	2.012	4.849	2.202
7	3.500	1.871	1.937	1.392	5.750	2.400	4.437	2.106	2.250	1.500
8	1.500	1.225	4.038	2.010	8.349	2.889	7.538	2.746	4.849	2.202
9	2.167	1.472	4.105	2.026	7.016	2.649	6.272	2.504	4.849	2.202

early start times and late finish times directly from the forward and reverse network simulations. The variance of the early finish time for an activity is equal to the variance of the early start time plus the variance of the activity duration. Similarly, the variance of the late start time is the sum of the variance of the late finish time plus the variance of the activity duration. These variance estimates are shown in Table 18-3. In deciding when to schedule an activity to be started, both the estimates of the mean start time and the variance of that time should be used. The start time can then be based on the risk associated with being able to achieve a prescribed starting date.

In Table 18-2, estimates of the average total slack and average free slack values were also given. An interpretation and use of average slack is required. Because of the random variation, we can no longer delay a project in accordance with the amount of slack without a probable change in the project completion time or the start time of the following activities. Such a delay may or may not cause problems. The degree of confidence on activity and project completion times depends on the amount of variation in the slack estimates.

A ranking of the activities by high value of average slack time is a possible method for ordering the activities that could be started later. A more appropriate ranking is based on the ratio of the average slack time to the standard deviation of the activity duration. This ratio provides an indication of the number of standard deviations that the average slack time represents. Higher values of the ratio indicate that there is less likelihood that the average slack time will be exceeded due to the basic variability inherent in the performance of the activity. A low value of the ratio indicates that there is little leeway in the start time for the activity. The ratio and activity ranking based on the ratio are shown in Table 18-4. Also given in Table 18-4 are the criticality indices

TABLE 18-4 Activity Criticality Assessment

Activity		Total Slack, TS_j		Ratio Index, TS_j/σ_j		Criticality Index, CI_j	
j	σ_j	Value	Rank	Value	Rank	Value[a]	Rank
1	0.816	0.58	1	0.71	2	0.6075	1
2	1.225	1.99	5	1.63	7	0.1975	6
3	1.871	2.85	7	1.52	6	0.1950	7
4	1.871	3.81	9	2.04	8	0.1200	(8, 9)
5	1.472	0.95	3	0.65	3	0.4875	3
6	1.764	2.38	6	1.35	5	0.2750	5
7	1.871	1.39	4	0.74	4	0.4100	4
8	1.225	3.78	8	3.09	9	0.1200	(8, 9)
9	1.472	0.72	2	0.49	1	0.6050	2

[a]Source: From Fig. 16-10.

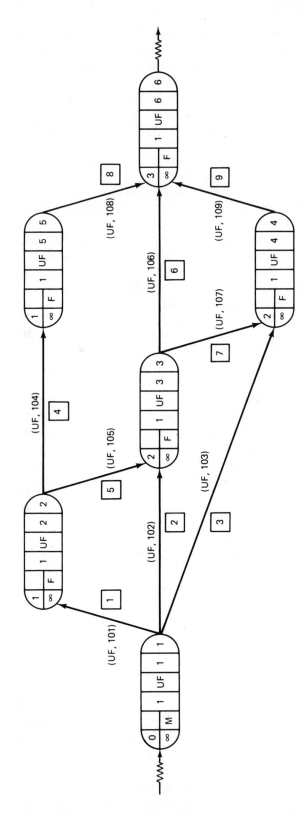

Figure 18-3 Q-GERT network for scheduling computations example.

computed in Section 16.6. It can be seen that there is a large positive correlation between the ranking of critical activities based on the ratio of average slack to activity duration standard deviation and the criticality index. It is conjectured that this will always occur.

18.5 USER FUNCTIONS FOR THE SCHEDULING COMPUTATIONS

The scheduling computations described in the preceding section can be performed automatically through the use of function UF and subroutines UI and UO. The basic requirement is the establishment of a data structure that provides information on (1) the activities incident to a node and (2) the start nodes for activities. This information can be read in or defined in subroutine UI. During the simulation, the activity times would need to be stored. In subroutine UO, the backward-pass computations can be made, and sample values obtained for a given run. By calling subroutine COL, statistical estimates for each of the variables estimated by the scheduling computations can be obtained. Alternatively, if only averages are desired, the sum of the values for each run can be maintained and a table similar to Table 18-2 could be printed when all runs are completed. In the following discussion, the latter approach is taken.

The Q-GERT network for calculating slack using user functions is shown in Figure 18-3. User function numbers greater than 100 are used for activities with the user function number set equal to 100 plus the activity number. User functions at a node have a user function number equal to the node number.

On each run of the network, the forward pass is made using standard procedures with the early realization time of the node, TE(N), computed as the node release time. This is shown in Figure 18-4, which gives a listing of function UF for this example. If the user function

```
        FUNCTION UF(N)
        COMMON /QVAR/ NDE,NFTBU(100),NREL(100),NRELP(100),NREL2(100),NRUN,
       1NRUNS,NTC(100),PARAM(100,4),TBEG,TNOW
        COMMON /SLACK/ NPPTR(6),NSPTR(6),NPS(50),DUR(9),NBRELP(6),
       1NBREL(6),NNBP(6),ES(9),EF(9),XLS(9),XLF(9),TE(6),TL(6),TS(9),FS(9)
        IF(N.GT.100) GO TO 100
C****
C**** FOR USER FUNCTION AT A NODE
C**** SET THE TE VALUE TO NODE RELEASE TIME
C****
        UF=0.
        TE(N)=TNOW
        RETURN
C****
C**** FOR USER FUNCTION ON BRANCH
C**** SET UF TO TRIANGULAR SAMPLE
C**** SAVE THIS DURATION
C**** DETERMINE EARLY START AND FINISH TIMES
C****
    100 N=N-100
        UF=TR(N)
        DUR(N)=UF
        ES(N)=TNOW
        EF(N)=TNOW+DUR(N)
        RETURN
        END
```

Figure 18-4 Function UF for performing scheduling computations in project planning.

number N is greater than 100, the user function refers to an activity. At statement 100 in function UF, the activity number is obtained by subtracting 100 from N. The duration of an activity is obtained as a sample from the triangular distribution. This sample is stored in the vector DUR(I). The early start time for activity I, ES(I), is then established as the current time. The early finish for activity I, EF(I), is the current time plus the duration. These computations are made in the same manner as those discussed in Section 18.4.

The backward pass is made in subroutine UO to compute the late start, late finish, and late release times for each node and the slack values for each activity. The procedure for making these calculations will be illustrated by example. Rather than present a general program that could be difficult to follow, a specialized program showing data values that are explicit for the repair network is given. The definitions of the variables employed in the user functions are shown in Table 18-5.

TABLE 18-5 Variable Definitions for Slack Computation

Variable Name	Definition	Initial Value
SES(I)	Sum of early start times, activity I	0.0
SEF(I)	Sum of early finish times, activity I	0.0
SLS(I)	Sum of late start times, activity I	0.0
SLF(I)	Sum of late finish times, activity I	0.0
STS(I)	Sum of total slack, activity I	0.0
SFS(I)	Sum of free slack, activity I	0.0
TL(N)	Latest release time, node N	10^{20}
TE(N)	Earliest release time, node N	
NNBP($\cdot$)	Order in which nodes are released in backward pass	(6, 0, 0,0,0,0)
NBREL(N)	Current release requirement for node N in backward paths	(3, 2, 2,1,1,0)
NBRELP(N)	Number of releases required in backward paths	(3, 2, 2,1,1,0)
NPS($\cdot$)	Activity predecessor nodes and successor nodes	See subroutine UI
NPPTR(N)	Pointer to location in NPS where incident activities and their start nodes are stored	See subroutine UI
NSPTR(N)	Pointer to location in NPS where activities emanating from node N and their end nodes are stored	See subroutine UI

```
      SUBROUTINE UI
      COMMON /QVAR/ NDE,NFTBU(100),NREL(100),NRELP(100),NREL2(100),NRUN,
     1NRUNS,NTC(100),PARAM(100,4),TBEG,TNOW
      COMMON /SLACK/ NPPTR(6),NSPTR(6),NPS(50),DUR(9),NBRELP(6),
     1NBREL(6),NNBP(6),ES(9),EF(9),XLS(9),XLF(9),TE(6),TL(6),TS(9),FS(9)
      COMMON /SUMS/ SES(9),SEF(9),SLS(9),SLF(9),STS(9),SFS(9)
      DATA HIVAL/1.E20/
      DATA NBRELP/3,2,2,1,1,0/
      DATA NNBP/0,0,0,0,0,0/
      DATA NPPTR/0,1,4,9,14,17/
      DATA NSPTR/25,32,37,42,45,0/
      DATA NPS/1,1,0,5,2,2,1,0,7,3,3,1,0,4,2,0,8,5,6,3,9,4,0,0,1,2,2,
     13,3,4,0,4,5,5,3,0,6,6,7,4,0,9,6,0,8,6,0,0,0,0/
C****
C**** THE ABOVE DATA STATEMENTS DESCRIBE THIS PARTICULAR
C**** NETWORK, ACCORDING TO THE FOLLOWING ARRAY DEFINITIONS
C****
C**** NBRELP - BACKWARD RELEASE REQUIREMENTS
C**** NBREL - REMAINING BACKWARD RELEASES
C**** NNBP - LIST OF NODES TO PROCESS IN BACKWARD PASS
C**** NPPTR - POINTERS TO LOCATION IN NPS WHERE PRECEDENT
C****         ACTIVITIES ARE STORED
C**** NSPTR - POINTERS TO LOCATION IN NPS WHERE SUCCEEDING
C****         ACTIVITIES ARE STORED
C**** NPS - ARRAY FOR NETWORK DESCRIPTION
C****
      IF(NRUN.GT.1) GO TO 10
C****
C**** INITIALIZE SUMS ON RUN 1
C**** MODIFY TRIANGULAR DISTRIBUTION PARAMETERS
C****
      DO 5 I=1,9
      SES(I)=0.
      SEF(I)=0.
      SLS(I)=0.
      SLF(I)=0.
      STS(I)=0.
      SFS(I)=0.
    5 CALL CPTR(I)
C****
C**** INITIALIZE TL VALUES TO LARGE NUMBER
C**** SET BACKWARD RELEASE REQUIREMENTS FOR THIS RUN
C****
   10 DO 15 N=1,6
      TL(N)=HIVAL
   15 NBREL(N)=NBRELP(N)
C****
C**** SET THE SINK NODE AS A NODE WHICH IS TO BE RELEASED
C**** ON BACKWARD PASS
C****
      NNBP(1)=6
      RETURN
      END
```

Figure 18-5 Subroutine UI for performing scheduling computations in project planning.

The values for the variables defined in Table 18-5 for the particular network under consideration are defined in subroutine UI, which is given in Figure 18-5. The vector NPS is established through a DATA statement and contains a summary of the network structure. In cells 1 through 23, information about an activity and its start node are stored. The data are grouped together by the node to which the activity is incident, that is, all activities incident to a given node are grouped together with a zero separating groups. In cells 25 through 47, data regarding an activity and its end node organized according to activities emanating from a given node are provided.

The vector NPPTR is used to indicate the cell in NPS where information on activities incident to a node are stored. For example, the values of NPPTR are as follows:

NPPTR(NODE)

Node	1	2	3	4	5	6
Pointer	0	1	4	9	14	17

The second value of NPPTR specifies that the incident activities to node 2 and their start nodes are maintained in the vector NPS beginning at cell 1. As another example, consider node 4. The activities incident to node 4 are stored in NPS starting at cell 9.

The first 23 cells of NPS are as follows:

NPS

Cell	1	2	3	4	5	6	7	8	9	10	11	12	13	14	15	16	17
Data	1	1	0	5	2	2	1	0	7	3	3	1	0	4	2	0	8

Cell	18	19	20	21	22	23
Data	5	6	3	9	4	0

Cells 1 and 2 of NPS specify that activity 1 is incident to node 2 [NPPTR(2)=1] and its start node is node 1. The 0 in cell 3 indicates that there are no further activities incident to node 2. In cell 9 of NPS we can see that activity 7 is incident to node 4 [NPPTR(4)=9] and that the start node of activity 7 is node 3. Since NPS(11) is 3, activity 3 is also incident to node 4 and activity 3's start node is node 1 as NPS(12)=1.

A similar procedure is used to store successor activities and the end nodes of emanating activities. Cells 25 through 47 of the vector NPS are used for this purpose as follows:

Cell	25	26	27	28	29	30	31	32	33	34	35	36	37	38
Data	1	2	2	3	3	4	0	4	5	5	3	0	6	6

Cell	39	40	41	42	43	44	45	46	47
Data	7	4	0	9	6	0	8	6	0

The vector NSPTR is used to point to the cell of NPS where an activity and its end node are stored for a given node. The vector NSPTR is:

NSPTR(NODE)

Node	1	2	3	4	5	6
Pointer	25	32	37	42	45	0

As an example of the use of NSPTR and NPS, consider node 3. The activities emanating from node 3 are stored in NPS starting at cell 37. Activity 6, whose end node is node 6, and activity 7, whose end node is node 4, both emanate from node 3. This data structure is employed in subroutine UO in order to make the backward pass required for computing slack values.

The listing of subroutine UO is shown in Figure 18-6. The first statement sets the latest realization time for the sink node (node 6) equal to the earliest realization time. In the next section of code, the vector NNBP is tested to determine the next node to consider in the backward pass. The first value is 6, as established in subroutine UI. If the next value is 0, the backward pass is completed.

At statement 5, the pointer to the location in NPS where activi-

```
      SUBROUTINE UO
      COMMON /QVAR/ NDE,NFTBU(100),NREL(100),NRELP(100),NREL2(100),NRUN,
     1NRUNS,NTC(100),PARAM(100,4),TBEG,TNOW
      COMMON /SLACK/ NPPTR(6),NSPTR(6),NPS(50),DUR(9),NBRELP(6),
     1NBREL(6),NNBP(6),ES(9),EF(9),XLS(9),XLF(9),TE(9),TL(6),TS(9),FS(9)
      COMMON /SUMS/ SES(9),SEF(9),SLS(9),SLF(9),STS(9),SFS(9)
C****
C**** SET TL OF SINK TO TE OF SINK
C****
      TL(6)=TE(6)
C****
C**** DETERMINE THE NEXT NODE TO CONSIDER
C**** IF NO NODE IN LIST, THEN FINISHED
C****
    2 DO 1 I=1,6
      K=I
      NODE=NNBP(I)
      IF(NODE.NE.0) GO TO 3
    1 CONTINUE
      GO TO 20
    3 NNBP(K)=0
C****
C**** CALCULATE LATE START AND TL VALUES
C****
C**** LOOP THROUGH NPPTR
C****      NP = ACTIVITY NUMBER
C****      NP1 = START NODE OF THE ACTIVITY
C****
    5 NPTR=NPPTR(NODE)
      IF(NPTR.EQ.0) GO TO 20
      NP=NPS(NPTR)
   10 IF(NP.EQ.0) GO TO 2
      NP1=NPS(NPTR+1)
      XLS(NP)=TL(NODE)-DUR(NP)
      IF(TL(NP1).GT.XLS(NP)) TL(NP1)=XLS(NP)
C****
C**** DECREMENT NUMBER OF BACKWARD RELEASES REQUIRED
C****
      NBREL(NP1)=NBREL(NP1)-1
      IF(NBREL(NP1).NE.0) GO TO 15
C****
C**** IF NUMBER OF BACKWARD RELEASES SATISFIED,
C**** ADD THIS NODE TO LIST TO BE CONSIDERED
C****
      DO 16 I=1,6
      K=I
      IF(NNBP(I).EQ.0) GO TO 17
   16 CONTINUE
      CALL ERROR(1)
   17 NNBP(K)=NP1
   15 NPTR=NPTR+2
      NP=NPS(NPTR)
      GO TO 10
C****
C**** CALCULATE LATE FINISH AND TOTAL SLACK VALUES
C****
   20 DO 25 I=1,9
      XLF(I)=XLS(I)+DUR(I)
   25 TS(I)=XLF(I)-EF(I)
C****
C**** CALCULATE FREE SLACK
C****
C**** LOOP THROUGH NSPTR
C****      NS = POINTER
C****      NA = ACTIVITY NUMBER
C****      NN = END NODE OF THE ACTIVITY
C****
      NS=NSPTR(1)
      NA=NPS(NS)
   30 NN=NPS(NS+1)
      FS(NA)=TE(NN)-EF(NA)
      NS=NS+2
      NA=NPS(NS)
      IF(NA.NE.0) GO TO 30
      NS=NS+1
      NA=NPS(NS)
      IF(NA.NE.0) GO TO 30
C****
C**** ADD OBSERVATIONS FOR THIS RUN TO SUMS
C****
      DO 60 I=1,9
      SES(I)=SES(I)+ES(I)
      SEF(I)=SEF(I)+EF(I)
      SLS(I)=SLS(I)+XLS(I)
      SLF(I)=SLF(I)+XLF(I)
      STS(I)=STS(I)+TS(I)
   60 SFS(I)=SFS(I)+FS(I)
C****
C**** RETURN UNLESS THIS IS THE LAST RUN
C****
      IF(NRUN.NE.NRUNS) RETURN
C****
C**** CALCULATE AND PRINT AVERAGES
C****
      WRITE(6,100)
      DO 70 I=1,9
      SES(I)=SES(I)/FLOAT(NRUNS)
      SEF(I)=SEF(I)/FLOAT(NRUNS)
      SLS(I)=SLS(I)/FLOAT(NRUNS)
      SLF(I)=SLF(I)/FLOAT(NRUNS)
      STS(I)=STS(I)/FLOAT(NRUNS)
      SFS(I)=SFS(I)/FLOAT(NRUNS)
   70 WRITE(6,200) I, SES(I),SLS(I),SEF(I),SLF(I),STS(I),SFS(I)
  100 FORMAT(1H1///1X,'ACTIVITY',6X,'EARLY',7X,'LATE',8X,'EARLY',7X,
     1'LATE',8X,'TOTAL',7X,'FREE'/2X,'NUMBER',7X,'START',7X,'START',6X,
     2'FINISH',6X,'FINISH',7X,'SLACK',7X,'SLACK'//)
  200 FORMAT(I6,4X,F10.2,5(2X,F10.2))
      RETURN
      END
```

Figure 18-6 Subroutine UO for performing scheduling computations in project planning.

ties incident to the next node to be considered, NODE, is established. The latest start time for this activity is then equal to the latest release time of NODE minus the duration of the activity. If the latest release time for the start node of the activity is greater than the value just computed, the latest release time for the start node of this activity is set equal to the latest start time for the activity. The number of releases required on the backward pass for the start node of the activity is then decremented by 1. If the start node of the activity is released, node NP1 is placed in the vector NNBP to be considered in the backward pass. At statement 15, the next activity number that was incident to the node NODE is established and the process is repeated by branching to statement 10. If no further activities are incident to NODE, the next node to be considered is established by a transfer back to statement 2.

Statements 20 through 25 calculate the late finish and total slack values based on the backward pass. Following statement 25, a second forward pass is made in order to compute the free slack. In this pass the activities emanating from a node and their end nodes are referenced through the use of NSPTR and NPS.

The DO loop through statement 60 sums the values calculated during the forward pass and backward pass for a single run. If all runs have not been completed, NRUN will not be equal to NRUNS and a return from subroutine .UO will cause the next run to be started. If all runs are completed, average values are obtained. At statement 70, a printout of the average values is made.

The final printout is shown in Figure 18-7. The values are similar to those presented in Table 18-2. The slight difference is due entirely to the use of the actual sample durations in Figure 18-7, whereas the theoretical expected durations were used in Table 18-2. As stated previously, the standard deviation, minimum and maximum values of the scheduling variables, and a histogram of the values could be obtained by calls to subroutines COL and HIS.

ACTIVITY NUMBER	EARLY START	LATE START	EARLY FINISH	LATE FINISH	TOTAL SLACK	FREE SLACK
1	0	.56	3.03	3.58	.56	0
2	0	2.00	5.98	7.98	2.00	1.48
3	0	2.96	13.89	16.85	2.96	2.24
4	3.03	6.80	11.06	14.84	3.77	0
5	3.03	3.87	7.14	7.98	.84	.32
6	7.46	9.78	18.52	20.84	2.32	2.32
7	7.46	8.72	15.59	16.85	1.26	.53
8	11.06	14.84	17.06	20.84	3.77	3.77
9	16.12	16.85	20.11	20.84	.73	.73

Figure 18-7 Scheduling computations printed in subroutine UO.

18.6 PROJECT PLANNING WITH LIMITED RESOURCES

Throughout the discussion of project planning, precedence between activities was established based on the order in which the activities had to be performed. When activities compete for limited resources, there exists an implicit set of precedence constraints which dictate that activities must be performed sequentially because of the lack of resources that can be allocated simultaneously. As we shall see, the addition of resources in project planning networks requires the specification of procedures, rules, or algorithms for allocating the resources.

Q-GERT can be used to model project planning with limited resources. The complexity of the decision processes associated with resource allocation in project networks may require specialized tools. The work of J. Wiest and his development of the SPAR programs [219] have been instrumental in fostering developments in this field. Commercially available packages for allocating resources in PERT-type networks are available [143]. Research on project planning with limited resources for GERT-type networks has also been explored, and specialized GERT programs have been developed for this purpose. The research by Wortman on START [222], Wortman and others on SAINT [223,225], and Hebert on R-GERT [76] have been significant.

In the next section, the example repair problem is extended to include resource requirements for each activity. Procedures for using Q-GERT to model this revised situation are illustrated.

18.7 REPAIRMAN MODEL WITH RESOURCE REQUIREMENTS

The network for the repair project is redrawn in Figure 18-8 with the addition of the number of repairmen required to perform an activity included below the branch in a triangle. It can be seen from Figure 18-8 that it requires two repairmen to perform activities 1 and 2 but only one repairman to perform any of the other activities. Questions that relate to the analysis of this network are similar to those previously presented but, in addition, we are now interested in the utilization of the repairmen. Decision making relates to the total amount of resources to be allocated to the project (in this example the two repairmen) and, once allocated, the manner in which they should be used to perform the activities. Tradeoffs clearly exist between resource capacity and project duration.

Figure 18-9 presents a Q-GERT model of the repairman project with the resource allocation decisions modeled explicitly on the network. Since resources are to be allocated, activities waiting for resources must be placed in queues in order for the allocation process to be performed. Thus, in addition to a start node for the project, three Q-nodes

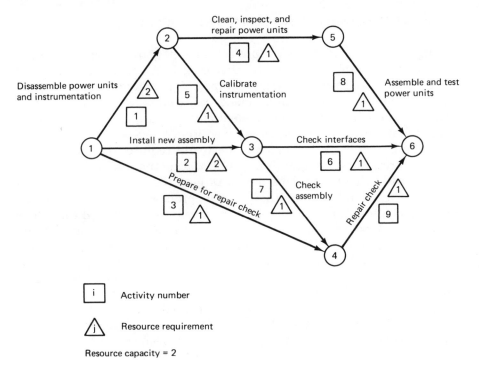

Figure 18-8 Network model of a repair project with resource requirements.

are used to hold transactions representing the released activities. Activities 1, 2, and 3 are waiting to be performed in Q-nodes 51, 52, and 53, respectively. ALLOCATE node 40 is used to allocate two repairmen to activities waiting in either Q-node 51 or Q-node 52. ALLOCATE node 41 will allocate one repairman to perform activity 3, which waits in Q-node 53. The first decision process involves the decision to allocate repairmen to either activity 1 or 2 or to activity 3. In the resource block shown in Figure 18-9, ALLOCATE node 40 precedes ALLOCATE node 41; hence, repairmen will be allocated to activities 1 or 2 before activity 3. The next decision involves whether the repairmen should be allocated to activity 1 or activity 2. At ALLOCATE node 40, the preferred order (POR) rule is prescribed and we decide to allocate to activity 1 first. This is specified in the description of the ALLOCATE node:

$$ALLOCATE,40,POR,1,2,51/1,52/11*$$

Since at the beginning of the project two repairmen are available, they will both be allocated to activity 1 and a transaction will move to node 1 and activity 1 will be started. At node 2, two units of resource 1 are freed. These two resource units are reallocated at node 40 as specified

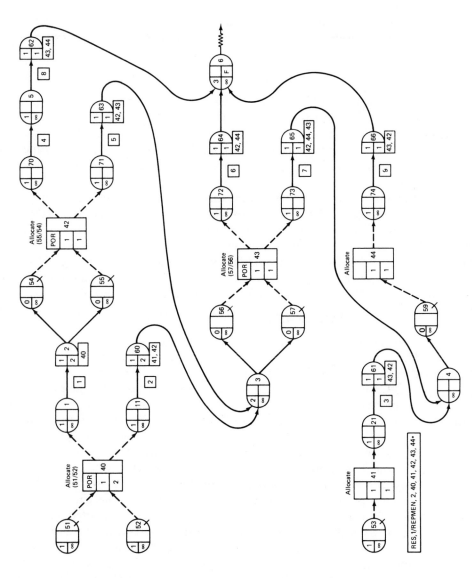

Figure 18-9 Q-GERT model of repairman project with resource constraints.

at the FREE node. Activities 4 and 5 can now be started and they wait in Q-nodes 54 and 55, respectively.

The two repairmen work on activity 2 and, when it is completed, they are made available at FREE node 60. Reallocation is made at ALLOCATE node 41, to start activity 3, and ALLOCATE node 42, to select between activities 4 and 5.

At ALLOCATE node 42, the transaction in Q-node 55 is selected since priority is established by the order of the Q-node numbers on the following statement:

$$\text{ALLOCATE,42,POR,1,1,55/71,54/70*}$$

When activity 5 is completed, the repairman is freed at node 63 and will be reallocated to perform activity 4 if activity 4 has not already been started. Otherwise, he will be reallocated at ALLOCATE node 43. The network model has incorporated a decision to use the same repairman on activity 8 as on activity 4 and that the two activities be performed sequentially.

Returning to when activity 5 is completed, a transaction is sent to node 3 to indicate that one of the release requirements for activities 6 and 7 has been satisfied. If activity 2 has also been completed, node 3 would be released, and transactions would reside in Q-nodes 56 and 57, representing the information that activities 6 and 7 are ready to be started. If a repairman is available, ALLOCATE node 43 is modeled to start activity 7 prior to activity 6 through the following statement:

$$\text{ALLOCATE,43,POR,1,1,57/73,56/72*}$$

A decription of the remainder of the network is similar to the above. The project is completed when SINK node 6 is released, which occurs after activities 6, 8, and 9 are completed.

The Q-GERT model of this project demonstrates the large number of decisions involved in project planning under limited resources. The outputs from the Q-GERT processor for the model presented in Figure 18-9 are shown in Figure 18-10. The estimate of the average time to complete the project is 38.58 time units. The estimated time to complete the project without resources given in Figure 16-3 was 20.74 time units. Thus, the addition of resource requirements adds approximately 17.84 time units to the project duration. Not only has the average project duration increased, but the range of possible project durations has widened, as indicated by the minimum and maximum values observed. For the resource case, the range is over 21 time units, whereas for the unconstrained resource case it was only 12.5 time units. From the histogram presented in Figure 18-11, we see that there is almost a 10% chance that the project will take greater than 43 time units, which is more than double the average project duration if resources are not considered.

The utilization of repairmen is estimated at 1.9; that is, on the

GERT SIMULATION PROJECT PERT-RESOURC BY PRITSKER
DATE 3/ 8/ 1982

FINAL RESULTS FOR 400 SIMULATIONS

AVERAGE NODE STATISTICS

NODE	LABEL	PROBABILITY	AVE.	STD.DEV.	SD OF AVE	NO OF OBS.	MIN.	MAX.	STAT TYPE
6	PROJCOMP	1.0000	38.5827	3.1886	.1594	400.	27.8505	48.9102	F
74	START 9	1.0000	31.1064	2.8099	.1405	400.	22.1953	39.0918	F
21	START 3	1.0000	9.0079	1.4914	.0746	400.	4.8463	12.8683	F
73	START 7	1.0000	22.7488	2.3226	.1161	400.	15.7761	29.7348	F
72	START 6	1.0000	27.0694	2.6762	.1338	400.	18.2440	33.9133	F
5	START 8	1.0000	21.1544	2.7742	.1387	400.	11.8280	28.8274	F
71	START 5	1.0000	9.0079	1.4914	.0746	400.	4.8463	12.8683	F
70	START 4	1.0000	13.1172	2.1151	.1058	400.	6.7390	18.7176	F
11	START 2	1.0000	3.0277	.8164	.0408	400.	1.2196	4.9198	F
11	START 1	1.0000	0	0	0	400.	0	0	F

AVERAGE NUMBER IN Q-NODE / **NUMBER IN Q-NODE** / **AVERAGE WAITING TIME**

NODE	LABEL	AVE.	STD.DEV.	SD OF AVE	MIN.	MAX.	NUMBER IN Q-NODE MAX.	WAIT AVE.	WAIT STD.DEV.	WAIT SD OF AVE
51	Q FOR 1	0	0	0	0	0	0	0	0	0
52	Q FOR 2	.0786	.0209	.0010	.0292	.1359	1.0000	3.0277	.8164	.0408
53	Q FOR 3	.2337	.0357	.0018	.1409	.3205	1.0000	9.0079	1.4914	.0746
54	Q FOR 4	.2613	.0459	.0023	.1323	.3775	1.0000	10.0895	1.9875	.0994
55	Q FOR 5	.1551	.0297	.0015	.0774	.2372	1.0000	5.9802	1.2134	.0607
56	Q FOR 6	.3619	.0433	.0022	.2407	.4716	1.0000	13.9522	1.9522	.0976
57	Q FOR 7	.2512	.0613	.0031	.0903	.4297	1.0000	9.6316	2.2366	.1118
59	Q FOR 9	.0060	.0213	.0011	0	.2110	1.0000	.2277	.7750	.0388

AVERAGE RESOURCE UTILIZATION / **NUMBER OF RESOURCES**

RESOURCE	LABEL	AVE.	STD.DEV.	SD OF AVE	NO. OF OBS.	MIN.	MAX.	NUMBER OF RESOURCES MAX.
1	REPMEN	1.9001	.0659	.0033	400	1.7148	1.9990	2.

Figure 18-10 Q-GERT output report for repairman model with two repairmen.

```
OBSV    RELA    CUML    UPPER         0         20        40        60        80        100
FREQ    FREQ    FREQ    BOUND OF CELL I....I....I....I....I....I....I....I....I....I....I
  1     .002    .002     30.00        I                                                    I
  2     .005    .007     31.00        I                                                    I
  7     .017    .025     32.00        I*                                                   I
  8     .020    .045     33.00        I*C                                                  I
  5     .012    .057     34.00        I* C                                                 I
 24     .060    .117     35.00        I***  C                                              I
 32     .080    .197     36.00        I****     C                                          I
 54     .135    .332     37.00        I*******        C                                    I
 43     .107    .440     38.00        I*****              C                                I
 47     .117    .557     39.00        I******                  C                           I
 47     .117    .675     40.00        I******                       C                      I
 39     .097    .772     41.00        I*****                             C                 I
 34     .085    .857     42.00        I****                                   C            I
 18     .045    .902     43.00        I**                                         C        I
 21     .052    .955     44.00        I***                                           C    I
 11     .027    .982     45.00        I*                                               CI
  4     .010    .992     46.00        I                                                   C
  1     .002    .995     47.00        I                                                   C
  0      0      .995     48.00        I                                                   C
  2     .005   1.000     +INF         I                                                   C
                                      I....I....I....I....I....I....I....I....I....I....I
TOTAL  400
```

Figure 18-11 Histogram of project completion times for repairman model with two repairmen.

average a repairman is busy 95% of the time. With only 2 repairmen, no free time has been built into the project and the only idle time occurs at the end of the project when one repairman finishes an activity and no other activities are to be performed. Thus, on each project realization one repairman will be busy 100% of the time and the other, on the average, has 10% idle time at the end of the project. For more complex projects, repairmen would normally wait for other repairmen to become available before activities can be started.

Also obtained on the output report presented in Figure 18-10 are estimates of the starting times for each activity (the time of first release of the start node associated with the activity) and the average time an activity is delayed because resources are not available (waiting time in queues). Comparing the values in Figure 18-10 with those in Figure 16-4, it is seen that the average start time in the resource case is much larger than in the unconstrained situation. In addition, there is a higher variability associated with the start times. With regard to the delay time for activities, it is seen that activity 6 waits in Q-node 56 on the average of 13.95 time units before a repairman is assigned to it.

For this project with two repairmen, it is possible to estimate some of these delay times. For example, the delay time in starting activity 2 is equal to the time to perform activity 1. Since the average time to perform activity 1 is three time units, we expect and obtain a three-time-unit delay in starting activity 2. Similarly, the delay in starting activity 3 is equal to the sum of the times to perform activities 1 and 2, which is nine time units. The delay in starting activity 5 is the time required to perform activity 2, or approximately six time units. It is not possible to estimate directly all the delay times, as they depend on the order in which activities are completed. By reviewing traces of different runs, the possible sequences of activity completions can be observed.

Number of Repairmen	Project Completion Time				Resource Utilization	
	Average	Std. Dev.	Min.	Max.	Average	Average Per Repairman
2	38.58	3.19	27.85	48.12	1.90	0.95
3	27.43	2.66	21.50	35.21	2.68	0.89
4	23.55	2.57	17.98	32.81	3.13	0.78
Unlimited	20.74	2.05	15.31	27.85	—	—

To investigate the effect of increasing the number of repairmen, the Q-GERT Analysis Program was rerun with the capacity of the repairmen resource increased from 2 to 3 and then to 4. A summary of the results from these runs is shown in Table 18-6. As expected, the average project completion time decreases and approaches the estimate obtained for the unlimited resource case. Also shown is the decrease in the standard deviation and the minimum and maximum of the project completion times. In analyzing the results of the runs made for the four-repairmen case, it was seen that only activities 3 and 5 were delayed because of limited resources. Thus, if a fifth repairman is employed, no activities would be delayed and the use of five repairmen would be equivalent to the unlimited resource situation.

The decrease in average project completion time is obtained at the cost of additional repairmen. Clearly, there are benefits for completing the project earlier, and these benefits must be compared against the increased cost of assigning repairmen to the project. Note that as the number of repairmen is increased, the utilization of each repairman decreases. This occurs because the repairmen are waiting for precedence activities to be completed before they can start work on their next assigned activity.

A common approach in project planning is to assign resources on an as-needed basis. In Q-GERT, this would be modeled by initially setting the capacity of the resource to a given value and then altering this capacity first by a positive amount and then by a negative amount to change the resource availability at specific times during the performance of the project.

From the analysis above it is seen that a significant amount of information is available in the Q-GERT Summary Report to enable project planning when resources are constrained and activity durations are random variables.

18.7.1 Alternative Q-GERT Model

An alternative way to model the repairman project with limited resources is shown in Figure 18-12. In this model, the decision re-

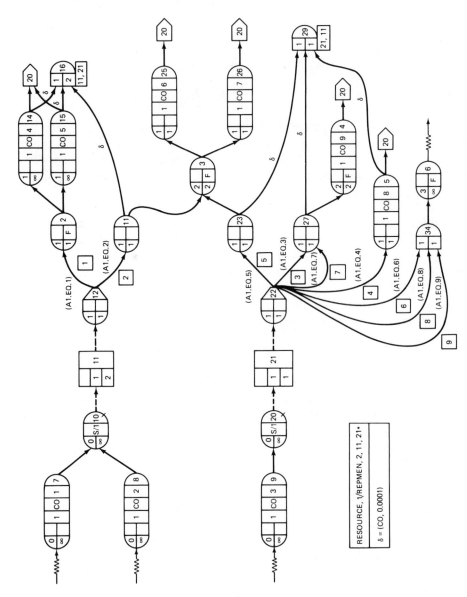

Figure 18-12 Alternative Q-GERT model of repairman with limited resources.

garding to which of the activities to allocate resources is accomplished by ranking activities that require the same number of resource units in a common queue. At Q-node 10, all activities are held that require two units of resource 1 (repairman) that have been released but not started.

In Q-node 20, all released activities that require one repairman are held. Those activities that have no predecessors are inserted into the Q-nodes through the use of source nodes. In this model, a waiting activity with the smallest activity number is given priority when allocating resource units.

When the required resource units are allocated to the activity, the activity is started at either node 12 or 22. After the activity is performed, other activities are released in accordance with the network predecessor relations and a transaction is routed back to the appropriate Q-node with attribute 1 defining the activity number. Also, following the completion of an activity, the resource units used by that activity are freed at either FREE node 16 or 29. Since we desire the freeing of the resources to occur after the released activities are inserted into the Q-nodes, a small time delay in freeing the resources is included in the network description. This is represented on the activities entering the FREE nodes by a δ, where $\delta = (CO, .0001)$.

The model presented in Figure 18-12 represents a general approach to project planning with limited resources. By changing the ranking attribute in the Q-nodes where activities are waiting to be started, different scheduling procedures can be modeled. Ranking attributes that could be used include:

1. Number of following activities
2. Total work content (the product of resource units and time units) of following activities
3. Slack measures
4. Activity duration

The computation of such priority values for activities without predecessors would be made in subroutine UI. When an activity is released, a user function would be employed to assign the computed priority to an attribute of the transaction representing the released activity.

Another approach is to write a user function that contains the logic to determine the order in which activities are to be performed. The user function could be employed to allocate the resources to waiting activities by calling subroutine IALOC and to free up resources when activities are completed by calling subroutine FREE (see Section 3.11.7). The activity to which resources are allocated could then be started by calling subroutine PTIN to put a transaction into the network at the start node of the activity. This approach to project planning would be used when activities have multiple resource requirements and complex allocation procedures are employed. Through the use of user functions, complex scheduling rules for modeling project planning with limited resources can be accomplished.

18.8 SUMMARY

In this chapter, scheduling and resource concepts associated with project planning with Q-GERT have been described. Methods for computing start and finish times and slack values are presented. Procedures and models for performing project planning when resources are limited are illustrated. This chapter establishes the foundation for using Q-GERT to make project planning decisions.

18.9 EXERCISES

18-1. Explain the differences in project scheduling when a due date for a project is prescribed versus the situation when one is not prescribed. Interpret the various slack measures for each situation.

18-2. Discuss the assumptions made when computing slack times using PERT/CPM procedures. Give a rationale for using such procedures and assess the impact of the approximations required.

18-3. Discuss the impact of project planning activities, including the allocation of resources to balance path times, on the probability of exceeding the expected completion time (a) when PERT is used and (b) when Q-GERT is used.

18-4. The following list represents the operations involved in a plant maintenance project to remove and replace a section of a pipe [84]. Draw the PERT network for this project, making appropriate assumptions regarding precedence requirements.

Activity	Description	Expected Duration (hours)
1	Prepare materials list	8
2	Deactivate line	8
3	Procure and deliver pipe materials	120
4	Procure and deliver valves	120
5	Procure and deliver paint	16
6	Procure and deliver insulation	16
7	Erect scaffold	12
8	Remove old pipe and valves	36
9	Prefabricate pipe sections (except valves)	40
10	Install prefabricated pipe sections and valves	24
11	Start insulation of pipe and valves	24
12	Pressure test pipe and valves	8
13	Complete insulation	8
14	Paint insulation	16
15	Remove scaffold	4
16	Reactivate line	8

Restrictions:

1. The scaffold is required for removing the old pipe but not for deactivating the line.
2. Operations 11 and 12 need to be done concurrently and must precede operation 13.
3. The pipe can be insulated after it is back in service.

Perform a detailed scheduling analysis on the network. Include the computation of slack time, early and late start and finish times, and the variability associated with the completion time.

18-5. For the network of Exercise 18-4, perform a detailed scheduling analysis using the Q-GERT processor. Compare the results with those obtained in Exercise 18-4.

18-6. For the network of Exercise 18-4, assuming exponentially distributed durations, evaluate the criticality of each activity based on total slack, the ratio index, and the criticality index.

18-7. For the network of Exercise 18-4, the following resources are required for each activity:

Activity	Plumbers	Helpers
1	0	1
2	1	1
3	0	1
4	0	1
5	0	1
6	0	1
7	0	2
8	1	1
9	1	0
10	1	1
11	1	1
12	1	1
13	1	1
14	0	1
15	0	2
16	1	1
Number available	1	2

In the face of these limited resources, plan the project so as to minimize the total time required to perform the project.

19

Project Planning – Applications

19.1 INTRODUCTION

This chapter describes three applications of project planning concepts and procedures. The applications selected are from actual case studies reported in the literature. Only the essential elements are presented and the literature cited should be consulted for complete details. The three applications relate to contract bidding and negotiations, research and development planning, and technological forecasting. There is a large overlap in these areas which is brought to light in the descriptions of management concerns for each application. Through these applications, we demonstrate the feasibility of expressing such concerns in network models and the quantitative assessment of alternative courses of action.

19.2 AN INDUSTRIAL CONTRACT NEGOTIATION PROCESS

This example concerns a construction firm that specializes in building gasoline plants that strip liquid hydrocarbons from natural gas. The firm's clients are large oil companies. These oil companies send out requests for bids on new gasoline plants to the construction firm and its competitors. The bidding process is costly and time consuming but obviously essential to the successful operation of the construction firm.

A study by Bird et al. [14] analyzed this bidding process from the viewpoint of the construction firm. The study provided management with a means for assessing the cost and effectiveness of the bidding process. In addition, alternative modes of operation were analyzed for the purpose of improving this key aspect of the business. Although this example involves the construction industry, the managerial concerns presented are common to a large number of industrial negotiation situations. In fact, Moore and Clayton present a GERT analysis of a similar situation from the vantage point of an oil company's management faced with the decision of deciding the number of vendors from which to request bids [128].

19.2.1 The System and Management Concerns

To introduce the contract bidding or negotiation process, consider the schematic diagram in Figure 19-1. The process begins with an initial client contact, which in this case is an oil company requesting a bid on the construction of a gasoline plant. The firm initiates a preliminary study of the proposed project. This involves initial reports to management as well as engineering, production, financial, marketing, and purchasing evaluations. Each evaluation may indicate that the proposed project is not in the best interests of the construction firm. It is management policy to decide against bidding if any evaluation is negative. If, however, all reports are positive, a management conference is held and more detailed studies ensue. If any of the detailed studies result in a negative recommendation, no bid is made. When this occurs, the costs of both the preliminary and detailed studies are considered as sunk costs. If no negative recommendation is made from the detailed studies, marketing and engineering plans are finalized and the client is presented with a detailed project proposal. The client may reject the bid, accept it, or request revisions. Any stated revisions are incorporated into the proposal, and the client evaluation process is repeated.

Each of the activities described above involves time and money and has an impact on the total effectiveness and success of the construction firm. The central questions that relate to the firm's profitability for this phase of its business are:

1. How much time and money does it take to obtain a successful contract?
2. How much time and money is spent on bidding for contracts that are lost?
3. What is the chance of winning (losing) a contract?
4. How much time and money is spent in each phase of the bidding process?

A Q-GERT model was constructed to provide data to assist in answering these questions. The model provided a vehicle for evaluating

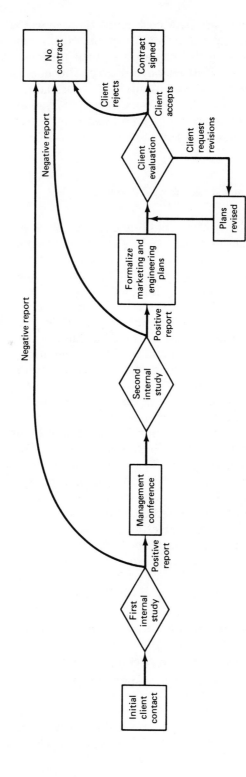

Figure 19-1 Schematic of contract negotiation process.

ways to redesign the current mode of operation. Important questions raised when considering alternative operating procedures were:

1. What is the effect on time and cost if initial report activities are resequenced such that activities with a high probability of rejecting a contract precede lower-risk activities?
2. What is the effect on time and costs from an increase in the expenditure of resources in the first report stage? How does this affect the probability of obtaining a contract?

The Q-GERT model for this example will now be described. The discussion concentrates on the network logic used to model the random time elements and the probabilistic outcomes of the negotiation process. Emphasis is placed on how network statistics provide answers to the questions posed.

19.2.2 The Q-GERT Model

Figure 19-2 is a Q-GERT network model of the negotiation process. Fixed and variable costs are associated with each activity. A fixed cost is charged each time an activity occurs, while a variable cost accumulates over the period of time required to complete the activity. In the description below, activity numbers are given in boxes ☐ to help relate to the project description.

'The process begins with the initial contact by a client [1]. A report to the marketing vice-president and to the president is then made [2], [3]. Current policy is to perform a preliminary analysis for the type of project being considered. As will be seen, an evaluation of this policy could be cost effective. Next, on the Q-GERT network, five parallel studies are performed beginning at node 5. These involve engineering[4], production [5], financial [6], marketing [7], and purchasing [8]. Except for the production report, the evaluation of the reports is performed at the nodes following the activities, as represented by activities [9], [10], and [13] through [18]. If any one of the reports is negative, the project is not negotiated further and the network terminates at node 22. Node 22 is placed in three locations in Figure 19-2 for graphical convenience. The evaluation of the production schedule is slightly more complicated in that the possibility for production subcontracting is available [11]. An unfavorable production subcontract could also occur [19], which would lead to termination of the negotiation process. When all five reports are favorable, node 12 is released. A user function is employed at node 12 to collect cost data with regard to the costs of the negotiation process up to the time at which five favorable reports are obtained. First statistics are also collected. Based on the five reports, corporate-level planning conferences are held [21]. Further information is then sought of a marketing and engineering nature [22], [23]. If either of these

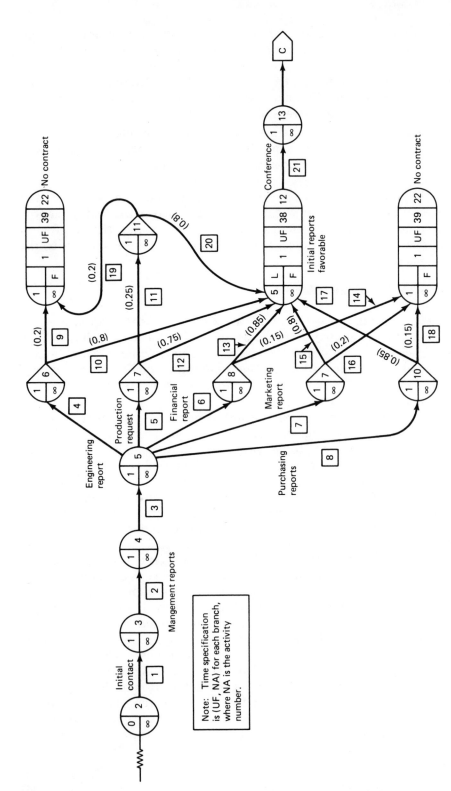

Figure 19-2 Q-GERT network for industrial negotiation study.

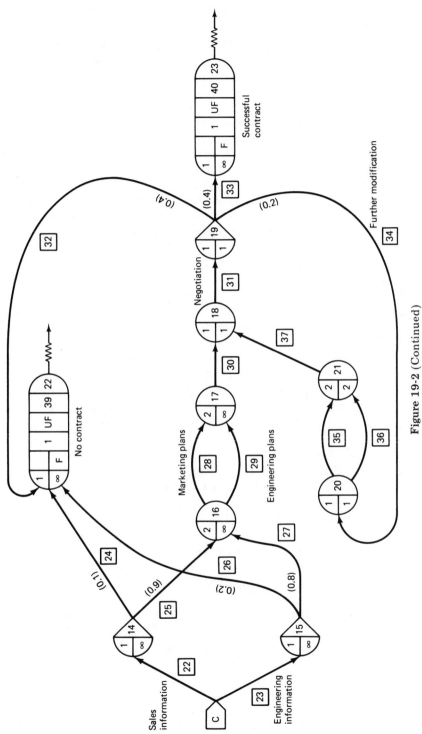

Figure 19-2 (Continued)

studies results in unfavorable information, the sales negotiation process will be terminated 24 , 26 . If positive information is obtained from the studies 25 , 27 , marketing negotiation plans and engineering design plans are formulated 28 , 29 . Based on these plans, corporate-level strategy is developed in a conference 30 . This strategy is implemented in a negotiation conference with the buying firm 31 . The results of the negotiation conference are: no sale 32 , contract awarded 33 , or further negotiations requested by the buyer involving plan modifications 34 . Marketing and engineering modifications are then performed 35, 36 . A corporate-level meeting to evaluate and reconcile the modifications is then held 37 . Following this, a return is made to node 18 of the Q-GERT network, where another negotiation conference with the buying firm is held 31 . At node 23, a successful sale has been made. Total costs when a successful sale is made are collected at node 23. Total costs of the negotiation when a sale has not been made are collected at node 22.

The network model for the negotiation process allows an analyst to include probabilistic outcomes as modeled by the probabilistic branching at nodes throughout the network. In addition, recycling of activities is permissible, as illustrated by the sequence of activities 31 , 34 , 35 , 36 , and 37 , which form a closed loop.

The details involved in obtaining cost estimates from the network model will now be described. In general, costs will be obtained using the concepts presented in Section 3.12.1. All activity times and costs for the negotiation process are calculated in user functions associated with the activities of the network. In this study, all activity times were prescribed by either a constant or a beta distribution. When all reports are favorable (node 12), user function 38 is employed to compute the total costs to achieve that milestone. At sink nodes 12 and 23, user function 39 and 40 are employed to compute total costs. At node 22, it is necessary to stop ongoing studies whenever a negative report is made.

Function UF is shown in Figure 19-3. Statement 1 is used for activities having a constant time, and statement 2 is used for those activities whose time is beta distributed. Statement 3 is used to obtain user-collected statistics at the three statistics nodes of the network. Statement 4 is used to stop any activities in progress when a lost contract occurs.

When UF is called and a transfer is made to statement 1, the time for the activity is taken as the value of the first column of row IFN of the PARAM array. These constants are read into PARAM on input and illustrate the use of Q-GERT input to read constant values. A transfer is then made to statement 100, where the total costs are increased by the sum of the setup and variable costs for the activity. The variable cost is the product of the cost per unit time and the activity time. The function number, IFN, used in statements 1 and 2 of UF is equivalent to the

```
      FUNCTION UF(IFN)
      COMMON/QVAR/NDE,NFTBU(100),NREL(100),NRELP(100),NREL2(100),NRUN,
     1NRUNS,NTC(100),PARAM(100,4)TBEG,TNOW
      COMMON/UCOM1/SETC(37),VARC(37),TOTALC
      GO TO (2,2,2,2,1,1,1,2,1,1,2,1,1,1,1,1,1,1,1,1,1,1,1,2,1,2,1,
     *2,2,2,2,1,1,1,2,2,2,3,4,3), IFN
C**** SET DURATION EQUAL TO A CONSTANT
    1 UF=PARAM(IFN,1)
      GO TO 100
C**** SET DURATION EQUAL TO A BETA SAMPLE
    2 UF=BE(IFN)
  100 TOTALC=TOTALC+SETC(IFN)+VARC(IFN)*UF
      RETURN
C**** FAVORABLE REPORTS OR SUCCESSFUL CONTRACT
    3 JJ=IFN-37
      CALL COL(TOTALC,JJ)
      CALL HIS(TOTALC,JJ)
      UF=0.0
      RETURN
C**** USER FUNCTION 39 - NO CONTRACT
C**** STOP ALL ON-GOING ACTIVITIES
    4 CALL SNACT(1,NACT,TIREM)
      IF(NACT.EQ.0) GO TO 3
C**** RETURN VARIABLE COSTS NOT SPENT
      TOTALC=TOTALC-VARC(NACT)*TIREM
      GO TO 4
      END
```

Figure 19-3 Function UF for negotiation model.

activity number of each branch on the network. Function numbers 38, 39, and 40 are used for user-collected statistics. When an activity time is beta distributed, the computed GO TO statement in UF causes a transfer to statement 2, where a sample from a beta distribution is taken as the value for UF. Total cost for the project is then updated by the equation specified in statement 100.

For this study, the setup cost and variable cost are added to the total cost when the activity is started. By changing statement 100, different or nonlinear cost relations as a function of time could be modeled.

When a contract is lost, node 22 is released and user function 39 is activated. In UF, this causes a transfer to statement 4. Since a lost sale can be caused by one negative report or by an unfavorable call from the client, other activities that are ongoing should be stopped as soon as possible after the determination is made that the contract is lost. To stop other activities, the Q-GERT subroutine SNACT is used. By setting the first argument to one, SNACT stops the next scheduled activity and provides the activity number and the time remaining on the activity. The statement to accomplish this is CALL SNACT(1,NACT,TIREM), where the 1 indicates the next event is to be stopped, NACT is returned as the activity number of the stopped activity (which will be zero if no activity is scheduled to occur), and TIREM is the time that was remaining on the activity.

If NACT = 0, no activity is ongoing, and a transfer to statement 3 in UF is made to collect the costs associated with the current run. If NACT is greater than zero, the costs that were added into the total cost variable, TOTALC, must be decreased because the dollars will be reappropriated before the activity is completed. The cost not expended on activity NACT is VARC(NACT)*TIREM, and this quantity is subtracted from TOTALC. A transfer back to statement 4 is made to stop all ongoing activities.

At statement 3, the index JJ is computed as the function number

```
      SUBROUTINE UI
      COMMON/QVAR/NDE,NFTBU(100),NREL(100),NRELP(100),NREL2(100),NRUN,
     1NRUNS,NTC(100),PARAM(100,4),TBEG,TNOW
      COMMON /UCOM1/SETC(37),VARC(37),TOTALC
C****  INITIALIZE TOTAL COST
      TOTALC=0.0
      IF(NRUN.GT.1) RETURN
C****  READ AND PRINT SETUP AND VARIABLE COSTS
      WRITE(6,101)
      DO 1 I=1,37
      READ(5,100) SETC(I),VARC(I)
      WRITE(6,102) SETC(I),VARC(I)
      GO TO (2,2,2,2,1,1,1,2,1,1,2,1,1,1,1,1,1,1,1,1,1,1,2,1,2,1,
     *2,2,2,2,1,1,1,2,2,2), I
C****  CHANGE VALUES OF PARAMETERS FOR BETA SAMPLING
    2 CALL CPBP(I)
    1 CONTINUE
      RETURN
  100 FORMAT(2F5.0)
  101 FORMAT(5X,'SETUP',5X,'VARIABLE'/6X,'COST',7X,'COST'/)
  102 FORMAT(F8.0,F12.0)
      END
```

Figure 19-4 Subroutine UI for negotiation model.

minus 37, where 37 is the number of activities that have function numbers. Function number 38 is prescribed for node 12; hence, a JJ value of 1 corresponds to the collection of total cost values at node 12. A JJ value of 2 corresponds to the collection of total cost statistics at node 22 (function number 39), and a JJ value of 3 corresponds to the collection of total costs at node 23 (function number 40). This completes the description of UF.

The initialization of the total cost variable for each run of the network is performed in subroutine UI. In addition, the cost variables, SETC(I) and VARC(I), for each activity are read in subroutine UI. Also required is the changing of the parameter values when the user samples directly from the beta distribution. The coding to perform these three tasks is shown in Figure 19-4. The first statement in subroutine UI initializes the total cost, TOTALC, to zero for each run of the network. Next, a check is made on the run number, NRUN, to ascertain if it is equal to one. If NRUN is one, the setup costs and variable costs for each activity are read. Since these costs are not part of the standard Q-GERT program, it is a good practice to print these values to obtain a written record of the values used. Since subroutine UI is called following the reading of the Q-GERT data input, the data corresponding to the setup costs and variable costs would follow the FIN card of the Q-GERT input.

For those activities for which sampling from the beta distribution is to be employed, a call is made to subroutine CPBE to change the parameters of the beta distribution. For this example, the parameter set number has been set equal to the activity number, which is equal to the function number. This equivalence between activity number, function number, and parameter set number is not required and is done in this example only for convenience. In fact, fewer activity numbers could be employed by using the same number for all the activities that have zero time and zero costs associated with them. This completes the discussion of subroutine UI. For the data input for this example, the reader should consult Refs. 14 and 154.

19.2.3 Model Output and Use

The Q-GERT model of the industrial negotiation process was analyzed for 500 runs. Summaries of the time and cost results are presented in Figures 19-5 and 19-6. The estimate of the probability of losing a contract, node 22, is 0.844. This indicates that over 84% of the negotiations end in failure.

Looking at node 12, favorable reports received, it is seen that approximately 43% of the potential projects result in all five reports being favorable. Thus, 57% of the negotiations are turned down for internal reasons. The time estimates indicate that it takes over 38 days to decide that negotiations should be carried beyond the internal report phase. The cost data indicate that it costs over $3050 when all favorable reports are obtained. This information can be extremely useful to a decision maker who is attempting to improve the sales negotiation process, as it provides trade-off data regarding the possibility of increasing the probability of favorable reports versus the time and costs required to obtain the favorable reports. By developing alternative networks up to node 12, such trade-offs can be made. An attempt should be made to develop procedures for detecting when unfavorable reports will be issued. Possibly, sequential reporting of the engineering, production, financial, marketing, and purchasing reports should be made. Since engineering and marketing have the highest probability of issuing a negative report, these two activities should perhaps be performed prior to the other reports. If this is done, the time required to reach the decision with regard to the preliminary reports would be extended.

The summary statistics for no contract (lost sale) indicate that it takes 62 days on the average to make this determination. Since node 22 can be reached from many points in the network, this time should have a wide variability, which is the case, as indicated by its standard deviation of 56.4 and its range of 23 to 288. The average cost associated with a lost sale is $4944. Comparing this value with project costs to obtain favorable reports, we see that, on the average, only $1900 is expended above the report costs when a lost sale occurs. When the project succeeds, which occurs only 15.6% of the time, the negotiation process takes a lengthy 182 days and costs on the average $11,947. Other statistical quantities concerning the time and cost when the negotiation is successful are shown in Figures 19-5 and 19-6.

In Figure 19-7, the time and cost histograms associated with node 22, lost sale, are presented. These histograms illustrate that the distribution function associated with node 22 has discrete breaks due to the different paths that can be used to reach node 22. For example, failed reports occurred on 283 runs [(1 - 0.434)500]. The histogram for node 22 shows 283 values in the range 20 to 50; hence, this cluster of values is associated with failed reports. The other values in the histogram for

GERT SIMULATION PROJECT SALES-14   BY PRITSKER
            DATE 3/ 15/ 1977

FINAL RESULTS FOR   500 SIMULATIONS

AVERAGE NODE STATISTICS

NODE	LABEL	PROBABILITY	AVE.	STD.DEV.	SD OF AVE	NO OF OBS.	MIN.	MAX.	STAT TYPE
22	LOST-SAL	.8440	62.1055	56.4425	2.7476	422.	22.6712	287.7906	F
23	SUCCESS	.1560	182.0164	48.1436	5.4512	78.	125.7381	425.7386	F
12	FAV-RPTS	.4340	38.1034	4.6936	.3186	217.	28.5247	50.9886	F

Figure 19-5 Summary report for times associated with negotiation model.

	AVE	STD DEV	SD OF AVE	MINIMUM	MAXIMUM	OBS
FAV-RPTS	3053.6797	141.4692	9.6036	2760.4418	3469.0602	217
LOST-SAL	4943.8782	3330.3886	162.1208	2475.4571	17774.4282	422
SUCCESS	11946.9841	2730.1616	309.1299	9524.0147	25238.0935	78

Figure 19-6 Summary report for costs associated with negotiation model.

F STAT HISTOGRAM FOR NODE   22

LOST-SAL

OBSV FREQ	RELA FREQ	CUML FREQ	UPPER BOUND OF CELL
0	0	0	10.00
0	0	0	20.00
0	0	0	30.00
138	.327	.327	30.00
133	.315	.642	40.00
12	.028	.671	50.00
3	.007	.678	60.00
43	.102	.780	70.00
17	.040	.820	80.00
0	0	.820	90.00
0	0	.820	100.00
0	0	.820	110.00
0	0	.820	120.00
2	.005	.825	130.00
8	.019	.844	140.00
8	.019	.863	150.00
9	.021	.884	160.00
11	.026	.910	170.00
10	.024	.934	180.00
7	.017	.950	190.00
21	.050	1.000	+INF

TOTAL   422

LOST-SAL

OBSV FREQ	RELA FREQ	CUML FREQ	UPPER BOUND OF CELL
0	0	0	2000.0000
203	.481	.481	3000.0000
80	.190	.671	4000.0000
0	0	.671	5000.0000
38	.090	.761	6000.0000
25	.059	.820	7000.0000
0	0	.820	8000.0000
0	0	.820	9000.0000
10	.024	.844	10000.0000
33	.078	.922	11000.0000
13	.031	.953	12000.0000
3	.007	.960	13000.0000
8	.019	.979	14000.0000
6	.014	.993	15000.0000
1	.002	.995	16000.0000
1	.002	.998	17000.0000
1	.002	1.000	18000.0000
0	0	1.000	19000.0000
0	0	1.000	20000.0000
0	0	1.000	INF

422

Figure 19-7 Histograms of times and costs associated with unsuccessful negotiation.

node 22 are for the times when a lost sale occurred after favorable reports were received.

Figure 19-8 presents the histograms for the time and costs associated with a successful negotiation. These histograms can be used to monitor company time and cost data associated with successful negotiations. From the histogram, we see that in over 20% of the runs, the total negotiation cost was greater than $14,000. Thus, we can expect one out of five negotiations to have this high cost, given that the nego-

```
          F  STAT HISTOGRAM FOR NODE   23

                    SUCCESS


      OBSV   RELA   CUML    UPPER         0      20      40      60      80     100
      FREQ   FREQ   FREQ   BOUND OF CELL  I....I....I....I....I....I....I....I....I....I....I
        0      0      0    100.00         I                                                  I
        0      0      0    120.00         I                                                  I
       10   .128   .128    140.00         I******                                            I
       20   .256   .385    160.00         I**************      C                             I
       14   .179   .564    180.00         I*********                       C                 I
       15   .192   .756    200.00         I**********                              C .       I
        4   .051   .808    220.00         I***                                        C      I
       10   .128   .936    240.00         I******                                        C   I
        0      0   .936    260.00         I                                              C   I
        3   .038   .974    280.00         I**                                            C  I
        0      0   .974    300.00         I                                              C  I
        0      0   .974    320.00         I                                              C  I
        1   .013   .987    340.00         I*                                             CI
        0      0   .987    360.00         I                                              CI
        0      0   .987    380.00         I                                              CI
        0      0   .987    400.00         I                                              CI
        0      0   .987    420.00         I                                              CI
        1   .013  1.000    440.00         I*                                             C
        0      0  1.000    460.00         I                                              C
        0      0  1.000    +INF           I                                              C
                                          I....I....I....I....I....I....I....I....I....I....I
            ---
TOTAL        78
```

```
              **USER HISTOGRAM NUMBER   3 AT TIME     30.0950 IN RUN    500**

                                    SUCCESS


      OBSV   RELA   CUML    UPPER            0       20      40      60      80     100
      FREQ   FREQ   FREQ   BOUND OF CELL     I....I....I....I....I....I....I....I....I....I....I
        0      0      0    8000.0000         I                                                  I
        0      0      0    9000.0000         I                                                  I
       12   .154   .154   10000.0000         I********                                          I
       31   .397   .551   11000.0000         I********************      C                       I
       11   .141   .692   12000.0000         I********                         C                I
        2   .026   .718   13000.0000         I*                                   C             I
        6   .077   .795   14000.0000         I****                                     C        I
       10   .128   .923   15000.0000         I******                                        C   I
        1   .013   .936   16000.0000         I*                                             C   I
        0      0   .936   17000.0000         I                                              C   I
        1   .013   .949   18000.0000         I*                                             C   I
        4   .051  1.000    INF               I***                                           C
            ---                              I....I....I....I....I....I....I....I....I....I....I
             78
```

Figure 19-8 Histograms of times and costs associated with successful negotiation.

tiation pattern follows the one described by the Q-GERT model. By making such comparisons, the company can maintain some control over the costs involved in their negotiation activities.

19.3 INDUSTRIAL RESEARCH AND DEVELOPMENT PLANNING

Effective analysis and planning of research and development (R&D) activities is vital to the success of many corporate endeavors. Corporate marketing and production strategies depend heavily on the outcome of R&D projects. Normally, long planning horizons are involved which, by their very nature, make R&D projects uncertain ventures. An analysis of such projects must account for the probabilistic nature of activity durations, the possibility of alternative strategies, the repetition of activities, and the possibility of project failure. As described in preceding chapters, these features can be modeled in Q-GERT. In fact, Q-GERT has been used as the modeling vehicle for diverse R&D planning activities [12,168,205]. An example from Moore and Taylor [30] is included here to illustrate the use of Q-GERT in R&D planning.

19.3.1 The System and Study Objectives

The organization to be modeled involves two research teams responsible for four R&D projects. The two teams work on different projects, but they begin at the same time and each team is capable of working on each of four projects. Each of the projects consists of five basic generic stages:

1. Problem definition
2. Research activity
3. Solution proposal
4. Prototype development
5. Solution implementation

For this example, each stage is represented in an aggregate manner as a single activity. Clearly, a detailed model of each stage could be developed.†

The study objective is to obtain estimates of the probability of success, cost, and time duration for the project. The estimates can be used to answer the following specific questions relating to research and development projects:

What is the chance of the project succeeding or failing?

When can a conclusion be reached concerning the impact of the project?

What is the range of costs to be expected on a successful or an unsuccessful project?

What is the effect of slowing down or speeding up the project through different budget allocations?

19.3.2 The Q-GERT Model

A Q-GERT network of the 5 stages is shown in Figure 19-9. The two possible project outcomes are represented by nodes 6 and 7. The five stages are represented sequentially; however, feedback branches emanating after nodes 2, 4, and 5 represent the possibility of repeated activities. Probabilistic branching from node 2 represents two possible outcomes: problem redefinition required or problem definition acceptance. In the latter case, the research stage (activity) can begin. After the research activity, an evaluation process ensues. The outcome of this activity is dependent on the branching probabilities at node 4.

---

†Alternatively, we can think of each stage being modeled in detail, with the time and cost values for each stage obtained as the output values from each of the detailed models. Q-GERT encourages this hierarchical modeling approach.

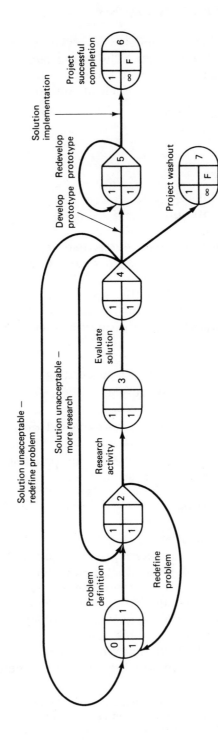

Figure 19-9 Q-GERT network of the stages in an R&D project (From Ref. 130.)

The possible outcomes include a determination of project failure (branch to node 7), a return to the problem definition stage (branch to node 1), a return to research activity (branch to node 2), or the initiation of prototype development (branch to node 5). The prototype developed may not be adequate, and redevelopment activities as represented by the loop around node 5 may be required. If the prototype is acceptable, the next activity is solution implementation.

Statistics for nodes 6 and 7 yield estimates of the probability and time for successful project completion and unsuccessful completion, respectively. Costs associated with each activity can be modeled as illustrated in the previous example.

For multiple R&D projects, it is necessary to link several networks of the type described in Figure 19-9. As one project ends (either by failure or successful completion), branching from the project sink node to the next project occurs. For the study described here, two research teams are employed, and it is necessary to include logic in the network that specifies the assignment of a team to a project. The Q-GERT model of the multiteam, multiproject R&D process is shown in Figure 19-10.

The network shows that one research team starts on project 1 (node 11) at the same time the other team starts on project 4 (node 41). When the first team finishes project 1, either by failure at node 17 or successful completion at node 16, it proceeds to project 2 (node 20). The same procedure describes the second team's movement from project 4 to project 3 (node 30).

Once either of the nodes 20 or 30 has been realized, representing a startup for the associated project, these nodes cannot be realized a second time (as signified by the infinite second release requirement). However, when either team terminates from its second project, it will move to a third project and begin work on that project if the source node for that project has not been realized. All network activity is terminated when four projects have been completed. This is accounted for by associating a final sink node (node 50) with each project completion event and specifying that four realizations of node 50 terminate a network run.

19.3.3 Model Output and Use

Moore and Taylor [130] provide the complete input for the model described above. The intent of this section is to review the model output in order to illustrate the types of responses that can be made to the managerial concerns discussed previously.

The Q-GERT program estimates the probability that a statistics node will be released at least once during a network realization. In the network described above we can use these values to estimate project success and failure for each of the four projects. Collecting statistics at node 50 provides statistics on total network performance.

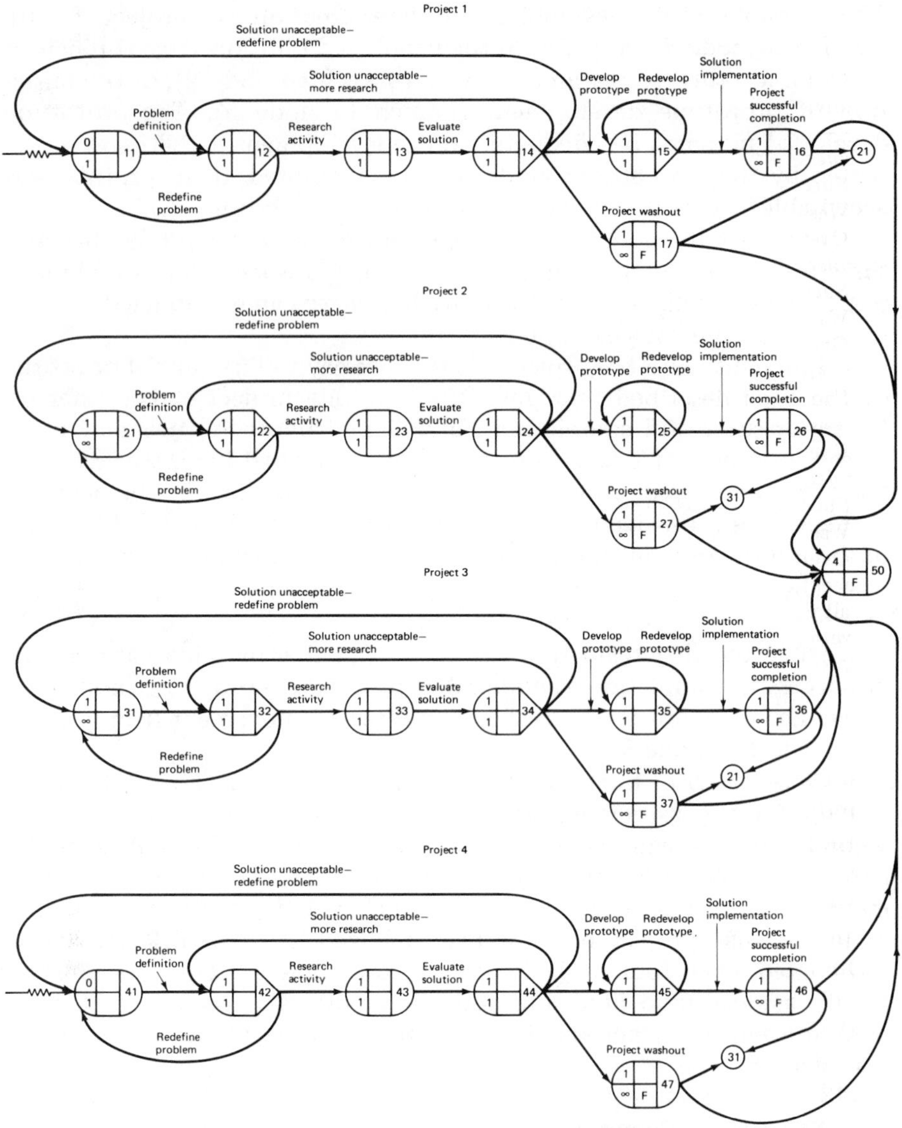

Figure 19-10 Q-GERT network of multiteam, multiproject team R&D process. Node numbers *ij* indicate project *i*, milestone *j*. (From Ref. 130.)

Mark nodes and interval statistics were used to collect statistics on the individual performance of projects 2 and 3. Tables 19-1 and 19-2 give a summary of time and cost statistics for the individual projects and the total network. Project success and failure probabilities are also given.

From Table 19-1, the expected completion time of the network is estimated at 982 days with a standard deviation of 252 days. The

TABLE 19-1 Summary of Time Statistics for Project Network

Individual Project Times	Prob.	Time (days)			
		$E(t)$	σ_t	Min. t	Max. t
Project 1					
Successful completion	0.745	419	125	277	1514
Washout	0.255	182	76	108	676
Overall project	1.000	358	154	108	1514
Project 2					
Successful completion	0.954	277	96	131	757
Washout	0.046	173	93	78	487
Overall project	1.000	272	99	78	757
Project 3					
Successful completion	0.638	717	207	453	1831
Washout	0.362	376	165	163	1218
Overall project	1.000	593	253	163	1831
Project 4					
Successful completion	0.970	371	120	208	1118
Washout	0.030	142	56	84	297
Overall project	1.000	364	125	84	1118
Successful completion: all projects	0.427	1096	224	758	2210
Overall network of projects	1.000	982	252	481	2210

Source: Ref. 130.

associated expected cost as given in Table 19-2 is $892,600 with a standard deviation of $180,600. Using these results, the R&D firm based their proposal estimates on a total duration of 1300 days at a cost of $1,100,000. These values correspond to a 90% chance of being within the time limitation and an 88% chance of being within the cost limitation, assuming that normal distributions pertain. Additionally, the firm computed a three-standard-deviation level (99.7%), which was 1738 days and $1,434,400. These values were within break-even points and this reduced the perceived risk of the projects.

One area of concern to the firm was the relatively low probability (0.427) of overall success for all four projects. Although the firm would not experience a substantial financial loss on a project failure, each failure did affect their return and affected their reputation. A sensitivity analysis of the results was conducted. The impact on the overall probability of success was studied when the probabilities for various stages of individual projects were varied. Of course, there is an attendant cost associated with such a probability improvement (Q-GERT could be used to model the R&D project necessary to improve the probabilities).

Similar probabilistic calculations were made for each individual project in terms of expected project duration and cost. This analysis revealed project 3 as the most risky, in terms of variation in project time and cost.

TABLE 19-2 Summary of Cost Statistics for Project Network

Individual Project Costs	Cost (thousands of dollars)				
	Prob	$E(c)$	σ_c	Min. c	Max. c
Project 1					
Successful completion	0.745	473.0	128.5	316.5	1147.9
Washout	0.255	195.1	72.1	129.9	663.4
Overall project	1.000	402.1	168.3	129.9	1147.9
Project 2					
Successful completion	0.954	290.8	92.1	103.5	759.1
Washout	0.046	185.6	95.5	86.0	515.7
Overall project	1.000	287.9	95.0	86.0	759.1
Project 3					
Successful completion	0.638	564.6	149.2	287.2	1247.4
Washout	0.362	329.5	119.0	129.1	827.0
Overall project	1.000	480.7	179.8	129.1	1247.4
Project 4					
Successful completion	0.970	411.5	129.4	231.9	1142.1
Washout	0.030	162.7	59.7	105.9	329.1
Overall project	1.000	404.0	134.7	105.9	1142.1
Successful completion: all projects	0.427	1008.7	148.5	726.6	1658.0
Overall network of projects	1.000	892.6	180.6	468.4	1658.0

Source: Ref. 130.

The statistical information provided by the Q-GERT network also enabled the firm to evaluate potential personnel, equipment, and capital needs. Specifically, the firm was concerned with possible bottlenecks at stages where there is a high probability of repeating a set of activities. This was particularly the case for the relatively high probabilities of failure on project 1 (0.255) and project 3 (0.362). It was felt that an influx of additional resources might alleviate this potential problem. However, after checking the original probabilistic branching estimates, it was determined that the high failure probabilities were a function of the nature of these individual projects. Thus, additional resources would not substantially reduce these probabilities. As a result, it appeared that no action should be taken to obtain extra resources. This was considered an important use of the Q-GERT model for future planning episodes and demonstrated the communication capabilities of the network procedure.

Sensitivity analysis was performed because of the subjective nature of some of the data estimates. In this way, the effect of data inaccuracies could be quantified. Key activity durations and node probabilities were identified and were adjusted to observe the overall effect on the outputs. The changes in activity durations had only a moderate effect. As expected [79,161], changes in node probabilities had a pronounced effect, especially for project 1 on the branches from node 14 and in project 3 on the branches from node 34. A sensitivity analysis was also performed to evaluate the effect of adding resources to the two teams. Based on time/cost trade-offs, the use of additional resources was not found to be economically justified.

In this example, the Q-GERT networking approach was used to evaluate different team strategies; prepare overall time and cost estimates; provide inputs to contract negotiations; plan and schedule personnel, equipment, and capital; and identify bottlenecks. The model presented above is for only one configuration, employing two research teams currently in use by the firm. With the model, alternatives were tested to determine the effect of adding additional research teams and several additional projects into the planning horizon of the firm.

19.4 TECHNOLOGY FORECASTING—
EVALUATING THE EFFECTIVENESS OF DIFFERENT
FUNDING LEVELS IN NUCLEAR FUSION RESEARCH

This study, performed by Vanston [205,206], demonstrates the use of a GERT approach to evaluate different funding alternatives of an engineering research project. This study differs from the one presented in the previous section in that detailed descriptions of the activities in the project were developed, including data collection procedures. Vanston refers to the total project approach, including the GERT networking as PAF, Partitive Analytical Forecasting. Important network concepts employed in the model are: the chance of failure in planned research, the repetition of unsuccessful tasks, and the alteration of planned activities as a result of new developments in related research efforts. The outputs from the model provide estimates of the probability of successful project completion for each funding alternative as well as time estimates for the realization of research goals. With such probability and time information for each funding alternative, decision makers can rationally evaluate and select a course of action that will best meet research objectives.

The following section gives a brief historical summary of nuclear power developments. A model of a particular project within fusion research is then described. A discussion is included on how the data were obtained to estimate probabilities and time durations. Finally, the use of the model in evaluating funding alternatives is explained. Throughout the section, a heavy reliance is made on the papers and reports of Vanston and his associates.

19.4.1 Historical Background
and Management Concerns [206]

Fusion reactors are expected to represent the third generation of nuclear power reactors. The first two generations of reactors are of the fission type which produce heat by splitting large atoms into pairs of lighter atoms. All U.S. nuclear plants are currently powered by first-generation reactors, also called "thermal" reactors. Fuel for these reactors is being used at an increasingly rapid rate. The second-generation reactor, still in a development stage, is the fast-breeder reactor, which produces more fuel atoms than it burns. Because they increase the recoverable energy from natural uranium by about 60 times, fast-breeder reactors are a prime hope for extending the world's finite fuel supplies.

The third generation of reactors will utilize the energy released when light atoms fuse together to form heavier ones. Since the early 1950s—when the uncontrolled, massive release of fusion energy in hydrogen bombs became a reality—scientists and engineers have sought to develop controlled fusion as a source of power. Although still in a developmental stage, research has made steady progress, and many researchers in the field hope to see fusion become a commercial reality by the end of the century. Although eventual success is not certain, the nature of both the obstacles and the potential solutions has become increasingly clear.

The primary fuels for fusion are deuterium and tritium, both hydrogen isotopes, that is, forms of the element with higher atomic weights than ordinary hydrogen. Deuterium can be extracted from seawater. The reactor produces tritium from the metal lithium. Controlled fusion is important because it not only promises a potentially "infinite" energy source, but also because fewer problems related to reactor operation and radioactive waste disposal are involved.

The principal obstacle to the development of fusion power is that the interacting nuclei are positively charged and strongly repel each other. Thus, to achieve fusion, the deuterium and tritium nuclei must be made to collide at velocities high enough to overcome this electrostatic repulsion. To attain this velocity, the nuclei must be raised to temperatures in the vicinity of 100 million degrees Celsius. At this temperature, the atoms are fully ionized and exist in the form of a "plasma" of positive and negative ions. Furthermore, in order to release a net output of energy, the fuel isotopes must be confined long enough to allow a large number of fusion reactions to occur.

To demonstrate that fusion power is scientifically feasible, researchers must be able to meet temperature and containment requirements simultaneously. Researchers are now working to produce the strong magnetic fields necessary to confine plasma while heating it to the high "ignition temperature" that will start the fusion process.

The Tokamak (an acronym for the Russian words for torus, room, and magnet) device is one of several potential methods for achieving magnetic confinement in a fusion reactor. Researchers differ on the exact sequence of events that might lead to a commercially successful Tokamak reactor. However, there is enough consensus to project and refine one probable scenario. Vanston et al. [206] modeled the Tokamak program to estimate the probability of success and the time to the completion of the first commercial fusion reactor.

19.4.2 Q-GERT Model Concepts

The Tokamak development project can be viewed in three successive stages: (1) the demonstration of scientific feasibility, (2) the demonstration of engineering feasibility, and (3) the completion of the first commercial reactor. Demonstrating scientific feasibility involves showing that plasma temperature and confinement requirements can be achieved simultaneously in an experimental device. The demonstration of engineering feasibility requires the development of necessary hardware for a continuously operated reactor. The final stage of the project involves the construction of the first demonstration plant designed to test economic or commercial feasibility of fusion power.

A hierarchical approach will be used to model this project to illustrate the iterative aspects of model building. This process is important to the maintenance of an overall perspective with respect to modeling objectives. In addition, communication among model builders and between model builders and decision makers is facilitated when one progresses from aggregate models to more detailed ones.

We begin with a network that models the three stages as shown in Figure 19-11. Demonstrating scientific feasibility, stage 1, requires the successful completion of plasma heating experiments as well as the testing of either a turbulent or nonturbulent heating method. This breakdown of stage 1 is modeled in Figure 19-12. The input requirement $(1,\infty)$ of node 16 specifies that the first activity to finish (either nonturbulent or turbulent heating testing) will release it. The output activity from node 16 signifies that successful completion of either activity results in successful completion of stage 1. At node 15, we require both the nonturbulent and turbulent approaches to fail before assessing a project (stage 1) failure. Plasma heating research is modeled as a single activity that can result in success or failure. Typically, this activity would be disaggregated and repeated experiments would be modeled.

To illustrate further the hierarchical approach, stages 2 and 3 are described in slightly more detail in Figure 19-13. Stage 2, demonstration of engineering feasibility, includes two parallel approaches, the deuterium–tritium (DT) process and the deuterium–deuterium (DD) process. The first of these is a fusion process using both tritium and deuterium atoms, whereas the second requires only deuterium atoms. The engineering problems of the former are easier to overcome. Since either process can lead to pilot plant design, stage 3, an "or" situation, exists so that only one input requirement is needed at node 3.

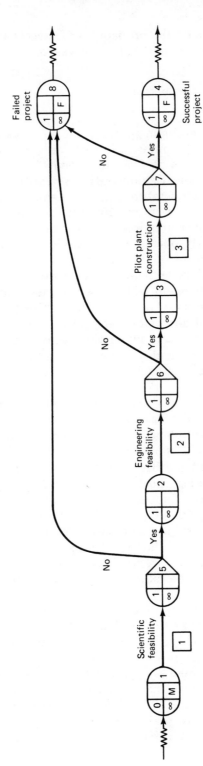

Figure 19-11 Aggregate model Tokamak project.

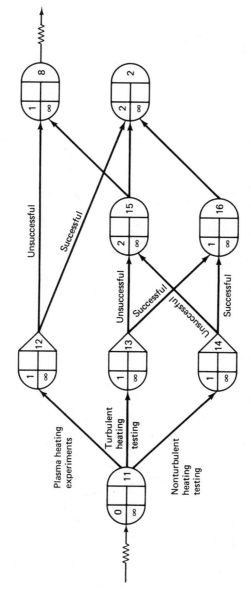

Figure 19-12 Breakdown of stage 1 activity description.

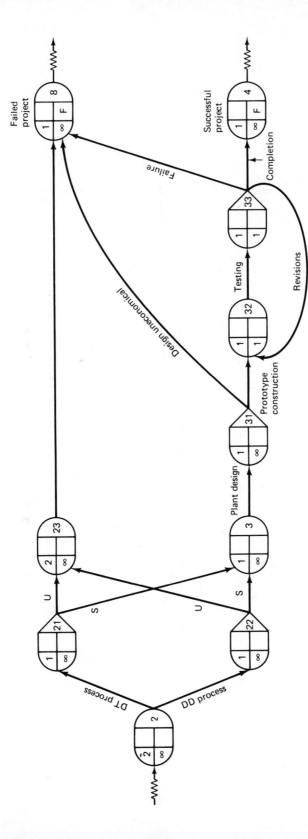

Figure 19-13 Breakdown of stages 2 and 3 of Tokamak project.

Stage 3 is modeled by the following three sequential activities: designing a pilot plant, constructing the plant, and testing the full-scale operation. There are two points of project failure identified, one in construction and one in testing. Testing has three possible outcomes: success, failure, or a requirement for retesting. For purposes of our discussion, the model need not be disaggregated further. It is clear that each process or design would consist of many subactivities. The interested reader should refer to Vanston [205], where a 300-node, 600-activity network is described. The discussion here will focus on data collection, model outputs, and their use in decision making.

19.4.3 Data Collection

To gather the activity time information and node probability data, Vanston conducted interviews with knowledgeable researchers and administrators associated with the Tokamak project.

A systematic sampling of informed judgments was designed which is akin to the Delphi family of techniques, where written questionnaires are used. Interviews allowed the interviewer to define carefully the information desired and permitted the participant to qualify answers in any manner deemed appropriate. Direct interviews are expensive in time, money, and effort, and their use must be justified based on the potential benefits.

Vanston employed the following procedure in the interviews. The interviewer presented the participant with a copy of the overall network and the specific subnetwork for his or her area of expertise. The use of the network put the data requests in an integrated context and greatly facilitated communication. The general nature of the interview was explained, together with an outline of how the information was to be used. Assurances of anonymity, if desired, were formally stated. For each activity to be estimated, the participant rated his or her experience on a scale of 1 to 3. This self-rating was later used to give added weight in favor of qualified experience. This ability to qualify their experience in each task area served to reduce the reluctance of participants to make estimates in areas where their competence was not extensive.

A major advantage of the structured interview technique was that it provided for individualized challenges; that is, the interviewer matched the participant's subjective responses against previous estimates. The interviewer must, of course, be thoroughly familiar with the network interrelationships and be alert to any inconsistencies in a participant's estimates. If a participant's estimate differed significantly from those of others, this fact was brought to his or her attention, and the participant was asked to explain possible reasons for the difference. If desired, the participant could change an estimate, but original estimates were also recorded for possible future analysis.

During an interview, the participant was asked to give three types of estimates: (1) the likelihood that each activity will be completed, (2) the probable time that will be required to complete each activity, and (3) the costs associated with such completion.

For each node with probabilistic branching, the participant was asked either to estimate the likelihood of an event's occurrence as a numerical probability or to choose the most appropriate of seven adjectival statements, such as "very probably will occur."

For each activity, the participant was asked to give a minimum and a maximum practical time for completion together with an indication of when, within that time span, the activity is most likely to be completed. This is done initially for the whole subnetwork under the assumption of a certain funding level. Later, similar estimates were requested based on different funding levels. The interviewer then compared the duration estimates for each activity for the different funding levels and brought apparent discrepancies to the attention of the participant for discussion. This technique adds a new element of self-challenge to the Delphi-type procedures.

19.4.4 Model Output and Use

In this project, there are three major milestones:

1. Demonstration of scientific feasibility
2. Completion of prototype (plasma test) reactor
3. Completion of first commercial reactor

The output of the Q-GERT program can be used directly to portray the probability of success for each of these milestones. Figures 19-14 and 19-15 are extracted from Vanston's report [205] and portray the probability of reaching the first milestone under two funding levels and the probability of successfully developing a commercial reactor as a function of time, respectively. From Figure 19-14, it is seen that increasing the funding level does not significantly increase the probability of success during early years and that the impact of increased funding occurs in the middle years (1983–1988). A decision maker must evaluate the increased cost due to higher funding against the gain of approximately five years in achieving milestone 1. Note that the increased funding results in only a slight improvement in the probability of successfully demonstrating scientific feasibility (the increase was from 0.727 to 0.758).

Figure 19-15 presents a different picture of the effect of increased funding. Here we see a large disparity in the times to complete a first commercial reactor. The difference in mean times under the two funding levels is approximately 18.8 years. In this situation, the decision maker must evaluate the investment in increased funding versus the potential payoff resulting from the more rapid availability of com-

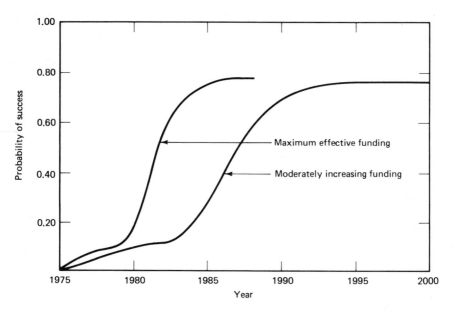

Figure 19-14 Probability of successfully demonstrating scientific feasibility under moderately increasing and maximum effective funding. (From Ref. 205.)

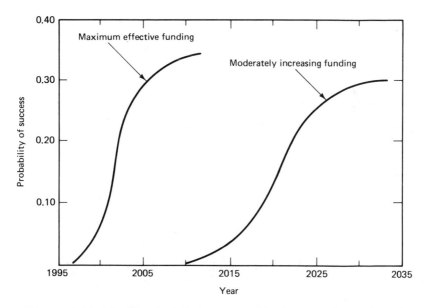

Figure 19-15 Likelihood of first commercial reactor under moderately increasing and maximum effective funding. (From Ref. 205.)

TABLE 19-3 Expected Times Required to Reach Key Milestones with Their Associated Probabilities of Success

Funding Strategy	Demonstration of Scientific Feasibility		Completion of Prototype (Plasma Test) Reactor		Completion of First Commercial Reactor	
	Mean Time in Years	Probability	Mean Time in Years	Probability	Mean Time in Years	Probability
MIF (Moderately Increasing Funding)	13.2	0.727	26.9	0.580	48.8	0.303
MEF (Maximum Effective Funding)	9.0	0.758	17.5	0.661	30.0	0.337
CPF (Continue Present Funding)	18.6	0.638	32.9	0.502	54.4	0.259
MIF with MEF of first wall R&D	13.2	0.716	24.0	0.590	45.8	0.290
MIF with MEF of blanket R&D	13.3	0.714	26.7	0.687	49.0	0.290
MIF with MEF of CMS R&D	12.6	0.742	26.7	0.666	46.5	0.314
MIF with MEF of CMS after DSF	13.2	0.732	26.9	0.652	46.9	0.325
MIF with MEF of first wall and blanket R&D	13.1	0.767	23.8	0.629	45.8	0.286
MIF with MEF of all supporting technology R&D	12.6	0.733	23.0	0.638	42.5	0.303
MIF with MEF after DSF	13.1	0.743	23.2	0.651	35.7	0.305

Source: Ref. 205.

mercial reactors. This decision is complicated by the estimate that there is only a 30 to 33% chance that the project will result in the completion of a first commercial reactor. Results like the ones presented in Figures 19-14 and 19-15 clearly identify the impact of budget allocations.

In addition to modeling the Tokamak project with two funding levels, Vanston et al. devised other funding strategies and simulated the network to determine the probability of success and mean time to success for the three milestones indicated [205]. Table 19-3 presents the results of these analyses. Soland et al. [184] extended the research described by performing optimization studies for the project described. The optimization study employed branch-and-bound techniques and attempted to maximize the likelihood that a successful demonstration reactor is completed before the end of year 2010 subject to an expenditure limit of 11 billion (1976) dollars.

19.5 SUMMARY

This chapter has presented three examples of the use of Q-GERT for project planning. The examples demonstrate that network models can be built at different levels ranging from the very aggregate to the very detailed. The examples demonstrate that in project planning there is a need for probabilistic and conditional branching, variability in the time description for project activities, and acyclic modeling capabilities. The examples clearly illustrate how the outputs from a Q-GERT analysis can assist in project planning and decision making.

19.6 EXERCISES

The exercises for Chapter 19 are to be performed for the following situation [106].

The National Center for Drug Analysis (NCDA) of the Food and Drug Administration (FDA) is an analytical laboratory specializing in the analysis of unit dosage forms of various pharmaceutical products. One of the primary functions of the center is to develop and test automated methods to be used in the analytical programs. After a decision is made to investigate a particular category of drugs, the research director begins the planning and scheduling process by reviewing the schedule of drugs, and noting the dosage levels, different product forms, the specific chemical and physical properties, and very important, the similarities to products previously analyzed. A flowchart of the research procedure used in NCDA is shown here. The flowchart provides guidelines to be used by the research chemists in performing projects related to drug testing. All of the steps, up to and including the Preparation of Reports of NCDA Methodology must be completed before the research

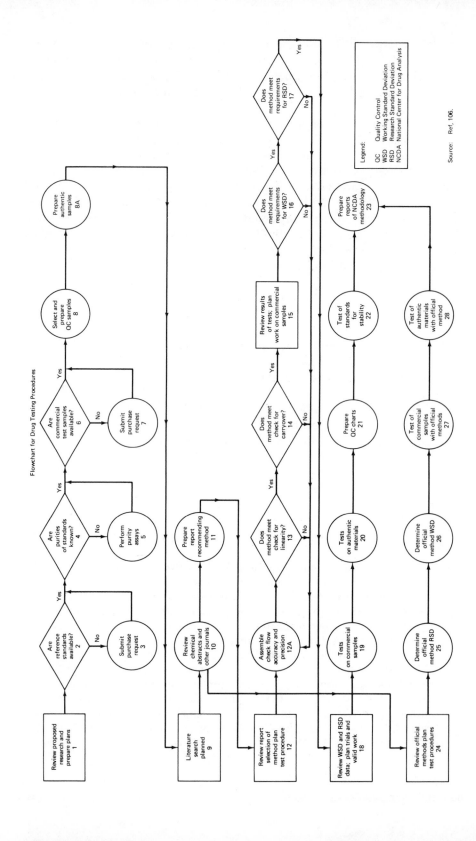

Flowchart for Drug Testing Procedures

Legend:

QC   Quality Control
WSD   Working Standard Deviation
RSD   Research Standard Deviation
NCDA National Center for Drug Analysis

Source: Ref. 106.

can be considered complete. A table of activities and time estimates is also provided.

Activity	Predecessor Activities	Time Estimates (days)		
		Opti-mistic	Most likely	Pessi-mistic
1. Review and assignment	—	1	1	1
2. Standards: supply	1	10	21	90
3. Purity known	2	1	4	10
4. Commercial samples:				
Requested	—	—	—	—
Received	1	5	10	20
5. Quality control samples prepared	4	0.25	0.5	3
6. Authentic samples prepared	3	0.5	1	3
7. Literature search	1	1	4	15
8. NCDA method: selected	7	0.5	1	5
9. Automated system assembled & checked	3	1	2	4
10. Linearity & carryover tests	3	2	5	20
11. Research standard deviation	10	0.5	1.0	2.0
12. Working standard deviation	11	10	12	15
13. Trials on commercial samples	5, 12	2	4	6
14. Validation samples	6, 13	1	2	3
15. Prepare quality control charts	14, 21	0.2	0.5	1
16. Determine standard stability	3	10	14	21
17. Prepare standard control chart	16	0.2	0.5	1
18. Official method: research standard deviation	3	0.5	1	2
19. Official method: working standard deviation	18	5	12	15
20. Trials on commercial samples	5, 18	2	4	6
21. Validation samples	6, 20	1	2	3
22. Preparation of reports: methodology	15, 17	3	5	10

19-1. (a) Without reference to the list of activities, convert the flowchart to a PERT diagram. List all assumptions required.
    (b) Prepare a PERT diagram from the list of activities.
    (c) Perform a PERT analysis on the PERT networks developed in parts (a) and (b).

19-2. (a) Develop a Q-GERT network from the flowchart for drug testing procedures. List any additional data requirements for the Q-GERT model.
   (b) Develop a Q-GERT model from the list of activities.
   (c) Compare the Q-GERT models developed in parts (a) and (b).
   (d) Develop procedures to obtain estimates for the additional information
required for the Q-GERT network. Assume values for the required additional data and perform a Q-GERT analysis.

19-3. Specify which activities you would allocate additional personnel or dollars in
order to shorten the project duration. Perform a Q-GERT analysis assuming
that the activities selected have been shortened. Select activity times so that
there are two or more paths that have approximately the same expected
completion time. Perform a Q-GERT analysis to estimate the criticality
indices for each activity.

VI

Network Graphics

20

Network Graphics

20.1 INTRODUCTION

Throughout this book, systems, decision situations, and problem statements have been portrayed in a network form. The graphical concepts of Q-GERT have aided in the understanding and communication aspects related to these areas. The advantages of graphical modeling and analysis have been presented. In this chapter we describe how the fast emerging field of computer graphics can be used to support the Q-GERT philosophy of systems analysis.

There are three main areas where graphics can supplement a Q-GERT analysis:

1. Assist in building Q-GERT models
2. Portray the operation of the system on the Q-GERT network
3. Display the outputs from the Q-GERT processor

Each of these areas is described in the following sections. The feasibility of the concepts presented has been established and in all cases prototypes of the graphics capability have been designed and developed. With the advent of more advanced and standardized graphics hardware and software, an integrated graphics capability for Q-GERT can be expected.

20.2 GRAPHICS FOR MODEL BUILDING

The current state of computer graphics allows symbols to be defined, placed on a computer screen, moved to a desired location, and connected with other symbols. Thus, Q-GERT nodes and branches can be defined and a model builder can, while sitting in front of a terminal, use the defined Q-GERT symbols to build a Q-GERT network model directly on the terminal screen. By building Q-GERT models at a terminal, it is possible to edit and revise the network directly, to prepare Q-GERT data input statements interactively, and to store the graphical network and input statements describing the network in a file or directly in a data base. A graphics model building system for Q-GERT, called Q-GRAF, has been developed by Sabuda [167].

Sabuda's approach to graphical model building employs a hierarchical structure. The model builder first selects a particular aspect or module of model building from a prescribed menu of options. Once a particular module is selected, another menu of choices is presented regarding the details of the module. This sequence of presenting a menu of options, requesting model builder decision making, presenting detailed options, and so on, provides for an interactive model building procedure. In subsequent sections of this chapter, the types of options available at each level of model building are described.

20.2.1 Module Selection Options

Eight basic modules were designed in Q-GRAF, and these are depicted in Table 20-1. When a model builder starts the model building process and requests the Q-GRAF program to be initiated, the command module selection options appear on the terminal screen. The model builder selects one of the eight options shown in Table 20-1 by keying in a value from 1 to 8. Once a module is selected, the options within that module are considered. When the model builder exits from a particular module, the module selection options are again displayed. A general description of each module is given next.

TABLE 20-1 Command Module Selection
Options

Keyset Value	Module
1	CREATE
2	EDIT
3	RESET
4	CHG. VIEWS
5	STORE
6	LOAD
7	SIM
8	EXIT

The CREATE module is used to construct Q-GERT networks by allowing the model builder to select nodes or branches and to draw the Q-GERT network directly on the terminal screen. Data values are also directly put on the Q-GERT network so that the data input statements for each Q-GERT symbol can be automatically prepared.

The EDIT module is used to replace or delete nodes and activities, to reposition them, or to change Q-GERT data. When a network is edited, the revised network is displayed automatically. The EDIT module may be used after any part of the Q-GERT network has been constructed. Thus, a portion of the network can be created, the CREATE module exited, and the EDIT module entered. Following an exit from the EDIT module, the CREATE module can be reentered and additional network portions created.

The RESET and EXIT modules provide model building restart and stopping options, respectively. The STORE module specifies that a created network is to be saved on a file, whereas the LOAD module specifies that a previously saved network is to be retrieved and made available for display on the terminal screen. The change view (CHG. VIEW) module allows the model builder to modify the dimensions of the display of the network by zooming in or zooming out or by graphically translating the network to the right, left, up, or down. The simulation (SIM) module is used to display dynamically the simulation of the network. The outputs from the Q-GERT processor are used to portray the movement of transactions over the graphical network. The movement of transactions over the activities and through the nodes provides a dynamic view of the operation of the system that is being modeled by the network.

In the following sections, the CREATE, EDIT, CHG.VIEWS, and SIM module selection options are described in more detail. Further description of the other module options is not warranted, as the functions performed by them are standard.

20.2.2 Creating Networks

In the CREATE module, the model builder has the option of selecting a Q-GERT symbol and placing it on the screen. In the Q-GRAF prototype, only the basic node and Q-node types were included. A menu of the symbol options available in the CREATE module is shown in Figure 20-1. These options are portrayed at the bottom of the terminal screen when building models.

At this point, a short description of the interface between the model builder and the Q-GRAF program may assist in understanding the ensuing discussion. The interface is designed to allow the model builder to focus his or her attention on the screen while manipulating input devices that provide decisions regarding the selection and placement of symbols. An SRI "mouse" is used to control the position of a

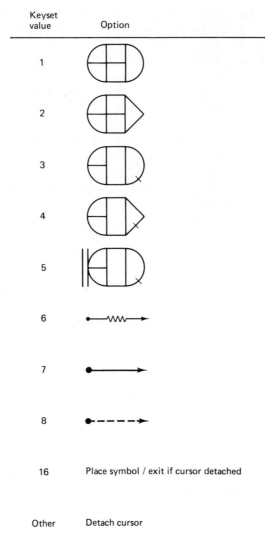

Keyset value	Option
1	
2	
3	
4	
5	
6	
7	
8	
16	Place symbol / exit if cursor detached
Other	Detach cursor

Figure 20-1 CREATE menu.

cursor on the screen. Basically, the SRI mouse provides analog input which corresponds to a position on the screen as the mouse moves across a horizontal surface. The cursor has multiple functions. In building a network, it is normally attached to a Q-GERT symbol and is used to move the symbol across the screen until the model builder decides on a specific position. In the EDIT mode, the cursor is used to select an existing symbol for editing or data input purposes. That is, placement of the cursor over an existing symbol specifies that the symbol is to be edited. By depressing the center button on the mouse, the model builder specifies that a change to the data describing the symbol is to be made. Data input specifications are made by the model builder through

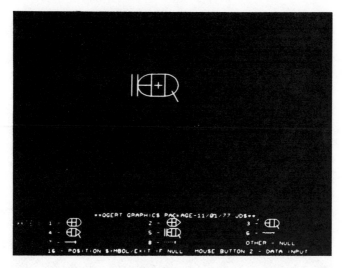

Figure 20-2 Selecting and positioning nodes.

the typewriter keyboard associated with the terminal. A third input device is a five-fingered keyset which is used to select options.

Referring back to Figure 20-1, an option is selected by specifying a keyset value. This causes a symbol to appear on the screen at the position defined by the cursor. Moving the cursor causes the symbol to move on the screen. The position of the symbol is fixed through the selection of a keyset value of 16. Figure 20-2 is a picture of the placement of a Q-node with blocking capability on the screen. Note that this is the first symbol being placed on the screen and that the CREATE options are shown at the bottom of the figure. After a node is positioned on the screen, default values associated with that node are placed in the appropriate locations of the Q-GERT symbol.

In the CREATE mode, option 7 places an activity on the screen. The menu of options at the bottom of the screen is replaced with the options shown in Table 20-2, which correspond to the positioning of an activity. In other words, a lower level in the hierarchical tree of model building has been activated. In the activity positioning mode, the cursor is used to select the point at which the line representing an activity is to begin. By placing the cursor on the right side of a node and selecting

TABLE 20-2 ACTIVITY Menu

Keyset Value	Option
1	Attach/position activity
4	Restart current activity
16	Exit
Center mouse button—data input	

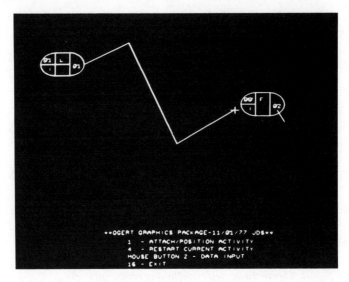

Figure 20-3 Sketching activities.

option 1, a model builder establishes the beginning point for a line. The line representing the activity is connected to the node and movement of the cursor prescribes the length of the line. Thus, as the cursor is moved, the line representing the activity starts at the start node specified and projects out to the position of the cursor. In graphics terminology this is called a "rubber-banded" line. By selecting option 1 again, a node at which the activity is to terminate or a breakpoint in the graphical display of the activity is set. A line with two breakpoints which connects nodes 1 and 2 on the screen is displayed in Figure 20-3. An example displaying a network built directly at a terminal is shown in Figure 20-4. Q-GRAF also makes it easy to draw networks by automatically aligning nodes and by attaching lines to nodes if they are within a specified tolerance.

20.2.3 Editing Networks

The modification of networks created using Q-GRAF is accomplished by selecting the EDIT option (keyset value 2) on the module selection menu. When this occurs, the EDIT menu shown in Table 20-3 is displayed. The options for editing are to select a symbol for editing

TABLE 20-3 EDIT Menu

Keyset Value	Option
1	Select symbol
16	Exit
Center mouse button—data input	

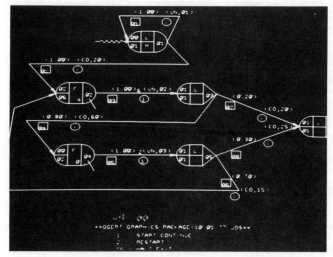

Figure 20-4 Q-GERT model on the terminal screen.

through the specification of keyset value 1 or editing the data input through the depressing of the button on the SRI mouse. Again, option 16 exits from this mode and would cause a return to the module selection menu.

By moving the cursor and pressing a 1 on the keyset, a symbol is selected. If a node is selected, the node, all associated activities, and balking routes are brightened on the screen. This is shown in Figure 20-5, where the repositioning of node 1 is illustrated. As seen in the figure, node 1 has been moved to a new location; however, the old

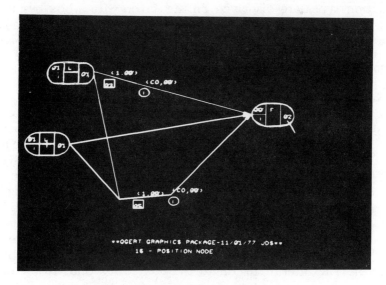

Figure 20-5 Moving nodes.

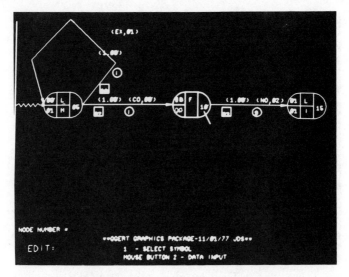

Figure 20-6 Editing data for a node.

location remains on the screen and is drawn with brightness of a lower intensity to distinguish it from the editing change that has been made.

When editing data inputs, the symbol to be edited is selected by the cursor and a sequence of questions is asked of the model builder. For example, if a node is selected, the model builder will be given a chance to change its node number. This is illustrated in Figure 20-6. In this case, a specific number would be input through the terminal keyboard. When all possible choices can be specified, the choices are listed. For example, when specifying a distribution type, all possible distribution types are displayed on the screen with a box beside each choice. The placement of the cursor within a box identifies the distribution type to be selected.

20.2.4 Viewing Network Segments

Networks may require more display area than the available space on the terminal screen. By displaying only a portion of a created network, Q-GRAF avoids this potential pitfall. Sections of the network can be moved off by shifting the midpoint of the screen to the left or right. Only that portion of the network which has not been shifted off the screen is displayed. In addition, the size of the network can be reduced or expanded. The commands used to perform the changing of the position or the size of the network are shown in Table 20-4. These options are displayed when the CHG.VIEW module is selected.

For the zoom-in and zoom-out options, the network size is selected by creating a box from the lines emanating from two settings of the cursor. The interior region to the box corresponds to the desired

TABLE 20-4 CHANGE VIEW Menu

Keyset Value	Option
1	Zoom in
2	Zoom out
3	Move screen center
4	View all
16	Exit

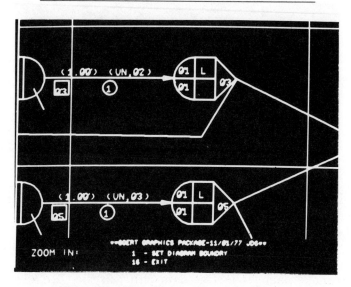

Figure 20-7 Illustration of zoom-in feature.

portion of the network to be displayed. An example of the zoom feature is shown in Figure 20-7. The zoom-out option allows for presenting more of the network, that is, making the elements of the network smaller. It is accomplished by repeatedly returning to the last display pictured.

The network can be translated by moving the center of the screen by selecting option 3 of the CHG.VIEW menu. The movement of the network to the left is illustrated in Figure 20-8. By continually moving the network to the left, larger networks can be built by adding new symbols to the right of the existing network. To view the entire network constructed to date, option 4 is selected and the network is redrawn on the screen to include all nodes and branches created. Again, option 16 is selected to exit from the CHG.VIEW module.

20.2.5 Data Input

Throughout the preceding sections, the procedures for inputting data for the network model on the screen were referenced. In this

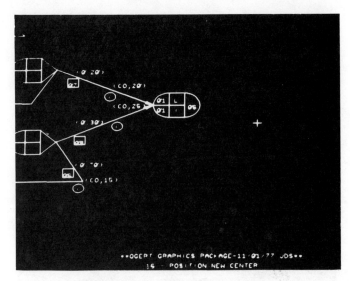

Figure 20-8 Translating networks.

section we present all the data input procedures. The data input procedures do not follow the hierarchical tree structure previously described, as it is necessary to allow a model builder to prescribe data values whenever he desires.

The basic approach in Q-GRAF is to display automatically the default data associated with each network symbol and to allow the model builder to make changes in this data either in the CREATE or EDIT modules. The selection of which piece of information to change on a created network is made by touching the piece of data with the cursor and depressing the center button on the mouse. Q-GRAF responds to this input by brightening the symbol containing that information and then prompting the model builder for the appropriate input. If numeric data are required, this prompt consists of the definition of the piece of data being changed, followed by an equal sign. By typing in the desired data, the network model is changed accordingly. A carriage return signal indicates that no change is to be made.

All numeric data are verified and, if admissible, the correction is made, which is then displayed to the model builder. If an illogical or uncorrectable data input or network construct is employed, an error message is displayed on the screen and a pause for correction is initiated.

If the required data input is nonnumeric, a display of the available options is given on the lower left-hand side of the screen. A selection is made by placing the cursor in the desired box representing the alternative desired. The design of the data input algorithms not only facilitates the preparation of the data input for Q-GERT, but also eliminates the need for extensive documentation regarding field definitions and other input specifications.

20.3 GRAPHICS FOR PORTRAYING SIMULATION TRACES

After a model is created using Q-GRAF, it is possible to request a simulation of the model by the Q-GERT processor. This is accomplished by selecting the SIM option on the module selection menu. When this option is selected, an interactive dialogue to define the fields for the GEN statement is initiated. A request can then be made to prepare and store the total data input for the Q-GERT model developed. A printout on a line printer of the data input is also made. If it is desired to display the running of the model, that is, a display of transaction movement through the network, a request for a trace on the GEN statement must be made. A trace contains all the information required to display transaction movement through the network. This trace is then used to display system operations after a simulation is completed.

In Figure 20-9, a picture of the screen displaying the operation of a nine-server, single-queue model is shown. Displayed on the screen is the current simulation time, which, for the illustration, is 14.70. The nine-server activity is represented by a line from node 10 to node 15 that has five segments. The broken branch helps to illustrate the movement of the transactions. Each transaction is represented by a transaction number. Thus, as depicted in Figure 20-9, transactions with the numbers 5, 7, 4, 3, 6, 10, 11, 12, and 2 are flowing over the service activity. Transaction 5 has the greatest fraction of its service time completed, and transaction 2 is just starting service. The rate at which the transactions flow over the activity is inversely proportional to the activity duration. Thus, a transaction with a long activity duration moves slowly over the line. In Q-node 10, below the queue ranking

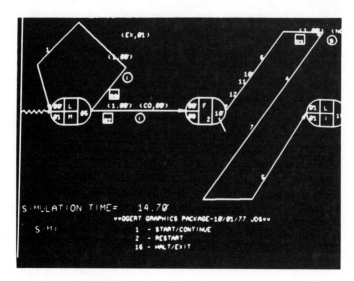

Figure 20-9 Transactions traversing a nine-server, single-queue model.

rule, the current number in the queue is shown. At time 14.70 there were two transactions in Q-node 10.

The arrival of the next transaction is modeled on the self-loop around node 5, where transaction 1 is seen returning to node 5. When transaction 1 returns to node 5, transactions will start on the two activities emanating from node 5: one representing the next arrival and the other representing a customer entering the system. Since the time to traverse the branch from node 5 to node 10 is zero, an instantaneous transfer occurs.

The viewing of the display of the trace information on the screen is an impressive sight. A keen understanding of the operation of the system as modeled by the Q-GERT network is obtained. Refined model building and communication regarding system operation among managers, engineers, and model builders is facilitated. Q-GRAF has demonstrated the feasibility of building Q-GERT models at a terminal, and the value of presenting graphical simulations of a model. Further developments of Q-GRAF-like techniques for the next generation of computer graphics equipment are forthcoming.

20.4 GRAPHICS FOR DISPLAYING OUTPUTS

In the discussion of Q-GERT outputs in Chapter 5, two types of variables were identified: variables on which observations were made, and variables which maintained a value over a period of time. For the former type of variable, a histogram displays graphically the frequency with which the values of the variable are within defined intervals. Printouts of the histograms are used to picture the underlying distribution associated with the observations. A discussion of the printing of histograms is given in Section 20.4.1.

For time-persistent variables, an understanding of their time-varying behavior can be obtained by plotting the variable as it changes during the simulation. These plots provide information regarding the dynamic behavior of the system and provide extensive information for understanding system operation and for redesigning the system for improved performance. A discussion of the plotting of time-persistent variables is given in Section 20.4.2.

20.4.1 Graphing Histograms

A program called AID has been written that can accept histograms generated by the Q-GERT processor as input [137]. A curve is drawn which depicts the relative frequency associated with the observed values. Figure 20-10 provides an illustration of a curve that was fit to histogram data.

There are many options associated with fitting a curve to observed

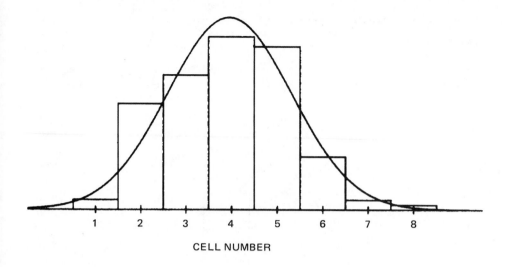

CELL NUMBER

CELL STATISTICS

CELL NO.	OBS. FREQ	REL. FREQ	CUM. FREQ	UPPER BOUND
1	2	.0147	.0147	51.54
2	22	.1618	.1765	53.13
3	28	.2059	.3824	54.73
4	36	.2647	.6471	56.32
5	34	.25	.8971	57.92
6	11	.0808	.9779	59.51
7	8	.0147	.9926	61.11
8	1	.0073	1.	62.7
	136	CELL WIDTH = 1.595		

SAMPLE STATISTICS:

MEAN =   55.46

STANDARD DEVIATION =   2.162

MINIMUM VALUE =   49.94

MAXIMUM VALUE =   62.7

HYPOTHESIZED DISTRIBUTION: NORMAL

PARAMETERS:

MEAN =   55.46

STANDARD DEVIATION =   2.162

NEW PARAMETERS:

MEAN =   55.46

STANDARD DEVIATION =   1.8

Figure 20-10 Sequence of displays showing the fitting of a distribution.

HYPOTHESIZED DISTRIBUTION: NORMAL

PARAMETERS:

    MEAN =   55.46

    STANDARD DEVIATION =   2.162

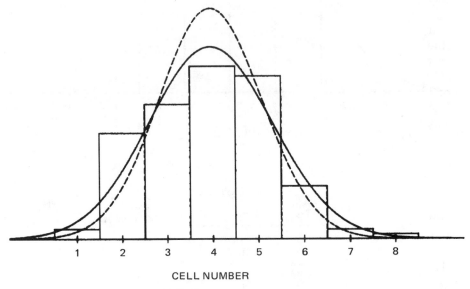

CELL NUMBER

SOLID LINE—OLD CURVE

DASH LINE—NEW CURVE

SAVE PLOT:

  1-YES, 0-NO : 0

Figure 20-10 (Continued)

values. One procedure for fitting a curve is to specify the form of the equation for the curve and to use the observed values to estimate the parameters of the curve. For example, a normal density function could be prescribed for the data and then the mean and the standard deviation would be estimated in order that a specific curve be drawn. The AID program has been developed to allow the standard distribution types provided in Q-GERT to be selected as candidates for fitting the observed data.

Procedures are also included in AID to allow the analyst to modify the curve in accordance with his or her perception of the discrepancy between the observed values and the curve fitted to the observed values. Upon inputting the desired changes to the curve, the picture on the screen is altered so that the effects of the change can be assessed graphically. A sequence of curves drawn for the same data is shown in Figure 20-10.

Also included in the program are tests of goodness-of-fit relating the curve and the observed data. The chi-square and Kolomogorov–Smirnov (K-S) goodness-of-fit test statistics are calculated by the program. These test statistics can be used to assess statistically the validity of a distribution type to represent the data.

The AID program for fitting curves to histograms allows an analyst to investigate interactively ways of summarizing simulation output values. Through the use of graphical techniques, insight into the characteristics of the outputs and the observations is obtained. The graphical analysis is seen as an adjunct to standard statistical procedures and is not intended to replace them. Experience has shown that the coupling of graphical techniques to statistical procedures results in improved analyses. An illustration of the graphical form for the K-S test is shown in Figure 20-11.

20.4.2 Plotting of Q-GERT Variables

The plotting of time-persistent variables is an excellent method for understanding how these variables change over time. Variables that are candidates for plotting are:

1. The number in the queue
2. The number of servers in use
3. The number of resources available and in use
4. The number of transactions in a network or subnetwork
5. The waiting times in queues
6. The time a transaction is in the network

The first three variables are maintained by the Q-GERT processor. The last three are not maintained in Q-GERT and would require the use of a user function to obtain their values over time.

For the number of transactions in a network, user functions would be employed at every source node to increase the number of transactions in the network at transaction arrival times. At every departure point for a transaction, this number would be decreased. A similar procedure could be used for determining the number of transactions in any portion of the network model.

Two procedures have been used to obtain plots of Q-GERT time-persistent variables. One method employs a plot subroutine which is called whenever a Q-GERT variable changes value. Alternatively, the data that are used to print a trace of a run can also be used to drive a plotting routine. In the latter mode, separate plots of variables of interest or combinations of variables can be obtained.

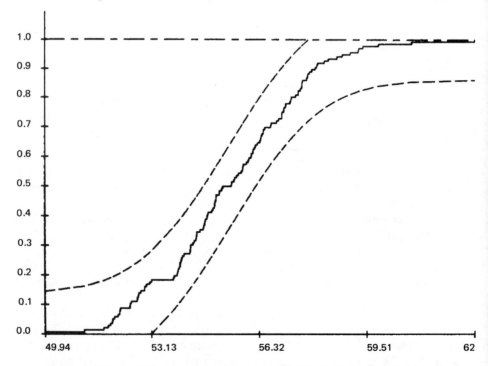

KOLMOGOROV-SMIRNOV TEST

SAMPLE SIZE =	136
LEVEL OF SIGNIFICANCE =	.01
CRITICAL VALUE =	.1398
K-S TEST STATISTIC =	.0435

THE K-S TEST STATISTIC IS
LESS THAN THE CRITICAL VALUE.

THERE IS NO SAMPLE EVIDENCE AGAINST THE
NULL HYPOTHESIS:

DISTRIBUTION:	NORMAL

PARAMETERS:

MEAN =	55.46
STANDARD DEVIATION =	2.162

Figure 20-11 Graphical representation of the Kolomogorov–Smirnov test.

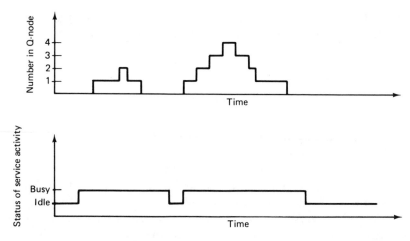

Figure 20-12 Time history of a service activity and its queue.

Figure 20-12 presents a plot of the number of transactions in a Q-node and the status of a following service activity. From the plot it can be seen that queue buildups are related to an increased rate of arrivals and potentially long service times. A plot of server utilization followed by the number in a queue that follows the server is displayed in Figure 20-13. In this situation, the times at which the server

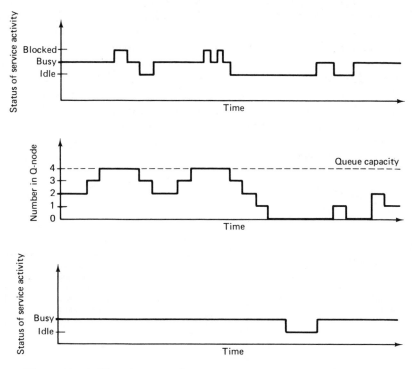

Figure 20-13 Time history of server–queue–server network segment.

is blocked, idle or busy are shown. SIMCHART [46] has been used in conjunction with the Q-GERT processor to plot time-persistent variables.

20.5 GRAPHICS AND DECISION MAKING

In a system analysis project in which Q-GERT is employed, there are three distinct functions: model building, output analysis, and decision making. These functions can be performed by a single individual or by a group of individuals. To avoid confusion between the function being performed and the individual performing the function, we will use the term "player" to describe the model builder, systems analyst, or decision maker. Thus, we will talk in terms of there being three players on a systems analysis project even though there may be 1, 2, or 40 individuals on the project.

In systems analysis, communication among the players is extremely important. A schematic diagram depicting the interaction among the players and the types of inputs to and outputs from the players is shown in Figure 20-14. Let us consider some of the joint interactions between each of the players.

The model builder and systems analyst work together to explain plot and trace outputs in terms of the model constructs. By explaining the statistical variation of the outputs in terms of the model, model revisions can be proposed. Such interaction facilitates the determination that the model performs as it was designed. This process corresponds to model verification. By graphically viewing the model, outputs from the model, and variations in the outputs due to changes in the model, the systems analyst can assess the sensitivity of the model even though he or she did not build it. Through the use of computer graphics, the systems analyst does not have to do everything and can rely more heavily on the model builder. The lack of reliance on other project partic-

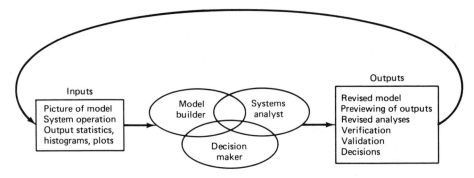

Figure 20-14 Project players, inputs, and outputs.

ipants can be a shortcoming of large systems and industrial engineering projects.

The main interaction between the model builder and the decision maker involves viewing traces of system operation. By illustrating system operation on a network model, the decision maker obtains an understanding of the modeling constructs. He or she gains confidence in the model builder's ability and sees how the modeling concepts relate to the system under study. With such information, the decision maker can propose changes to the model to make it reflect more accurately system operations. In this way, the decision maker is brought into the model building process, which is extremely advantageous for the model builder. Not only is the model builder's work better understood, but it captures the decision maker's experience, knowledge, and understanding of the system. This interaction between the model builder and decision maker is oriented toward demonstrating that the model reflects reality. This is part of the validation phase of systems analysis and leads to the decision maker having greater confidence in the outputs from the model. With increased confidence, the decision maker will be more forceful in decision making and implementation. The end result is a greater use of the model and its outputs, which for many model builders is sufficient to demonstrate validity.

The last set of interactions is between the decision maker and the systems analyst. Communication between these players involves the examination of histograms, plots, and statistical estimates. By storing the outputs from the simulation using a data base system such as SDL [190], statistical analyses for a set of runs can be revised or investigated from different points of view. By examining the outputs together and recognizing that a data base supports both outputs and other types of information, conditional analyses can be requested by the decision maker and can be easily performed by the systems analyst. Since both the decision maker and systems analyst have communicated with the model builder about the modeling details, they will be comfortable about requesting new runs, model changes, and model embellishments.

The foregoing discussion portrays some of the communications and interactions made possible by computer graphics [218]. Q-GERT as a network/graphic modeling language encourages and fosters such interactions.

20.6 ALC AIRCRAFT MAINTENANCE MODEL

Musselman and Hannan, working in conjunction with Lt. Col. R. Mortenson and his staff at McClellan AFB, developed an integrated network/data base/graphics model of aircraft maintenance for an Air

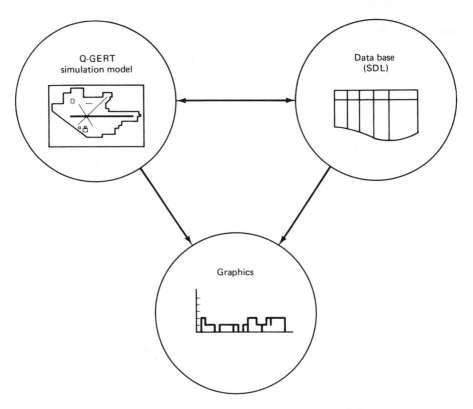

Figure 20-15 ALC aircraft maintenance model.

Logistics Center (ALC). The model is described in this section, with emphasis on the integration and graphics aspects of the project [136].

The ALC Aircraft Maintenance Model, depicted in Figure 20-15, is composed of three major components: a Q-GERT network model, an SDL data base, and a graphics capability. The Q-GERT network describes all the possible paths an aircraft can take in flowing through the ALC aircraft maintenance process.

SDL manages the data needed to run the model as well as to describe its performance. Both the incoming aircraft schedule and the aircraft status report are stored in this data base. The incoming aircraft schedule specifies when aircraft are scheduled to arrive at the facility. This schedule drives the ALC Aircraft Maintenance Model in the sense that the next aircraft arrival to the model is determined on the basis of this report. Included in this report are the aircraft's identifier (referred to as its MDS), tail number, work package number, arrival date, and scheduled completion date. An example of an incoming aircraft schedule is shown in Figure 20-16.

The aircraft status report states what the current load condition is at each work center within the facility. Figure 20-17 shows an example

MDS	Tail number	Work package	Arrival date	Scheduled completion date
FB111A	8241	23	140	297
CT39A	4488	60	140	341
CT39A	658	60	140	341
F111A	7113	3	145	217
F111D	8090	15	145	263
F4D	774	71	147	176
A10	264	55	480	523

Figure 20-16 Incoming aircraft schedule.

MDS	Tail number	Work package	Arrival time	Scheduled completion time	Current location	Remaining service time
F111A	7104	2	111	206	MOD–ASSY	6
FB111A	7163	24	90	222	MOD–ASSY	18
CT39A	653	61	1	143	FLTPREPF	3
F106A	40	83	73	151	FNLSL	2
F4D	701	70	7	160	PAINT	6
A10	205	50	106	181	MOD–ASSY	27

Figure 20-17 Aircraft status report.

of this type of a report. For any aircraft currently in the system, the status report states its MDS, tail number, work package number, arrival time to the ALC, scheduled completion time, current work center location, and the remaining service time at the work center. When the ALC model begins execution, this report is read in and the work centers are loaded in accordance with this report.

The data base also contains the data needed to describe the performance of the ALC maintenance system. As the model is executing, information concerning queue status, facility space status, aircraft work center arrival, and start and completion times is stored. To display and interpret this information, the graphics component of the model is used. The graphic capability provides modelers, analysts, and decision makers with information to recognize and compare key characteristics in the data patterns. The information obtained from a run is stored in the data base and is used to produce a standard Q-GERT output report,

TABLE 20-5 Selected Output Performance Measures

Q-GERT output
  Time in system
  Number in facility queue
  Waiting time in facility queue
  Number of aircraft unable to go directly to paint work center
  Facility utilization
Data base output
  Aircraft work center scheduled
  Identification of aircraft in a facility queue
  Schedule/actual completion time, time in system, total waiting time
Graphic output
  Facility utilization over time
  Number in facility queue over time
  Individual aircraft trace
  Time in system by aircraft type
  Ability to meet deadlines
  Picture of aircraft movement through a facility
  Diagram of the base

specialized data base output reports, and various graphical outputs. Table 20-5 lists selected outputs from each of these areas.

The graphics module contains the capability to interactively fit distributions to histogram outputs from the Q-GERT program. This enables an analyst to test different distribution types and parameters for a specific distribution at a computer terminal as described in Section 20.4.1. The graphics plotting capability described in Section 20.4.2 was used to display selected values of variables over time. An example of this type of output is shown in Figure 20-18.

Other interesting plots showed the time in the system for an aircraft at its time of departure by displaying a vertical line whose length represented the time in the system. This plot depicted correlations between aircraft system time as a function of Julian days and amount of congestion. A similar plot was used to display the ability to meet deadlines. For this situation the length of the vertical line was related to the amount of time the aircraft was early or late, with the former displayed above the horizontal axis and the latter below the axis. Another plot that was of interest to decision makers displayed the movement of aircraft through a facility model of the base. By numbering in sequence each location visited, a trace of locations was viewed on the terminal screen. This pictorial view of system operation provided understanding to the analysts and helped to verify the model for the decision makers.

To demonstrate the ability of the system to be functional in a dynamic operating environment, several scenarios were developed. The purpose of these scenarios was twofold. The first was to demonstrate the ability to make changes to various model parameters which re-

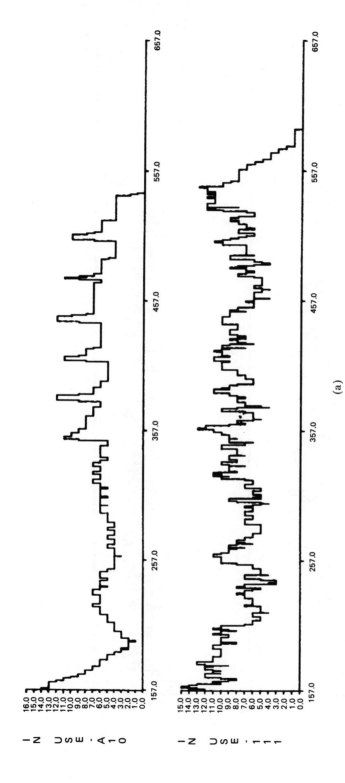

Figure 20-18 Time-varying behavior of selected variables for scenario 1, aircraft maintenance model.

(a)

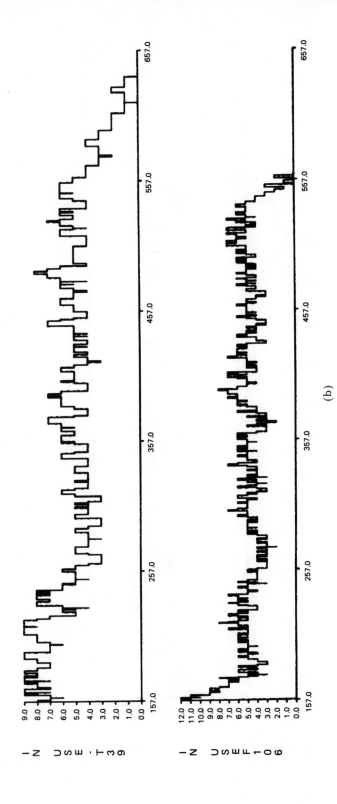

Figure 20-18 (Continued)

496

TABLE 20-6 Scenario Description and Summary

Scenario	Description
1	This scenario is the basic model which was initially provided; it is run using the system configuration, initial status, schedule and work flow days described by historical data
2	This scenario depicts the system behavior when there is a 25% reduction in the work flow days at the paint work center; this demonstrates the ability to change work flow times at the work centers
3	This scenario depicts the system behavior when five A10s that are currently in the system require additional time at the MOD CENTER; this demonstrates the ability to change the initial system status
4	This scenario depicts the system behavior when six A10s are rescheduled to avoid a bottleneck in the system; this demonstrates the ability to change an aircraft's schedule
5	This scenario depicts the system behavior when the space at the paint work center is reduced from 4 to 3 units; this demonstrates the ability to change the system configuration

flected changes in the operating environment at the ALC maintenance facility. Typical changes included:

1. Work flow times at work centers
2. Current system status
3. Schedule changes
4. Work center space availability

The second purpose for developing the scenarios was to demonstrate the ability to evaluate the effects of these changes through direct comparisons of system behavior at the work centers. Table 20-6 describes the scenarios that were developed. A demonstration of outputs that depicted system behavior at the various work centers was presented, and the interaction between analysts, modelers and decision makers was extensive. The project clearly showed that graphics used in conjunction with modeling and simulation will result in improved decision making.

20.7 SUMMARY

In this chapter, the feasibility of employing computer graphics within systems analysis studies has been demonstrated. The basic forms of outputs and how they may be used in systems engineering projects have been portrayed. The degree of improvement in decision making that is possible through the use of computer graphics is unlimited. Clearly, better decision making results when a decision maker has confidence in a model and its attendant statistical analysis.

20.8 EXERCISES

20-1. Design a graphic capability as described in Section 20.2 for the computing system with which you work.

20-2. The types of traces indicated in Section 20.3 present one type of display of Q-GERT outputs. Different types of traces that could be produced organized according to a specific Q-GERT concept are: nodal, activity, event, resource, and transaction number. Specify how each of these traces could be used for communication between decision makers, analysts, and model builders.

20-3. Discuss the advantages and disadvantages associated with a graphical system for portraying the outputs from a network simulation. Include in your answer a discussion of the data base requirements, competence of the decision maker, and the display equipment requirements.

20-4. Describe how the procedures and outputs discussed in Section 20.6 for the ALC Aircraft Maintenance Model can be used within the manufacturing environment to improve the scheduling of work orders.

20-5. Develop a decision-making support system that is network based that allows a production supervisor to access a data base to perform analyses on problems associated with order releases, job scheduling, and machine allocations.

References

1. Adam, E. E., Jr., and R. J. Ebert, *Production and Operations Management: Concepts, Models and Behavior.* Englewood Cliffs, NJ: Prentice-Hall, Inc., 1978.

2. Albala, A., "Stage Approach for the Evaluation and Selection of R&D Projects," *IEEE Transactions on Engineering Management,* Vol. EM-22, No. 4, November 1975, pp. 153–164.

3. American National Standards Institute, *American National Standard FORTRAN,* ANSI X3.9-1966.

4. Archibald, R. D., *Managing High-Technology Programs and Projects.* New York: John Wiley & Sons, Inc., 1976, pp. 204–215.

5. Archibald, R. D., and R. L. Villoria, *Network-Based Management Systems (PERT/CPM).* New York: John Wiley & Sons, Inc., 1968.

6. Arisawa, S., and S. E. Elmaghraby, "Optimal Time–Cost Trade-Offs in GERT Networks," *Management Science,* Vol. 18, No. 11, July 1972, pp. 589–599.

7. Auterio, V. J., "Q-GERT Simulation of Air Terminal Cargo Facilities," *Proc. Pittsburgh Modeling and Simulation Conference,* Vol. 5, 1974, pp. 1181–1186.

8. Auterio, V. J., and S. D. Draper, "Aerial Refueling Military Airlift Forces: An Economic Analysis Based on Q-GERT Simulation," Material Airlift Command, *Chicago ORSA Conference,* 1974.

9. Ayoub, M. A., R. J. Smillie, et al., "A Computerized Approach for the Assessment and Evaluation of Job Performance Aids," *Proc. Human Factors Society Meeting,* 1976, pp. 466–478.

10. Baker, K. R., *Introduction to Sequencing and Scheduling*. New York: John Wiley & Sons, Inc., 1974.

11. Bandy, D. B., and S. D. Duket, "Q-GERT Model of a Midwest Crude Supply System," *Milwaukee ORSA/TIMS Joint National Meeting*, October 1979.

12. Bellas, C. J., and A. C. Samli, "Improving New Product Planning with GERT Simulation," *California Management Review*, Vol. 15, No. 4, Summer 1973, pp. 14–21.

13. Berry, W. L., "Priority Scheduling and Inventory Control in Job Lot Manufacturing Systems," *AIIE Transactions*, Vol. 4, No. 4, December 1972, pp. 267–276.

14. Bird, M. M., E. R. Clayton, and L. J. Moore, "Industrial Buying: A Method of Planning for Contract Negotiations," *Journal of Economics and Business*, Vol. 26, 1974, pp. 209–213.

15. Bird, M. M., E. R. Clayton, and L. J. Moore, "Sales Negotiation Cost Planning for Corporate Level Sales," *Journal of Marketing*, Vol. 37, No. 2, April 1973, pp. 7–13.

16. Bonczek, R. H., C. W. Holsapple, and A. B. Whinston, "The Evolving Roles of Models in Decision Support Systems," *Decision Sciences*, Vol. 11, 1980, pp. 337–356.

17. Bonham, T. W., E. R. Clayton, and L. J. Moore, "A GERT Model to Meet Future Organizational Manpower Needs," *Journal of Personnel*, Vol. 54, 1975, pp. 402–406.

18. Branson, M. H., and B. Shah, "On GERT Modeling of a Class of Finite Queueing Processes," *AIIE Transactions*, Vol. 4, No. 1, 1972, pp. 43–48.

19. Brounstein, S. H., "An Adjudication Research Simulation Model (ARSM)," Institute of Law and Social Research Paper, Washington, DC, 1975.

20. Buffa, E. S., *Modern Production Management*, 3rd ed. New York: John Wiley & Sons, Inc., 1969.

21. Burgess, R. R., "GERTS Models of a University," M.S. thesis, Virginia Polytechnic Institute and State University, 1970.

22. Burt, J. M., Jr., and M. Garman, "Monte Carlo Techniques for Stochastic Network Analysis," *Fourth Conference on the Application of Simulation*, 1970, pp. 146–153.

23. Burt, J. M., D. P. Gaver, and M. Perlas, "Simple Stochastic Networks: Some Problems and Procedures," *Naval Research Logistics Quarterly*, Vol. 17, December 1970, pp. 439–460.

24. Busacker, R. G., and T. L. Saaty, *Finite Graphics and Networks*. New York: McGraw-Hill Book Company, 1965.

25. Byers, J. K., "Application of GERT to Reliability Analysis," Ph.D. dissertation, University of Arkansas, 1970.

26. Callahan, L. G., Jr., "Brief Survey of Operational Decision Support Systems," School of Industrial and Systems Engineering, Georgia Institute of Technology, February 1979.

27. Case, K. E., and K. R. Morrison, "A Simulation of System Reliability Using GERTS III," *Virginia Academy of Science Meeting*, May 14, 1971.

28. Chapman, C. B., "Large Engineering Project Risk Analysis," *IEEE Transactions on Engineering Management*, Vol. EM-26, No. 3, 1979, pp. 78–86.

29. Churchman, C. W., "Managerial Acceptance of Scientific Recommendations," in *Quantitative Disciplines in Management Decisions*, eds. R. I. Levin and R. P. Lamore. Belmont, CA: Dickenson Publishing Company, Inc., 1969.

30. Clayton, E. R., and L. J. Moore, "GERT vs. PERT," *Journal of Systems Management*, Vol. 22, No. 2, 1972, pp. 11-19.

31. Clymer, A. B., "The Modeling of Hierarchical Systems," *Proc. Conference on Applications of Continuous System Simulation Languages*, 1969, pp. 1-16.

32. Cobb, H. C. Jr., "A Q-GERT Model and Analysis of the Communications in a Mechanized Brigade Covering Force," Masters' thesis, Naval Postgraduate School, Monterey, CA, March 1979.

33. Conway, R. W., W. L. Maxwell, and L. W. Miller, *Theory of Scheduling*. Reading, MA: Addison-Wesley Publishing Co., Inc., 1967.

34. Cooper, R. B., *Introduction to Queueing Theory*. New York: Macmillan Publishing Co., Inc., 1972.

35. Crowston, W., and G. L. Thompson, "Decision CPM: A Method for Simultaneous Planning, Scheduling and Control of Projects," *Operations Research*, Vol. 15, No. 3, 1967, pp. 407-426.

36. Dabaghian, L., Y. Akiba, and W. W. Happ, "Network Modules to Simulate Quantized Entity Flow," *Joint Automatic Control Conference*, Austin, TX, June 19, 1974.

37. Dabaghian, L., Y. Akiba, and W. W. Happ, "Simulation and Modeling Techniques Using GERTS IIIQ: An Introductory Account for Prospective Users," *Seventh Asilomar Conference on Circuits, Systems and Computers*, Monterey, CA, November 27-29, 1973.

38. Davis, E. W., *Project Management: Techniques, Applications and Management Issues*. AIIE Monograph 3 in Production Planning and Control Division, AIIE-PP&C-76-1, 1976.

39. Davis, E. W., "Project Scheduling under Resource Constraints—Historical Review and Categorization of Procedures," *AIIE Transactions*, Vol. 5, No. 4, 1973, pp. 297-313.

40. Dean, B. V., and M. J. Nishry, "Scoring and Profitability Models for Evaluating and Selecting Engineering Projects," *Operations Research*, Vol. 13, No. 4, July-August 1965, pp. 13-21.

41. Devor, R. E., G. L. Hogg, and M. Handwerker, "Analysis of Criminal Justice Systems with GERTS IIIQ: A Case Study," *Proc. Pittsburgh Modeling and Simulation Conference*, Vol. 5, 1974, pp. 1193-1199.

42. Dijkstra, E. W., "A Note on Two Problems in Connection with Graphs," *Numerische Mathematik*, Vol. 1, 1959, pp. 269-271.

43. Dreyfus, S. E., "An Appraisal of Some Shortest Path Algorithms," *Operation Research*, Vol. 17, No. 3, May-June 1969, pp. 395-412.

44. Drezner, S. H., and A. A. B. Pritsker, "Network Analysis of Countdown," The RAND Corporation, RM-4976-NASA, March 1966.

45. Duket, S., and D. Wortman, "Q-GERT Model of the Dover Air Force Base Port Cargo Facilities," MACRO Task Force, Material Airlift Command, Scott Air Force Base, IL, 1976.

46. Duket, S. D., A. F. Hixson, and L. Rolston, *The SIMCHART User's Manual*. West Lafayette, IN: Pritsker & Associates, 1981.

47. Duncan, A. J., *Quality Control and Industrial Statistics*. Urbana, IL: Richard D. Irwin, Inc., 1965.

48. Eilon, S., I. G. Chowdhury, and S. S. Serghiou, "Experiments with the SI^x Rule in Job Shop Scheduling," *Simulation*, Vol. 24, 1975, pp. 45–48.

49. Eisner, H., "A Generalized Network Approach to the Planning and Scheduling of a Research Project," *Operations Research*, Vol. 10, No. 1, 1962, pp. 115–215.

50. Elmaghraby, S. E., "An Algebra for the Analysis of Generalized Activity Networks," *Management Science*, Vol. 10, No. 3, 1964, pp. 494–514.

51. Elmaghraby, S. E., *The Design of Production Systems*. New York: Reinhold Publishing Corp., 1966.

52. Elmaghraby, S. E., *Network Models in Management Science*. Lecture Series on Operations Research. New York: Springer-Verlag, 1970.

53. Elmaghraby, S. E., "On Generalized Activity Networks," *Journal of Industrial Engineering*, Vol. 18, No. 11, 1976, pp. 621–631.

54. Elmaghraby, S. E., "On the Expected Duration of PERT Type Networks," *Management Science*, Vol. 13, No. 5, 1967, pp. 299–306.

55. Elmaghraby, S. E., "Theory of Networks and Management Science: I and II," *Management Science*, Vol. 17, Nos. 1 and 2, 1970, pp. 1–34, No. 1, and pp. B54–B71.

56. Emshoff, J. R., and R. L. Sisson, *Design and Use of Computer Simulation Models*. New York: Macmillan Publishing Co., Inc., 1970.

57. Enlow, R. A., "An Application of GERT Network Techniques to the Selection and Management of Research and Development Projects," Ph.D. dissertation, Arizona State University, 1970.

58. Evans, G. W., II, G. F. Wallace, and G. L. Sutherland, *Simulation Using Digital Computers*. Englewood Cliffs, NJ: Prentice-Hall, Inc., 1967.

59. Faurie, B. R., "A Q-GERT Approach to a Requisition Processing Simulation at Naval Supply Center San Diego," Masters' thesis, Naval Postgraduate School, Monterey, CA, September 1980.

60. Federal Power Commission Exhibit EP-237, "Risk Analysis of the Arctic Gas Pipeline Project Construction Schedule," Vol. 167, Federal Power Commission, 1976.

61. Feller, W., *An Introduction to Probability Theory and Its Applications*, Vol. 1. New York: John Wiley & Sons, Inc., 1957.

62. Feller, W., *An Introduction to Probability Theory and Its Applications*, Vol. 2. New York: John Wiley & Sons, Inc., 1972.

63. Fishman, G. S., *Concepts and Methods in Discrete Event Digital Simulation*. New York: John Wiley & Sons, Inc., 1973.

64. Fishman, G. S., *Principles of Discrete Event Simulation*. New York: John Wiley & Sons, Inc., 1978.

65. Freeman, R. J., "A Generalized PERT," *Operations Research*, Vol. 8, No. 2, 1960, p. 281.

66. Fulkerson, D. R., "Expected Critical Path Lengths in PERT Networks," *Operations Research*, Vol. 10, No. 6, 1962, pp. 808–817.

67. Gallagher, D. J., "A GERT Network Approach to the Study of Queueing Phenomena," Ph.D. dissertation, Arizona State University, 1970.

68. Gere, W. S., "Heuristics in Job Shop Scheduling," *Management Science*, Vol. 13, No. 3, 1966, pp. 167–190.

69. Giffler, B., G. L. Thompson, and V. Van Ness, "Numerical Experience with the Linear and Monte Carlo Algorithms for Solving Production Scheduling Problems," in *Industrial Scheduling*, eds. J. Muth and G. L. Thompson. Englewood Cliffs, NJ: Prentice-Hall, Inc., 1963.

70. Grant, F. H., III, and A. A. B. Pritsker, "GERT Network Model of Burglary Resistance," NSF Grant No. GI 34978, Purdue University, December 1973.

71. Hahn, G. J., and S. S. Shapiro, *Statistical Methods of Engineering*. New York: John Wiley & Sons, Inc., 1967.

72. Halpin, D. W., "An Investigation of the Use of Simulation Networks for Modeling Construction Operations," Ph.D. dissertation, University of Illinois, 1973.

73. Halpin, D. W., and W. W. Happ, "Digital Simulation of Equipment Allocation for Corps of Engineering Construction Planning," U.S. Army, CERL, Champaign, IL, 1971.

74. Hammond, J. S., III, "The Roles of the Manager and Management Scientist in Successful Implementation," *Sloan Management Review*, Vol. 15, No. 2, 1974, pp. 1–24.

75. Hartley, H., and A. Wortham, "A Statistical Theory for PERT Critical Path Analysis," *Management Science*, Vol. 12, No. 10, June 1966, pp. 470–473.

76. Hebert, J. E., III, "Critical Path Analysis and a Simulation Program for Resource-Constrained Activity Scheduling in GERT Project Networks," Ph.D. dissertation, Purdue University, 1975.

77. Herald, M. J., and S. Y. Nof, "Modeling Analysis and Design Issues in a CMS with a Closed Loop Conveyor," Report No. 11, School of Industrial Engineering, Purdue University, June 1978.

78. Hespos, R. F., and P. A. Strassman, "Stochastic Decision Trees for the Analysis of Investment Decisions," *Management Science*, Vol. 11, No. 10, August 1965, pp. B244–259.

79. Hill, T. W., "System Improvement: A Sensitivity Approach Using GERT," Master's Engineering Report, Arizona State University, 1966.

80. Hogg, G. L., "An Analysis of Labor Limited Queueing Systems with a GERT's Simulation," Ph.D. dissertation, University of Texas, Austin, 1971.

81. Hogg, G. L., et al., "GERTS QR: A Model of Multi-resource Constrained Queueing Systems, Part I: Concepts, Notations, and Examples," *AIIE Transactions*, Vol. 7, No. 2, 1975, pp. 89–99.

82. Hogg, G. L., et al., "GERTS QR: A Model of Multi-resource Constrained Queueing Systems, Part II: An Analysis of Parallel Channel, Dual Constrained Queueing Systems with Homogeneous Resources," *AIIE Transactions*, Vol. 7, No. 2, 1975, pp. 100–109.

83. Holloway, C. A., and R. T. Nelson, "Job Shop Scheduling with Due Dates and Variable Processing Times," *Management Science*, Vol. 20, No. 9, May 1974, pp. 1264–1275.

84. Horowitz, J., *Critical Path Scheduling*. New York: The Ronald Press Company, 1976.

85. Huang, P. Y., E. R. Clayton, and L. J. Moore, "Analysis of Material and

Capacity Requirements with Q-GERT," College of Business, Virginia Polytechnic Institute and State University, Blacksburg, VA, 1981.

86. Hulme, B. L., "Graph Theoretic Models of Theft Problems, I. The Basic Theft Model," Sandia Laboratories, Albuquerque, NM, SAND 75-0595, November 1975.

87. Iwersen, A. Jr., R. R. Berry, and J. E. Brawner, Jr., "A Cost Analysis of the KT-73 Inertial Measurement Unit Repair Process Using GERT Simulation," Masters' thesis, Air Force Institute of Technology, Wright-Patterson Air Force Base, January 1975.

88. Jackson, J. R., "An Extension of Johnson's Results on Job-Lot Scheduling," *Naval Research Logistics Quarterly*, Vol. 3, No. 3, September 1956, pp. 201–203.

89. Jaglinski, T., *Program Management Plan for Ground Target Attack Control System Assault Breaker* (3rd draft). Unpublished document, HQ Electronics Systems Division, Hanscom Air Force Base, Bedford, MA, April 1980.

90. Johnson, S. M., "Optimal Two- and Three-Stage Production Schedules with Setup Times Included," *Naval Research Logistics Quarterly*, Vol. 1, No. 1, 1954.

91. Johnston, R. E., *Discrete Event Simulation as a Management Tool for Planning and Scheduling Overhauls of U.S. Navy Ships*. Masters' Project, Purdue University, December 1980.

92. Kaimann, R. A., "Coefficient of Network Complexity," *Management Science*, Vol. 21, No. 2, October 1974, pp. 172–177.

93. Kamins, M., "Two Notes on the Lognormal Distribution," RM-3781-PR, The RAND Corporation, Santa Monica, CA, 1963.

94. Kao, E. P. C., "Computational Experience with a Stochastic Assembly Line Balancing Algorithm," *Computers and Operations Research*, Vol. 6, 1979, pp. 79–86.

95. Kase, S., and H. Ohta, "An Application of Sampling Inspection to Correcting Plan for Semi-Markov Production Process," *AIIE Transactions*, Vol. 6, No. 2, 1974, pp. 151–158.

96. Kastenberg, W. E., et al., "On Risk Assessment in the Absence of Complete Data," NSF Grant GI-39416 and OEP75-20318, University of California, Los Angeles, CA, July 1976.

97. Keen, P. G., and G. R. Wagner, "DSS: An Executive Mind-Support System," *Datamation*, November 1979, pp. 117–122.

98. Keen, P. G. W., and M. S. Scott Morton, *Decision Support Systems: An Organizational Perspective*. Reading, MA: Addison-Wesley Publishing Co., Inc., 1978.

99. Kennedy, K. W., and R. M. Thrall, "Planet: A Simulation Approach to PERT," *Computers and Operations Research*, Vol. 3, 1976, pp. 313–325.

100. Kleijnen, J. P. C., "Generalizing Simulation Results Through Metamodels" (Working paper, Katholieke Hogeschool, Tilburg, S. Netherlands, December 1977.)

101. Kleijnen, J. P. C., *Statistical Techniques in Simulation, Parts I and II*. New York: Marcel Dekker, Inc., 1974.

102. Kleijnen, J. P. C., Van den Burg, and Van der Ham, "Generalization of

Simulation Results: Practicality of Statistical Methods," *European Journal of Operational Research*, Vol. 3, 1979, pp. 50-64.

103. Kleindorfer, G. B., "Bounding Distributions for a Stochastic Acylic Network," *Operations Research*, Vol. 19, No. 7, 1971, pp. 1586-1601.

104. Knuth, D. E., *The Art of Computer Programming*, Vol. 2: *Seminumerical Algorithms*. Reading, MA: Addison-Wesley Publishing Co., Inc., 1969.

105. Koch, D. P., "Iron and Steelmaking Facility Planning Simulation Model," *Proc. 1979 Winter Simulation Conference*, San Diego, CA, December 3-5, 1979, pp. 259-266.

106. Kwak, N. K., and L. Jones, "An Application of PERT to R&D Scheduling," *Information Processing and Management*, Vol. 14, 1978, pp. 121-131.

107. Lawrence, K. D., and C. E. Sigal, "A Work Flow Simulation of a Regional Service Office of a Property and Casualty Insurance Company with Q-GERT," *Proc. Pittsburgh Modeling and Simulation Conference*, Vol. 5, 1974, pp. 1187-1192.

108. Lee, C., and L. P. McNamee, "A Stochastic Network Model for Air Cargo Terminals," *Ninth Annual Allerton Conference on Circuit and Systems Theory*, 1971, pp. 1140-1150.

109. Leverenz, F. L. Jr., E. T. Rumble, et al., "Role of Computers in Reactor Risk Analysis," *Proc. 1976 Summer Computer Simulation Conference*, Washington D.C., July 12-14, 1976, pp. 173-176.

110. MacCrimmon, K. R., and C. A. Ryavec, "An Analytical Study of the PERT Assumptions," *Operations Research*, Vol. 12, 1964, pp. 16-38.

111. McNamee, L. P., and C. Lee, "Development of a Standard Data Base and Computer Simulation Model for an Air Cargo Terminal," U.S. Army, CERL, Champaign, IL, 1973.

112. Magee, J. F., "Decision Trees for Decision Making," *Harvard Business Review*, Vol. 42, No. 4, 1964, pp. 79-96.

113. Maggard, M. J., W. G. Lesso, et al., "GERTS IIIQR: A Multiple Resource Constrained Network Simulation Model," *Management Datamatics*, Vol. 5, No. 1, 1976, pp. 5-14.

114. Maggard, M. J., W. G. Lesso, et al. "Network Analysis with GERTS IIIQR," *Industrial Engineering*, Vol. 6, No. 5, May 1974, pp. 24-29.

115. Malcolm, D. G., J. H. Rosenbloom, C. E. Clark, and W. Fazer, "Application of a Technique for Research and Development Program Evaluation," *Operations Research*, Vol. 7, 1959, pp. 616-669.

116. March, J. C., and H. A. Simon, *Organizations*. New York: John Wiley & Sons, Inc., 1958.

117. Mastov, A. A., "An Experimental Investigation and Comparative Evaluation of Production Line Balancing Techniques," *Management Science*, Vol. 16, July 1970, pp. 728-742.

118. Medeiros, D. J., R. P. Sadowski, D. W. Starks, and B. S. Smith, "A Modular Approach to Simulation of Robotic Systems," *Proc. 1980 Winter Simulation Conference*, Orlando, FL, December 3-5, 1980.

119. Meier, R. C., W. T. Newell, and H. L. Pazer, *Simulation in Business and Economics*. Englewood Cliffs, NJ: Prentice-Hall, Inc., 1969.

120. Miller, George A., "The Magical Number Seven, Plus or Minus Two: Some Limits on Our Capacity for Processing Information," *The Psychological Review*, Vol. 63, No. 2, March 1956, pp. 81-97.

121. Mize, J. H., and J. G. Cox, *Essentials of Simulation.* Englewood Cliffs, NJ: Prentice-Hall, Inc., 1968.

122. Moder, J., R. A. Clark, and R. S. Gomez, "Applications of a GERT Simulator to a Repetitive Hardware Development Type Project," *AIIE Transactions,* Vol. 3, No. 4, 1971, pp. 271–280.

123. Moder, J. J., and S. E. Elmaghraby, *Handbook of Operations Research: Foundations and Fundamentals.* New York: Van Nostrand Reinhold Company, 1978.

124. Moder, J. J., and S. E. Elmaghraby, *Handbook of Operations Research: Models and Applications.* New York: Van Nostrand Reinhold Company, 1978.

125. Moder, J. J., and C. R. Phillips, *Project Management with CPM and PERT,* 2nd ed. New York: Van Nostrand Reinhold Company, 1970.

126. Moder, J. J., and E. G. Rodgers, "Judgment Estimates of the Moments of PERT Type Distributions," *Management Science,* Vol. 15, No. 2, October 1968, pp. B76–B83.

127. Moore, L. J., "Business Systems Analysis with GERTS IIIZ," *Proc. Pittsburgh Modeling and Simulation Conference,* Vol. 5, 1974, pp. 1177–1179.

128. Moore, L. J., and E. R. Clayton, *Introduction to Systems Analysis with GERT Modeling and Simulation.* New York: Petrocelli Books, 1976.

129. Moore, L. J., D. F. Scott, and E. R. Clayton, "GERT Analysis of Stochastic Systems," *Akron Business and Economic Review,* 1974, pp. 14–19.

130. Moore, L. J., and B. W. Taylor III, "Multiteam, Multiproject Research and Development Planning with GERT," *Management Science,* Vol. 24, No. 4, December 1977, pp. 401–410.

131. Morris, W. T., "On the Art of Modeling," *Management Science,* Vol. 13, No. 12, 1967, pp. B707–717.

132. Morris, W. T., *Analysis of Management Decision Making.* Homewood, IL: Richard D. Irwin, Inc., 1964.

133. Morris, W. T., *Implementation Strategies for Industrial Engineers.* Columbus, OH: Grid Publishing, Inc., 1979.

134. Morrison, K. R., "A Heuristic Algorithm for Multi-project, Limited Resource Compressible Activity Networks," Ph.D. dissertation, Virginia Polytechnic Institute and State University, 1973.

135. Mortenson, R. E., "R, M, and Logistics Simulations Using Q-GERT," *1980 Proceedings Annual Reliability and Maintainability Symposium,* pp. 1–5.

136. Musselman, K. J., and R. J. Hannan, *Description and Documentation with the Sacramento ALC Aircraft Maintenance Model with Supporting Program.* West Lafayette, IN: Pritsker & Associates, Inc., January 1981.

137. Musselman, K. J., W. R. Penick, and M. E. Grant, *AID:, Fitting Distributions to Observations: A Graphical Approach.* West Lafayette, IN: Pritsker & Associates, Inc., 1981.

138. Nelson, R. T., "A Simulation Study of Labor Efficiency and Centralized Labor Assignments in a Production System Model," *Management Science,* Vol. 17, No. 2, October 1970.

139. Otway, H. J., and R. C. Erdmann, "Reactor Siting and Design from a Risk Viewpoint," *Nuclear Engineering Design,* Vol. 13, 1970, p. 365.

140. Ozan, T., "Design of Complex Flow Line System by Simulation," *Computers and Industrial Engineering,* Vol. 4, 1980, pp. 75–85.

141. Papageorgiou, J. C., *An Application of GERT to Air Force Systems Develop-*

ment *Planning*. Unpublished paper, AFOSR/AFSC Contract F49620-79-C-0038, University of Massachusetts (Boston).

142. Perry, C., and I. D. Greig, "Estimating the Mean and Variance of Subjective Distributions in PERT and Decision Analysis," *Management Science*, Vol. 21, No. 12, August 1975, pp. 1477–1480.

143. Petersen, P., "Project Control Systems," *Datamation*, June 1979, pp. 147–162.

144. Phillips, D. T., *Applied Goodness of Fit Testing*, AIIE Monograph Series, AIIE-OR-72-1, Atlanta, GA, 1972.

145. Phillips, D. T., and A. A. B. Pritsker, "GERT Network Analysis of Complex Production Systems," *International Journal of Production Research*, Vol. 13, No. 3, 1975, pp. 223–237.

146. Phillips, D. T., A. Ravindrin, and J. Solberg, *Introduction to Operations Research*. New York: John Wiley & Sons, Inc., 1976.

147. Phillips, D. T., and R. F. Slovick, "A GERTS IIIQ Application to a Production Line," *Proc. 1974 AIIE National Conference*, pp. 307–318.

148. Polito, J., Jr., and C. C. Petersen, "User's Manual for GRASP," Purdue Laboratory for Applied Industrial Control, Report Number 75, April 1976.

149. Porte, H. A., and W. W. Happ, "Activity Networks to Model Transportation Systems Subject to Facility Constraints," *Ninth Annual Allerton Conference on Circuit and Systems Theory*, 1971, pp. 1151–1160.

150. Pritsker, A. A. B., "Applications of Multichannel Queueing Results to the Analysis of Conveyor Systems," *Journal of Industrial Engineering*, Vol. 17, No. 1, 1966, pp. 14–21.

151. Pritsker, A. A. B., "GERT: Graphical Evaluation and Review Technique," The RAND Corporation, RM-4973-NASA, Santa Monica, CA, April 1966.

152. Pritsker, A. A. B., "GERT Networks," *The Production Engineer*, 1968, pp. 499–506.

153. Pritsker, A. A. B., *The GERTE User's Manual*. West Lafayette, IN: Pritsker & Associates, Inc., 1974.

154. Pritsker, A. A. B., *Modeling and Analysis Using Q-GERT Networks*, 2nd ed. New York: Halsted Press, 1979.

155. Pritsker, A. A. B., *The Precedence GERT User's Manual*. West Lafayette, IN: Pritsker & Associates, Inc., 1974.

156. Pritsker, A. A. B., and W. W. Happ, "GERT: Graphical Evaluation and Review Technique, Part I. Fundamentals," *Journal of Industrial Engineering*, Vol. 17, No. 5, 1966, pp. 267–74.

157. Pritsker, A. A. B., and C. D. Pegden, *Introduction to Simulation and SLAM*. West Lafayette, IN: Systems Publishing Corporation, 1979.

158. Pritsker, A. A. B., and C. E. Sigal, *The GERT IIIZ User's Manual*. West Lafayette, IN: Pritsker & Associates, 1974.

159. Pritsker, A. A. B., L. J. Watters, and P. M. Wolfe, "Mathematical Formulation: A Problem in Design," *Proceedings 19th AIIE Conference*, May 1968, pp. 205–210.

160. Pritsker, A. A. B., and G. E. Whitehouse, "GERT: Graphical Evaluation and Review Technique, Part II. Applications," *Journal of Industrial Engineering*, Vol. 17, No. 5, 1966, pp. 293–301.

161. Raju, G. V. S., "Sensitivity Analysis of GERT Networks," *AIIE Transactions*, Vol. 3, No. 2, 1971, pp. 133–141.

162. Randolph, P. H., and R. D. Ringeisen, "A Network Learning Model with GERT Analysis," *Journal of Mathematical Psychology*, Vol. 2, No. 1, 1974, pp. 59-70.

163. Richard, J. H., "Q-GERT Model of Planned Product Distribution Network," *Proc. 1981 Winter Simulation Conference*, Atlanta, GA, December 1981.

164. Roberts, S. D., and T. E. Sadlowski, "INS: Integrated Network Simulator," *Proc. Winter Simulation Conference*, 1975, pp. 575-586.

165. Rochette, R., and R. P. Sadowski, "A Statistical Comparison of the Performance of Simple Dispatching Rules for a Particular Set of Job Shops," *International Journal of Production Research*, Vol. 14, No. 1, January 1976, pp. 63-75.

166. Runner, J. S., and F. F. Leimkuhler, "CAMSAM: A Simulation Analysis Model for Computer-Aided Manufacturing Systems," *Proc. 1978 Summer Computer Simulation Conference*, Newport Beach, CA, July 1978.

167. Sabuda, J., "A Study of Q-GERT Modeling and Analysis Using Interactive Computer Graphics," M.S. thesis, Purdue University, December 1977.

168. Samli, A. C., and C. Bellas, "The Use of GERT in the Planning and Control of Marketing Research," *Journal of Marketing Research*, Vol. 8, August 1971, pp. 335-339.

169. Sauls, E., "The Use of GERT," *Journal of Systems Management*, Vol. 23, No. 8, 1972, pp. 11-21.

170. Schrage, L., and K. R. Baker, "Dynamic Programming Solution of Sequencing Problems with Procedence Constraints," *Operations Research*, Vol. 26, 1978, pp. 444-449.

171. Schriber, T., *Simulation Using GPSS*. New York: John Wiley & Sons, Inc., 1974.

172. Seaberg, R. A., and C. Seaberg, "Computer Based Decision Systems in Xerox Corporate Planning," *Management Science*, Vol. 20, No. 4, 1973, pp. 575-584.

173. Settles, F. S., "GERT Network Models of Production Economics," *Proc. 1969 AIIE National Conference*, pp. 383-394.

174. Seum, C. S., "The Addition of Queue Nodes and Server Nodes to Precedence GERT," Master's thesis, Purdue University, 1975.

175. Shannon, R. E., "Simulation: A Survey with Research Suggestions," *AIIE Transactions*, Vol. 7, No. 3, 1975, pp. 289-301.

176. Shannon, R. E., *System Simulation: The Art and Science*. Englewood Cliffs, NJ: Prentice-Hall, Inc., 1975.

177. Sigal, C. E., "Stochastic Shortest Route Problems," Ph.D. dissertation, Purdue University, December 1977.

178. Sigal, C. E., S. Duket, and A. A. B. Pritsker, *New Additions to Q-GERT*. West Lafayette, IN: Pritsker & Associates, Inc., 1976.

179. Sigal, C. E., and A. A. B. Pritsker, "SMOOTH: A Combined Continuous-Discrete Network Simulation Language," *Simulation*, Vol. 22, March 1974, pp. 65-73.

180. Sigal, C. E., A. A. B. Pritsker, and J. J. Solberg, "Cutsets in Monte Carlo Analysis of Stochastic Networks," *Mathematics and Computers in Simulation*, Vol. 21, No. 4, December 1979.

181. Sigal, C. E., A. A. B. Pritsker, and J. J. Solberg, "The Stochastic Shortest Route Problem," *Operations Research*, Vol. 28, No. 5, September–October 1980.

182. Simon, H. A., "How Big Is a Chunk?," *Science*, Vol. 183, February 8, 1974, pp. 482–488.

183. Smith, R. L., "Stochastic Analysis of Personnel Movement in Formal Organizations," Ph.D. dissertation, Arizona State University, 1968.

184. Soland, R. M., J. H. Vanston, Jr., and S. P. Nichols, "Optimal Resource Allocation in the Nuclear Fusion Development Program," *ORSA/TIMS National Meeting*, November 1975.

185. Souder, W. E., "Achieving Organizational Consensus with Respect to R&D Project Selection Criteria," *Management Science*, Vol. 21, No. 6, February 1975, pp. 669–681.

186. Souder, W. E., "Utility and Perceived Acceptability of R&D Project Selection Models," *Management Science*, Vol. 19, No. 12, 1973, pp. 1384–1394.

187. Sprague, R. H., Jr., and H. J. Watson, "A Decision Support System for Banks," *OMEGA*, Vol. 4, No. 6, 1976, pp. 657–671.

188. Sprague, R. H., Jr., and H. J. Watson, "MIS Concepts-Part I," *Journal of Systems Management*, Vol. 26, No. 1, 1975, pp. 34–37.

189. Sprague, R. H., Jr., and H. J. Watson, "MIS Concepts-Part II," *Journal of Systems Management*, Vol. 26, No. 2, 1975, pp. 35–40.

190. Standridge, C. R., *SDL: Simulation Data Languages Reference Manual*. West Lafayette, IN: Pritsker & Associates, Inc., 1981.

191. Standridge, C. R., and A. A. B. Pritsker, "Using Data Base Capabilities in Simulation," *Proc. Simulation "80" Course on Modeling and Simulation Methodology*, June 23–24, 1980, pp. 73–78.

192. Stidham, S., Jr., "A Last Word on $L = \lambda W$," *Operations Research*, Vol. 22, No. 2, 1974, pp. 417–421.

193. Swingle, D. W., Jr., "A Probabilistic Network Analysis of the Advanced Fuel Recycle Program's Receiving and Storage Task," Report No. K/OP-247, Union Carbide Corp., Oak Ridge, TN, June 1978.

194. Swingle, D. W., Jr., E. H. Gift, and F. M. Bustamante, "Utilization of Probabilistic Network Analysis in Planning Long-Range Engineering Projects," *Proc. 1979 Winter Simulation Conference*, San Diego, CA, December 3–5, 1979, pp. 569–575.

195. Taha, H. A., *Operations Research: An Introduction*. New York: Macmillan Publishing Co., Inc., 1971.

196. Taylor, B. W., III, and K. R. Davis, "Evaluating Time/Cost Factors of Implementation via GERT Simulation," *OMEGA*, Vol. 6, 1978, pp. 257–266.

197. Taylor, B. W., III, and A. V. Keown, "A Network Analysis of an Inpatient/Outpatient Department," *Journal of the Operational Research Society*, Vol. 31, 1980, pp. 169–179.

198. Taylor, B. W., III, L. M. Moore, and R. D. Hammesfahr, "Global Analysis of a Multi-product, Multi-line Production System Using Q-GERT Modeling and Simulation," *AIIE Transactions*, June 1980, pp. 145–155.

199. Thornton, J., "Use of Computer Simulation Is Expanding," *Tech Update, American Metal Marketing Metalworking News*, June 9, 1980, p. 10.

200. Thrall, R. M., C. H. Coombes, and R. L. Davis, eds., *Decision Processes*. New York: John Wiley & Sons, Inc., 1954.

201. Tocher, K. D., *The Art of Simulation*. New York: D. Van Nostrand Company, 1963.

202. Townsend, T., "GERT Networks with Item Differentiation Capabilities," Masters' thesis, Purdue University, 1973.

203. Velenzuela, C. A., and G. E. Whitehouse, "The Application of Q-GERT to Materials Handling Problems in Open Pit Mining," *Proc. Ninth Annual Pittsburgh Conference,* April 27–28, 1978, pp. 273–278.

204. Van Slyke, R. M., "Monte Carlo Methods and the PERT Problem," *Operations Research,* Vol. 11, September–October 1963, pp. 839–860.

205. Vanston, J. H., Jr., "Use of the Partitive Analytical Forecasting (PAF) Technique for Analyzing of the Effects of Various Funding and Administrative Strategies on Nuclear Fusion Power Plant Development," University of Texas, TR ESL-15, Energy Systems Laboratory, 1974.

206. Vanston, J. H., Jr., S. P. Nichols, and R. M. Soland, "PAF—A New Probabilistic, Computer-Based Technique for Technology Forecasting," *Technological Forecasting and Social Change,* Vol. 10, 1977, pp. 239–258.

207. Wagner, H., *Principles of Operations Research with Applications to Managerial Decisions.* Englewood Cliffs, NJ: Prentice-Hall, Inc., 1969.

208. Watters, L. J., and M. J. Vasilik, "A Stochastic Network Approach to Test and Checkout," *Proc. Fourth Conference of Application of Simulation,* 1970, pp. 113–123.

209. White, J. A., J. W. Schmidt, and G. K. Bennett, *Analysis of Queueing Systems.* New York: Academic Press, Inc., 1975.

210. Whitehouse, G. E., "The Choice between GERTS and Simulation Modeling for Industrial Systems," *Proc. Pittsburgh Modeling and Simulation Conference,* Vol. 5, 1974.

211. Whitehouse, G. E., "GERT, A Useful Technique for Analyzing Reliability Problems," *Technometrics,* February 1970.

212. Whitehouse, G. E., *Systems Analysis and Design Using Network Techniques.* Englewood Cliffs, NJ: Prentice-Hall, Inc., 1973.

213. Whitehouse, G. E., and E. C. Hsuan, "The Application of GERT to Quality Control: A Feasibility Study," (NASA Contract NAS-12-2079) Department of Industrial Engineering, Lehigh University.

214. Whitehouse, G. E., and A. A. B. Pritsker, "GERT: Part III—Further Statistical Results: Counters, Renewal Times and Correlations," *AIIE Transactions,* Vol. 1, No. 1, March 1969, pp. 45–50.

215. Whitehouse, G. E., and L. J. Riccio, "Application of GERT to Determine Effective Check-Out Procedures and Failure Diagnosis in Microcircuits," (NASA Contract NAS-12-2079), Department of Industrial Engineering, Lehigh University, Bethlehem, PA.

216. Whitehouse, G. W., "Extensions, New Developments, and Applications of GERT: Graphical Evaluation and Review Technique," Ph.D. dissertation, Arizona State University, 1966.

217. Wiest, J., and F. Levy, *Management Guide to PERT-CPM.* Englewood Cliffs, NJ: Prentice-Hall, Inc., 1969.

218. Wiest, J. D., "Computer Graphics for Project Management," *Proc. Seminar–Symposium of Project Management Institute,* St. Louis, MO, 1970.

219. Wiest, J. D., "A Heuristic Model for Scheduling Large Projects with Limited Resources," *Management Science,* Vol. 13, No. 6, Feb. 1967, pp. B359–B377.

220. Wiest, J. D., "Project Network Models Past, Present, and Future," *Project Management Quarterly,* Vol. 8, No. 4, December 1977, pp. 27–36.

221. Wolfe, P. M., E. B. Cochran, and W. J. Thompson, "A GERTS-Based Interactive Computer System for Analyzing Project Networks Incorporating Im-

provement Curve Concepts," *AIIE Transactions*, Vol. 12, No. 1, March 1980, pp. 70–79.

222. Wortman, D. B., "A Simulation Technique for Allocating Resources to Tasks," Master's thesis, Purdue University, December 1977.

223. Wortman, D. B., S. D. Duket, and D. J. Seifert, "Simulation of a Remotely Piloted Vehicle/Drone Control Facility Using SAINT," *Proc. Summer Computer Simulation Conference*, San Francisco, CA, 1975.

224. Wortman, D. B., and C. E. Sigal, *Project Planning and Control Using GERT*. West Lafayette, IN: Pritsker & Associates, Inc., October 1978.

225. Wortman, D. B., C. E. Sigal, et al., *New SAINT Concepts and the SAINT Simulation Program*, AMRL-TR-75, Aerospace Medical Research Laboratory, Wright-Patterson Air Force Base, April 1975.

226. Yancey, D. P., and K. J. Musselman, *Critical Statistics in General Project Planning Networks*. West Lafayette, IN: Pritsker & Associates, Inc., September 1980.

Index

C

CAPQ (function), 52, 53, 130
Caterpillar Tractor Company, 228, 232
Chance decision, 342, 344
Check processing facility, analysis of, 244-51
Chi-square test, 487
Choice decision, 341-42, 345
Clayton, E. R., xx, 293, 439
CLEAR (subroutine), 60, 62
COL (subroutine), 59, 60, 80-81, 119, 171, 224, 316, 320, 329, 383, 389, 421, 426
COLC (subroutine), 59, 60-61, 62
COLP (subroutine), 59, 60
Combined parallel-series systems, reliability of, 290-91
COMMON block QVAR, 47, 52
Computer graphics (*See* Graphics)
Computerized manufacturing systems: analysis of, 226-36
Conditional routing and branching, 23-25, 35, 68, 147-50, 210-11, 345, 399, 400
Continuous product flow: pipelines and, 182-84
Continuous review procedure: inventory control and, 311, 314-20
Contract negotiation process, 438-50
Conveyor systems, 176-82
COPYQ (subroutine), 52, 53
Costs, inventory control and, 311-13
Count variables, statistical estimates for, 89
CPBE (subroutine), 446
CPM (critical path method), 373, 376, 394
CPTR (subroutine), 391
Criticality indices, 384-85
    example of estimation using Q-GERT, 385-88
Cycle time, 167-71

D

Data base, 11
    storing Q-GERT outputs in, 96-101
Decision and risk analysis, 341-71

cost in place of time, use of, 343-44
decision networks, 346
decision trees, 344-46
new product introduction:
    decision tree model of, 347-51
    Q-GERT analysis of, 351-55
risk assessment, 355-56
stochastic shortest-route analysis, 356-68
    for equipment replacement, 361-65
    estimating path optimality, 357-61
    Q-GERT approach to, 357
    for safeguards system design, 365-68
value associated with outcome, 341-42
Decision logic, representation of, 399-403
Decision making, graphics and, 490-91
Decision networks, 346
Decision process, 3-5
Decision support system (DSS), 6
Decision trees, 344-46
    model of new product introduction, 347-51
Demand processes, 327-28
    bulk, 333
    characterizing interdemand time, 328-30
    differentiating among, 333
    interdemand time distributions specified by user-defined histogram, 331-32
    predetermined demand sequences, 330-31
    seasonal, 332-33
Detailed scheduling, 140, 141, 161-62
Deterministic routing and branching, 23, 25, 35, 68, 195, 246
Direct experimentation, 4
Distribution of counts, 328
Double sampling plan, 300-305
Dover Air Force Base, analysis of logistics system at, 275-85
DPROB (function), 126, 328, 331-32
DRAND (function), 213
Due dates, meeting, 117-19
Duket, Steven D., xx, 177*n*, 238*n*, 244, 275
Dummy subprograms, 64
Dynamic slack, 154-55